SOCIOPSYCHONOMICS™

Enjoy!

SOCIOPSYCHONOMICS™

HOW SOCIAL CLASSES THINK, ACT, AND BEHAVE
FINANCIALLY IN THE TWENTY-FIRST CENTURY

LAWRENCE FUNDERBURKE, MBA and CFP®

AUTHOR'S NOTE

This publication is designed to shed light on the unique differences among social classes and embedded subsets in America. It is sold with the understanding that the author, book contributors, and publisher are not engaged in rendering financial, investment, legal, accounting, tax, medical advice, or other professional services. If financial planning advice or other expert assistance is required, the services of a competent professional should be sought.

Library of Congress Control Number: 2017956820

ISBN: 978-0-9980203-0-3

Funderburke, Lawrence.
Sociopsychonomics™: How Social Classes Think, Act, and Behave Financially in the Twenty-First Century

Printed in the United States
10 9 8 7 6 5 4 3 2 1

To those ready for the sacrifices, demands, and legacy
benefits of an upgraded Sociopsychonomic filter.

CONTENTS

FINANCIAL MANAGEMENT AND WELLNESS

INVESTMENT PLANNING

INSURANCE PLANNING

INTRODUCTION

This book examines the economic dynamics and differences embedded in each social class and relating subsets. However, my main reason for writing *Sociopsychonomics* is to raise awareness of how our psychological temperament, memories, and life experiences drive our current (and future) expectations, habits, and tendencies around financial matters. We act and behave in concert with how we think, or more specifically, how we were taught to think. The good news is that we can upgrade our frame of reference by fine-tuning our Sociopsychonomic filter.

A brief description of each social class's income statement and balance sheet profile follows. Keep in mind, though, these two financial yardsticks or scoreboard measures do not tell the whole story. However, they can serve as a barometer of one's despondence, ambivalence, or insistence on fulfilling his or her economic potential.

The impoverished class benefits from or relies solely on economic subsistence, which includes government and nonprofit assistance to secure basic necessities (food, shelter, and clothing), part-time employment with minimal pay and few (if any) benefits, and a decent education for their children. The traditional middle class enjoys or pursues economic stability, which includes a comfortable living environment (homeownership in a middle-class neighborhood), full-time employment with reasonable pay and adequate benefits (or business ownership that pays the bills), and a quality education for their children. The affluent class takes solace in or anticipates economic freedom, which includes lifestyle accoutrements (suburban living in a gated community and country club memberships), white-collar employment with exceptional pay and significant benefits (or business ownership that creates wealth), career advancement, and an elite-level education for their children.

The working poor and those receiving financial support from the federal government's Supplemental Nutritional Assistance Program (SNAP, also known as food stamps) must stretch a dollar to cover $1.50 of obligations each month. It's not surprising that they use nontraditional banking methods, such as payday loans, pawn shops, and reluctant neighbors to absorb the shortfall. Obviously, these revolving debt traps create more problems than they solve for economically distressed households.

The U.S. Census Bureau's poverty threshold in 2015 for a family of four was slightly more than $24,000.[1] The annual income for a middle-class individual or family typically falls between $35,000 and $150,000. People in the lower middle class are at the bottom end of the range, with incomes between $35,000 and $49,000. They may literally be one paycheck away from falling into poverty. The middle of the middle class earns a modest to above-average income that ranges between $50,000 and $100,000 per year. Depending on their city's standard of living costs, middle-income earners may have to watch every penny to avoid financial ruin. Upper middle-income earners have salaries between $101,000 and $150,000. Their high incomes can shield them from economic turmoil—though there is no guarantee.

The moderately wealthy have employment incomes that exceed $250,000 annually. For the mega wealthy, six- and seven-figure incomes are the norm, not the exception. Income-generating assets provide an additional boost to their already impressive salaries. Their balance sheets or net worth statements are more important than their income statements for several reasons. One prominent reason is asset allocation, or the process by which an investor spreads money among asset classes. This is an investing strategy's primary driver and, according to industry experts, accounts for roughly 90 percent of a portfolio's success in achieving financial goals.

The informed wealthy don't shun riskier asset classes. In fact, they use these classes to add increased diversification, protection, and profit potential when the economy shifts gears and less risky assets, such as bonds and dividend-paying stocks, check out of the wealth game. In addition to stocks, bonds, and mutual funds, the mega wealthy add real estate, private equity, venture capital, art and vintage collectibles, precious metals, and commodities to their mix of investment assets. Their team of financial advisors or coaches shift players in and out of the wealth game when economic conditions dictate.

Affluent Americans don't fear risk. They embrace it. As Marcellus Wiley, a former NFL player and current ESPN analyst, says, "Scared money don't make no money." The informed wealthy seize opportunities when others become fearful. They take profits off the table when unsophisticated stock market investors become recklessly greedy. Good fortune, expert advice, and even smarts aren't wealthy investors' biggest investment advantage. Their success has everything to do with emotional regulation, which the poor and middle class often struggle with as they navigate the world of wealth accumulation and cash flow management.

Net worth, which is the true measurement of wealth, is the difference between assets and liabilities. Assets fall into three categories: cash and cash equivalents (savings and checking accounts, certificates of deposit, and money market accounts), investable (stocks, bonds, mutual funds, exchanged-traded funds, rental real estate, private equity, and commodities), and use (personal property, automobiles, and homes). In the majority of cases, net worth is negative or less than $25,000 for impoverished individuals or families. Net worth may also be negative for many lower middle-class households, fall between $0 and $249,000 for middle-income families, and exceed $250,000 for upper middle-income households that focus on building their savings and income-generating assets—for example, bonds and dividend-paying stocks. Incidentally, affluent Americans do not usually include use assets in their net worth calculation. I'll discuss the reasons for this in a later chapter, but Robert Kiyosaki, author of the *Rich Dad, Poor Dad* book series, classifies homeownership as a liability or maintenance debt.

Let's deviate for a second to explore the catalyst that initially compelled me to study our most prized asset (or biggest liability): connecting our mind and body in a way that we often take for granted.

A FULL-COURT PRESS TO SAVE OUR SON

The brain is the most awe-inspiring and perhaps most misunderstood part of the human body. It contains billions of neurons that let us learn challenging math concepts, navigate our environment, and be uniquely different from any other person who has ever walked the earth. This command center processes our thoughts, emotions, mindsets, behaviors, and movements. It has always intrigued me, but none more than when our precious son Eli, then five years old, was diagnosed with sensory integration disorder (SID). SID is a condition in which the brain and the body can't sync up. Most people have never heard of this disorder; however, they've probably seen some kids exhibit noticeable symptoms, as more American children get autism-spectrum diagnoses.

Our son was never diagnosed with an autism-spectrum disorder. Nonetheless, he did display many of the common characteristics shared by most kids on the autism spectrum who also have sensory integration disorder. Although they are two distinct (but interconnected) conditions, it's fairly common for people to interchange autism-spectrum disorder and sensory integration disorder. His symptoms and challenges once included, among many others, picky eating, social awkwardness, unusual clumsiness and tiredness, spatial disorientation, poor eye tracking, substandard handwriting, torso and large muscle-group weakness, compromised immune system, and perfectionism. (Poor gut health may be the underlying culprit behind many cognitive disorders. The connection between the brain and gut flora is undeniable. Urine and blood tests revealed that our son had a yeast overgrowth or fungus in his gut, which likely contributed to many of his behavioral problems. How each social class deals with health and related matters will be covered in greater detail in Chapter 15, "Wellness.")

We went on a full-court press to save our son after he told my wife one evening, "My bones won't allow me to move my body right." Additionally, I was heartbroken when Eli yelled at me before storming out of the gym, "I hate basketball! I just can't do it!" Two years later we had a different son, thanks in large part to dietary changes, a customized nutritional protocol, an intense mental and physical exercise regimen, and of course, constant prayer. We watched in amazement as his brain and body merged into one integrated unit. Our entire family had to adapt to his immediate needs, or else any gains would be short-lived. It was worth the sacrifice of both money (a little) and time (a lot). We also vowed to help him overcome his sensory challenges without using prescription drugs, with their inevitable side effects. Most people who see him today have a hard time believing that Eli couldn't catch a football or do five pushups just a few years ago. My wife and I know that the brain is pliable and can change for the better if it's exercised diligently, efficiently, and nutritionally.

Here is an abbreviated list of the areas of improvement our son experienced in the four lobes of the brain, a highly complex and interdependent system: the cerebral cortex, which includes the frontal lobe, parietal lobe, temporal lobe, and occipital lobe. Each lobe is responsible for specific tasks, actions, and functions:

Frontal Lobe	Parietal Lobe
weighing the consequences of actions and behaviors that could result in pain or injury	being aware of his body as it relates to people and objects
writing neatly and legibly, which are fine-motor skills	navigating his environment without being told what to do
becoming a more refined planner and problem-solver	overcoming a stuttering problem to become a confident and bodacious communicator
learning to organize his thoughts and actions constructively	respecting the space and territorial rights of others
sitting still and paying attention in a distracting environment when the reward or payout is low	processing information and acquiring knowledge through his senses

Temporal Lobe	Occipital Lobe
normalization of appropriate responses to perceived threats that are fueled by fight-or-flight reactions of the amygdala	understanding the importance of visual acuity to stationary or moving objects to avoid bumping into them
reacting normally to certain smells instead of overreacting to them, which the olfactory bulb handles	projecting future goals without a visual representation

Temporal Lobe	Occipital Lobe
learning to regulate disappointment when denied access to an intensely pleasurable action, for example, not getting angry when he can't play video games	perceiving and interacting with objects in motion, such as catching a football without crossing his arms
being more balanced in his range of emotions (happiness, surprise, disgust, sadness, fear, and anger)	processing visual information, color and spatial distance of objects notably, correctly and efficiently
improvement in how he hears and processes auditory information	being able to clarify and articulate how he "sees" his future world

WHY *SOCIOPSYCHONOMICS*?

Socioeconomic classifications are often defined from a myopic, income-oriented vantage point with little or no emphasis on the individual psychological habits and tendencies that allow us to upgrade our monetary frame of reference, and thus, our income and wealth picture. Still further, within each social class there are nontraditional subsets or categories with clearly defined walls of separation. Without these, distinctions between classes would blur somewhat. With more than 25 years of anecdotal research as an obsessive student of social class dynamics, I'm firmly convinced that these boundaries do not prevent anyone from achieving social mobility (as measured by income and wealth), nor should they. Any barrier to upward mobility, outside of racism (overt and covert) or verifiable prejudice, has its roots in human psychology, where perception holds reality hostage.

You might be surprised that social studies was my least favorite school subject throughout my educational experience. The rationale for it wasn't obvious back then, but it is now.

As a child, I took tremendous pride in my intellectual capabilities, enjoying the challenges of learning every school subject—except social studies. It did not excite my soul. As a result, I don't have any fond memories of this topic from my formative years. Math? You bet. Mrs. Johnson, my second-grade teacher, inspired my fascination with numbers and was instrumental in shaping the mathematical formula I needed to succeed in life, particularly as an inner-city child. My sixth-grade math teacher, Miss Devers, inspired me to new heights in math, because she refused to allow "mediocre efforts in class from a gifted student." English? Yes, ma'am. Miss Brown, my eighth-grade teacher, didn't like my sloppy penmanship, but she did push me to express myself through creative writing. In high school at Wehrle Memorial, Miss Wiseman forced me to take my language arts skills to a new level. What about science, history, health, physical education, and art? Absolutely! I excelled in all of them.

I earned A's in social studies, but without feeling any driving ambition to learn the subject. Looking back, I see why. Studying America's social systems and cultures was too personal, too painful. This field of study explains how human beings think, act, and behave from a civic, economic, historic, and geographic perspective. This is the underlying premise of *Sociopsychonomics*: to differentiate each social class and their subsets based on financial interactions and habits and life experiences.

I've spoken to more than 10,000 elementary and middle-school students who took part in the Mr. Fundy's Math Basketball Jam, a one-hour interactive presentation combining humor, emotion, math, and (of course) basketball activities. I discuss my life story and love of math through powerful illustrations and exciting basketball drills. Students come alive as they see math from a different point of view. We verbally and visually highlight the correlation between education, earnings, and quality of life, as well as the importance of academic balance in all the core subjects. The students correctly guessed my favorite subject in school: math. Then I tell them my least favorite school subject: social studies. They laughed hysterically and immediately turned toward the social studies teacher for a reaction. I turned down the volume of their hysteria with these heartfelt words: "It was my least favorite school subject as a child, but now, it is a close second to my favorite." (Ironically, my wife's two favorite school subjects in childhood were social studies and history. She says, "I was fascinated by them because I was trying to find my identity and heritage growing up in a small town, Chillicothe, with ties to the Underground Railroad.")

I couldn't articulate this as a child because social studies touched my *poverty nerve*. Who wants to study a subject that mirrors humiliation, embarrassment, and inequality? Contrasts in cultures and social class distinctions can lead to apathetic, judgmental, and prejudicial attitudes. I knew better, but I sometimes succumbed to these detrimental forces whenever I viewed poverty through the lens of economic unfairness.

Before I discuss the subsets within each social class, let's spotlight some glaring (and not so bright) socioeconomic beliefs. Many of these are based on misconceptions. Here are the big ten.

SOCIAL CLASS BELIEFS AND FALLACIES

Belief #1

A dramatic increase in income must automatically mean an upgrade in socioeconomic status.

Why the belief?
- Some people believe that more money means greater social acceptance.
- Government data and economists use income to determine social status.

Why is this belief a fallacy?
- Income doesn't automatically change behaviors; thoughts, mindsets, and newfound vantage points do.
- Social status conversion doesn't happen by osmosis; it is a planned or calculated event.
- Money brings out the best or worst in you (and oftentimes in those around you).

Belief #2

Affluence is elusive and abstract. The poor and middle class cannot become affluent, except through a "lucky break" or fortuitous event: lottery winnings, inheritance, professional sports, or a music contract.

Why the belief?
- A lack of income and wealth-generating opportunities make affluence hard to reach.
- Many people feel that wealth is inherently evil. Or they believe they are swimming upstream against the currents of economic advancement. Why try when you're doomed to failure?
- People feel that wealth is too abstract to be part of their reality. Fear and anger—internal images of a perpetually glooming and troubling outlook—keep them stuck in their current situations.

Why is this belief a fallacy?

- The tenets of wealth creation do not discriminate on the basis of race, religion, or gender.
- Sowing and reaping apply to every aspect of life, including wealth.
- With the right tools, resources, mentors, and game plan, anyone can amass wealth, though the learning curve may be steeper for some than for others. (Check your motives before pursuing personal or financial wealth. It'll be well worth it.)
- Misperception just might be the biggest hindrance to wealth-generating opportunities, a failure to see them in their proper perspective.

Belief #3

Wealth comes only from tangible things, and money is a way to keep score.

Why the belief?

- This belief is based solely on how we define and create assets. Tangible assets include cash and cash equivalents—things we can invest and spend. But intangible assets, including intellect, creativity, compassion, and faith, are significantly more valuable.
- People who hold this belief feel inadequate because they compare their financial situations to those of other people and decide that they don't measure up.
- This belief explains why inner-city communities place so much emphasis on material possessions as a way to "pay back the haters" when they experience a financial "come-up" or breakthrough.

Why is this belief a fallacy?

- Intangible assets are often the engine behind tangible financial assets. Intangible assets create intellectual property, personal and professional networks, emotional regulation, legacy continuity, and the ability to recognize and fulfill one's life purpose.
- The truly wealthy don't keep score, because they operate under the law of prosperity. (More on this later in the book.)
- The informed wealthy look at value, not market price, as they provide for children, grandchildren, and philanthropic causes that are near and dear to their hearts and intellectual proclivities.

Belief #4

An individual's or family's socioeconomic status is a permanent condition that children and grandchildren will replicate.

Why the belief?

- The generationally affluent see this as a natural progression, one based on their histories of family legacy.
- "This is as good as it gets for our family tree and heritage." Many people in poverty or the middle class assume the economic ladder of wealth has missing rungs, believing they cannot climb any higher than their current financial standing.
- We tend to presume that people in all classes are content with the status quo, a cruise control state of existence.

Why is this belief a fallacy?

- People who create wealth typically have strong ambition and work ethics. Their children and grandchildren may not share those qualities, and so may squander family wealth. To prevent this, affluent families must spend as much time on financial education as on degree-oriented educational programs. They should include spendthrift and incentive provisions in estate trusts, though once beneficiaries have access to assets, there isn't much that can prevent mismanagement. And they need to spend time with family members, creating the relationships that are vital to legacy continuity. Hired help—nannies and caregivers—can't replace the love of a biological parent or grandparent, though they can supplement that love.
- People can change their incomes and degree of economic mobility if they are committed to the tasks and responsibilities required. It's always more expensive to pursue a worthwhile goal than we originally estimate.
- The global economic landscape, free trade in particular, has forever changed the comforts of our nation's middle-class lifestyle.

Belief #5

A substantial or permanent reduction in income (or, more specifically, lifestyle comforts) means an automatic downgrade in socioeconomic status.

Why the belief?

- Poverty is one of the middle class's biggest fears. Financial disequilibrium would shatter what they have worked so hard to achieve.

- Middle-class workers who lose jobs may be unable to find comparable work with commensurate pay.

- An unexpected event, such as divorce or death, can mean a reduced lifestyle, particularly for stay-at-home parents.

Why is this belief a fallacy?

- A life and financial plan can sustain an individual or family through economic setbacks. A plan should include adequate savings, investable assets, and insurance to replace lost income. It can also mean monetizing a skill-set to start a (side or standalone) business.

- Improved skills and abilities (and refinement of talents) often mean more employment and entrepreneurial opportunities. More education, personal brand enhancements, and an extended network can lead to better job prospects and higher pay.

- Don't let emotions dictate behavior. We tend to exacerbate financial problems when feelings overwhelm logic.

Belief #6

A college degree means a good job and at least a modest standard of living.

Why the belief?

- Educational advancement (with an outdated trust in the benefits obtained from a degree) is the hallmark of the middle class. Detractors point to ballooning student debt, but a four-year degree can significantly boost lifetime pay, compared to just a high school diploma.

Why is this belief a fallacy?

- The wrong degree creates significant debt (an average of roughly $25,000 for a bachelor's degree) and runaway stress.

- It's important to choose study programs wisely in a dynamic, globally connected world.

Belief #7

More money means more happiness.

Why the belief?
- Outflows (uses of income) are greater than inflows (sources of income) to cover living expenses.
- The media and music industry glamorize the lifestyles of the rich and famous as problem-free.
- Financial stress has a devastating effect on physical and mental health, relationships, and work productivity.

Why is this belief a fallacy?
- More money often brings more problems. Many lottery winners, musicians, and professional athletes emit faux happiness. Pain or internal turmoil often lies under the facade.
- Better money management habits are more valuable than more money.
- The informed wealthy work to fulfill their lives' purpose and economic potential. Money is a byproduct.

Belief #8

In retirement, individuals and couples will enjoy at least the same standard of living they have now.

Why the belief?
- Projections suggest that Social Security and Medicare safety nets will make up the shortfall for most Americans in retirement.
- Middle-class people believe time is on their side to save for retirement, as more pressing matters take precedence now.
- The stock market's historical average—a gain of roughly 10 percent per year—proves the power of compounding to fund lifestyle demands in retirement and stay ahead of inflation. (To determine the nest egg you'll need to avoid running out of money in retirement, multiply projected annual expenditures today by 25, a rule-of-thumb tool to gauge retirement readiness. Scary, right?)

Why is this belief a fallacy?
- The middle class is in denial about how much they'll need to cover

lifestyle expenditures in retirement. Most middle-class people have not even considered long-term care costs, which can exceed more than $75,000 per year in today's dollars.

- We will need drastic measures to plug the gaping holes in Social Security and Medicare, including means testing, raising taxes on the wealthy (chiefly federal and payroll taxes), or reducing retirement benefits. Neither Democrats nor Republicans want to deal with this demoralizing problem, which disproportionately hurts the middle class.

Belief #9

The mega wealthy are selfish and indifferent to the plight of the poor.

Why the belief?
- The wealth gap is growing wider; the richest 1 percent in America own 33 percent of our nation's wealth.[2]
- President Lyndon Johnson's war on poverty in the 1960s, and anti-poverty measures at the federal level that followed, have made only incremental gains against generational poverty.
- Generationally affluent donors support nonprofit organizations in keeping with legacy values, not in response to a need.
- Seclusion in gated communities and prestigious neighborhoods immunizes the mega wealthy from the problems and struggles facing their inner-city counterparts.
- Political candidates demonize the wealthy as contributing to the plight of the poor and struggling middle class, lamenting that "They win while you lose."

Why is this belief a fallacy?
- I'm not a fan of some of the organizations they support, but wealthy Americans do donate billions to domestic and international charities each year. In fact, many situationally and generationally affluent Americans have pledged to donate most, if not all, of their fortunes to social causes at death.
- Small-business owners create approximately 70 percent of new jobs.
- Super-affluent donors give strategically, diversifying to fund goals across different values, interests, and sometimes continents. Emotional pleas for financial support are rarely an influence.

- Many wealthy Americans and impoverished voting blocks support the same political candidates.

Belief #10

People living in poverty are lazy and lack the ambition to achieve a better life.

Why the belief?
- Despite the economic recovery since the Great Recession, the number of Americans living in poverty in 2015 was 43.1 million.[3]
- Over 40 million Americans are currently receiving food stamps.[4]
- The plight of inner-city communities has gotten worse as gangs, drugs, fatherlessness (or children born out of wedlock), teen pregnancies, and academic indifference cycle through from one generation to the next.
- Elected officials use political banter to point out societal ills plaguing impoverised areas of the country.

Why is this belief a fallacy?
- People in poverty aren't privy to the scaffolding blueprint to economic liberty—verifiable opportunities and available mentors that precede the buildup of meaningful financial wealth. They don't necessarily lack ambition or personal drive.
- Poverty's structural challenges often handicap the poor, who lack positive role models, endure neighborhood blight and dysfunction, and have inadequate coping mechanisms to counteract stress.
- The shift from a manufacturing economy to a service economy requires different educations and skill-sets. Even with government assistance, this change disproportionately affects the poor more than their middle-class and wealthy peers.
- Part-time, minimum-wage employment proves that the poor will work, even for an extremely low financial reward.
- My wife and I have worked with thousands of young people and families from impoverished backgrounds through LFYO, our nonprofit organization. Their capacity to learn complex subjects is never an issue when they're motivated and in a conducive and non-threatening setting. The formula for economic liberty follows:

[Inspiration + Information] x Preparation = Emancipation

- I'm living proof that a hand up is more empowering than a potentially disempowering handout!

PRE GAME

CHAPTER

1

CLASSES AND SUBSETS

*Affinity markers used to define an individual's or
family's group identity and emotive association with a
socioeconomic classification or embedded subset*

Sociopsychonomics separates each social class—the poor, the middle class, and the wealthy—into three distinct subsets: generational, situational, and functional. These distinctions are based on identifying traits and habits that are fairly common among social class subsets. People very often aren't even aware of displaying these qualities.

I use semantic references for each socioeconomic group interchangeably throughout the book. I characterize poverty-stricken Americans, welfare recipients, and the working poor as economically distressed Americans, or EDAs. I describe the middle class, blue-collar workers, and middle America as income-stability Americans, or ISAs. I call affluent Americans, the mega wealthy, high-net-worth individuals and families, the super rich, and the 1 Percent as affluent-positioned Americans, or APAs. Unless I note otherwise, I look at social class from a generational perspective.

Most people see generational subsets as the face of a social class, where customs, traditions, and norms are passed down from one generation to the next. (The middle class is an exception.) Discomfort occurs when their way of living—the status quo—is interrupted. Depending on their social class, generationally speaking, people respond to incoming distress signals in ways that are predictable, and at times, perplexing.

Situational subsets receive the bulk of any compassion, because a misfortune bumped them into a lower social class. Praise for self-determination and hard work goes to those who move up a social class, from poverty to the middle class or from the middle class to affluence. Social class mobility is the badge of economic success in America.

Functional subsets are a quagmire because their actions and attitudes are often manufactured (which isn't a bad thing in every case) to assimilate within a socioeconomic class. Group identity and emotive association are critically important to their images and egos. The methods people use to display social class allegiance are amusing, confusing, defusing, and bemusing.

I'll first examine poverty, my childhood abode.

THE POOR

Subset #1

Generational Economically Distressed Americans (GEDAs)

It's not easy to attain structural wealth through post-secondary education and career-advancement efforts, especially for people from impoverished backgrounds. Law, finance, architectural design, and business probably offer more realistic roads out of poverty, but poor people often shun these career paths in favor of professional sports and entertainment, where the odds of success are infinitesimally small. Illogic aside, this explains why poor and middle-class parents in search of a meal ticket will make tremendous sacrifices to invest in their children's athletic potential. High-end designer sneakers and apparel, Amateur Athletic Union (AAU) fees, weekend tournament expenditures, and shopping excursions to reward a child's performance in basketball, football, or baseball are burdensome financial outlays. To these parents, the expected payoff is worth the expense. They must make sacrifices, they reason, to help their children reach the pinnacle of athletic success: a college scholarship or career in pro sports.

All this diminishes the responsibility a child feels to perform outside of sports. The law of unintended consequences punishes the poor more than the middle class and wealthy, because the repercussions hit them harder. (I held a life and financial planning workshop for nearly a dozen African-American female school teachers in March of 2016. The issue of the law of unintended consequences came up. One teacher remarked in frustration, "I don't understand why a parent would buy her son a pair of Air Jordan shoes when he doesn't even have school supplies to advance his educational development.")

THE FACE OF POVERTY

Poverty's legacy—recurring traumatic events, contentment in current circumstances, skepticism toward outsiders, and fatalistic attitudes—is hard for people without comparable life experiences to understand. Perpetual stress, lack of opportunities, and unimaginable neighborhood violence take a tremendous toll on children and adults in economically distressed communities. Emotions drive behaviors, and that can and often does mean repeating the very same actions and inactions that people should avoid. I'll highlight this point throughout the book: high, sustained levels of stress create psychological and physiological imbalances. The brain bypasses the prefrontal cortex, home to sequential reasoning and logic, to deal with more immediate threats, real or perceived. Resulting behavior includes impulsivity, indifference, retaliation, hostility, or insubordination. None of these responses lead to favorable economic conditions. In fact, people magnify poor financial habits to minimize the pain and other effects of stressful situations. They spend what little money they have on feel-good purchases: food, clothing, and entertainment. That perpetuates poverty, creates more debt, and handicaps delayed gratification.

Still other impoverished people see education as an unnecessary, long-term burden. Economic success and income mobility are a process that punishes the impatient and rewards the diligent. The journey must start in the mind; appropriate behaviors follow. Since 2000, my wife and I have worked with thousands of impoverished youth. We've learned that a lack of confidence and parental affirmation means that we hold a lot of hands as students encounter the world of personal finance and wealth accumulation.

Teachers carry the entire burden of educating children when many poverty-stricken parents abdicate their roles in their children's educational development. Without that parental support, student motivation starts to dissipate after the third or fourth grade. In dozens of conversations with public- and private-school teachers, I've heard that third grade may be the most academically challenging school year for poor children, especially in higher-level mathematical thinking, reasoning, and articulation skills. The brain is growing and so are the options to tune out education. Earning easy money by selling street drugs becomes more enticing, fantasy careers in professional sports seem more real, and academic gaps grow more pronounced. The educational journey becomes too daunting to navigate as feelings overwhelm logic, and millions of disadvantaged students exit high school without a diploma. I am haunted by the tagline from the United Negro College Fund commercials I watched as a child: "A mind is a terrible thing to waste." We spend billions of dollars to incarcerate, medicate, and alienate impoverished Americans. It's time we emancipate!

A CEO of a large nonprofit organization here in Central Ohio, where employees live in the same neighborhoods as the constituents they serve, told me, "People in poverty have an extremely difficult time with trust." He is correct. With violated innocence and the resulting pain at deafening levels, people default to self-preservation. I used the same tactic (and still do, to a certain extent) to keep people from invading my inner sanctuary of the soul.

The world of generational poverty is full of anger, pain, stress, and fatalism. A profound sense of unfairness, accompanied by an unhealthy dose of skepticism toward outsiders who, in most instances, really do come to help, is pervasive in historically impoverished communities across the country. (People in their inner circles make promises to uplift their broken spirit, but rarely keep those promises—and the downward spiral of despair and depression continues unabated.)

People give their trust and take it back when family members, friends, or acquaintances exploit them. Affirmation and validation are scarce on the home front, but gangs and drug dealers offer these identification markers in abundance to impressionable youth who have no father figures or role models. Self-preservation and little or no regard for the welfare of others can lead to disastrous consequences. Hurting people hurt other people.

Impoverished children may have food, yet that food is devoid of the nutrition children need to focus in school. Empty calories, some people assume, are better than no calories. Nonprofit organizations offer supple-mental services, but how can recipients capitalize on job skills training and credit repair offerings without adequate transportation? The proliferation of e-learning does not excite the poor, who have trouble seeing rewards that are years in the future. They live in and for the moment, which can produce endorphins, boost happiness, and help (temporarily) assuage the pain of being seen as second-class citizens. Generational poverty makes very little sense to mezzanine observers, who are quick to criticize the poor but provide no economic solutions that help people escape poverty. America needs to bridge the wealth gap before the curtain closes and revolution spills into our streets.

Subset #2

Situational Economically Distressed Americans (SEDAs)

Middle-class and wealthy people are most sympathetic toward situational poverty, where reckless financial behaviors did not apparently contribute to an individual's or family's economic demise—a triggering event did. A lack of compassion would appear callous and indifferent. Who wants to wear any of these labels when observing financial distress in the lives of hardworking Americans? The following two hypothetical examples have real-world implications today.

ONE STEP DOWN TO POVERTY

Michael is 46, single, and an unemployed carpenter. His company laid him off several years ago during an economic downturn. Low interest rates, lax lending standards, and eager builders and developers flooded the housing market with "affordably priced" homes. Michael assumed his job security and modest pay as a blue-collar worker would last several more years. It didn't. Unfortunately, boom and bust cycles are part of the financial landscape, as policymakers and the Federal Reserve work to keep economic growth trending upward and consumer borrowing costs low. (Ultimately, an economy should grow organically, without manipulation and intervening efforts.)

Economics 101 teaches us that supply doesn't automatically equal demand. When we assume that it does, the collateral damage usually hits the middle class hardest and millions lose their jobs and lifestyle comforts. Lack of planning, insufficient transitional job skills, and complacent strategic thinking are income-stability Americans' (ISAs) most glaring weaknesses during periods of economic turmoil.

Michael doesn't have health insurance, and he is depleting his savings to cover bills and groceries. Although he qualifies, pride prevents him from seeking and receiving government assistance, welfare, and Medicaid. When he was a teenager his father, a former assembly line worker for an automobile manufacturer, told him, "Son, earn your keep by working hard. I'm not against welfare by any means, but to take from the government when you have the capacity to work is theft. Plain and simple. And our family ain't no thieves!" These words still resonate with Michael, the oldest of four children. His employment options are minimal. He has a high school diploma and one year of college; these can't take him very far in a dynamic, global environment. A stellar work ethic is laudable. But physical labor is no match for intellectual capital when economic forces (domestically or internationally) shift from manufacturing to service. Reluctantly, Michael sells his car and moves back home to care for his aging parents. He must wait for the economy to recover before his employment prospects get better.

TWO STEPS DOWN FROM AFFLUENCE TO POVERTY

Monica, a recently divorced mother of three children, is struggling financially. The money and lifestyle she was accustomed to over the past decade have vanished. Her ex-husband, John, is a former professional athlete who earned more than $30 million during his ten-year playing career. A reckless lifestyle, bad investment deals, and financial mismanagement led to economic ruin.

Monica was complicit, too. She spent extravagantly on herself and their three kids. Shopping sprees at a local mall, where she spent tens of thousands of dollars with her girlfriends while John was on the road, were a regular occurrence. The family kept a live-in nanny, chef, personal trainer, massage therapist, chauffeur, life coach, wardrobe consultant, bill pay specialist, agent, attorney, investment advisor, and entourage on their monthly payroll. Private schooling for the children, country club memberships, a jet timeshare, exclusive vacations, and loans to family members who never paid them back were additional financial outlays. John and Monica owned six automobiles, two residences (in-season and out-of-season homes), and other depreciating assets that gave the appearance of economic success. Taxes, agent fees, and union dues shrank the $30 million guaranteed contract to $12 million. Then came the shocking reality of economic distress, a fall from situational wealth to situational poverty. It sounds far-fetched that this happened in the world of professional sports, but many players and their families are no better off in retirement than when they began their careers.

John and Monica were divorced two years after he retired. Depression, gambling, lingering injuries, and a lack of employable skills outside sports crippled John's ability to transition away from the game he loved. Sports were his life and his identity. Neither he nor his advisors planned for the fateful day that awaits every professional athlete, when the horn sounds and the game is truly over. By force or choice, every sports career ends. Monica, John's high school sweetheart, never attended college.

Monica was a gifted student, but her higher-education goals went on permanent hold to support John's professional sports career. Of course, she now regrets this decision, especially after signing a prenuptial agreement that limited her assets and income in a divorce. What few assets they still had went to pay creditors and John's gambling debts. John filed for Chapter 7 bankruptcy protection, which will stay on his credit report for ten years. He must pay child and spousal support, which can't be expunged through the bankruptcy laws. However, Monica may not receive any financial support from John for the foreseeable future, because he doesn't have an income. As she sobs uncontrollably, Monica swallows her pride and signs the necessary paperwork to collect welfare benefits. She made a vow that this would be a temporary measure until her circumstances change for the better.

> One of the worst things in the world is to face a future that you are not prepared for.

Other leading contributors to situational poverty include illness, death, and denying financial reality. Bankruptcies caused by an illness or unexpected surgery were commonplace before the Affordable Care Act, also known as Obamacare. When a spouse dies, the income loss can combine with long-term grief to paralyze a family for years. Stress and depression can create financial and emotional wounds that are too deep to overcome. Caring for aging Baby Boomers while simultaneously raising young children can push a family from the middle class to situational poverty. Long-term nursing care costs can exceed $75,000 annually. Ninety-five percent of Americans cannot afford long-term care for their aging parents or relatives, never mind their own future needs. We care for loved ones who can't care for themselves, even when it hurts us financially. When we ignore our financial realities, paralysis sets in and we lose the chance to mitigate the fall to situational poverty. Life insurance, wealth-protection strategies, and estate-preservation techniques can all help avert financial calamity.

Subset #3

Functional Economically Distressed Americans (FEDAs)

Functional poverty prevents people from enjoying financial success. FEDAs find it hard to relinquish the habits of poverty. They don't live in poverty in the physical realm, but in their own heads. Some FEDAs are extreme cheapskates. Frugality is too generous a word to describe their penny-pinching ways. Others spend money frivolously. Middle-class and affluent people from impoverished backgrounds may repeat the foolish spending patterns their parents used to gain an emotional high or appease other people's expectations. Fear and guilt drive the two extremes.

"TO REALLY KNOW THE DIVINE, YOU MUST BE POOR"

Some faith-based circles preach the humility of poverty, literally. "Be on your guard against the snares of riches, lest you fall into a sudden trap," the message goes. Religious and nonreligious people alike should avoid get-rich-quick schemes and too-good-to-be-true investment opportunities. Too many sheep in wolves' clothing have led people of all faiths astray. Scam artists don't discriminate in making a fast buck. Their victims run the gamut from elderly couples who lose their life savings to single mothers raising children on part-time incomes. CNBC's "American Greed" has aired countless segments on the betrayals of hard-working Americans who can least afford to lose money in investment scams.

In my associations with wealthy and poverty-stricken communities, I've known people who were incredibly greedy and ruthless in their pursuit of money. Glorification of wealth and material possessions are matters of the heart, not the mark of a particular social class. Debt and poverty don't mean spiritual freedom. Quite the contrary—financial distress can lead to economic bondage and contribute to poor health, strained relationships, and an agitated spirit. Differences over money are perhaps the biggest single contributor to marital discord, which is so pervasive today. Money can be a productive tool or a destructive weapon.

> ## SOCIOPSYCHONOMIC FILTER
> When your lifestyle is reckless, your money and financial habits soon follow.

'HOOD CARD REVOKED

Fictitious rapper Nico (aka "Kool Breeze") signed a multimillion-dollar record deal with Next Level Entertainment. Although he lives in a gated community with highly successful doctors, lawyers, and influential business leaders, Nico can't relate to his white-collar neighbors. Yes, he does have seven cars, along with the bling of diamond-studded earrings and several Rolex watches. His posse, rolling six deep, make weekend trips back to Kool Breeze's neighborhood on the city's south side, the Jamison Housing Projects. His fear of losing his street credibility is difficult to overcome. He tells himself, "I'll lose my 'hood card if I forget where I came from." To feel emotionally secure, even in the suburbs, Kool Breeze surrounds himself with an entourage of neighborhood peers whose primary responsibility is to keep him afraid of abandoning his impoverished origins. They keep his mind at the street level, even as he rises to the top of the Billboard charts.

Nico has his share of critics in the 'hood. The accusations are wrapped in guilt. At the barbershop, on social media, in the nightclub, they let it be known that Kool Breeze is full of hot air:

> **'Hood Critic #1**: He Hollywood now! Dude forgot about the little people.

> **'Hood Critic #2**: Man, Kool Breeze ain't from the projects. He fake.

> **'Hood Critic #3**: He didn't keep his word—he promised me a new car with some 30-inch rims!

Nico's confidence drops to a new low after he reads these words spray-painted on the side of his former apartment complex: "Kool Breeze—stay in the 'burbs, homeboy. You ain't welcome here no mo.'"

A LESSON IN ECONOMIC SELF-PRESERVATION

Here's another example that illustrates the power of guilt and fear in functional poverty. Jim was a tenured professor at State University for more than three decades. Now a widower, he is in relative good health and lives frugally in retirement. Jim's parents grew up during the Great Depression and remember meal rationing, alcoholism, and even suicide as people tried to cope with the pain of one of our nation's darkest periods. Even after the Great Depression ended and economic conditions normalized, a permanent transformation occurred in the hearts and minds of middle-class Americans who saved every penny while living well below their means. They reasoned, "If economic chaos happened once, it can certainly happen again."

> ### SOCIOPSYCHONOMIC FILTER
> Glorification of wealth and material possessions are matters of the heart, not the mark of a particular social class.

Economic self-preservation is a way to protect ourselves from real or perceived financial threats. Jim's parents lost their family farm. Fortunately, Jim's father, John, found a factory job when World War II revived U.S. manufacturing. The security of a good job appealed to Jim's internal compass, which directed him to higher education. His former wife, Sally, didn't indulge herself in shopping sprees or pampering salon sessions. She was the proverbial Plain Jane. With no debt, the couple owned a home in an up-and-coming, middle-class neighborhood of educators, police officers, and government workers. Their financial advisor tried unsuccessfully to persuade Jim and Sally to spend more. Their retirement nest egg was on solid footing, he assured them. They could more than afford a fine-dining experience at an upscale restaurant each month and an annual vacation to an exotic destination. They refused his overtures. The substantive empirical data, with its modest growth and risk projections, weren't enough to convince these two unshakable believers in economic deprivation. Financial paralysis prevents people from enjoying their economic success. Again, fear or guilt is the likely culprit.

THE MIDDLE CLASS

Subset #1

Generational Income- Stability Americans (GISAs)

The traditional middle class is in a state of flux. Their three economic pillars have obvious foundational cracks. The first pillar, a stable job with modest pay, annual wage increases, and good benefits, has undergone a tremendous shake-up as our economy shifted over the past century from agriculture to industry to manufacturing and now to service and technology. Far too many Americans, especially GISAs, have not adjusted to globalism's rapid changes over the past quarter century. Wage increases have been anemic for the middle class and employers expect workers to cover some (if not all) of the rising healthcare costs and fund their retirements. Just as a coach makes tactical adjustments as game conditions dictate, GISAs must also use a calculated playbook to compete.

The second pillar of middle-class economic success is a comfortable living environment with homeownership. It's awfully difficult to enjoy labor's fruits as we lose more jobs to corporate restructuring, downsizing, and outsourcing. Companies and industries have to reinvent themselves when the situation demands it, or die. Kodak, Blockbuster, and Borders are painful reminders of outdated business models that didn't (and still don't) work in the new economy. Unfortunately, those companies' workers lost their jobs, benefits, and lifestyles.

During the housing collapse that led to the Great Recession, banks extended loans to Americans who bought homes they couldn't really afford. Of course, lenders and homeowners were also culpable. Financial planners use a simple rule of thumb to determine how much house someone can afford: 2.5 times annual income. A couple earning a combined yearly income of $90,000 can afford a $225,000 house. During the housing bubble, people bought homes that cost five to ten times their annual incomes. (When the economy is expanding, realtors may encourage buyers to consider purchasing a home that costs 3.5 to 4 times annual income. Just because you can doesn't mean you should.)

A secure retirement is the third pillar of economic success. If you're in the middle class, even the thought of planning for retirement may create incredible stress. Check your pulse now and compare it to your resting heart rate if you don't believe me. Sadly, most Americans don't have a clue about what they'll need to avoid running out of money in retirement. Here's another rule of thumb. First, close your eyes, take a deep breath, and exhale slowly. Estimate the annual living expenses that you (and your partner) will likely have in retirement. Use today's dollars. Expenses should include housing, lifestyle expenditures, insurance, and supplemental healthcare, among others. Now multiply your estimated annual living expenses in today's dollars by 25. That's the nest egg you'll need to retire, generally speaking, to avoid depleting the portfolio. Shocking, isn't it?

Assuming a generous 8 percent annual return, an individual or couple with projected retirement living expenses of $100,000 in today's dollars will need $2.5 million to avoid running out of money in retirement. The average American family's retirement account balance in 2013 was $95,776, but the median retirement savings was only $5,000.[5] Still today, on the whole, Americans are woefully unprepared for retirement.

The middle class should have seen the writing on the wall in the early 1990s, when the great shift in retirement benefits began. Very few people were listening. Employers have put the onus of preparing for retirement squarely on employees' shoulders. A staple of blue-collar employment before 1990, employees expected employer-provided pensions.

In an employer-provided defined benefit plan, the employer or sponsor pays employees a promised future benefit and assumes the risk of the plan's performance. In retirement, an employee receives a set amount with a cost-of-living adjustment (COLA) each month for the rest of his or her life. Combined with Social Security, this is the deal blue-collar workers signed up for and would enjoy until their death. Since 1990, employers have gradually shifted to employer-sponsored defined contribution plans. With defined contribution plans, employees—not employers—are responsible for selecting investments inside their retirement accounts, as well as for those investments' underlying performance. Also, employees forfeit matching employer contributions when they don't participate at all or to the rewarded degree.

Employees and the self-employed alike must start saving diligently for retirement. Given Medicare and Social Security's obvious shortfalls—current Social Security recipients take out roughly three dollars for every dollar they contributed during their working years—people under 50 will be in big trouble if they haven't adequately planned for retirement. It's going to be really ugly for the vast majority of Americans: the traditional middle class.

> **SOCIOPSYCHONOMIC FILTER**
> Nothing paralyzes the traditional middle class more than the law of diminishing returns: too many monthly bills and debts, and too few income sources to cover them.

Like other social class subsets, generational income-stability Americans share characteristics. They are loyal, compliant, diligent, reliable, dependable, and prompt. They prefer to be employees rather than employers. They prefer to invest in income-oriented stocks that pay dividends instead of growth-oriented stocks that do not pay dividends. They strongly value education for their children, assuming that it will help their offspring achieve the same comfortable, middle-class lifestyle in adulthood. The traditional middle class willingly sacrifice for the greater good, even if this means taking a steep pay cut to keep their company's cash flow situation positive and shareholders happy. Unfortunately, GISAs are increasingly being asked to make concessions with their time and money. Nothing paralyzes the traditional middle class more than the law of diminishing returns: too many monthly bills and debts, and too few income sources to cover them. This creates an incredible amount of anxiety and stress, forcing them to block out other equally or more important matters, such as protecting an asset from a large-scale loss, funding their retirement, and creating a rock-solid estate plan to prevent family members from feuding over possessions.

A STARR SHINES BRIGHT

In my interview with Starr Powell, a family friend, she shared a profound truth about the middle class: "We don't lack vision, but our vision of what's financially possible is limited. We only see ourselves going so far in life, stopping well short of affluence." How true.

I've known Starr for years, but didn't know about her middle-class upbringing until she participated in a financial wellness seminar at FunderMax Fitness. In one of the sessions, I was describing the middle class and their singular focus on finding solutions to pending financial problems. Sitting directly in front of me, Starr laughed, saying, "That's me, that's me. Nothing else matters to me—just a solution to my financial situation."

Next, I discussed the concept of financial disorientation, which is a recurring headache for GISAs. When people don't know where they stand financially, it prevents them from taking the necessary steps to achieve lasting economic freedom. Their financial navigation system is missing the appropriate latitudinal and longitudinal coordinates. No location. No movement. Just spinning around in the same spot, getting dizzier and going nowhere. Welcome to the world of the traditional middle class, where an ever-changing landscape of macroeconomic conditions can short-circuit their monetary vestibular system. It's amazing what shows up when anxiety and fear dominate our lives, even in the midst of favorable circumstances—a pay raise, bonus, tax refund, or investment gain.

Starr's monetary frame of reference came from her parents, Jeannie and Karl Lockett. Jeannie managed the family's finances with religious fervor. She rarely deviated from the budget. Needs, not wants, were always met first. Starr recalls, "My mother and her siblings received an allowance in childhood. Although not rich, they had more than other families in the neighborhood. Money was never scarce." She adds, "My father grew up very poor. As a result, he doesn't deprive himself now when he wants something. It has to be the best—'top of the line' is his motto. He'll buy a car that's fully loaded. At restaurants, he's had enough of the scraps and feels he has earned the right to order what he wants, a prime cut of steak instead of chicken." It's not uncommon for spouses to balance one another, as Starr's parents did.

Starr reflected on the approaching Third Quarter of Life, the time when wealth accumulation should shine brightest. She says:

> "I grew up in a middle-class neighborhood where I *knew* I'd get good grades in school; this was not optional in our household. I *knew* that I would go to college and graduate with a four-year degree. I *knew* that I'd get a good job. However, nothing in me ever *said*, 'You're going to own this asset and achieve this level of affluence.' Even now, I place limitations on my financial health— it's a certain comfort level. I don't *feel* that I want the responsibility

that wealth brings. Given what's already on my plate, I *feel* I have enough responsibilities: work, kids, and relationships. Where is there room to add? Then I *see* other people and ask myself, 'How do they do that?' I don't *get* it because I don't *see* it." (My emphases are italicized.)

Starr's words communicate a powerful story. In the context of our discussion about the four lobes in the cerebral cortex, "knew" and "said" are code words that describe her internal dialogue center: the temporal lobe. She exuded confidence about her childhood educational prospects, which culminated in a bachelor's degree at The Ohio State University. But Starr didn't tell herself a positive story about what was possible for her financially. We tell ourselves and others what we imagine about our future economic reality. Childhood beliefs can birth or abort our financial dreams (or nightmares).

Now to the action verbs: "feel" and "get." These deal with perception (or intuition) and sensation (particularly touch) and orientation (or current standing in life), which are key parietal lobe attributes. The parietal lobe, or internal GPS, is a danger zone for the middle class, who often base economic success on measures they can reasonably control: educational attainment, work ethic, and reliability. What they can't measure or quantify in full is difficult to fully imagine, and thus is difficult to achieve.

What we "see," literally or figuratively, is housed in the occipital lobe, along with depth perception and visual acuity. Vision is the catalyst for financial freedom. It drives our interpretation of what we believe is possible or impossible. It motivates us to plug in the appropriate GPS coordinates to reach our destination, or paralyzes us to stay where we are, stuck in neutral. We'll cover the cerebral cortex in greater detail in Chapter 4, "Your Fascinating Brain."

AN IMPROMPTU VISIT

I'm a huge fan of the middle class, thanks in large part to my wife, Monya. She was born in one of the bluest of blue-collar small towns in our state's first capital, Chillicothe. This city currently boasts approximately 22,000 residents, most of whom presumably earn less than $60,000 per year. Chillicothe is rich in history and heritage, as the city was named after one of the tribal divisions of the Shawnee indigenous nation. My wife's family includes African-American, Native-American, and European-American heritage. In fact, my wife is a descendant of Madison Hemings, the slave child of Sally Hemings and former president Thomas Jefferson. Monya's great-grandmother on her mother's side, Emma Jane, was Madison Hemings' daughter. This town was one of the key passageways on the Underground Railroad. Runaway slaves from the South and free blacks found solace in Chillicothe. Many stayed here and made Ohio their permanent refuge, while others continued their trek north to Canada, where blacks were accepted into mainstream society.

My first visit to Chillicothe was surreal. I felt as if I'd been transported back in time. It was so strange to hear black people who lived one hour south of Columbus speaking with a southern dialect. They were also a decade or two behind in their wardrobe selections. I called Monya, whom I had just started dating, from a convenience store pay phone. She answered, "Hi. What are you doing here?" I sheepishly replied, "I've come down to see you and meet your parents." (In poor, inner-city communities, it's fairly common to show up at someone's house or apartment unannounced. This social faux pas is called being *ghetto fab*.)

Unlike me, Monya is not the confrontational type. She is quiet, reserved, polite, and calm, a person who cares deeply about social decorum. Surprisingly, in spite of our associations with millionaires, billionaires, and dignitaries through the years, Monya still feels out of place at times. With a painful expression on her face, she says, "Sometimes, and certainly not like I did initially, I feel inadequate being in the presence of super-wealthy people because of my middle-class background. I just don't feel like I fit in." Regardless of the social class or subset, I feel equally comfortable with Pookie and Ray Ray in poverty, Mary and John Thomas in the middle class, or the Hoffsteins in mega affluence. My comfort level remains high, diction quite flexible, and topics of interest adaptable. (Yes, I did grow up with people named Pookie and Ray Ray, as well as Rock Head, Peaches, Wingback, Man Man and Wawn Wawn, Tuffy, Poochie, Dirty Bert, Buggie, Stretch, Yuck Mouth, and many other interesting nicknames.)

Monya's parents, Cheri Hicks and Chris Fairrow, worked on the assembly line at two local factories. In the 1960s and 1970s, an unspoken quota system kept many blacks from obtaining good jobs in the areas surrounding Chillicothe, as well as in the continental United States. Even the appearance of minor transgressions could result in job loss. Monya says, "My mom and dad were so adamant about being compliant workers who showed up ahead of time and didn't cause problems. They also didn't want to be portrayed as blacks who were lazy. And this, too, is how I feel as a black woman in America. I don't ever want to be viewed in an unflattering light."

The traditional middle class is quick to distance themselves from poverty stereotypes. The difference between generational economically distressed Americans and generational income-stability Americans is significant. People in traditional poverty question everybody: parents, teachers, law-enforcement officials, doctors, even social workers. Skepticism is always present, no matter the circumstance or person, especially when feelings dominate decision-making abilities. In the traditional middle class, you never question anyone above you: doctors, lawyers, financial advisors, company executives, or other white-collar professionals in positions of authority. To do so would be akin to a soldier breaking rank or falling out of line, a disrespectful move subject to punishment by humiliation, degradation, alienation, insubordination, or termination. Better to stay in your place and keep quiet than risk embarrassment or lost income, they reason. However, the traditional middle class must question their current apprehension around wealth accumulation to meet current and future lifestyle demands.

SOCIOPSYCHONOMIC FILTER
Social Security and Medicare have shortfalls in the trillions of dollars, which rightly creates additional angst for middle-income earners.

Cheri and Chris are retired now, rewarded for their labor with guaranteed pension and Social Security benefits. Fortunately for them and their colleagues over age 62, these two income sources are paying their promised obligations. For middle-class workers under age 50, though, retirement income guarantees are either phased out or exhausted to meet current retiree obligations. Companies say they can't afford to finance pension or legacy assets decades into the future. Of course, white-collar executives and their lucrative benefits packages will be paid as promised. Blue-collar workers will have to fend for themselves. The earlier they realize this, the better off they'll be. Social Security and Medicare have shortfalls in the trillions of dollars, which rightly creates additional angst for middle-income earners. We'll revisit the pension and Social Security conundrum in the "Game-Time" section of the book.

Subset #2

Situational Income-Stability Americans (SISAs)

Situational income-stability Americans move up or down the socioeconomic ladder as fortune dictates. First-generation college graduates with meaningful degrees escape poverty and secure gainful employment with above-average pay. Their aspirations rise with their income levels and options. A timely mentor, an inner goal, or a fortuitous opportunity can be the key that propels an individual or family from economic distress into the safe arms of middle-class living, or so it appears. The challenges facing blue-collar Americans are glaringly real, but these pale in comparison to the torment of perpetual lack and financial misery that beset those in poverty. Trust me, the poor would gladly trade troubles with the middle class.

Those moving up from poverty to the middle class are applauded for their efforts, but those moving down from affluence to the middle class, for whatever reason, typically receive very little sympathy from outside observers. A job loss, illness, divorce, or even the death of a breadwinning partner could push a situationally affluent person or family firmly into the class below. Poor or struggling middle-class people may have a hard time feeling sorry for someone who previously had a very comfortable life. Lifestyle accoutrements such as country club memberships, weekend shopping sprees, or lavish vacations dwindle or vanish. Children attend public school instead of an elite private school. Home maintenance services, such as lawn and pool care, aren't outsourced anymore; family members do those tasks themselves to save money. (Of course, wealth does not immunize a person or family from hardship. In some instances, affluence exacerbates it, as we'll discuss later in the book.)

A PROUD MENTOR

I'm extremely proud of Joe Smith and Joseph Easley, who were teenagers in 2005, when they participated in our nonprofit's personal and financial development programs at the Milo-Grogan Boys and Girls Club. Milo-Grogan is a predominantly African-American neighborhood in Columbus, Ohio. In

2015, area homes had median incomes of roughly $33,000, just a few thousand dollars above the poverty level for a family of five.[6] By contrast, Columbus as a whole had a median household income in 2015 of over $47,000.[7]

Fast food restaurants dominate the intersection at Fifth and Cleveland Avenues, the epicenter of this corridor of the city, just a little more than a mile from downtown Columbus. Like most inner-city communities in America, drug addiction and violence are part of life here, and many residents have low expectations for the area's young people.

Joe and Joseph refused to believe the lie that they couldn't succeed in life. With determined spirits and shatter-proof vision, both overcame enormous odds to reach the middle class. Many of their neighborhood peers spent time in jail or died at a young age. It would have been easy for them to take the same path.

Teasing is common in impoverished communities when some residents envy others' success. Joseph recalls the teasing that he and Joe endured:

> "We were teased by our friends for taking part in your program. They would tell us that the only reasons why we hung out with you and Mrs. Fundy were because you liked us and you two were established and had money. However, you instilled in us that we could achieve millionaire or even billionaire status, outside of career pursuits in sports and entertainment. You opened our eyes to a professional world that included law, medicine, real estate, and business. I'm so grateful because you and Mrs. Fundy taught us about life and how to have structured goals. My present goals include being a lawyer and senator one day. The knowledge you provided us allowed our dreams to become reality."

Each of these young men received college scholarship assistance from the Lawrence Funderburke Youth Organization (LFYO) and the generous donors who support our mission.

A SPECIAL PLACE IN MY HEART

Sue Kaufman enjoyed a comfortable life for several decades in Upper Arlington, one of the most desirable suburban communities in Central Ohio, complete with pristine landscaping, excellent schools, white-collar professionals, and above-average incomes. I met Sue on a college summer job, working for Larry Kaufman, her former husband. Larry, a hard worker who came up from a humble childhood in blue-collar Cleveland, owned two dozen pharmacies in Columbus, Cincinnati, Dayton, and Lancaster.

Larry stood just 5'9", but his larger-than-life personality, smile, and words of encouragement attracted people. Sue, with her compassion and sunny personality, was his match. Together, the two demonstrated what was economically possible for me through education, diligence, determination, and an extended network.

Larry will always have a special place in my heart. When I transferred from Indiana University to Ohio State as a sophomore in early 1991, he didn't prejudge me for my previous basketball missteps. He didn't assume that my tumultuous past would follow me like a dark shadow into the new environment or interrogate me about what went wrong when I lasted only six games under the watchful eye of basketball legend and enigmatic coach, Bobby "The General" Knight. We shared a love of life.

SOCIOPSYCHONOMIC FILTER

A big heart goes a long way when an upper-class family allows the poor to enter their world, an environment free of economic limitations and full of networking interactions.

Unfortunately, Larry didn't see an urgent need for a comprehensive estate plan, one that would have taken care of his loved ones if he passed. "I'd ask if he had everything in order, but he'd tell me not to worry about it," Sue says. Larry died unexpectedly of a heart condition on April 1, 2006. Too numerous to count, his funeral was attended by family members, close friends, and colleagues. Buckeye sports stars were present as well, and Heisman Trophy winner Troy Smith wore a decal on his helmet throughout the 2006 season in his memory.

Sue sold their home, made substantial lifestyle adjustments, and took a part-time job. She thinks twice before making purchases, diligently searching for bargains and sales. She is the proud mother of three wonderful kids and now lives with her son Mike. "When a spouse who handles all aspects of a family's finances tells his wife that everything is taken care of if he dies, get documented proof that this is actually the case," Sue says. "It's critical that you know where to locate the will, life insurance documents, and investment accounts." Her son Mike adds that several people got in touch after his father's death to say that they had created or updated their estate plans.

Subset #3

Functional Income-Stability Americans (FISAs)

Functional income-stability Americans (FISA) operate with traditional middle-class mindsets, habits, and tendencies, even though their incomes, net worth, and other factors don't firmly anchor them in the middle class. FISAs may be extremely poor or significantly wealthy, but they have middle-class, blue-collar characteristics.

Someone with a low-paying job may receive praise for her efficiency, work ethic, and dependability. Management sees her as an unfortunate outlier and a candidate for promotion, not one of poverty's casualties.

Other people might live in upper-class neighborhoods and have incomes and assets that exceed middle-class levels, but they feel more at home associating with the people and places of middle America, including houses of worship, restaurants, grocery stores, faith-based schools, entertainment venues, and vacation destinations. FISAs may have ample resources to frequent five-star dining establishments, but are more comfortable eating at more modest venues.

Blue-collar attributes were (and still are) instrumental in my personal development. Teachers, social workers, and middle-class families let me follow in their footsteps; I watched and duplicated what they did.

My very first substantive job occurred at the age of 12 as a vendor selling popcorn, peanuts, and watered-down Cokes at Cooper Stadium, home of the Columbus Clippers. When I was 14, management singled me out for a one-time gig that, at the time, seemed to be the opportunity of a lifetime. A man from the Clippers front office approached me to sell pictures of the San Diego Chicken, the mascot who entertained adoring fans throughout the game. They were more interested in his antics than in the action on the field, particularly when he played a prank on the umpire or opposing team.

It took eight long innings and I started nearly an hour before the first pitch, but I sold every San Diego Chicken picture I had. It was the most money I ever earned as a Cooper Stadium vendor. I was terrified as I walked back to Sullivant Gardens with nearly $100 in my pocket. Robbery was a way of life in my neighborhood; the victim's age and gender didn't matter. When I walked through our front door, my stress level dropped precipitously.

Let's dig deeper into why significantly wealthy FISAs tend to have middle-class tendencies and habits. The reasons vary, of course. Some avoid the trappings of materialism, preferring a simpler life. These people are often avid philanthropists, giving away wealth instead of hoarding it. Other affluent FISAs still focus on finding good bargains. These people avoid the appearance of wealth because they fear that others will take advantage of them. Still other cost-conscious FISAs were reared in an era when thriftiness was a way of life, not a choice. It is difficult for this group to enjoy their financial success. A wealthy individual can have qualities from all three income-stability subsets.

SOCIOPSYCHONOMIC FILTER
Feeling out of place in the land of affluence is a real phenomenon for some transplants who've climbed up the economic ladder, thus their comfort level with the traditional middle-class experience.

Affluent FISAs typically care less about titles or possessions, and more about people and relationships. For them, wealth is not a yardstick; it is a tool to empower others. Materialism, as they see it, is a trap. Embracing a simpler life clarifies and affirms their lives' purpose: the betterment of humanity. New or updated homes, expensive cars, designer clothing, and electronic gadgets are distractions. Intangible assets are priceless and timeless; these include compassion, philanthropy, and love for those less fortunate.

A LIFE OF SIMPLICITY AND PHILANTHROPY

Robert Sr. and Missy Weiler are pillars of the Central Ohio community. They have supported hundreds of philanthropic causes throughout the years, receiving dozens of awards for their devotion to helping disenfranchised people. The Robert Weiler Company is one of the area's leading commercial real estate enterprises, with a knack for buying land where economic growth will one day thrive.

I met Robert Sr. in 2001, when we were both receiving the Fisher College of Business Community Service Award at our alma mater, The Ohio State University. I told him that I was interested in learning more about real estate. With just a few more years left in my NBA career, it was time to explore investment and career-transitioning options. For some reason, most professional athletes gravitate to real estate ventures, perhaps because land and property are tangible. I was no different, though other asset classes interested me as well. Robert put me in touch with his son, Robert "Skip" Weiler, Jr., and he and I have been friends and business partners ever since.

> ## SOCIOPSYCHONOMIC FILTER
> The accumulation of wealth has a three-pronged litmus test: Don't let it define you; don't let it change you; and don't let it stop you from being a blessing in the lives of those less fortunate.

Robert and Missy Weiler are genuine, down-to-earth people, thanks in large part to their middle-class values. In spite of their real estate fortune, the Weilers never relocated to one of the city's wealthy suburbs, even as their neighborhood changed for the worse around them. They sent their four children to public school. They refused to allow affluence to set the terms of their contented life.

FINANCIAL PSYCHOLOGY'S DEEP ROOTS

Tony Payne is a successful, fee-only certified financial planner who works with a variety of clients. He believes that money psychology forms in childhood. "Some of my most affluent clients grew up during the Depression. One drove an older Buick with very high mileage. Possessions weren't a big deal to him," Tony says.

Ric Dillon, who makes a longer appearance later in this book, is also an investment advisor. His stepfather, a former educator, had trouble enjoying the fruits of his success. He was an incessant worrier who struggled with investing stage fright, particularly when it came to the stock market. According to Ric, frugality and fear shaped his consumption habit—but the thrift and modest living he learned helped him achieve his financial goals. Fortunately, Ric's expertise in equity analysis and behavioral finance guided his stepfather through the 1987 stock market crash.

THE WEALTHY

Subset #1

Generationally Affluent-Positioned Americans (GAPAs)

In the book *Outliers*, author Malcolm Gladwell postulates that the super wealthy became generationally affluent by seizing opportunities at strategic moments in history. Financial outliers become greedy when others are fearful. Known as contrarians, they are the exception to the rule. Emotional intelligence is critical to wealth accumulation, which is arguably financial outliers' primary attribute. (It should be yours, too, if this is the goal.)

The generationally affluent are the first responders when the flames of economic turmoil burn the brightest. If calculated correctly, the risk-reward payoff can be stratospheric. Unlike the poor and middle class, GAPAs do not let emotions dictate how they handle financial opportunities that come disguised as economic calamity.

The dozen or so generationally wealthy individuals and families that I know seem to share the following characteristics or habits, which I will cover extensively throughout the book:

- an unwavering belief in and allegiance to the law of compound interest (aka the Rule of 72)
- a geographic framework with a global outlook and physical footprint
- an innate sense of their altruistic and philanthropic responsibilities, as aligned with their core values
- a confident but humble belief in the virtues of fulfilling their economic potential
- an obsessive commitment to time and situation management

- a calm demeanor when assessing financial opportunities and economic challenges
- a holistic approach to life and financial planning
- a seamless legacy transition from one generation to the next
- an interconnected network of social, professional, personal, educational, and financial relationships
- an internal compass to stay the course financially, no matter how turbulent the times

Contrary to accounts portraying them as financial vultures, people with multigenerational wealth do not have a death grip on money. In fact, GAPAs go to great lengths to ensure they and their families aren't captive to money's entanglements, installing safeguards designed to prevent money from controlling those who have it. To a large extent, financial well-being is tied to emotional well-being and our ability to regulate emotions, not suppress them.

The generationally affluent take a measured approach to growing their balance sheets, employing the three T's: team, temperament, and time. The poor and middle class often let their feelings sabotage their financial well-being. The informed wealthy avoid overreacting to stock market disruptions and negative economic data. Having a team of highly compensated advisors does add an additional layer of emotional protection, because strategic planning is key to preventing irrational investment decisions. A team of competent advisors, an understanding of the cyclical nature of boom and bust financial markets, and legacy values (which transcend time) help GAPAs stay composed, stay confident, and stay the course.

Fear, guilt, and anxiety are the biggest hindrances to accumulating and preserving wealth. They affect each social class and subset in different ways. Let's explore a few of them.

Fear paralyzes a blue-collar employee, keeping her from monetizing a unique idea and skill-set that, with a rock-solid business plan, available mentor, modest start-up capital, and a large dose of confidence, could bring a lifetime of residual income. A comfortable job with above-average benefits in a highly competitive labor market offers security and peace of mind. Unfavorable economic conditions are too risky for a contemplative entrepreneur with GISA roots. She waits for the most ideal time to start a side or primary business. Of course, that time is never now.

Guilt demoralizes an impoverished African-American teenager living in a crime-ridden neighborhood whose peers mock him for his intelligence. He is labeled a nerd, a sellout, and a white wannabe by peers with attitudes that stifle educational achievement and personal responsibility. An agitated spirit magnifies financial obstacles and minimizes income-stream opportunities— another hurdle for the poor and middle class.

IMMUNIZATION FROM AFFLUENZA

The generationally wealthy do have a hidden anxiety: protecting their offspring and wealth from the entitlement virus. Affluenza is not a recent phenomenon. It's the biggest threat to legacy continuity for mega-affluent families. Children suffering from affluenza display:

- a reckless disregard for the family's good name and brand capital
- disillusionment about their life's purpose and how it aligns with the family's legacy template
- frivolous, wasteful financial habits
- addictive behavior that can lead to injury or death
- an arrogant attitude toward others
- a lack of compassion toward poor and economically challenged communities

Legacy continuity is a pledge wealthy family members must make, explicitly or covertly, to be good stewards of the family's values, brand, and financial assets. Most of them take that pledge. GAPAs are extremely diligent in not handicapping their ancestral lines. To ensure that affluenza doesn't infect family members, many wealthy people plan to distribute the bulk of their estates to charity. In effect, they will legally avoid millions or billions in estate taxes while supporting philanthropic causes with their accumulated or inherited wealth.

Most of the teenagers who attend our financial summer camps live in upper middle-class to affluent homes with two involved, biological parents. Monya and I have learned that moderately to super-wealthy children often know as little about financial matters as their impoverished peers, because the family doesn't openly discuss money. "Mom and Dad do very well and that's all you need to know," these parents implicitly communicate to children. Participants are somewhat familiar with financial terms and concepts, but not their application or relevance. (Practical tips and suggestions to help GAPA parents and grandparents discuss financial matters, and other sensitive topics around wealth, with children and grandchildren are highlighted in the chapter "Primary Sensory-Learning Drivers.")

A note before I move on to situationally affluent-positioned Americans: I didn't anticipate that so many generationally wealthy individuals and families in my network would decline to be interviewed. They have been incredibly generous in their support of our nonprofit organization, the Lawrence Funderburke Youth Organization (LFYO). They're incredibly busy, yet they make time to take my calls when I contact them. However, the majority of them respectfully declined to be interviewed for this book and share insights on their financial profiles. The greatest challenge facing significantly wealthy individuals and families is not to donate more money to charity or pay higher taxes to close the wealth gap in America. It's to share the ways of wealth. Trickle-down *Sociopsychonomics*, where information and application flow from the wealthy to the middle class and poor, works! I should know.

I suspect most of my mega-wealthy contacts chose not to be interviewed because they weren't sure whether this book would enhance or detract from their personal or family brands. Also, the vast majority of GAPAs do not want or need any additional attention. They prefer anonymity, especially when wealth and inequality are mentioned in the same sentence. Nonetheless, it is very important that they help narrate their financial profiles, which I have given them carte blanche to do throughout the book.

Subset #2

Situationally Affluent-Positioned Americans (SAPAs)

The "1 Percent," a group that includes the most affluent wage earners and wealth generators in America, are easy targets in discussions of income or wealth inequality. Interestingly enough, however, this vitriol isn't usually directed at situationally affluent-positioned Americans, or SAPAs for short.

Our larger culture sees professional athletes, entertainers, inventors, and entrepreneurs as laborers who generate significant wealth through hard work and perseverance. They don't appear to have taken advantage of someone else on their climb up the wealth ladder, and they weren't born in affluence with the proverbial silver spoon in their mouths, either. It's relatively easy to cheer for someone who looks, acts, and dresses like your middle-class, next-door neighbor.

RISE TO WEALTH: MODERN-DAY EXAMPLES

The situationally wealthy give poor and middle-class people hope because their paths to prosperity can be replicated. Incremental and overnight millionaires and billionaires have made their fortunes in fields from business to sports to technology to finance. Some are household names; other SAPAs fly under the radar, motivated by a childhood in poverty or a blue-collar upbringing where they barely got by.

In the wildly popular television show *Shark Tank*, average Joes and Janes pitch their business ideas to investors Mark Cuban, Daymond John, Kevin O'Leary, Lori Greiner, Barbara Corcoran, and Robert Herjavec. Presenters compete for the cash, connections, and coaching that they hope will turn their business into a multimillion-dollar success story. *Shark Tank* is the epitome of the American Dream, where calculated risks are rewarded, innovative ideas are applauded, and free-market principles are accepted. I love what Chris Johnson, a serial entrepreneur, said after securing a deal with one of the Sharks: "To build wealth, it's all about proximity. You hang around four broke people, you'll be the fifth. You hang around even just one billionaire, that proximity can impact your life."

A SMALL-TOWN SUCCESS STORY

Ric Dillon, chairman of the board and former CEO of Diamond Hill Capital Management, a firm with more than $15 billion in assets under management, is a hero of mine. He's also a portfolio manager for the firm's long-short funds and one of the most brilliant minds in the world of value investing. Value investors use a systematic approach, made famous by Warren Buffett and Benjamin Graham, to estimate a stock's intrinsic value. The stock may be selling at a premium (expensive) or discount (cheap) to the actual price. Value investors look to buy a stock when the current price is significantly below its intrinsic value, and sell a stock when the price goes above that value.

I met Ric the summer after my fourth year in the NBA, when I was an intern at Diamond Hill. His brilliance for selecting bargain stocks impressed me, as did his humble roots.

He grew up in the blue-collar, middle-class town of Newark, Ohio, which is 30 miles due east of Columbus but worlds away in terms of upward mobility. His mother, a frugal, determined woman who grew up during the Great Depression, was a school teacher. His father was a State Farm insurance representative. The family moved from Bloomington, Illinois, to Newark in 1960 as part of a State Farm relocation assignment. In 1966, his parents divorced; Ric was ten years old.

Divorce was quite uncommon back then. Ric was the youngest of four children and the only boy in a household dominated by women. His mother told him, "You have to step up and be the man of the household." That put Ric on the fast track to manhood, and he embraced the challenge.

His entrepreneurial spirit and keen sense of frugality were planted in childhood and blossomed during his teenage years. He mowed lawns and did odd jobs for neighbors, saving his money and working hard in school.

When he entered high school, Ric began spending summers in Newark and academic years in Sewanee, Tennessee. He received a scholarship to St. Andrews Preparatory School, a private boarding institution with a connection to the Episcopal Church. About 80 percent of the students came from affluent families. The remaining 20 percent were scholarship students. The formal education he received consisted of a regimented daily schedule, stellar academics, and high student achievement, a combination that would have been difficult or impossible to replicate in his hometown. Ric became just as comfortable around wealthy students as he was with poor students, most of whom were African-Americans from the Deep South.

Not surprisingly, most of Ric's charitable giving focuses on education. He says, "It is incumbent upon me to assist economically challenged students in their academic pursuits. My financial support will always be oriented to education." It is easy to see why this situationally influent individual is so passionate about learning. It changed his life for the better.

THE EVAPORATION OF SITUATIONAL WEALTH

One of the biggest concerns generationally wealthy families face is preventing children and grandchildren from catching the entitlement bug and its symptoms: rebellion, boredom, a lack of ambition, and unfulfilled potential.

As if those things weren't bad enough, children suffering from affluenza do considerable damage to their family's brand when their character flaws become pronounced. GAPAs use complex estate trusts and unlimited charitable deductions, among other comprehensive planning strategies, to ensure that future generations don't squander family wealth.

The situationally wealthy often have an intragenerational mindset that almost guarantees that their wealth will evaporate within the next two generations. Children and grandchildren don't know or fulfill their responsibilities in carrying the family legacy of affluence forward. Instead, they spend recklessly, without any safeguards to stop them. In essence, this is generational theft.

FINANCIAL FACT

According to the Williams Group, a wealth consultancy firm, "70% of [affluent] families lose their wealth by the second generation, and a stunning 90% by the third."

–Chris Taylor
Time Magazine

The following fictional account shows how a SAPA's fortune can dissipate within a matter of years, or even months, after the wealth generator's death.

John, a seventy-something Baby Boomer, amassed his financial empire through several strategic real estate ventures. It was the late 1970s and white Americans were moving to the suburbs in droves to avoid newly integrated schools and neighborhoods. Suburbs extended their boundaries to accommodate future homeownership growth, thriving school districts with high tax bases, and state-of-the art shopping experiences. John capitalized on a gut instinct and bought hundreds of acres of land from farmers. He took a second loan on his home, borrowed money from family members, and persuaded his best friend to become a partner in the business. His intuition was handsomely rewarded.

John repaid his second mortgage, as well as the family members who trusted him with their life savings. He bought out his business partner right before completing his most lucrative deal, which pushed his net worth over $50 million—not bad for someone who dropped out of high school in the tenth grade.

As he climbed the economic ladder, John paid little attention to planning his legacy. He assumed that his children would be good wealth stewards. That proved to be a terrible miscalculation. After John's death, his third wife and four biological children exhausted the family's wealth through lavish living. Michael, John's eldest son and estate executor, bought a Lamborghini and Maserati within three months of his father's demise. He didn't have his father's golden touch for investment success and lost millions of dollars in several ill-conceived business ventures. But Michael did have an insatiable appetite for unfettered risk-taking and get-rich-quick schemes.

John's financial legacy evaporated under the guidance of those John thought he could trust the most. At times, the best sports defense is a great offense. The situationally affluent must pass principles and values, not just dollars, to their children to keep the legacy money ball in play. Every generation must follow the ways of wealth, a systematic process that rewards diligence and punishes negligence.

Subset #3

Functionally Affluent-Positioned Americans (FAPAs)

I watched the sitcom *The Jeffersons* every Sunday evening in the late 1970s and early 1980s. On the show, Sherman Hemsley played the temperamental George Jefferson, who was obnoxious, ostentatious, and outrageous. (Looking back, it's astonishing that a black man could act like this on television, just a decade after the Civil Rights Movement.)

George Jefferson had it going on, or so it appeared. The character flapped his arms in concert with rhythmic shoulder and head movements when he walked, body language that screamed, "Check me out! I've arrived."

George itched to make a quick buck, so it's not clear how wealthy the character really was. Still, he tried desperately to fit in with the mega-wealthy socialites in his building, the Whittendales in particular. What he lacked in class and grace, he hoped to buy with humor and money. George was the master of distraction, a common behavior pattern in poverty, which, according to the storyline, he had escaped.

In one of my favorite episodes, "A Charmed Life," George sulks because he wasn't invited to Mr. and Mrs. Whittendale's party. He invites a newspaper columnist who wrote about the Whittendales' party, Morgan Kingsley, to his own party. Morgan Kingsley has no idea that he will be the only guest. Then George hires Louis Alfred Grayson III to give him a crash course in etiquette, manners, and appropriate conversation. The behavioral change, as usual, is short-lived, and George is exposed as a fraud.

As he leaves, Morgan Kingsley stops mid-stride and turns to George, saying, "Mr. Jefferson, you are obviously a man who has made some money—some money—and is now trying to pass himself off as a man of breeding. You think after appearing in my column, you will gain social respectability?"[8] Ouch. George missed the life lesson: If you're out of class, you will never be welcomed into their school. Social respect can't be bought in situational or generational affluence; it is learned, earned, and affirmed on a daily basis.

KEEPIN' UP WITH THE SUPERSTARS

As George Jefferson demonstrates, functionally affluent people can find it painfully difficult to enter their preferred social groups, held out by an abundance of crass, a lack of class, or insufficient cash. This group of FAPAs try to keep up with the Joneses, even if it means an upside-down balance sheet, where liabilities far exceed assets. They prefer looking the part over being the real thing.

This is the negative side of functional wealth, and it shows up glaringly in professional sports. My first NBA contract was a two-year deal for $1.1 million, which I signed in 1997. I had made a good living before this by playing professional basketball for three years in Greece and France. The National Basketball Association was altogether different. The competition was more intense, both on and off the court. Even teams at the bottom of the conference standings had players with exceptional talent. The game was faster, players were quicker and stronger, and internal stress levels were significantly higher. Rookies often feel the pressure to show off in lockstep with highly paid veterans. Fortunately, I never felt obligated to duplicate the lifestyle habits of our team's superstars, most of whom earned well over $5 million per season back in the late 1990s, though I was tempted. If I had, it would have meant financial ruin.

In 2012, ESPN's *30 for 30* aired the documentary, "Broke," which cast a spotlight on how and why professional athletes in our country's four major sports end up financially destitute after earning millions and millions of dollars during their playing days. It's very easy to succumb to peer pressure when veteran players indulge themselves. Gullible rookies get caught up; they're too eager to appear successful, buying high-priced cars with aftermarket accessories, expensive jewelry, designer clothing, and meals at five-star restaurants for themselves and their entourages. It's one thing to fund a lifestyle when you can afford it, and still another when you can't. (You can read more about the financial challenges facing today's mega-paid professional athletes in my book *Hook Me Up Player!* I wrote this book nearly a decade before the "Broke" documentary aired.)

THE DANGERS OF CAMOUFLAGE WEALTH

In prestigious communities across the country, many more people look wealthy than actually are wealthy. The facade can last only so long. Who can forget the shocking discovery when Toto, the most unlikely character, exposes the Wizard of Oz as a fraud? The self-proclaimed great and powerful Oz stayed on the microphone in stunned disbelief as the curtain opened. He told them, "Pay no attention to the man behind the curtain!"[9] His personal identity was finally revealed, resulting in a dose of humility and apologies for misleading Dorothy and her friends.

Image-conscious people pursue conspicuous consumption. In return, they get rising debt levels, stress, recklessness, strained relationships, and internal chaos. If you have to take out a 40-year mortgage with a very low down payment when interest rates are at historic lows, then you can't really afford your home or your lifestyle. A home with furniture in only the few rooms that guests are allowed to see is a classic sign of economic distress.

THE POSITIVE SIDE OF FUNCTIONAL WEALTH

Fortunately, functional wealth has a positive side, too. FAPAs who are not guided by pretense or flamboyance generally have personal net worths that far exceed their financial net worths. Eventually, their monetary balance sheet will grow, but not at the expense of their marketable character traits. Anyone can identify with the wealthy, as long as you:

1. Don't make excuses or blame others for your current predicament.

2. Be passionate about fulfilling your personal, educational, financial, and charitable potential.

3. Celebrate the financial accomplishments of others. You cannot become what you hate. Poverty awaits those who despise economic liberty.

4. Be your own cheerleader. Setbacks come with the territory.

5. Learn and follow the laws of wealth creation, without being captivated or entangled by the covetous trap.

In spite of my toxic, poverty-stricken environment, I never thought I couldn't succeed in life. My opportunity lens didn't depend on favorable circumstances. Intuitively, I knew success was procedural, involving vision, patience, and movement toward a worthwhile goal. As I daydreamed, I imagined how my life would eventually turn out if I followed the right game plan. Patience was not one of my strongest virtues—it still isn't—but veering off course wasn't an option; I had a destiny to fulfill.

My mother nicknamed me Huckleberry Finn, after Mark Twain's fictional character, because I was always on the go. I only ate meals and slept in our apartment, particularly after starting high school. I worked every spring and summer in the early to mid-1980s as a Cooper stadium vendor for the Columbus Clippers. This job taught me how to manage money, interact with different (and difficult) people, and get paid for my efforts. Although the stadium was walking distance from my housing projects, Sullivant Gardens, I was the only teenager from my neighborhood who worked there, though I tried unsuccessfully to recruit others to join me. They told me, "Why are you wasting your time selling popcorn and peanuts and Cracker Jacks. You're crazy!" They failed to appreciate the life lessons in play.

A MAN ON A SPIRITUAL AND FINANCIAL MISSION

Jason Tyree is a man on a spiritual and financial mission. His faith comes first, then family, then finances. His economic goals: become a millionaire within 10 years. He's already developed an impressive personal balance sheet of character traits and attributes developed through years of sweat equity in overcoming a difficult childhood. Jason's upbringing, like that of so many black children from impoverished, inner-city communities, was full of pain and psychological turmoil. Now a devout Christian and committed father, he has pledged, "We will win as a family. Our history of poverty and dysfunction will be replaced with financial freedom and unity. The cycle of economic bondage and hopelessness must end."

"I grew up in Dayton, Ohio, an hour west of Columbus," Jason says. "Of course, I never met my biological father. He and my mother were drug addicts.

I heard stories that he would tie my mother to a tree and savagely beat her, for no apparent reason at all. My birth name was Jesus Coleman. They named me Jesus, a spiritual euphoria of sorts, because they were so high one day. I was in my mother's womb during this drug-induced escapade. Later, I learned that my mother would beat me since she hated my father so intensely; she paid him back by abusing me. I have four siblings, and each of us has a different father, a common problem in the black community. Marijuana, heroin, and cocaine were the drugs of choice for my mother. Children's services would intervene because she was an unfit mother. I was in and out of foster homes for a large part of my childhood."

Mary, Jason's mother, was a strikingly beautiful woman. Half Cherokee and fair-skinned, with light eyes and long, curly hair, she attracted a great deal of attention back in the disco era of the 1970s. She even dated one of the members of the R&B group, The Ohio Players. Jason adds, "My mother also shoplifted for herself and others. She stole clothes, jewelry, and fur coats from department stores. On several occasions, I acted as her lookout. If I didn't do my job correctly, I'd get a beatdown from her when we got home."

Mary partied throughout the week and weekend. Momma Lou's, a restaurant by day and night club at dusk, was a popular destination. Outside, drug deals and other illegal activities occurred. Obviously, this wasn't the place for children. "Me and my brother would have to sit in the car and wait for our mother. She'd party from 5 p.m. to 1 a.m., coming to the car intermittently to provide us with something to drink and eat," Jason says. "It would be the middle of summer and we would have sweat dripping from our faces. I will never forget these memories, no matter how hard I try."

In spite of her challenges and compromised self-esteem, Jason notes, Mary was a fabulous cook, had a magnetic and energetic personality, and could display a keen sense of humor at just the right moment. He gravitated to women who reminded him of his mother.

Mary was placed in hospice care in 2001 and died of complications from a seizure at 56. The effects of drugs and a fast-paced lifestyle finally caught up with her, Jason points out.

An accomplished cook himself, food has literally been medicine to Jason's soul. "The spirit of poverty will be broken in our ancestral tree through my culinary gifts," he says. He's on track to create multiple income streams to supplement his current job as a cook and part-time Uber driver. He operates a full-service catering business and is creating a line of desserts and other comfort foods. A clothing line will come next, then a real estate empire. He envisions building a community of affordable housing with thriving schools in a safe environment, free of drugs and deviant activities.

He is fully entrenched in the ways of wealth creation. Jason is a regular attendee at our financial empowerment classes. Before saving up enough money to purchase a reliable automobile, he would catch the city bus to get to FunderMax Fitness in the suburbs. He'd stand outside for 30 minutes, sometimes in temperatures below freezing, waiting for the Saturday morning workshops to begin.

Jason's daughters already have better childhoods than he had, and he hopes to give them still more. "I not only want them to get a better education by attending a school with stellar academics, but also expose them to situations and opportunities that will improve their lives," he says.

Jason Tyree is a FAPA who will one day transition to SAPA or GAPA status. I'm confident that he will reach his wealth and legacy goals. Many fans along the way will cheer for him, starting with me. I might be the tallest.

CHAPTER

2

OUTSIDE IN:
THE SIX PRIMARY EMOTIONS

*How the landscape and emotional world of
poverty shaped my Sociopsychonomic filter*

C ore memories are inextricably tied to life's unforgettable moments: an embarrassing situation that could have been avoided, a horrific tragedy, a heated argument, the aroma of our favorite foods, the touch of a loved one's hand. These memories, good and bad, are firmly embedded in the mind's deep recesses, waiting to be activated by a thought or sensory stimulus. It's nearly impossible for us to forget them; sometimes, though, we wish the bad memories would simply just go away.

In Pixar's blockbuster animated film *Inside Out*, a girl named Riley deals with a wide range of emotions as she struggles to make friends and fit in. Her family moved from Minnesota to San Francisco, with cultures and climates that are polar opposites in many respects. Fear, anger, disgust, and sadness battle against joy to control Riley's thoughts and feelings. Eventually she adjusts to her unusual surroundings, one year after the dreaded move to the land of the unfamiliar. Like Riley, we resist what we don't know. My environment, and the resulting emotions I inherited and developed around finances, shaped me from the *Outside In*.

THE PAIN OF POVERTY

Negative emotions dominate the lives of generational economically distressed Americans (GEDAs). I can speak from experience, having lived in abject poverty myself for nearly two decades. Money was scarce in the Funderburke household. This created incredible stress for me, my three older sisters, and our mother. My childhood fear of running out of food before the month ended and the next welfare check arrived, combined with the deplorable conditions of my living environment, did profoundly affect my current economic and possibility filter.

My resting heart rate is about 57 beats per minute, according to my last checkup. Just thinking about my childhood makes that rate jump to more than 100 beats per minute. These memories make my heart beat faster, raise my stress level, and make my body tense up—all normal reactions to the threat of immediate danger. In this case, though, there is no threat. I triggered the emotions with my mind.

Fear

Poverty is a breeding ground for fear. Fear is contagious and paralyzing, rendering victims disillusioned, agitated, frustrated, disengaged, isolated, aggravated, alienated, marginalized, and chronically stressed. It is detrimental to a person's health and wealth.

Toxic thoughts and poor eating (and coping) habits are common in economic distress, and along with genetic predispositions, can lead to illness and disease. I developed a duodenal ulcer during my freshman year in college from incessantly worrying about how my basketball career would unfold after I left Indiana University in the middle of the season. The backlash and negative media attention were enormous, which added to my anxiety.

As a certified financial planner, I have watched adults experience tremendous fear and disorientation, even in a game setting using hypothetical money. Those emotions bring out the very behavioral responses they wish to avoid.

Fear surveys the scene to find a problem. Where none exists, it creates a problem in order to stay alive. Fear contaminates relationships and destroys confidence. Some of the common fears of poverty include:

- fear of running out of money before the month ends
- fear of not having enough food
- fear of being labeled an inadequate family provider
- fear of being robbed, assaulted, injured, or murdered
- fear of a child getting caught up in the gang or drug game
- fear of being verbally, emotionally, financially, or physically abused
- fear of losing much-needed government benefits or support from nonprofit organizations
- fear of being rejected or abandoned by a parent or lover
- fear of going to jail over a case of mistaken identity
- fear of being treated like a second-class citizen because of race, appearance, group identification, or grammar
- fear surrounding the mood swings of neighbors and guardians (usually mothers and grandmothers, because fathers are often an endangered species) in impoverished communities

I won't address all of these fears, just the ones that had the biggest affect on my psyche and wallet.

"BOY, WHAT TOOK YOU SO LONG?"

My teenage years were a time of deep introspection and soul-searching, particularly as my body outgrew my clothes. As a tall and lanky kid, I was incredibly self-conscious. Poverty didn't help assuage my sensitivities; it exposed my vulnerabilities in a way that I went great lengths to avoid. Being a fair-skinned black, really tall, and extremely poor made me feel as though I were on public display, providing others the opportunity to critique me. I kept outsiders (and even some insiders) at arm's length, a default mechanism I used (and still do) to protect myself from real or perceived threats. I became obsessed with the notion of success; girls and other interests common to most boys going through puberty didn't interest me. These passions had to be contained if academics and basketball were to be my ticket out of the projects. Girls were distractions, or so I thought. So were the efforts some teenagers expended to become popular. Neither of these concerned me. I was a young man determined to complete a mission that demanded my absolute focus.

I felt particularly fearful and on display when someone from my neighborhood saw me using food stamps at the grocery store. It didn't matter that 95 percent of residents were also on welfare or received some kind of government benefit. My amygdala or emotion filter didn't respond to logic. I only knew that I needed to save face.

My long walks to and from the grocery store provided therapy to my aching soul, a breath of fresh air to imagine the life I would live in adulthood, when I could take matters into my own hands. No longer would I depend on the government to take care of me.

The grocery store we frequented, IGA, was just a little over a mile away, from our front door to the corner of Greenlawn and Harmon Avenues. One afternoon, I was ready to check out and abruptly stepped out of line when someone from Sullivant Gardens entered the store. Two other residents of my housing project entered as well. I walked around the store for half an hour until they left, pretending to look for the purchase that would complete my grocery list and becoming acquainted with every item on the grocery shelves in the process. I finally checked out. When I returned home, my annoyed mother asked, "Boy, what took you so long to get just a few things?" I didn't dare tell her the truth.

THE GHETTO VERSION OF THRIFT

Every economically distressed American lacks money. That's obvious. To an outsider, however, the anxiety that this lack of money creates in every aspect of life is less obvious. Managing resources was more art than science for our family. Without a spending or meal plan, impulsivity ruled the day. This perpetual state of immediacy was the root of many of our fears in poverty, perhaps none more debilitating than an inadequate food supply. Quantity over quality was the rule. The volume of food took precedence over its nutritional value. Full bellies, which we usually had, didn't mean a healthy body. (More on this later and how it contributed to my manic obsession to provide my wife and kids with gluten-free, all-natural, and organic foods.) We never discussed food's health benefits back then. We only cared about having enough food throughout the month to feed a family of five.

The last few days of the month brought a combination of creativity and ingenuity in *ghettonomics*. In poverty, you have to be resourceful. Add a little water to milk, ketchup, hot sauce, and other malleable liquids to extend their usefulness. When we ran out of milk entirely, we substituted evaporated milk.

(The taste of water and evaporated milk in cereal is disgusting.) When we couldn't find a substitute for a particular food item—a rare occurrence, as my mother did an admirable job of managing resources—the youngest person in the family often had the task of borrowing necessary items from neighbors. That was me. I would go from one apartment to the next until I found a willing lender. The anxiety was so intense that it made me sick to my stomach. The fear of being turned down or worse, having a door slammed in my face, was unnerving. Returning home without the goods would have been even more problematic.

Imagine being a 10-year-old child who has to face an adult neighbor who is mad at the world and must protect precious resources for her own family. You approach the front door, knowing that someone is probably at home. Only a handful of neighbors had part-time jobs, with the remainder on public assistance, so residents spent the majority of their time in or around their apartments. Before you raise your hand to knock on the door, someone closes the curtains. You hear her telling others, "Shh, be quiet! We don't want him to know we're home." You see a faint image peeping through a curtain slit. She notices that you have a cup in your hand. You knock and knock and knock. You stand waiting for another few minutes for a response, to no avail. It's time to move on to the next neighbor. That happened to me on several occasions. It was frightening to return home with nothing to show for my efforts. Depending on her mood, my mother might issue a harsh rebuke.

THE CURRENCY OF RECIPROCITY

In the ghetto, borrowing food or other items from neighbors happens on a quid pro quo system: the law of reciprocity. Favors were a bankable commodity, a reserve to draw on when the lenders needed something. The items loaned didn't have to be paid back in kind—only in a similar gesture of goodwill. Failing to lend when you had the power to do so—an admonition in the Bible as well as the unspoken neighborhood code of conduct—could mean verbal assaults and denial of future borrowing requests. The Almighty forgives, but Sullivant Gardens residents weren't so generous. We played our fair share of hide and seek when neighbors came to borrow. But if we had the item—and we usually did—we generally loaned it, because what goes around comes around in the ghetto.

The law of unintended consequences pervades poverty. People consume precious resources without the slightest thought about the consequences.

"Enjoy now, I'll deal with the costs later" is an ingrained mindset. Repercussions are an afterthought in a scarcity-led environment. Crises, particularly those involving food, are a normal part of the ebb and flow. People deal with them, but don't plan for them.

In general, the middle and affluent classes don't understand GEDAs' ways. In poverty, sanity and sense are not mutually exclusive terms. Here's what I mean. Poor people are never out of survival mode. Economic behaviors are not rationally motivated; they're emotionally and socially driven. People accept and conform to established group norms, which often take the form of either-or propositions:

> "Either I live life to the fullest now, or let the moment pass me by. Who knows when it'll be offered again?"

> "Either we starve at the end of the month, or borrow from neighbors to feed our family."

THE COSTLY MISTAKE OF SELF-PRESERVATION

Gangsta rap, which was popular during my college years, reminded me of the fear I felt as a little boy, when I witnessed senseless acts of violence and horrifying tragedies in Sullivant Gardens. They desensitized me, at times, to the pain and suffering of others. It's true that hurting people hurt other people. It's also true that fearful people fear other people. Before I realized it, I was engulfed in paranoia, which is common in poverty. I trusted no one and questioned everything, especially after I joined the NBA. Instead of trying to sort friend from fraud, it's easier to dump both in fear's dungeon, bound with chains of distrust. A popular song back then by the Geto Boys, "Mind Playing Tricks on Me,"[10] is filled with fear-based lyrics and paranoia references.

I was cool with teammates in high school and college, but distant off the court. I treated coaches with a bit more skepticism, using "Don't divulge too much information, appease them where necessary, and see them more as foe than friend" as my motto. As Debbie Cacchio, secretary to Randy Ayers, my former coach at Ohio State, told me two years ago, "You had a wall up when you first came to OSU to keep people—even the coaching staff and university administrators—at arm's length. It was so hard to figure you out."

Fifty players were selected ahead of me in the 1994 NBA draft, because teams misinterpreted my distance as an attitude problem. An NBA executive told me, "Lawrence, you have lottery talent, but no team would select you there; you're too big of a risk." The late pick cost me a conservative $25 million over the course of my professional basketball career. Self-preserving paranoia can be very expensive.

Anger

Anger was both the most toxic and the most beneficial emotion of my childhood. Inner-city boys without fathers are ships without rudders. The vessel may temporarily stay afloat, but your guess is as good as mine as to what direction it goes. One day, a child is bright and sunny, a joy to be around, compliant and full of contained energy. The next day, he transforms into a raging inferno. It's perplexing and terrifying, but it's also understandable.

When people are marginalized, society pays the bills for the pain they inflict through anger. As I tell our donors, "You can pay now or pay later. The choice is yours. Financial and non-monetary support can be provided at the front-end to grassroots organizations like LFYO, which are changing the trajectory and legacy of disenfranchised populations through compassion and cutting-edge, empowerment-based programs. Of course, you can pay at the back-end, locking these young men and women up in prisons—literally and figuratively—or seeing them have one child after another out of wedlock, where the cycle of welfare, hopelessness, and lack of purpose that future generations are inevitably doomed to follow."

CAPTAIN OF MY SHIP

Elementary school teachers, most of whom are women from middle-class backgrounds, have a difficult time dealing with these boys. Most inner-city kids capsize their vessels and drown in a sea of hopeless despair. Our inner-city communities and prisons are filled with damaged goods, products that appear serviceable but contain tangled webs of disconnected wiring. They are malfunctioning males, guided primarily by untamed anger and aggression. Their destructive actions and erratic behaviors make perfect sense to them. I should know.

Like most boys from impoverished settings, I had a problem with authority figures. When I left Sullivant Gardens to attend Indiana University and play basketball for Bobby "The General" Knight, my anger didn't dissipate. In fact, it escalated. My relationship with Coach Knight didn't last very long. The problem child and The General didn't see eye to eye. I was the proverbial poor kid from the projects who wasn't going to be told what to do by any coach, famous or infamous. If told to jump, I didn't reply, "How high?" I'd respond, "For what?"

Runaway anger and hostility can't be coached. It was me against the basketball world from 1990 to 1992, until I landed at Ohio State to play for Randy Ayers, who was a father figure to me and other black players. Half of the Buckeye fans didn't think I'd be a good fit and the other half were only willing to accept me because interior players, Perry Carter and Treg Lee, had exhausted their collegiate eligibility. I didn't win in the court of public opinion, and it cost me a fortune. My reputation and wallet took a beating, as I would later find out.

THE GYM BAG OF ANGER

My gym bag was full of anger, and not even that fully reflected the effect poverty had on my mind and dignity. We depended on the government for food and shelter. The first of the month was the most important date to our family, because that was the day the mail carrier delivered a welfare check and food stamps. We left the front door open to anticipate his arrival and dissuade a would-be thief in hot pursuit of our government benefits. (Thieves and even some welfare recipients sold food stamps for 50 cents on the dollar to buy drugs or alcohol. Food stamps, as the name implies, or an electronic benefit transfer card today, can only be used to buy consumable, nonalcoholic groceries.) Of course, sometimes the mail carrier was slow, maybe because he had so many checks to deliver. That made residents angry, too. It was an entitlement, and it belonged to them.

Our family also depended on benevolent programs and nonprofits to survive economically. For more than 100 years, Charity Newsies has provided clothing to children from needy families. We were grateful for the support from this wonderful organization, but my three sisters and I still were incredibly embarrassed when a peer noticed us wearing Newsie clothes. We denied every accusation and lied about where we got our back-to-school clothes. I remember an exchange between me and a friend about a checkered black-and-red coat I was wearing. It was indeed from Charity Newsies and kept me warm that winter.

Friend: Man, where did you get that coat, from Charity Newsies?

Me: My mother bought this for me at Hart's. (Hart's was a department store chain where lower- and middle-income families typically shopped. We frequented the Central Point Shopping Center location after cashing our welfare check at Big Bear's, an adjacent grocery store. Both of these chains no longer exist.)

Friend: (laughing) You're lying, dude. C'mon.

Me: Nah man, I'm serious. This from Hart's.

Friend: Why you gotta lie? Be honest!

Me: I am.

Friend: That coat don't even have the same pattern as a Hart's coat.

Me: Shut up stupid! It does. (I walk away.)

My embarrassment turned to humiliation and from there to anger. In the projects, when your peers make fun of you, you either laugh along with the joke or stand your ground. Accepting poverty was never an option for me. I refused to drown in self-pity, academic indifference, and the blame game. As Monya, my wife, observes, "You were in an environment where anger was a natural reaction to a grossly unfair predicament; your environment and upbringing taught you how to be angry. In a good way, though, righteous anger drove you to succeed in life."

THE WAY IT WAS

I was angry that many Sullivant Gardens residents saw public assistance as a generational birthright instead of a situational stumbling block. I'll never be against welfare. Children should not be punished when their parents (mothers usually) refuse or are unable to work and fathers disappear. A part-time job with a minimum-wage paycheck isn't enough for a single parent to take care of her family. Welfare can be a temporary measure, not a permanent solution, to assist an impoverished mother until she gains skills, improves her education, or starts a business. (Men impregnate vulnerable, impoverished women and then refuse to support their children financially, leaving it up to mothers and taxpayers to handle this responsibility. It's shameful. Manhood does not start in the bedroom; it begins in the boardroom of a responsible life, which should precede the birth of a key stakeholder: a precious child.)

Mom did the best she could with the welfare benefits she had. It takes two to tango, and the men who fathered my mother's children vanished when we needed them.

My sophomore year at Worthington Christian High School (WCHS) ended and my transfer to Wehrle Memorial was, as it turned out, just a couple of months away. Good friends and teammates Chris Homoelle and Mike Anthony gave me rides to and from school, open gym, and practice at WCHS. We usually listened to the radio in the car. Whenever Bruce Hornsby's 1986 #1 Pop Chart hit came on the radio, "The Way It Is,"[11] I strategically diverted attention to avoid several of the lyrics, which cast a spotlight, or so I thought, on our family's reliance on welfare benefits to survive from one day to the next. The song touched my poverty nerve.

During his State of the Union address on January 8, 1964, United States President Lyndon B. Johnson, a Democrat, introduced his signature War on Poverty initiative.[12] His ambitious goal was to provide relief for needy families and hopefully, eradicate poverty in America. The poverty rate then was almost 20 percent. Both Chris and Mike were two highly intelligent individuals who could make the connection between Hornsby's '64 reference to welfare, and me, the guy in the passenger seat who received a welfare benefit every month since the day he was born. This was probably the farthest thing from their mind, but I still kept to my master-of-distraction plan and avoidance strategy. (I tolerated the song, which I liked, but only when alone in my room listening to the radio.)

By early 1987, I was 6'6", rail thin, and wore a size 16 sneaker. I stood out in a crowd of average-size people. My mother begged me to go with her to the welfare office, a dreary day in March that I'll never forget. In spite of my embarrassment, I did accompany her. When someone in line recognized me as a high school basketball star, I stormed home, leaving my mother alone in line. I couldn't take it anymore. Though I would remain on welfare with my mother for two more years, until I graduated from high school, I distanced myself from economic misery as best I could. I only slept and ate in Sullivant Gardens after 1987. Otherwise, I was with friends and their families: the Anthonys, Wilsons, Johnsons, Sommers, and Coopers. This was difficult, because my mother relied heavily on me for emotional support. To protect my own sanity, I neglected hers at a time when my mother needed me the most. I am deeply sorry that I indirectly abandoned her.

WHERE ARE THE CO-SIGNERS?

As I grew up in poverty, I felt utterly disrespected by people around me. They were stuck in poverty and believed that I would never escape, either. Maybe they couldn't dream big and push themselves. Or maybe it's just hard to imagine what's possible when a frame of reference is missing.

With average physical skills and above-average intellectual abilities, I had a vision for my life. My neighborhood peers, and even the adults I encountered at school or recreational centers, could not bring themselves to sign on.

Essentially, I needed a co-signer. A co-signer promises to pay back a loan if the borrower defaults. Young borrowers or those with a subpar credit score and low down payment, may need a co-signer in order to get a loan. When you co-sign, you vouch for someone else's ability, character, and credibility when a financial institution is skeptical.

Feelings and perceptions matter more in poverty than reality. On several occasions, people in Sullivant Gardens told me, "You ain't never going to be nothing but a poor kid from the projects." It was a lonely road, but what did I have to lose? I couldn't go any lower than poverty. So I forged ahead.

I received a "C" on one of my report cards in middle school, which meant I wouldn't be on the honor roll. Devastated, I held my head down as I walked to my school bus seat. A classmate from Sullivant Gardens took notice. He asked, "What's wrong with you?" I replied dejectedly, "I got a 'C' on my report card. No honor roll this grading period." Stunned by my disdain for the grade, which he'd gladly have taken, he commented, "You trippin'; a 'C' ain't bad. Education don't mean nothing. Why you trying to be white?"

To leave poverty for something better is never an issue of capability, but of accessibility and opportunity. I needed to access the opportunities that seemed far-fetched to others, but not to me. I didn't have a frame of reference, and neither did anyone else in my neighborhood, so I developed my own internal compass of a world beyond Sullivant Gardens. As Monya says, "Most people in your neighborhood didn't have a vision of what was possible beyond where they presently were. They couldn't see past their current circumstances, thus it was impossible for them to co-sign for you. They couldn't take you somewhere, in their mind, that they had never been before."

To release anger, there are three requirements. First, we must recognize the root cause(s) of the anger. Second, we must surrender ownership of the attached emotion and learned behavioral responses. Third, we must change course by circumventing negative thoughts, and instead, replacing them with positive ones. Recognize, surrender, and change. It's never too late. The beauty of being human is that our circumstance can change for the better. (This healing formula can be used to break free from any primary or secondary toxic emotion, including fear, anger, disgust, sadness, despair, bitterness, resentment, envy, hatred, anxiety, worry, or depression.)

Sadness

The perpetual invisibility loop occurs when poor people anticipate being treated as if their lives don't matter. When you grow up in an environment of five-finger discounts and mindless assaults, you're labeled a malcontent, whether you deserve it or not, because of your association with the world of poverty. You're guilty as charged, though no trial ever happens. You're seen and judged, but never acknowledged. Inner-city kids across the color spectrum feel sadly invisible. I did as a child.

THE INVISIBLE KID

Poverty made me feel invisible, whether that was a figment of my imagination or a genuine reaction from people with higher social standings. Even though my clothes were clean, at times, I looked unkempt, and people made judgments about my social standing, intellect, character, ambition, and outlook on life as a result.

Psychologists think we form impressions about strangers within a split second. No need to read the book's contents; the cover tells the complete story.

I couldn't articulate this as a teenager, but being judged in an unflattering light simply because of my attire and skin color was deflating.

Between the ages of 12 and 16, I worked as a vendor selling popcorn, peanuts, Cracker Jacks, and soft drinks to fans attending Columbus Clippers games at Cooper Stadium, a twelve-minute journey from my front door to the main entrance gate. The Clippers, then the AAA-affiliate of the New York Yankees, were a popular attraction in the spring and summer months for Central Ohio families with discretionary income. This job taught me a great deal more besides counting money and working hard; I learned how to read people who treated me as invisible.

One muggy summer day, I went up an aisle minutes before the start of the game. I made eye contact with the large, predominantly white crowd, pausing every five or six seconds to bellow, "Coke, Sprite here. Get your ice-cold Coke and Sprite here!" I didn't sell very many soft drinks in that aisle. I quickly made my way to the next aisle. Time was money, and I needed to earn as many George Washingtons and Abraham Lincolns as I could. I glanced over to find a white vendor selling soft drinks in the aisle I left no more than two minutes earlier. His tray was almost gone. I couldn't believe my eyes. Either fans in that section had sudden-onset thirst or they just didn't want to buy any soft drinks from me. I was deeply hurt, but quickly dismissed the incident and walked briskly to the other side of the stadium.

In college, I tried to pay back those who treated me invisibly when I was a *Nobody*. Now I was a somebody, a household name in Columbus and a nationally known Ohio State basketball player. I treated fans who wanted to shake my hand as though they had leprosy. At other times, I acted as though I didn't hear a word fans said. I didn't sign very many autographs. "Don't even think about asking me to take a picture with you," I communicated with my cold glance. I was nicer to children, women, and black people. I treated any white man I didn't know with contempt. Never once did I regret these actions. I was called a jerk (and other names too degrading to repeat in this book). Didn't bother me at all. The revenge felt good.

To hurt others intentionally is a strategy to assuage your own pain. Unfortunately, this remedy never truly works. In poverty, retaliation is a common way to combat extreme sadness and disrespect. It's cold, calculating, and costly. I paid a huge price for it. I lost in the court of public opinion and lost millions of dollars as a late-round NBA draft pick as a result. As a person of faith now, I'm deeply saddened that I once hurt innocent people intentionally. (Today, I am a huge germaphobe, mysophobiac to be technical, who does not like to shake anyone's hand—man, woman, or child. As an alternative, I do give daps and hugs.)

Intense sadness in poverty can also lead to depression and self-loathing. Rarely, it can inspire someone to introspection and self-motivation, which precedes a change in circumstances. My journey to a better life was lonely, with very little support from other people. I had to be my own cheerleader, coach, teammate, trainer, and where necessary, opponent. I couldn't afford complacency. Giving up would have meant forfeiting the life I wanted, a life that matters in substance and meaning.

My wife, a woman who knows me better than anyone, says this:

> "Sadness propelled you because of the pain of humiliation and feeling ashamed by how you were treated growing up very poor. Today, you make sure that people know you are well-educated in spite of an impoverished upbringing, and that you weren't some poor kid who just happened to make it out of the ghetto because of basketball. You go to great lengths to distance yourself not from poverty, but from the negative associations that surround it. Your experiences in poverty shaped you into the man you are now, which you are grateful for."

In July 1992, one month after I met Monya in college, we took a ride through my former neighborhood. With tears streaming down her angelic face, she told me, "I would have never guessed you could have grown up in an environment like this." Street entrepreneurs—a euphemistic description for drug dealers—openly sold their goods. Zombies walked the streets, high on drugs. Grown men stood on the corners, drinking malt liquor from 40-ounce bottles. They had nothing else to do. Trash was strewn around the neighborhood. Sullivant Gardens looked like a war zone.

THE FORGOTTEN SON

I remember when my mother told me, "Son, your father is coming to see you today." I was elated, but he left me deflated. I stayed in, looking out the window and interrupting my mother's television shows to ask, "When is he coming? Will it be soon?"

"I dunno," she responded. I waited and waited and waited. He never showed up. My father was not a man of his word.

My father did stop by occasionally, unannounced and reeking of alcohol. I never saw him sober. The smell of alcohol leaking through his pores was unbearable. He passed out on the couch late one evening; my sisters and I stole money from his pocket to order a pizza.

My father cared more about that bottle than about the emotions I had bottled up inside me. He had a negative balance in the father-son account. He never spent quality time with me or took an interest in anything I did. He and my mother were never married, but this should not have exempted him from fatherhood's responsibilities.

He did take me to the corner store on two occasions to buy me some candy. I rode in the car, in stunned silence, with an inebriated man who shared one-half of my DNA. What does a father say to a son that he doesn't want? What does a son say to a father he doesn't know? When we entered the convenience store, I headed for the candy aisle and he walked to the adult beverage cooler for another 40 ounces of malt liquor. He'd regulate how much candy I could have—most of what I chose stayed behind when we left the store—but not how much alcohol he drank. After age 9, I never saw him again. (I believe alcohol was his coping strategy to deal with life and a son he saw as a burden.)

I had just returned from playing basketball with a neighborhood friend as a high school sophomore. Before I could place my gym bag on the floor, my mom gave me the bad news: "Your father just passed away. Do you want to attend the funeral? It's out-of-state." I was stunned, not by my father's death, but by my mother's question. I couldn't believe she would ask if I wanted to attend the funeral of someone I hadn't seen or heard

I didn't forgive my father until I became one myself, 16 years after his death.

from in more than seven years. Mom didn't pursue the question again after I responded, "For what? He didn't want to be involved in my life, and it's not necessary to travel hundreds of miles to pay my respects to someone I never knew. I don't even have his picture. My father never once told me that he loved me. He passed at the age of 40 from liver failure. Isn't that number ironic?

Unfortunately, my mother didn't always show up for me, either. At the last home football game I played for the Westside Boys Club Dolphins, parents escorted their children across the field before the game, to fans' applause. Of course, my father was missing in action. My mother, recovering from a late night of partying, told me, "Son, I'll be there." She never showed up. The game announcer called my name, but stopped short of saying, "accompanied by his mother, Laura." I walked across the field alone in front of the capacity crowd. There were other no-shows for school assemblies and sporting events during my childhood. I don't hold any personal animus toward my mother; she suffered immensely through the years while dealing the best she could with her physical and emotional challenges. Even so, this was one of the saddest and most humiliating moments of my life. My wife and I make it a point to attend all of our children's ceremonial activities and sporting events.

Disgust

Poverty made me feel dirty, even though I bathed daily. I don't feel dirty anymore. However, the stench of poverty is still with me. The memories will never go away.

The olfactory bulb, located deep within the brain's temporal lobe, is responsible for our sense of smell. Smell and emotions are famously connected, with pleasant odors conjuring positive emotions and unpleasant odors triggering negative emotions.

Aspects of my neighborhood make me nauseous when I think about them in detail, even decades later. The path to our apartment's back door went past a huge, brownish-green dumpster. Dirty diapers littered the ground around the dumpster. I could smell rotted food and rancid cooking grease from 100 feet away. Late at night, neighborhood alcoholics used the dumpster as a urinal. Rodents rummaged through the garbage in the wee hours of the morning, looking for something to eat. When I took our trash to the dumpster, I held my nose with one hand and used the other to toss our bag, sprinting back afterwards to get away from the filth and sickening odor.

FLYIN' SCARED

Hundreds of bats shared our housing project. At dusk they emerged from under the roof gutters, flying high and swooping low as if to intimidate residents with their erratic aerial patterns. I kept a watchful eye on the little brown bats that terrorized Sullivant Gardens. These bats eat flying insects, which is good for us and our ecosystem, but it's still hard to imagine that they aren't out to suck our blood. I made sure never to wear red when shooting hoops late at night, to dissuade bats from gravitating to my "blood colors." (It's also important to be aware of your clothing selection and social interactions in a gang-infested neighborhood, where the wrong colors could cost you a visit to the hospital or county morgue.)

Bats slept just a few feet from my bedroom window. Late at night, I could hear them squealing and making weird noises as they jockeyed for position in a tight space. It freaked me out. Somehow they made their way inside our home, probably by coming down the chimney. We complained repeatedly to the office manager, but he did very little to remove the bats from our apartment.

As if in a real-life horror flick, bats turned up inside our home at the most inopportune times: mealtime or right before we went to bed. My mother, a super-spiritual woman, screamed, "Satan, get out of here! We bind your evil spirit in the name of Jesus!" Her exorcism scared me more than the bat itself. The poor bats were just as afraid of us as we were of them. They flew upstairs and down, with us screaming hysterically (and right on cue) every time a bat flew near us. Sometimes bats crawled on our kitchen floor. Other times they hung upside down from our curtains until daybreak. We were the only neighborhood household that reported bats in their apartment. Very strange, and this still gives me the creeps thinking about it.

YOU'RE NOT WELCOME

In high school, I tried hard to hide my economically distressing situation from coaches, teammates, and friends. I didn't want them to see my world for even one second. I thought, "Why would I want anyone to see where I sleep, eat, and live? How will they judge me now that they know how poor I really am?" Hearing about poverty is one thing; smelling and seeing poverty in person is another. I was utterly ashamed. The more attention I received for playing basketball, the more embarrassed I became.

Rides home were excruciating. I pre-planned where I wanted to be dropped off, how far it needed to be from Sullivant Gardens, and what alternate routes the driver should take to avoid the faintest glimpse of extreme poverty. Of course, I couldn't account for every conceivable circumstance, and sometimes my plan imploded:

> **Me:** (showing my nervousness) Hey, I'll let you know when we are getting close.

Teammate: (unaware of my scheme and anxiety) Okay, great.

Me: (agitated) Don't go that way. Turn here. My house is just around the corner.

Teammate: (worried about my safety) I don't mind dropping you off at your front door.

Me: This is fine right here.

Teammate: I insist.

Me: Well, all right. Here it is. Thanks for the ride!

Teammate: Sure, you bet.

I exit the vehicle. He waits while I open a random family's garden gate. I look back, wave, and signal for him to leave. When he turns the corner, I sprint toward my housing project, taking a breather while walking under the freeway viaduct. I notice a car driving by. It was my teammate, waving good-bye again. I can only imagine what he was thinking—my scheme didn't fool him.

I transferred from Worthington Christian to Wehrle Memorial High School at the end of my sophomore year. It was difficult to fit in with the upper-middle-class and affluent students at Worthington Christian. I was one of five blacks in the high school, and the only African-American student from an impoverished background.

My junior year at Wehrle was magical. We won a state championship and finished as one of the top teams in the *USA Today* rankings. I was one of the top five high school basketball prospects in the country, and had multiple offers to play basketball in college. Hall of Fame coaches Bobby Knight and Dean Smith recruited me hard, as did Gary Williams of Ohio State and Jerry "The Shark" Tarkanian of the University of Nevada Las Vegas. I vehemently refused to let coaches meet with my mother and me in our apartment.

I was too ashamed to invite famous coaches into my world of extreme poverty. I didn't want my living conditions to influence their opinion of me.

In the controversial *Sports Illustrated* article, "Funderburke vs. Knight," Curry Kirkpatrick wrote:

> "Much of Funderburke's life has been anything but a laughing matter. His father left home before Lawrence got to know him; his

mother, Laura, is something of a recluse whom college recruiters never saw. They only talked to her on the phone. Says one college coach. 'None of us ever got a home visit. It was obvious Lawrence was embarrassed with his home life.'"[13]

My high school friends didn't come into our home, either. One of my closest friends back then, Ernest Stromer, tried to come inside on one occasion, but I stopped him. "Hold up, dog," I barked. "I'll be out in a minute." Our living room housed a kaleidoscope of mismatched furniture: a gold chair, a blue sofa, a multicolored couch with a hospital bed frame standing in for its missing legs, and a television with a coat hanger doubling as the antenna. I could not allow anyone a glimpse of my living arrangements.

Surprise

It was a dreary spring day in the early 1980s when I heard my mother pleading with a man to return something he had taken. This scumbag, who I'll call Jimmy, stole our welfare check and food stamps. Jimmy ran for his life as I, my mother, and my older sisters screamed for him to return our benefits. He didn't oblige. Jimmy didn't care whether we were able to pay our bills or had enough food. What a jerk! But Jimmy did leave us a token of appreciation: an R&B cassette tape. We were unusually hungry that month, but at least we were able to get our boogie on!

My mother is a fair skinned African-American woman with long curly hair and a 6'0" frame. Men were attracted to her physical beauty. Some of them gravitated to her for another, more sinister reason. She was single and taking care of four children in a setting where mothers got a welfare stipend for each fatherless child they were raising. These predators wanted money, not love. Unfortunately, there were plenty of similar men around our neighborhood. Some of them were serial batterers; they verbally and physically abused women and children unable to defend themselves.

A ROLL OF THE DICE

Growing up in poverty could be an action-packed movie full of intrigue and suspense. These forms of entertainment depended on the main characters, their roles, testosterone, bravado, and how the wind blew on a particular day. I watched an assailant wearing a cast knock out a guy before he hit the pavement. The sound I heard when the back of his head hit the concrete was chilling. I witnessed neighborhood bullies savagely beat random people who were simply passing through Sullivant Gardens. Obviously, they didn't get the memo that uninvited strangers risked bodily harm if they stepped foot inside our housing project. I saw a group of male residents, too old to play softball against their younger white competitors, hit home runs and then hit their opponents with baseball bats after the game.

One resident hit the visiting team's head coach, a bodybuilder with layers of muscle, hard in the head with an aluminum baseball bat. The sound literally vibrated through my body, even though I was standing more than thirty feet away. It was surreal, a slow-motion scene in a horror movie. I thought the blow was fatal or caused brain damage at the very least, but perhaps his muscular build and will to live saved him. He staggered to his van with blood dripping down his face before exiting our neighborhood. Horrified, I sprinted home, ran upstairs to my room, and cried uncontrollably. I was nine years old. Why this all-white team agreed to play a softball game in our housing project is a question I find myself asking even today. Sullivant Gardens was the most dangerous neighborhood in the city.

> Poverty's scars are noticeably present. Of course, they never let you forget how brutal this life is.

I watched the ghetto dice game, also known as "street craps." The players were brave enough to risk losing money on a roll of the dice, and more importantly, willing to be arrested for illegal gambling. Most of them had been in and out of jail throughout their adult lives.

The antics they displayed were fun to watch. Street craps was a game of rituals and clever sayings, none of which actually improved players' chances of winning. It was about humor, street cred, raw emotion, and reputation. Mama jokes were rarely, if ever, allowed unless the players were blood relatives or best friends. If someone else said a mama joke, it meant a fight. With no involved fathers in their lives, Mama was the only parent most of them had, and they protected her good name even when they were high or in a speech-slurring, drunken stupor.

I vividly remember one participant, who I'll call Dicey D, playing with a pair of shiny green dice. He seemed to win more than his share of games, which brought accusations that he'd rigged the dice. Rigged, weighted dice weren't uncommon, and greatly improved a player's chances.

Let's dig deeper into the game of craps to gauge the likely (or unlikely) outcome that a particular number would be rolled. On any given roll, the odds of success were as follows:

Number Rolled	Combination	Odds
1	N/A	0%
2	1 + 1	4.8%
3	1 + 2	4.8%
4	1 + 3; 2 + 2	9.5%
5	1 + 4; 2 + 3	9.5%
6	1 + 5; 2 + 4; 3 + 3	14.3%
7	1 + 6; 2 + 5; 3 + 4	14.3%
8	2 + 6; 3 + 5; 4 + 4	14.3%
9	3 + 6; 4 + 5	9.5%
10	4 + 6; 5 + 5	9.5%
11	5 + 6	4.8%
12	6 + 6	4.8%

On each roll, there's a 19.1 percent likelihood that the numbers on the two dice will total 7 or 11. Those are bad odds, but most of the players saw this as the best bet. The key word here is "felt," because in poverty, feelings often guide behaviors. The odds of the dice totaling 2, 3, or 12 is 13.1 percent, for even worse odds. A player has a 66.6 percent chance of rolling a total of 4, 5, 6, 8, 9, or 10—good odds, but bad omen.

I watched a player make and then refuse to keep a $2 side bet. The counterparty and his posse stomped and kicked the player. It could have been even worse. Most of the players carried guns. He could have very easily been shot by the out-of-control counterparty. Given the broken malt liquor bottles nearby, he could have been stabbed, too.

Someone on YahooAnswers! wanted to learn more about street craps. Another commenter responded, "Fool, you have to be black and you learn the rules on the street!" You also must have an above-average tolerance for risk. Money might not be the only thing you lose; in the ghetto, loss of life is a distinct possibility as well, though it is rarely considered by game participants.

A LESSON IN PRACTICAL INTELLIGENCE

It was a cool day in March 1983 when my mother gave me $15 to purchase a rain jacket at Schottenstein's department store. She told me, "Go straight there, purchase the rain jacket, and come right back home. And don't do something stupid and spend the money on anything else but a rain jacket." Unfortunately, I didn't follow her instructions.

Halfway to the Northern Lights Shopping Center, a black man in his late twenties approached me while sitting in the back of the COTA bus, our city's public transportation. Earlier I had noticed him moving a tiny rubber ball back and forth under three small plastic cups that sat on top of a folded newspaper. He asked, "My young brother, do you want to play a game where you can make some quick money? Just pick the right one—the cup the ball is hidden under—and you win. What do you have to lose?" Sounded simple enough, a slam-dunk opportunity I presumed with a guaranteed payout.

"When I win," I said to myself, "I'll have plenty of money left over after purchasing the raincoat to play arcade games and get something to eat at Wendy's."

> ### SOCIOPSYCHONOMIC FILTER
> The lure of easy money is an obvious trap for the poor. A favorable economic outcome is expected. Risks are minimized or downgraded, while the financial rewards get amplified or upgraded.

The man walked to the front of the bus to ask the bus driver a question, leaving the game on his seat. His accomplice, sitting behind us, quickly gets my attention. He said, "Brother man, I know exactly where it is. It's right here—you can't lose!" His partner in crime returned to his seat. "Young buck, you ready to play?" he asked. I nodded. He said, "That'll be $10." I point to the cup that the accomplice had indicated. The ball wasn't there. My heart sank. The accomplice shook his head in disbelief.

I exited the bus and headed straight for the arcade. I had no reason to go inside Schottenstein's now that I didn't have enough money to purchase the $12 rain jacket. I spent several hours playing arcade games and had just enough left over to get something to eat and catch the bus home.

Before I share my mother's reaction to my lapse in judgment, let me pause and provide you with some context for this game, though some readers may be familiar with it. Five things are needed to make the bait-and-switch game work:

1. **Shady characters:** secretly working together, these smooth-talking hustlers lure their victims with ersatz philanthropic benevolence and a kindred connection. ("Hey, I'm looking out for you!")

2. **The bait**: this is a can't-miss opportunity to double, triple, or even quadruple an investor's money. ("What do you have to lose but a lost opportunity?")

3. **Gullible investors**: people who are in desperate need of a financial breakthrough but can least afford to invest in grand cons. ("I'm due for a lucky break!")

4. **The switch**: the distraction used to separate the investor from his money, as well as perception from reality. ("There's no way you can lose!")

5. **The venue**: a transitory setting with lots of unsuspecting, down-on-their-luck investors who would be embarrassed to turn the scam artists in to police. ("Our rendezvous was meant to be!")

Now back to the story. My mother asked to see the rain jacket as soon as I got home. I sheepishly replied, "Some guy on the bus scammed me out of $10, and I ..." Irate, my mother interrupted me and shouted, "Boy, you have lots of book smarts, but no common sense. Go to your room!"

I didn't get a rain jacket that day, but I did get an eye-opening tutorial in practical intelligence, also known as common sense. I also learned something about navigating the world of emotional and financial intelligence, too. Emotional intelligence is the ability to wisely manage competing emotions. Financial intelligence helps us make or maintain good monetary decisions as circumstances change, and is critical to managing cash flow and accumulating wealth. Once I began playing professional basketball, people pitched me countless can't-miss investment opportunities. Most were such outrageous, far-fetched scams that it's hard to believe anyone would invest money. Some people did and lost every penny. Losing $10 as a kid instead of hundreds of thousands of dollars as a grown man—that's a fortunate break. (For more insight on the outlandish scams presented to professional athletes, please read my book *Hook Me Up, Playa!*)

Happiness

I actually have plenty of fond childhood memories. On my twelfth birthday, my mother gave me a shiny Spaulding basketball, though made of plastic, not leather. I gave her a big hug and promised her that I would graduate from college and then play in the NBA. "You are gonna be so proud of me, Mommy," I said. She cried, saying, "I know you will, son! I believe you."

HAPPY (OR SAD) OR CONTEMPLATIVE, SHOOT SOME HOOPS

In spite of the chilly morning, after dressing warmly, I sprinted outside for an imaginary, epic showdown between Larry Bird and Earvin "Magic" Johnson. To this day, if I'm feeling a bit depressed, I go to the basketball court and shoot some hoops. This always lifts my spirit.

Decades later, I still have those same feelings when I step on the basketball court. This game, as many inner-city kids can attest, is a sanctuary, an opportunity to briefly push aside life's stressors. We needed just a ball, a hoop, and creativity to imagine a world of boundless opportunities.

Basketball is the ghetto sport of choice. Nearly every housing project in America has at least one basketball court. The ghetto represents bondage; this game represents freedom, a chance to shake off the shackles and show off your athletic skills. A liberated soul isn't afraid to try a new move or take a risky shot. A popular saying sums up the game: "You miss 100 percent of the shots you don't take."

Today, shooting hoops lets me go back to where my escape from poverty began, more than 30 years ago. Shot after shot, now I think about what it takes to help others break free from the shackles of economic misery and unfulfilled potential.

THE COMPROMISE OF SPLURGING

We didn't often spend money on things that weren't bills or groceries. During the week after the first of the month, however, Mom might splurge on a movie night out with the family at a nearby drive-in theater or order an extra-large pizza for four hungry kids. We did have a ritual, though, before we entered the parking lot of the drive-in theater. First, we made popcorn at home, added lots of butter, and placed it in a brown paper grocery bag. We stopped by Big Bear, another now-defunct grocery store, to pick up a pack of peanut butter cups. Then we made our way to the drive-in theater, where an attendant peaked inside the car to make sure we weren't bringing in any outside food, candy, or soft drinks. We hid these items well.

When our family goes to the movies, a rare occurrence today, to save a few bucks I still sometimes hide bottled water and healthy snacks in coat pockets or my wife's purse. If I could sneak in a big bucket of organic popcorn, I'd do that, too.

HAPPY INSIDE, FULFILLED OUTSIDE

Happiness is not about making a lot of money or accumulating substantial assets, though these things can accentuate true happiness. A tropical vacation can strengthen family unity, and it's a blessing to support a favorite charity with a six-figure gift. Financial success can also be used to mask unhappiness. We purchase luxury items to get people to like us or to fit in with the "in" crowd, whoever they are. No, true happiness has everything to do with fulfilling the potential God has placed inside us and the purpose to which we are called. This is our *happiness mandate*.

I'm reminded of the significance of reaching my full potential when I peruse our car's owner's manual. As I flip through the pages to troubleshoot a problem, I quickly conclude that we've shortchanged our driving experience. The options at our disposable, with additional insight on how to use them, would make the driving experience even more enjoyable. Unfortunately, I am only inclined to look inside the manual when I have an obvious problem with a car. Big mistake. Most of us go through life on cruise control, challenging ourselves to aspire to new heights only when the situation calls for it. How do we know the depths of our talents and capabilities if we don't dig deep inside to uncover them? Our schools, at every level, need to teach students how to find true happiness by maximizing their TAP—talents, abilities, and passions.

> Without a life of purpose, true happiness will be a fleeting and aimless endeavor.

THE TRUMP CARD OF HAPPINESS: USE IT OR LOSE IT

Happiness can trump fear, anger, disgust, and sadness. The joy of getting paid for my childhood labor did create a state of bliss that insulated me from many of my peers' toxic mindsets and actions. I saw the world not through the microscope of scarcity, but with the magnifying glass of opportunity. This vantage point, along with the humiliation of living in economic distress, propelled me to seek opportunities that extended beyond the borders of Sullivant Gardens. I shoveled snow, mowed lawns, and sold newspapers with my cousin Ricky White outside the OSU football stadium in the early 1980s. We'd wake up early on a Saturday morning, eat breakfast, and catch the COTA bus with just a few dollars in our pockets. With no guarantees, we purchased a few dozen newspapers at wholesale prices, which we then sold to OSU fans at a markup. This served as an early lesson in entrepreneurship.

I didn't deny (and still don't) the detrimental effects of racism, low expectations, parental abandonment, and lack of compassion in dealing with the plight of the poor. Injustices will always exist; it's how we respond to them that shapes and defines the life we choose to live. We can't control other people's actions or inactions, but we can regulate our own happiness filter. If we don't, we have only ourselves to blame.

The pursuit of happiness in America is an inalienable right that our founding fathers—themselves flawed men—were adamant about protecting under the Constitution. But how do you pursue an abstraction without appropriate role modeling?

A true constitutionalist advocates and creates conditions in which the poor and middle class have a legitimate shot at living decent, humane lives. The argument shouldn't be political, Democrats versus Republicans. This is about the happiness of every American citizen, regardless of their socioeconomic standing. I've been hungry and I've been well fed. In every circumstance, I controlled my personal happiness meter. America is one of the few places that people can still overcome challenges, change their flight paths toward success and away from failure by adjusting their GPS coordinates of what's possible, and break the curse of generational poverty. I'm living proof!

CHAPTER

3

I DID WHAT?

Behavioral finance: a look under the hood

W e are creatures of habit with death grips on our preconceived notions, especially those around money. Our financial comfort zone, we think, protects us from monetary and non-monetary threats. However, most of our economic headaches are self-inflicted mishaps. A faulty belief system is largely to blame.

Behavioral finance is best understood in the context of real-world experiences that involve money, ego, class, race, biases, and upbringing. It's rare that a single example can illustrate a myriad of financial decisions, attitudes, and actions. I have the ideal candidate.

Kioshi Smith, a single parent and father of four, is a school bus driver and barber. He's black, middle age and middle class, insightful, and a hard worker. In an interview he discussed a financial decision that he later regretted, made when he was in his early thirties. Its effects lingered for two decades. He revisits his decision through the lens of behavioral finance, considering overreaction, inadvertent blindness, confirmatory bias, overconfidence, anchoring, loss aversion, and hindsight bias.

OVERREACTION

> a state of unrelenting panic that leads to irrational thoughts, decisions, and actions

It was the summer of 1994 and things were good in the American economy. The recession of 1991 was a distant memory. The Federal Reserve was aggressively raising interest rates, a sign that our gross domestic product (GDP) was on solid footing. Investors felt confident enough to take bigger risks and stay ahead of inflation.

Black folks saw improved financial prospects that year. Tangible assets—our preferred capital deployment strategy then as now—dominated our investment choices. My cousin Kioshi spent $1,200 for a paint job on his 1978 Cadillac Sedan Deville. The automobile was a collector's edition, and he was sure it would gain value. It would be his big break. Unfortunately, it wasn't.

Like many African-Americans from similar backgrounds, Kioshi never learned the importance and power of money. With no frame of reference to protect him from financial mishaps (or build meaningful wealth), he got caught up in the got-to-have-it-now syndrome: mortgage your economic future now and pay the debt later. Being on the wrong side of compound interest during a period of rising interest rates is a terrible predicament. Kioshi says, "When you're in your twenties and even early thirties, you think irrational, not rational. You think time is on your side to recover from financial malfeasance. Not true."

He has two image-conscious teenage children. They, too, want what other cool kids have—the latest sneakers, clothes, and electronic gadgets. "I'm trying to get them to postpone their wants for a later date," he affirms. "These things are not necessities; they can wait." Delayed gratification is a hard concept for adults to grasp, let alone children.

INADVERTENT BLINDNESS

> a failure to see the blind spots that hinder a successful outcome

Investor euphoria shows up (and eventually fizzles out) during favorable economic conditions when people don't perform enough due diligence before taking on risk. It seems that the odds of a successful investment outcome are higher than usual. It's a classic case of tunnel vision.

We see everything, but we choose what gets our immediate attention. We can see financial blind spots clearly in our rearview mirrors, but we don't take them seriously until things inevitably go wrong.

Financial blind spots cloud our judgment, short-circuit our money filter, and disrupt our economic navigational system. The side effects become painfully obvious when we can no longer deny them.

Arguably, inadvertent blindness is the most punishing behavioral finance concept, because logic automatically takes a back seat to runaway emotion. In the world of financial well-being, emotional frivolity and carefree monetary habits are two unrelenting, sabotaging forces. "It was about the moment," Kioshi says, "not my future." Now 53, he regrets that paint job. "I couldn't foresee how this lapse in judgment would haunt me to this day, but it has," he laments.

CONFIRMATION BIAS

> the tendency to interpret new evidence as confirmation of one's existing beliefs or theories

Kioshi sought other opinions to confirm his thoughts about the newly painted classic automobile's future value, a classic case of confirmation bias. His conversational starters were intentionally optimistic, and he shot down critiques with precision-guided rebuttals. His older brother Kenneth, a mentor and confidant, commented, "That could happen. You could have a great return if you sold the classic car for a lot of money." The key word here is *if*. Possible (it could happen) does not mean probable (it's likely to happen).

Semantics is confirmation bias's biggest ally, because we often hear what we want to hear. The absence of conflicting data and differences of opinions strengthens our resolve to stay the course. We welcome new insights if they align with our flawed predispositions.

Kioshi's analysis bypassed normal investment due diligence. He should have considered strategic goals (How will this decision affect my short- and long-term financial objectives?), opportunity costs (What are the tradeoffs?), time horizon (When will I have or need the money?), risk assessment (What could go wrong?), and return on investment (What rate of return can I reasonably expect?). Kioshi considered only the rate of return. According to his analysis, it far exceeded what he could have received from a certificate of deposit or dividend-paying stock. That alone was good enough for him.

OVERCONFIDENCE

> a haughty attitude in a skill or tightly held position that can cloud a person's judgment

The freshly painted 1978 Cadillac Sedan Deville made Kioshi feel great. It enhanced his image. "It gave me a false sense of security," he says. "I was the guy driving around in a big car. In a shallow way, it gave credibility to my image—temporarily. I assumed the car would also get me out of a financial rut in the future. Man, was I wrong. We, inner-city black folks, are our own worst enemy. We believe perception and reality are always interchangeable. They're not." Revisiting financial mishaps is never easy, even decades later. It takes a brave man to subject himself to this type of scrutiny.

Let's pause for a moment and dig a little deeper into the overconfidence trap. The world of investing is very unkind to egocentricity. Left unchecked, it has dire financial consequences on four fronts. First, it magnifies alleged investment gains, yet minimizes the associated risks. Second, overconfident investors suffer from inflamed egos. They believe divine investment knowledge escaped others, but somehow, mysteriously found them. Third, egocentricity can (and often does) threaten financial well-being. Fourth, overconfidence is a breeding ground for the three behavioral finance concepts that follow.

ANCHORING

> an entrenched position or determination to stay the course in spite of changing circumstances or conditions

When facts change, change your mind. It's good advice and so hard to take, because we tend to stick to our old beliefs and decisions.

Kioshi's car was going to be his next big break. People anchor themselves by buying lottery tickets, gambling at casinos or racetracks, or investing in outlandish, get-rich-quick schemes. The lure of a financial windfall is captivating, and anchors them even more. They convince themselves that a profitable outcome is nearly guaranteed. "I got suckered into the same mental trap," he says. "Big mistake."

Researchers estimate that it takes 21 days to form a habit, 63 days to form a mindset, and a more extended period to shape a belief system. Each of these is difficult (although not impossible) to change once an individual reaches adulthood.

We derive our beliefs and attitudes from our mindsets. Our economic frames of reference and Sociopsychonomic filters guide our financial decisions. You can't correct a debilitating behavior pattern until your mindset changes. For this to happen, though, you must introduce and diligently follow a new frame of reference or vantage point.

LOSS AVERSION

> the inability to give up a valued possession because of time, money, or emotions already invested in it

Kioshi admits that the car's sentimental value, as well as the time and money he'd already spent on it, kept him from selling the vehicle much sooner. It also served as a symbol of racial progress and economic pride. "It's so hard to let go of something when we feel such an intense attachment," he adds. "It was my first Cadillac." He knew better, but held out hope for a successful outcome.

The car was a money pit. Whatever could go wrong, did go wrong. "Something was always breaking down: the brakes, transmission, air-conditioning system, muffler. You name it, something went bad," Kioshi says. The more he convinced himself to keep the car, the more money he lost.

Finally, Kioshi sold the car. "Sometimes you have to cut your losses and move forward. Take the loss, move on, learn from it, and never repeat the same mistake again. If I would have substituted my sentimental value for financial value, how much further along would I be today?" he asks.

Loss aversion is not just about an underperforming asset. Sometimes it may be perfectly appropriate to sell an investment position at a profit. Let's pretend that Kioshi invested the money in a conservative, dividend-paying index fund with a five-star rating. He purchases 100 shares at $25 per share, for an outlay of $2,500.

Two years later he liquidates the position after extensive research and on the recommendation of a registered investment advisor (RIA) who believes dividend-paying stocks are headed for a correction as investors anticipate a shift to growth-oriented sectors, including real estate, industrials, commodities, and precious metals.

Not including fees and expenses, his realized gain is $2,000, because each share sold for $45. Had he not liquidated the position, his position could have dropped precipitously in changing economic conditions and investor whims. Here, loss aversion is seen in the context of emotional loyalty to achieve an even bigger investment payoff, not hold on to an underperforming dud.

HINDSIGHT BIAS

> the ability to see an event or predicament with greater clarity and focus, but only after the fact, and the erroneous assumption that this insight was available and entirely predictable all along

Hindsight bias is the I-knew-it-all-along bias. We eventually see the factors that led to our errors in judgment and imagine that, had we only listened harder or done better research, we might have avoided them.

"I knew this decision wasn't smart to do. To make matters worse, my ex-wife repeatedly warned me not to do it! It's so frustrating, and comical, really, thinking about such a stupid thing to waste money on," Kioshi says.

Kioshi invested thousands to buy the car, and another $1,200 on the paint job. Eventually, a junkyard paid him $300 for his former pride and joy.

If he could make the investment over again, Kioshi says, he'd set up a college fund for his oldest daughter, Cylon, who was then six years old. He could have put the money in an investment vehicle with a successful track record. "I'd be in the six figures right now, had I made the right moves financially in my twenties and thirties," he asserts. "Nobody ever told or showed me how to invest wisely."

It's never too late to learn. Throughout this book, my intention is to help economically distressed and income-stability Americans create personal, financial, and emotional wealth. None of this happens without a mindset change and upgraded Sociopsychonomic filter.

4

YOUR FASCINATING BRAIN

The four lobes of the cerebral cortex

Author's Note

I'm not a specialist in any field of brain science and readily acknowledge that this chapter, for illustrative purposes, is an oversimplification to help readers grasp a general understanding of the cerebral cortex. My analysis is based on classes I took during my undergraduate, graduate, and professional coursework that described neural activity in the context of consumer and investor behavior. I do have years of experience documenting the mindsets and corresponding habits of thousands of people across the socioeconomic spectrum, including my clients and my precious son Eli.

E ven the brightest minds in psychology and neuroscience admit that we are just beginning to scratch the surface in our understanding of how the human brain works. Scientists are clear, though, that the brain operates as an integrated unit, performing billions of cross-regional calculations in a split second. We give the parts of the brain different names, and it's possible to have a dominant cerebral lobe and learning style. But outside of a cognitive dysfunction or traumatic injury, the parts of the brain always work in concert.

Our minds produce kinetic chains of neural activities, guided by our attitude—optimistic, pessimistic, or somewhere in between. Children often mimic their parents' mindsets and behaviors in a variety of areas, especially around money.

You may have a gloomy outlook (*occipital lobe*) on your economic future that causes you to speak negatively (*temporal lobe*) about yourself and others and behave impulsively (*frontal lobe*) in the grips of out-of-control emotional (*temporal lobe*) and sensory experiences (*parietal lobe*). If you are stressed and confused about your life's direction, that affects your breathing and digestion (*brain stem*), short- and long-term memory (*hippocampus*), hormones (*hypothalamus* and *pituitary gland*), and circadian rhythm (*pineal gland*). Limbic system and endocrine disruptions can combine with poor eating and lack of exercise to create disastrous outcomes. The ways that you imagine your financial future have a profound effect on your overall wealth and health.

> ## DID YOU KNOW?
> The cerebral cortex makes up approximately 70 to 80 percent of the brain's mass.

Let's explore the cerebrum, also known as the cerebral cortex, in greater detail. Some observers postulate that the detail-oriented side of the cerebrum occurs in the left hemisphere and is microscopic in interpreting how the human brain processes what it sees, hears, smells, tastes, or touches. The right hemisphere, by contrast, sees, interprets, or gathers data from a big-picture perspective. The corpus callosum, the bridge between the two hemispheres, is the communication channel that helps each side of the brain make sense of the other. It helps one side translate the big picture into smaller, more focused tasks, and helps the other magnify sequential details into a sense of the whole. Using sports terminology, the overall game plan, to a large extent, centers in the right brain. Each diagrammed play has a natural or more comfortable home in the left brain. (To be fair, evidence suggests that both sides of the brain interpret or carry out the same tasks or neural processes from coordinated vantage points, which highlights the differences in opinions among psychologists, neuroscientists, and exercise specialists regarding the left- and right-brain dichotomy. It's possible opposing viewpoints may, in fact, be describing this hemispheric quagmire from a two-sided lens.)

When one hemisphere is overly dominant, this can create imbalances in the brain. Our son Eli's brain had a dominant left side, and he wasn't happy when life wasn't arranged to his satisfaction in a sequential fashion. Today, thank God, his right and left hemispheres (and the lobes within them) have a more symbiotic or balanced relationship.

The Frontal Lobe

Code Name: Analytical Processing Center

The frontal lobe is also known as the executive command center. Its functions include higher-order brain tasks, including planning, organizing, decision-making, weighing consequences, problem-solving, communicating, reasoning, controlling and regulating emotions (particularly during times of stress), modulating impulses, and representing one's personality to the outside world. These attributes are critically important in the world of life planning, cash flow management, and wealth accumulation.

Dr. Ian Krajbich, a neuroeconomist at The Ohio State University, believes that the frontal lobe has an important role in helping people stick to a financial plan. He says that the dorsolateral prefrontal cortex is high and off to the side in the front of the head. "This is where decisions are made for higher-order goals, for example, self-control. In fact, we know that the dorsolateral prefrontal cortex works to counteract, control, or influence other parts of the prefrontal cortex," he says. This is where people silence background noise and bypass immediate gratification. We tend to make more thoughtful financial (and personal) decisions when we filter goals through our dorsolateral prefrontal cortex and not emotional whims.

SEQUENTIAL PROCESSORS: ORDERING A CHAOTIC WORLD

Sequential processors often learn and operate best when the world around them is structured, logical, and orderly. They do very well in tasks that benefit from taking time to think, such as planning to meet a long-term financial goal or other situations in which the processor can control or reasonably predict variables and outcomes. But when a sequential processor is in an environment that rewards instinct, that processor is a fish out of water.

Improvisational sports such as soccer, lacrosse, basketball, and skilled positions in football are incredibly challenging, but they're also the best way for a sequential thinker to grow more balanced. Improvisational sports require spontaneity, creativity, and maneuverability. These things are outside the comfort zone for people with dominant left brains, who are most comfortable in a structured setting with predetermined tasks, assignments, and responsibilities. They may prefer to coach or even teach themselves, especially if they're disciplined and driven. (In poverty, frontal lobers are often shunned and mocked. They are la-

> In an environment of scarcity or improvisation, logic doesn't make a whole lot of sense.

beled geeks, nerds, brainiacs, oddballs, and weirdos. They prefer reason and logic over sensation and movement, so they stand out from peers who make sense of their world through music, sports, and social interaction.)

Sequential processors typically gravitate to technique or stop-start sports: swimming, chess, golf, and cross-country running. By and large, these are individual sports with clearly defined rules and boundaries. Sequential learners are naturally gifted in math, science, and rote memory, with natural inclinations to career paths in engineering, accounting, medicine, law, computer programming, research, and business.

Quite often, analytical thinkers struggle in social settings where interaction with others, especially random people, is required. These people are usually quiet, reserved, and introspective. They may experience difficulty with big-picture thinking, navigating strange or unusual environments, and public speaking. They prefer behind-the-scenes work roles and are adept at quickly deflecting attention and praise when others recognize their efforts.

Sequential processors are ideal financial planning clients. They tend to be detail-oriented and goal-driven, organized, emotionally stoic, methodical (though sometimes hard to figure out), and disciplined. Charts, diagrams, and illustrations can help them make sense of financial strategies. They readily understand deductive reasoning and logical explanations.

Financially speaking, sequential processors have predictable strengths and weaknesses.

Strengths

- They prefer substance to pretense, seeing the latter as uncouth, and are comfortable with modesty and simplicity.
- They prefer substance to style. For example, they never add after-market accessories to their automobiles.

- They carefully plan even mundane activities, such as grocery shopping or a child's activities.

Deficits

- They may be rigid and inflexible in thought, action, or time management.
- They may lack genuine empathy and unwittingly become judgmental in their understanding of the less fortunate. (They tend to believe that the poor can change their economic circumstances by just following a series of calculated steps.)
- They see the world in absolutes, although the world of economic distress is often open to interpretation.

Interestingly enough, the generationally affluent (and those with a wealth-accumulation mindset) often have many characteristics of frontal-lobe thinkers. They follow well-constructed financial plans with religious fervor, subdue emotions when economic conditions change or an investment loses value, and regulate counterproductive impulses that can derail their families' fortune and legacy.

The Parietal Lobe

Code Name: Internal GPS System

Privilege alone does not guarantee financial freedom, nor does an upbringing in economic distress have to be an impediment to achieving it. The lessons we learn in affluence or poverty help or hinder us on the road to fulfilling our economic potentials. We learn about managing sensory inputs, orienting to our physical and mental selves, and navigating risk on the way to an intended destination.

In America, wealthy kids' navigational aptitude for success is pre-set, thanks in large part to this carefully crafted and followed template: first-class experiences, elite-level education, and precision-guided expectations. GAPA (and many SAPA) parents don't take chances with their lineage. Too much is at stake.

Now, for children from generational poverty, the navigational path to success must be felt—literally. It must produce a warm, fuzzy feeling to stay in the intellectual moment at school as the painful urge to check out becomes more

intense. An escape route is offered, free of academic torment. It is very enticing, and unfortunately, many poor students take the bait. (This phenomenon
is covered extensively in Chapter 7, "Academic Enrichment.")

On the home front, GEDA parents may want what's best for their kids but
lack the personal ambition and financial resources and professional role models
to bring this to fruition. The result: Children get sidetrack by unrestrained
feelings and never reach their success destinations. Of course, these academic-
and economic-potential casualties get stuck in the maze of a coulda-woulda-
shoulda life. Guided by a sensory-driven landscape assessment, they *feel* there
is no legit way out. Fait accompli.

Without an upgrade to their Sociopsychonomic filter, the poor—children
and adults—will be held captive for the rest of their lives by a physical (and not
a mental) GPS system that seeks pleasurable experiences at every turn, and
to their detriment, avoids pain-generated growth initiatives. This is the crux
of the ever-expanding wealth and health conundrum in which GEDAs find
themselves, a dangerous predicament our nation needs to address, right now,
at the grassroots level. Time is running out.

SEEK AND YOU SHALL MOVE

People with dominant parietal lobes, also called *sensory seekers*, are easy to spot.
They are tactile, interactive learners. They engage with learning and athletics
through sensation and movement, their preferred learning style. Perception,
or intuitive reasoning based on external stimuli, is their default, decision-
making mechanism. They are often natural athletes, fashionable dressers, and
charismatic personalities. They even have a rhythm and rhyme to their daps
and handshakes!

Sensory seekers are often empathetic, feeling other people's pain and
joy. This doesn't necessarily bode well for their wallets. Their generous,
compassionate hearts are often guided by gut reactions, which can be very
misleading. Impulsive giving or investing attracts scam artists, and sincere
pleas for help mixed with lies. It's not easy to distinguish between the two.

Sensory seekers care a lot about image, a priority that can conflict with
the achievement of true financial freedom. They prioritize the goals of inward orientation and outward validation. Some buy approval or statement
assets—cars, clothes, shoes, handbags and other wardrobe accessories, and
electronics—to boost their image and perceived social standing. They like the
way designer clothes, shoes, and other products make them feel. They may

even marry a person they think will impress others. Looking the part instead of being the part offers faux security.

These gregarious people are often personable, gifted, or musically inclined. They seek career paths that require movement, human touch and inspiration, or ingenuity: professional athlete or coach, CEO, performer, public speaker, artist, chef, musician, or inventor. Sitting in a classroom may bore them, especially when information is presented sequentially, and they may feel trapped in a dead-end job or relationship. When their backs are against the wall, they tend to move quickly through the nearest exit.

Sensory seekers appreciate (and sometimes actually crave) applause and adulation. They prefer highly visible work or support roles where their efforts are recognized and, more importantly, lead to successful outcomes. They can light up a room with their electric and eclectic personalities; people are drawn to their natural leadership and relationship management skills.

Although their feelings should be respected, sensory seekers can be challenging clients for financial planners. They are apt to move in and out of investment positions and defy conventional recommendations when instincts, sensations, and emotions become their guides. Scheduled appointments are moving targets. Parietal lobers' transitory nature can be problematic for even the most patient financial representative. It can be incredibly hard to keep them on course when the stock market experiences abnormal volatility.

All is not lost in working with sensory-seeking clients, however. For instance, MoneyGuidePro is an interactive financial planning tool that offers what-if scenarios and variable analyses that can move clients to act or stay put. Real-world simulations offer the stimulation sensory seekers need to pursue financial well-being. To them, feeling is believing.

People with dominant parietal lobes have predictable strengths and weaknesses:

Strengths

- They embrace change if it feels right. (If it doesn't feel right, they are prone to wonder aimlessly.)
- Their sense of spontaneity thrives on new experiences and invigorating sensations.
- Their magnetic personalities can inspire themselves and others to new heights.

- An empathetic nature helps them connect with others on social and emotional levels. (This might explain why some people can jump out of a marriage and into someone else's arms.)

Deficits

- They may confuse movement with progress.
- When sensory seekers touch or try on a shirt or pair of sneakers, out comes the cash or credit card!
- Delayed gratification is hard for sensory seekers to master.
- They may be too generous with their time, money, emotions, and relationships.

Several social class subsets have their fair share of temporal lobers. Generational economically distressed Americans (or GEDAs) have the largest proportion of sensory seekers. They gravitate to feel-good experiences that temporarily diffuse the pain (while often adding to the heartache) of economic distress: dead-end relationships, sports, fast food, and deeply emotional music genres (rap and R&B for inner-city poverty, and heavy metal and country music for Appalachian poverty). They spend what little money they have on short-term enjoyment instead of long-term betterment.

Situational income-stability Americans (or SISAs), situational affluent-positioned Americans (or SAPAs), and functional economically distressed Americans (or FEDAs) who have roots in poverty may shift back and forth between their present reality and former world because it feels like the right thing to do. Guilt, shame, fear, or empathy drives their affinity connection with those left behind.

When people from the 'hood experience a financial come-up, they typically make cameo visits back to their old neighborhood, decked out in statement assets and driving high-end automobiles to keep their ghetto card up to date. Only a few lucky individuals from their former lives are permitted to get in touch with them, and those chosen few get specific instructions about who can and can't have their

> Cameo visits back to the ghetto keep your 'hood card up to date and sellout diatribes by the haters out of mind.

contact information. Breach that trust, and the relationship ends. These spokespeople, mainly for SAPAs and FEDAs, serve as buffers and validation channels to broadcast a compelling message. Some of them may even be on

SAPAs' and FEDAs' payroll. They tell residents that those fortunate enough to escape economic hardship haven't forgotten where they came from. Sports camps, concert tickets, Thanksgiving meals, and Christmas gifts for the needy add credibility and underline affinity, though the donor may not be present. These acts of kindness show that home is only one good deed or arm's length transaction away.

WHO ARE YOU?

Positional standing—physically and mentally—resides in your parietal lobe. The parietal lobe borders all of the other lobes and works in rhythm with them. Find your purpose. When you do, you will understand more about who you are and the steps you might take to reach your personal, professional, and financial potential.

A number of factors influence your physical and mental self: your upbringing, environment, genetics, and spiritual life. Your outlook on life (occipital lobe) and ability to manage your life (frontal lobe), balance your internal dialogue (temporal lobe), and navigate your internal landscape (parietal lobe) define who you are: the self that you and the world see. You are constantly affirming or redefining your sense of self: the good, the bad, and the ugly. Your financial condition, and to a large extent, your economic potential, can be a mirror image of your positional standing. Answer these five questions to find your economic center:

1. **Sensation:** How do your senses influence and shape your financial decisions?

2. **Perception:** How do you perceive your current or future financial situation?

3. **Orientation:** Where do you stand financially?

4. **Navigation:** What tools and steps are you currently using to reach your financial goals?

5. **Destination:** How likely are you to reach your financial goals based on your present economic playbook?

You might not have one ounce of rhythm, but if you answered these five questions with clarity and conviction, then you have a framework of financial rhythm. This is more important to your economic future than any ability to dance the night away.

The Temporal Lobe

Code Name: Internal Dialogue Center

The temporal lobe regulates sound, smell (or olfaction), spoken language recognition, auditory processing for external and internal words, and equilibrium, a critical factor in our realization and perception of physical or financial balance. Memory and emotions also reside in this lobe.

The hippocampus stores visual and verbal memories. The amygdala, which houses our fight-or-flight response, lives deep in the temporal lobe, along with the basal ganglia (or reward filter). All these structures are part of the limbic system, which handles fear, anger, and intensely pleasurable feelings. A memory can trigger the same physiological reaction the original event once did, even if the event happened years or decades ago.

"WHAT'S WRONG WITH OUR SON?"

When our son was an infant, we knew something was terribly wrong. He experienced severe developmental delays in his speech and gait. Eli was nearly four years old before he could walk satisfactorily. His speech was incoherent well past the age of five. When he heard loud noises, including vacuum cleaners, sirens, and horns, Eli covered his ears, writhing in pain. He was hypersensitive to smells no one else noticed. Between the ages of four and seven, his balance and proprioception (or spatial awareness) got worse. Eli bumped into walls and other stationary objects in ways that defied logic. "How did you not see that wall?" we asked him. Poor coordination meant that he couldn't enjoy or excel in sports. Strangely, he didn't get dizzy after swinging on the playground continuously for more than 30 minutes at a time.

Complimentary words excite Eli and convicting words usually aggravate him. Best-selling author and relationship expert, Dr. Gary Chapman, has written extensively about communication and love languages. Our son primarily expresses love through words of affirmation. Eli's face lights up when we compliment him for doing a good job in school, sports, or chores around the house. Temporal lobers, also called *sensitivity internalizers*, love and desperately need words of affirmation. For them, affirming words create a sense of harmony. Auditory processing and olfaction are huge factors in equilibrium. How an individual interprets a smell or even innocent comment can create a nauseous or euphoric feeling inside. Inner sickness from hurtful words or bad news can affect our sense of balance. It happens when someone faints after hearing that a loved one has tragically died.

Eli can still be incredibly hard on himself when he's having difficulty in a given area. He's quick to share his feelings, which we immediately correct when he blurts out: "I'm terrible at everything … I'm so stupid … I'll never be able to learn this."

THE GRAMMAR KING

Eli, now a fifth grader, is a grammar king. His love of reading and writing is extraordinary, and he has a masterful understanding of language structure. He immediately corrects any family member whose English falls short of grammatical perfection, even when meals or cartoons distract him. He also opposes lackluster pronunciation. Say "maff" instead of "math," and he'll correct you instantly. The rest of the family spiffs up our speech when Eli is around. His rebukes aren't belittling. They're more amusing than convicting, and quite telling about how his brain works.

> "The language our kids are exposed to often dictates how they'll perform in school."
>
> **–Geoffrey Canada, President**
> Harlem Children's Zone

Eli's obsession with diction and syntax isn't surprising given his proclivity toward left-brain thinking and its signature trademark: orderly precision. Between ages four and six he'd line up his toys so precisely that he'd notice a half-inch position change (and went ballistic if the formation was altered, even accidentally). No detail escaped his memory. His ability to recall obscure facts and figures was, and still is, remarkable. Although his hemispheric abilities are more balanced now, external and internal dialogue still have a major effect on our son.

Eli's classmates appreciate his humor, encouraging spirit, and compassion, three distinguishing qualities of interpersonal intelligence, which is the ability to connect with others. Effective coaches, teachers, CEOs, and U.S. presidents, many of whom are temporal lobers, often have a natural gift for establishing rapport and motivating people. Our son is self-motivated, largely because of his inner dialogue and intrapersonal intelligence. (In poverty, self-talk was my second most valuable intangible asset. As a child, my mother wondered with whom I was having such intense conversations. Today, my wife laughs at me because I still do this. When other people happen to hear my inner dialogue, they give me a few strange looks.)

WHAT'S YOUR MONEY LANGUAGE?

Our self-talk needs constant supervision. Temporal lobers can talk themselves out of financial success with repetitive, negative commentary on what might go wrong instead of what could go right. According to their faulty emotional controls, their efforts probably won't pay off. Mission aborted. Financial freedom denied.

Your money language is the conversation you have with yourself about finances. It can dominate your monetary thought life and the economic horizon you envision. It's primarily shaped by your past experiences and present reality, but it's also guided by the world you anticipate (future possibility).

Our money language reflects the financial destinies we imagine for ourselves: economic distress, income stability, or positional affluence. It can trap us in dependency, with our financial prospects under someone else's control, or serve as a launching pad to financial bliss, pushing us to earn enough to provide for ourselves and for those under our care. Good or bad, we spend, save, invest, protect, and donate financial resources in accordance with our money language. We even gravitate to people who share our financial compass; we think alike and often arrive at the same economic destination, though perhaps by different paths. Our money language reflects how money makes us feel, what role it plays in our lives, and why we are attached to or detached from it.

Christopher H. Fairrow, my wife's father, was an assembly line worker at a major company for 31 years. As the stock market began its frantic decline before its Black Monday crash on October 19, 1987, Chris heard a company engineer complain about the thousands of dollars his investment account had lost. Chris panicked; he immediately sold all of his company's stock.

In a declining market, single-stock investors typically lose more than do those with well-diversified investment portfolios. Chris's entire investment was in his company's stock, which dropped substantially in value. The market eventually recovered, and so did his company's stock, but Chris was scarred for many decades. (The Dow Jones Industrial Average, a composite of 30 large and well-known U.S.-based companies, lost nearly 23 percent of its value on Black Monday.)

It took Chris nearly 30 years to invest in the stock market again. He prioritizes safety and security over appreciation, putting most of his savings in money market accounts and a few dividend-paying stocks. He says, "I panicked. I didn't understand the stock market. Had I understood the process of investing better, like I do today, things would have been different. Then again, I'd rather be safe than sorry."

The experience was deeply painful, and it will always be a core memory for Chris. Unfortunately, it affected his ability to build retirement wealth, which he could be using today. "I may not have retired as a millionaire, but had I invested more diligently in something other than a money market account, who knows, perhaps I would have had $500,000 to $700,000 right now to use in retirement," Chris says. "Had I taken education more seriously, things would have been different for me, too."

Unlike the poor, middle-class people have resources to invest, even if these are limited. Their money language, however, can prevent them from taking the risks necessary to really grow their money. Middle-class investors fear losing principal, and this fear—the amygdala in motion—can paralyze their ability to take calculated investment risks, even when they can improve the odds of success with the right professional guidance, due diligence, and emotional profile.

Interestingly enough, a friend of Chris's who was also an assembly line worker retired a millionaire. He earned slightly more per hour than Chris, but the catalyst of his retirement nest egg's real secret was the law of compound interest.

The Internet is full of compound interest calculators, but you can get a good approximation by using the Rule of 72. This rule-of-thumb tool tells investors the time it will take to double their money. Just divide 72 by the interest rate. For example, a $10,000 investment earning 10 percent annually will double every 7.2 years. Chris's millionaire colleague also understood the stock market's volatile nature and didn't panic when it dropped precipitously. Compound interest favors the time-compliant and emotionally stable investor, but it can still provide incremental benefits to those who arrive late to the money-making party.

ARE YOU THE SENSITIVE TYPE?

Temporal lobers often remember obscure facts and details that don't get more than a cursory glance from most people. They appreciate people who speak their language. If they're comfortable, they enjoy talking. They also like reading, writing, journaling, and recalling pleasant memories and experiences.

Language arts and history tend to be their favorite subjects in school. They often find math and science uneventfully boring.

They can be hypersensitive to words, sounds, smells, and injustices. An argument that a child hears between parents, an innocent correction from a teacher in front of peers, a foul odor from spoiled food, or an unkind action toward a minority group can trigger an immediate emotive and physiological response, leading to a host of feelings and autonomic reactions: anger, apathy, indifference, fear, isolation, agitation, hopelessness, depression, or ambivalence to new information.

Like parietal lobers, people with dominant temporal lobes can be empathetic when pleas of support are directed their way. Their compassionate hearts let them act as intervention specialists. Unfortunately, they can fret incessantly about things beyond their control. Worry can be a debilitating condition for them.

They can be emotional wrecking balls or ticking time bombs when discomfort sets in. Emotional wrecking balls always show their frustration, agitation, or annoyance with something said, heard, remembered, or experienced, particularly if their educational, personal, or financial well-being is (or will be) threatened. They might interpret laughter as a put down. My wife, son, and father-in-law are temporal lobers. They may interpret prolonged laughter as a slight. They don't take jokes very well. My daughter, a parietal lober, often points this out. I have seen this reaction in many other internalizers as well.

Temporal lobers like the status quo, and abrupt change can be very unnerving for them. Our sense of equilibrium is in our ears. The threat of a job loss or other upsetting economic news can make it harder to achieve a positive financial goal. Cortisol, a hormone released in response to stress, can wreak havoc on the body and balance sheet during prolonged periods of uneasiness.

Two distinct social class subsets, the generationally poor (GEDAs) and traditional middle class (GISAs), find safety and security in group identity. Temporal lobers living close to one another have a shared mindset, value system, and economic orientation. Poor, inner-city, and Appalachian communities contain like-minded people with similar survival strategies. These groups rarely trust outsiders and keep them at bay. Insiders must follow strict, self-imposed codes of conduct, and violators can be punished on hearsay alone. Residents consume an abundance of comfort foods with negligible nutritional benefits, as well as sugary beverages.

For the traditional middle class, group preservation is about economic stability, a foundation built on three financial pillars: a reliable job with good benefits, homeownership in a comfortable neighborhood, and secure retirement benefits. Shake these pillars and you create incredible angst in the minds and lives of generational income-stability Americans (or GISAs).

SOCIOPSYCHONOMIC FILTER
You can free an ex-convict from prison, but his mind can still be imprisoned as he integrates back in to mainstream society.

Some of the most talented temporal lobers I've known were people who lived alongside me in poverty: urban blacks and Appalachian whites. They were funny, artistic, smart, athletic, and creative. Unfortunately, most of them lacked the internal and external support systems required to improve their economic lives in adulthood. In 2008 I visited the London Correctional Institute, a medium-security prison, with Lonnie Jones, a former high school teammate who was an inmate there himself for nearly a decade. Inmates, some of whom we knew personally and the vast majority from impoverished backgrounds, showed us their artwork. We were amazed. They were geniuses, trapped behind bars.

Ironically, many working poor, temporal lobers choose jobs in food services, custodial care, nursing assistance, and sanitation. They often gravitate to work environments that amplify or desensitize their sense of olfaction. Menial labor as cooks, cleaners, trash collectors, or caregivers is financially debilitating, mentally draining, personally frustrating, physically demanding, and emotionally exhausting. It's also smelly.

For GISAs, job and career paths cover the gamut, from social services to education, law enforcement to nursing to sales to manufacturing. One thing is certain: Most GISAs are content and comfortable as employees, rather than as employers. I've been on both sides. It's more stressful when you are directly responsible for generating profits and paychecks.

People with dominant temporal lobes have predictable strengths and weaknesses:

Strengths

- They are not afraid of or disgusted by menial work.
- They understand what true contentment means.
- Empathy and compassion are among their defining attributes.
- They are aware of their own limitations, which can lead to authentic humility.
- They are personally and financially resilient and battle-tested.

Deficits

- They can become their own worst enemies when their internal dialogue turns negative.
- They prefer to bypass personal growth when it's uncomfortable. They sometimes see change as a setback rather than as an opportunity to break free from complacency or mediocrity.
- Emotional meltdowns can and often do prevent them from taking calculated risks.
- Their fear of losing guaranteed income (or government benefits) is greater than the joy of potentially earning more money while taking on more risk.

As I've said, the poor and traditional middle class have the largest concentrations of temporal lobers. Financial planners who want to work with either or both groups must speak directly to the fears of middle-market Americans. Economically distressed Americans benefit from basic money-management principles, with scaffolding programs to follow that reach higher-level, wealth-building concepts. A steep discount for the working poor is one way for financial planners to help this population. In theory, pro bono offerings sound good, but the poor rarely respect free services outside food, clothing, income assistance, or entertainment.

In closing, I must reiterate a few important points about many temporal lobers. They prefer paycheck security over income variability. They believe that a steady drip of money is better than an unforeseen downpour. GISAs are risk averse, or indifferent to risk when they are the working poor. They see wealth attainment as a fantasy only available to those with a well-connected network, a group they assume doesn't include them. They are content with their circumstances because they believe that something better is not an option. It's hard to convince them otherwise, but this is why I wrote *Sociopsychonomics*.

The Occipital Lobe

Code Name: Visual Processing Center

The occipital lobe, located in the posterior or back of the cerebral cortex, regulates sight, depth perception, color variation of real and imagined objects, visual topography, and to a certain extent, visuospatial intelligence. This region of the cerebral cortex helps us imagine, gain clarity, avoid road hazards, and see the obvious and not so obvious detours we need to take to accomplish our goals. The occipital lobe can be a unifying or destructive force in our lives; it all depends on our vantage point for a given situation.

THE HUE OF YOUR GOAL COLOR PALATE

Visual topography, the ability to navigate a mental landscape through illustrations and pictoral representations, is the most important skill people in either poverty or the middle class can cultivate economically. By and large, both groups give very little thought to their financial futures.

Vision is the ability to plan a future goal without an external model. It requires vivid imagery (How bright is your color palate?), spatial sensitivity (How deep is your imagination, and how hard are you willing to work to reach a goal?), and unfettered creativity (How will you stay motivated when your circumstances turn negative?).

Vivid imagery puts the clothes on your goals, giving them meaning and context. Imagery lets you create a masterful financial portrait where each hue adds a unique dimension of artistic brilliance. Red, yellow, and orange create energy, action, and excitement. Dull goals have bland colors. Blue stands for the depths of unlimited economic possibilities, as the clouds in the sky can attest. Only vibrant goals are welcome here.

Purple, historically a color for royalty, communicates a legacy of transgenerational values. Pink soothes an anxious, financially stressed spirit. Add pink to goals that require a great deal of patience and tenacity. Gold shines brightest when stability and accountability are key pillars of a well-crafted, goal-driven plan.

Of course, green represents money, or the ability to create multiple income streams. Be aware, though, that wealth-accumulation goals can create envy. Share your goals selectively. Not everyone will be a fan; critics come disguised as wise counselors and exuberant cheerleaders.

CAN YOU SEE THE FINISH LINE?

You can picture your goal. You understand the requirements for reaching it. What's next? You'll need a creative, enduring spirit to inspire you, encourage you, and help you reach your goals. Your creativity might help you do something as simple as learning to laugh at missteps. This book documents several of mine. Take your goals seriously, but not yourself. Lighten up, because you're going to need a dose of humor along the way!

> **SOCIOPSYCHONOMIC FILTER**
> When your vision for the future doesn't extend beyond tomorrow, you will live an unfulfilled and status quo existence today.

Setbacks are inevitable, but they need not be fatal. Over the years, I've visualized and planned many goals that first appeared relatively straightforward. But I made miscalculations along the way. The remedy? Time for a gut-check moment. That image of who you are (or want to be) will be instrumental in motivating you to keep going. Mentors or accountability partners can also provide creative solutions to help us reach our goals. Many have helped me stay focused on my goals, getting me back on track personally, professionally, and spiritually. Their insights and wisdom have been priceless.

Spatial sensitivity is a heightened awareness of what's required to reach a goal. This speaks to internal resources, the stamina to remain steadfast when we're most tempted to quit.

Worthwhile financial goals stretch us beyond our comfort zone, and many people are quick to return to what they know: the land of familiarity, comfort, and convenience. Even a dismal situation can seem secure, while the cost of achieving a life-changing goal can seem insurmountably high. They've got insufficient funds in their internal bank accounts to pay the price and forge ahead. Comfort and convenience are more important than economic freedom. They enter the race, but they're not committed to finishing it.

CAR TROUBLE

Reliable transportation is key for college students who live off campus. During my first year back in Columbus as a non-athletic scholarship student at Ohio State, I drove a hooptie: an older car with high mileage and likely maintenance problems. In-conference transfer rules stipulated that I could not receive an athletic scholarship at Ohio State. Like most of my peers, I had to take out loans, find grants, and secure academic scholarships to pay for college.

To save money that first year, I lived with my former Little League basketball coach and surrogate father figure, Nate Mitchell. I worked in the summer at a pharmacy owned by Larry Kaufman, whom I highlighted earlier in the book. I finally had enough money to buy a car. It was a 1987 Honda Accord with relatively low mileage, and was both reasonably priced and reliable. There was just one major problem. It had a manual transmission, which I didn't know how to drive.

Before I bought the Honda, Larry's son, Mike, spent two hours teaching me to drive a stick shift. I struggled mightily, although he was generous with his compliments. "You're doing very good," he said, as the engine crunched its disapproval. We primarily drove around his Upper Arlington neighborhood, rarely shifting out of second gear. (The speed limit was 25 miles per hour.) Mike assured me that I would be fine. I was so excited that I forgot everything he had told (and showed) me.

I barely slept the night before I picked up the car. I signed the paperwork and handed over a small down payment, and the sales associate gave me the keys. It was rush hour on a Friday. I visualized timing all the lights, slowing down when the light was red and speeding up when it was green. My plan was to avoid the freeway, though I lived on the other side of town, a 30-minute drive from the dealership. Didn't matter. I had to stay in my comfort zone.

I shook the sales associate's hand and thanked him for his efforts. Then I put the key in the ignition. First gear is the hardest part of driving a stick shift. "What did Mike tell me again?" I thought to myself. The car screeched as I drove away.

My plan worked for roughly five miles. When my first red light turned to green, the car wouldn't move. Frustrated drivers blew their horns at me. I was visibly distraught. An African-American gentleman got out of his car and approached my stalled vehicle. Our conversation went like this:

Good Samaritan: Aren't you Lawrence Funderburke?

Me: (embarrassed) I am.

Good Samaritan: (laughing) Are you having car trouble?

Me: Yes. I just bought this vehicle and I don't really know how to drive a stick shift.

Good Samaritan: Okay, what gear is it in?

Me: Dunno.

Good Samaritan: (He takes the wheel.) It wasn't moving because you're in third gear. Where do you want to go?

Me: Let's go to the parking lot of St. John Arena. It's about two miles down on the same street.

Good Samaritan: (arriving at our destination) Okay, we're here.

Me: My brother, thanks so much.

Good Samaritan: No problem—glad to help. Look forward to watching you in a Buckeye uniform next season.

For the next three hours, I practiced driving in the parking lot. Finally, I felt comfortable enough to drive the car on the freeway. The moral of the story: Be sure to visualize how you'll handle both the triumphs and setbacks of a far-reaching goal, because you're likely to deal with them both. Of course, difficult moments show up at the most inopportune times, regardless of your plan. Fine-tune your visual acuity to overcome them.

THE ROAD LESS TRAVELED

I was looking for an escape route and the opportunity, unbeknownst to me at the time, presented itself before my 19th birthday. Coach Bobby Knight kicked me out of practice for lackluster play as an Indiana freshman, just five days after I scored 26 points in a game against Long Beach State—my career high at the time. He told me to go home, that he wanted to enjoy the rest of practice without me "messing" it up. (Actually, Coach Knight used a different word than "messing." You can probably figure it out.) Joby Wright, an assistant coach, met me at my apartment as I was packing up to go home. I took The General's command literally, although that's not what he intended. Coach Knight sent Joby to massage my bruised ego and fragile emotions. It didn't work.

I left Bloomington and traveled south through the backwoods of Kentucky to Madisonville, where I stayed for one week with Travis Ford and his family, whom I'd visited 18 months earlier. Travis was an all-state guard and good friend (and now the current head basketball coach at St. Louis University). He was in college at the University of Missouri when I knocked on his parents' front door. Shocked to see me, his mother asked, "Lawrence, what are you doing here at this time of the night?" I don't know how I remembered the way to Madisonville. An angel must have been with me. I never stopped once even to ask for directions.

Next I traveled east to Lexington, Kentucky, to stay with Dwane Casey for several days. He was a former assistant coach at the University of Kentucky and is now the NBA head coach of the Toronto Raptors. He recruited me in high school for two years.

I finally made my way back home to Columbus, Ohio. When I walked through my mother's front door, she gave me an earful. She said, "Son, what are you trying to do, throw away your basketball career before it starts? Reporters have called here throughout the day and evening hours looking for you. I told them that I didn't know where you were, which was true. Lawrence Damon, you have to stop running from life's challenges. It's time to step up: Be a man, not a mouse."

The image of me, standing 6'9", contrasted with that of a mouse, barely a few inches in height. It forced me to take a close look at how my future would unfold. What I saw was dark, dreary, and debilitating. A mouse scatters when trouble comes, but a real man stands tall in the face of adversity. My mother's observation was exactly the visual stimulation that I needed. Hearing it was the first step in repairing a personal brand that I had spent years crafting to fit my narrative of ghetto triumph. To prove my critics wrong, I just needed to get out of my own way. Course corrected.

ARE YOU A SENSORY VISUALIZER?

Occipital lobers (*sensory visualizers*) have personalities that shine brightest when others are present. They are not afraid of the spotlight. They are imaginative, optimistic, passionate, colorful, loud, charismatic, exciting, memorable, charitable, friendly, opportunistic, adaptive, entertaining, fearless, driven, and unintentionally rebellious.

Leadership is an inborn trait, though sensory visualizers welcome opportunities to refine it. They are not afraid to lead others (or themselves) through difficult moments. They don't fear failure, because occipital lobers believe every problem has at least one solution. They often visualize a successful outcome before they even have a plan to accomplish it, assembling resources and a team to carry out the mission.

Sensory visualizers specialize in practical intelligence; they are masterful at getting people to see things their way. They use visual topography—a representative map or blueprint—to go through, around, or past a challenging situation. They inspire colleagues and subordinates with their call to action.

Occipital lobers tend to move fast when others move slowly. They are not afraid to communicate their points of view, even in a room full of conflicting opinions. How so? They rehearse. Rehearsal is a mental exercise routine that preps them to deal with difficult personalities, stay calm under pressure, and focus on the task at hand.

They are never boring; they're always remembered. They always make a statement with their presence. They command attention when they enter a room, regardless of their height or physical stature.

Visionaries reinvent themselves when a setback rocks their professional or financial world. Instead of feeling sorry for themselves and wallowing in self-pity, they realize it's time to change, even asking accountability mentors to do forensic audits on their shortcomings.

Envisioned goals become completed goals, where their words and actions produce imaginative landscapes of boundless possibilities and friendly terrains. They walk toward their ambitious goals instead of running from them. To visionaries the glass of opportunity is always half-full. You don't have to tell them when to drink; they've already taken the first sip.

Occipital lobers can see gifts in other people, including gifts that friends, family members, and colleagues haven't noticed in themselves. They push people toward personal and professional growth, sometimes wanting it more than the intended recipients do themselves. They do not like complacency, which can clash with temporal lobers' internalized sensitivity. As big-picture visionaries, people with dominant occipital lobes can feel pushback (and rightly so in some cases) from frontal lobers, who process information sequentially, analytically, and microscopically.

The symbiotic relationship between sensory visualizers and their biggest ally, sensory seekers (parietal lobers), is a fascinating one. Sensory seekers crave movement, which conveys intent, destination, and sometimes impulsivity. Even if they haven't created action plans, occipital lobers are still moving toward their goals. Parietal lobers move with their heart, while occipital lobers move through imagination. It's easy to confuse the two.

Career paths for occipital lobers include CEO, manager, coach, professional development specialist, entrepreneur, financial planner, architect, pastor, administrator, graphic designer, and artist, among others. It takes vision, intestinal fortitude, charisma, charm, and tough love to be an occipital lobe leader. Effective visionaries inspire themselves and others. This involves change, a mandate to be better than you were in the past. It's not an easy task to pull off, by any means, but sensory visualizers are not afraid to try!

People with dominant occipital lobes have predictable strengths and weaknesses:

Strengths

- They are not afraid to dream big and challenge conventional wisdom.
- They don't fear failure, because it offers opportunities for growth.
- They have an innate ability to come up with innovative solutions and strategies to solve a problem.
- They see obstacles as work clothes in disguise.
- They embrace change if it looks right to them.
- They see the end goal before taking a single step to achieve it.

Deficits

- They can get caught in a fantasy of financial grandeur.
- Their visionary creativity can seem self-serving, opportunistic, or arrogant to others.
- They can become too narrow-minded when others don't see things their way.
- They may face stiff resistance from non-occipital lobers who aren't ready for change, especially frontal and temporal lobers.

- In their pursuit of an ambitious goal, they can lose sight of current matters that deserve their immediate attention.

How Each Dominant Lobe Responds to Change
Frontal Lobers: respond to change through logic or empirical evidence
Parietal Lobers: respond to change through gut instincts or feelings
Temporal Lobers: respond to change through emotions or words
Occipital Lobers: respond to change through imagination or mental pictures

Which social class subsets contain the biggest proportion of occipital lobers? The answer is somewhat complicated. Many GAPAs and SAPAs are sensory visualizers by nature, because the majority of them are in white-collar leadership roles. Also, with wealth accumulation and asset preservation, it takes vision to come up with creative strategies to handle and protect monetary blessings. Some SEDAs and SISAs, the two situational classes for poverty and the middle class, can be occipital lobers, though they may be waiting to climb up the wealth ladder. Functional subsets of each class have their fair share of occipital lobers, too. They identify with a representative class for affinity reasons, while their financial statements show a different picture.

Financial planners enjoy working with occipital lobers, because these clients see the big picture. Colorful illustrations of financial goals go over well with this group. Challenges come when they don't stick to the script, preferring improvisational strategies to conventional advice. The good news: They can be reined back in once their focus is reset.

GAME TIME

LIFE PLANNING

CHAPTER

5

MINDSET

*The thought process and information filter
used by social classes to shape their
beliefs, attitudes, and behaviors*

Scarcity

Poverty is often a state of perpetual scarcity. Scarce resources. Scarce opportunities. Scarce role models. Scarce hopes and dreams that tomorrow will be brighter than today. How do you cope when hope is missing? You cling to an oversupply of toxic emotions and unrelenting sensations to deal with the disappointments and criticisms.

The Good Book says, "Hope deferred makes the heart sick, but a longing fulfilled is a tree of life" (Proverbs 13:12, New International Version). When one rejection results in a chain reaction of predictable outcomes, consternation is the natural response the poor employ to cover up intense disappointment. They will gravitate toward food, beverages, entertainment, clothing, or relationships seeking a remedy. Whatever resources are at their disposal, they will need to deploy the time, energy, emotional capital, or money to feel better. The poor are conditioned and convinced into believing that a change in mindset will automatically follow a financial breakthrough or major change in circumstances. Not true. The mindset change must precede a change in circumstances. Patience and learning a different way of thinking are the keys.

Having a scarcity mindset leads to contradictory and questionable behaviors that may make no sense to those outside the walls of poverty. However, for those on the inside (or who once were), it makes perfect sense. The poor try not to make sense of the pain they feel in being treated as second-class citizens in a country that supposedly offers first-class options to every man, woman, or child. Life has dealt the poor a lousy hand, so GEDAs immediately seize the opportunity to satisfy a physical need while ignoring the urgent pleas to upgrade their mindset.

STILL ROOM FOR MORE

Tim and Mike were two teenage boys that I mentored many years ago who we invited to our home for a five-course meal prepared by one of our city's finest chefs, Jim Warner. My goal with this dinner was to get to know Tim and Mike better, expose them to a neighborhood of working professionals with intact families where both biological parents are present in the home, and to eat some deliciously healthy food.

On the car ride over from their housing project to our home, they expressed trepidation over what to expect. They were use to sit-down meals where everything was served at once, regardless of how much food was available. My coaching advice was short and light. I urged them to be themselves and pace their eating while also leaving room for dessert.

Walking into the house, their faces lit up as the aroma of well-seasoned food softened their fears. They couldn't wait to eat, although the first course wouldn't get served for another hour. We head to the kitchen and introductions to Chef Jim are made. Tim and Mike were cordial but understandably quiet as their eyes soaked up the experience of seeing a professional chef in action. We went downstairs to pass time until dinner was served.

Most observers wouldn't have noticed the hoarding behavior of the teenagers during that dinner, a habit I mirrored as a boy that is quite common in households of poverty. When the first course arrived, the boys each grabbed four pieces of bread within seconds after it was placed on the table. Now, these were far from being bite-sized servings, and one piece would have been sufficient for most adults. They forgot my advice to pace themselves as their eyes wanted more food than their stomachs could hold. With each course presented, Tim and Mike added more and more to their plates. Stuffed, they could barely walk to the car when it was time to go home. Surprisingly, they passed on the dessert. I did pace myself, which allowed me to eat their dessert as well as mine.

My wife never picked up on their hoarding behavior until I brought it to her attention. As we discussed it, we started recalling other times when we fed those from impoverished backgrounds and witnessed that same hoarding behavior from children and adults alike.

Hoarding is an instinctive reaction in an environment of scarcity. The volume to hoard remains at excruciating levels even when urges to satisfy a sensation dissipate. Grabbing what you can is an internal conversation repeated over and over in the temporal lobe of GEDAs, deflecting them away from more reasoned action.

Hoarding addresses scarcity in impoverished households, while protecting one's food from real or imagined predators is a defense mechanism that's hard to abandon. I still find myself doing it unintentionally to anyone within arm's length of my food. Table etiquette aside, forearms and elbows are placed around the food as shields, just in case someone tries to snatch something off the dinner plate. For GEDAs, an environment of perpetual lack drives behaviors to protect a cherished commodity, in this case food—by any means necessary, even if the food is bad for you.

EXTREME FRUGALITY NO MATTER HOW IT'S SLICED

Generational poverty leaves some obvious scars; not all of them are bad, but they do tell an interesting story. Behaviors that should have been buried in poverty often follow the social class transplant up the economic ladder. They are mostly harmless, but these actions can lead to some quizzical looks from the observant eye of another. You know better, but still find yourself slipping back into a scarcity mindset even when economic distress is nowhere in sight.

A popular saying in the 'hood is that you can take the brother out of the ghetto, but you can't take the ghetto out of the brother, which stands out as an embedded truth that says some habits are hard to break because we simply choose not to correct them. Behaviors that are normal in one environment may not fit in another environment.

Scarce availability of high-quality food in my childhood still influences me today. I never let a single tidbit go to waste. I'll nibble around apple and pear cores like a rabbit that has found hidden goodies buried in the snow, while food nearing its expiration date must be consumed immediately or frozen. Monya accepts my "po'etiquette," though she thinks my actions are extreme. My mother never allowed her kids to leave the kitchen table unless our plates were spotless, with nary a crumb remaining.

I still hear my mom's guilt-driven admonition for us to eat our food because less fortunate people in other countries would love having it. This plea always worked on me whether I was full or the food didn't taste good. Conversely, my three sisters hated oatmeal, and what they refused to eat would get scooped into my bowl or dumped behind the refrigerator. They'd threaten to beat me up if I told mom. Of course, I kept my mouth shut and ate the extra oatmeal. Even today, oatmeal is my favorite meal of choice. I'm sure Adele, Gina, and Tamara had something to do with this.

Nothing irks me more than to see people waste good food, especially children. I've admonished kids from affluent households in our summer camps after seeing them dump food on their plates into the trash can. Children living in affluent households are not forced to eat every item on the plate. Frugality is less of a concern than it was in our home.

I'm even frugal where my golf game is concerned.

My handicap is a generous 23, and I get invited to play in charity golf tournaments all the time. In a scramble format, two teams are often paired at one hole and require you to move pretty fast because there's an unspoken limit on how long the round should last. You don't want to hold up the next team. So bad shot, move on. Lost ball, keep it moving.

You don't want me as a team member because my frugality, groomed in the scarcity environment of my youth, dictates that I retrieve lost golf balls after hitting a bad shot—and those can add up. That's right, I search for every single lost golf ball, which I warn my teammates about before we tee off. My athletic skills are such

> Scarcity-laden behaviors are hard to contain, even when you are years or decades removed from abject poverty.

that I'll hit my fair share of Tiger Woods shots. But as a golf hack, my Tiger Whoa Whoa shots keep me humble when they venture off the fairway, deep into the woods. Although my teammates might joke about the warning, my actions make perfect sense to me. Anyways, a round of golf provides ample time to share with those who may have a cursory understanding of generational poverty what that hellish experience was like.

"YOU GOT ME, RIGHT?"

Ghetto poverty is something that's hard to shake. You revert back to behaviors that cast a spotlight on obvious social faux pas. You should be embarrassed, but you're not. You respond at times to still being all the way in even when you're clearly on the way out.

I never felt ashamed to pull out my you-got-me-right? card when hanging out with two friends back in college. During those days, I'd intentionally forget—not plan on—to toss a few dollars into my pocket before we headed out for a night on the town. I even felt justified in my actions at the time, knowing their situation was better than mine and taking advantage of it. They were from the suburbs and I grew up in the projects.

There is an expectation or anticipation among the poor that exists, mostly on a subliminal level, where subtle hints match sympathy-driven facial expressions they infer to mean someone else is going to look out for them. As a matter of fact, you're sure of help being extended when in the presence of someone who can provide it. A sheepish gaze downward can generate legitimate or contrived sensitivity from others when financial support is most needed. A head tilt exposing the neck can elicit compassion, an act of vulnerability to move a person to intervene on your behalf. Government safety nets and charitable organizations are ready to help, but is that always wise? Robert Lupton points out in his controversial book, *Toxic Charities*, that sometimes charity does more harm than good when we do for others what they are perfectly capable of doing for themselves. I agree.

One-way generosity can lead to disempowerment if beneficiaries aren't given the skills and tools to provide for themselves. In other words, the help should have an expiration date to wean the poor off the mindset of perpetual dependency, educationally or financially. This may very well be the most difficult task to accomplish in bridging the academic and economic gaps in our country.

Good friends Danny Levitt and David Harris got a good taste of my you-got-me-right? strategy at Ohio State and even called me out after about the sixth or seventh time. My usual reply was, "My bad—I forgot."

Not only did they supply the ride, they always kept some extra cash on hand for me, their celebrity friend from the projects. Living in a scarcity environment can lead to a sense of entitlement and make it easy for a person to rationalize that others should help because their situations are so much better.

I embraced two-way giving more than two decades ago and have never looked back. However, it remains a battle with some close friends who embody authentic generosity, the kind without reciprocity strings attached. They won't let me pay for meals even though I now have the cash to do so.

APPALACHIAN POVERTY IS A MIRROR IMAGE OF INNER-CITY POVERTY

Famous Americans from Appalachian Ohio include Ulysses S. Grant, Clark Gable, Dean Martin, John Glenn, and Sarah Jessica Parker, to name a few. Located in the southeast quadrant of the state, the region has been rapidly deteriorating over the last two decades as drugs and hopelessness have engulfed this once thriving, blue-collar community fed by plentiful factory jobs.

Most Southern Ohio residents failed to change with the times as the economy shifted gears from manufacturing to service in the late 1980s, and to technology post-2000. Hours got cut and more people received pink slips. The writing on the wall was faint, but noticeably legible. What people could not have anticipated was the frustration and despair their offspring would embrace as coping mechanisms to fill a widening void of shrinking opportunities.

I'll always have a special place in my heart for Appalachian Ohio, a connection made the day I married my wife, a native of Chillicothe, which is an hour's drive south of Columbus. She attended school with and befriended many Appalachian children from poverty. This small town has undergone big changes as economic distress has grown. A keen observer and stakeholder in the nonprofit arena described the landscape "as a cultural depression of diminished expectations, individually and collectively." So true.

Immediacy of needs is often what drives actions and reactions in poverty, and it matters not whether it's rural, urban, or generational poverty. Once filled, that temporary moment of satisfaction is what preoccupies them until the sensation dies down. Feelings match their level of contentment or obvious disinterest.

Fred Fairrow is Monya's first cousin and a Chillicothe native. He, too, was reared in a middle-class household. He has a rugged work ethic, and is a pastor to boot. His generosity to help those less fortunate is commendable, but Fred looks around his city with guarded optimism. He wants the best for others, but accepts the fact that many impoverished residents may not want what's best for themselves. The poverty mindset that has taken hold of this small town is a quagmire.

"Children inherit this mindset from their parents and grandparents. Getting by is a day-to-day adventure," he says. "As long as they have a $100 in their pocket on a Friday night, they're good. If they can sit on their front porch and talk with friends or play video games throughout the day, life is swell. They have no desire for anything else beyond this level of contentment; at least, this is how it appears on the surface."

To illustrate his thought, Fred tells the story of two men from Appalachian poverty that worked odd jobs for him. They fixed various items around the rental properties Fred owned, but eventually the pair began stealing from him. His grace is extensive, but it does have limits, although Fred never saw the worth in pressing legal charges against the men. It was an easy decision to make.

"For what?" he asks rhetorically. "What really breaks my heart more than anything, not as a pastor but as a human being, is that they were interested only in earning enough money to spend on an immediate fix. When the high is over, what's next?"

Fred is not a fire and brimstone kind of guy. He loves people and is quick to overlook a transgression. However, the experience did leave a bad taste in his mouth. He says, "It was baffling because they couldn't see beyond the moment. I've tried to understand their way of thinking, but I couldn't."

If you like the direction your life is going, you're never going to want something different or know how to change course to get it. Sometimes, deep introspection can be the catalyst to compel (and hopefully propel) GEDAs toward that different course. How do we encourage them? By speaking their language of emotion, but forcing them to deal with logic. Consequences with severe repercussions can move their behavior needle. It shouldn't come down to this, but fear of loss creates enormous pressure, a form of internal pain that they desperately try to avoid.

Security

A comfortable and convenient life free of constant change fits neatly into the middle class's narrative of safety, security, and stability. They want to feel safe in their country, community, cash flow, and careers. They prefer a safe job with benefits, rather than business ownership with inconsistent profits.

Generational income-stability Americans, or GISAs, want to go to bed at night knowing that their job will be there the next day, an uninterrupted work routine that is entirely predictable. They also want to feel protected from hostile foreign or domestic enemies hell-bent on destroying our commitment to life, liberty, and the pursuit of happiness. Our armed services have a significantly higher concentration of troops who hail from middle-class households than do either the poor or wealthy.

GISAs bleed red, white, and blue. They proudly display the American flag on their vehicles, around their yards and homes, and in their work cubicles. They gravitate toward safe communities and neighborhoods with good schools so their children can experience living in an environment that respects the rights of others and values education.

Financial stability is an economic tenet of the middle class. Disruptions in their cash flow or monthly budget can be unnerving. They may not admit this, but GISAs revere banks and credit unions perhaps second only to a church or house of worship. Though most of their accounts fall well below the FDIC guarantee-protection thresholds, $250,000 per individual account and $500,000 for joint accounts, this doesn't stop them from fretting about money. Forget about identity theft, problems accessing an account online, or low interest rates. That stuff is important, but may not be at the top of their financial comfort wish list. GISAs just need to know that their money is safe and the institution holding their cash has adequate reserves to cover withdrawals.

The underlying theme of safety, security, and stability is peace of mind. Wealth-building responsibilities may be more hassle than benefit to them, but it's the one logical choice to take for GISAs to avert dire financial outcomes. The reality is that most Americans are woefully unprepared for retirement, so they must implement a life and financial planning playbook now to avoid being pushed down to the social class below them.

A CHANGING LANDSCAPE OF MIDDLE-CLASS COMFORTS

In decades gone by, the middle class was clearly in the middle. Not today. The lines between the poor and traditional middle class are blurring. GISAs see economic calamity in the rearview mirror, with blue-collar wages stagnant, healthcare costs rising, and college costs unaffordable for most middle-income households. More frightening is change the middle class doesn't acknowledge in a timely manner. They might get a whiff that change is coming but refuse to navigate around it. GISAs also tend to have more difficulty with change compared to the other classes. The generationally poor may remain economically distressed, for instance, but they deal with change on a regular basis.

Poverty is a breeding ground for certain forms of transiency. Relationships are short-term while commitments are sensory driven and change with the individual's feelings. Low-paying jobs come and go on a carousel of fleeting employment opportunities. Housing accommodations are temporary. Many impoverished children are forced to enroll in up to three different schools in a calendar year as their families move from one apartment to the next.

The informed wealthy welcome change since it is often accompanied by growth. Setbacks, professional or financial, are empowering. Lessons are learned and lost opportunities quickly forgotten. Also, SAPAs and GAPAs can beckon legions of professionals to help them when change is difficult.

Not so much for the middle class. They are racked with fear of the unknown that distresses and immobilizes them. Negative outcomes are pondered, which creates even more discomfort. Change is a disruptive force to GISAs' sense of financial or personal equilibrium. They don't like it unless the outcomes are positive. (I cover the phenomenon of financial disequilibrium in the next chapter, "Time.")

The big change for GISAs during the last two decades is that they have adopted part of the GEDA playbook and are pessimistic about their economic prospects; the odds of financial survival are stacked against them. This creates a snowball effect where they worry more about what they can control: their kids' education, their job, and economizing at home.

Jobs outsourced overseas disproportionately affect the middle class more than the poor and wealthy. The poor have social safety nets to rely on, while the wealthy have impressive balance sheets to protect them during economic storms. President Trump promises a renaissance of manufacturing jobs to squelch palpable fears. We'll see, but I am inclined to give him the benefit of the doubt about helping the struggling middle class (and working poor), as I did with President Obama.

GUARDIANS OF THE PERSONAL AND EDUCATIONAL DEVELOPMENT COMPASS

Sports can teach us a great deal about life. From inspirational coaches and trainers, players learn discipline, teamwork, and how to persevere under competitive pressure. But they also reveal the role parents play in a child's cognitive development and decision-making ability.

Tennis prodigies Jennifer Capriati, Venus and Serena Williams, and golf's Tiger Woods offer examples of parents who helped or hurt their child's personal, professional, moral, and financial compass along the way. The GPS coordinates our children plug in will likely be mirror images of those used by the adults in their lives.

Far too many lower- or middle-class parents make a huge mistake when they invest in a child's academic or athletic development: They only coach or convince a child to arrive at a pre-selected destination or resting place, but not to pursue a lifelong journey that ends when death begins. To attain a college degree or sports fame offers temporary security, while learning financial life skills will help children fulfill their long-term purpose. None of these outcomes, though, happens by chance.

Attorney Eric Seabrook, who is also a life coach to several professional athletes and personal mentor of mine, offers a revealing look into how Richard Williams, father of Serena and Venus, helped mold their holistic perspective of the world and themselves beyond the tennis court.

"Some people's transition is reflected by their kid. In reshaping his children's frame of reference, Richard's was transformed, too. His out-of-the-box playbook to produce two amazing tennis stars in Venus and Serena Williams was seen as extreme at the time," Seabrook says. "Richard did manically train his kids to be tennis champions, but more importantly, he also challenged them to be well-rounded women. He prevented them from going pro early even though the family needed the money. His shortcomings aside, Richard made sure Venus and Serena developed other interests outside of sports. In essence, he enlarged their vantage point by exposing them to the characteristics of affluence, all while growing up in a lower-income environment. When Serena won the French Open, she gave her acceptance speech in French. Now, meditate on how powerful this is in the context of her upbringing. It's not a coincidence that their success has been so amazing."

> "Some parents know too much for their kids to know so little about life."
>
> **–Eric Seabrook**
> Life Coach and Attorney

Middle class decision-makers have the arduous task of providing programming to help their constituencies develop necessary educational, personal, and professional skills. Unfortunately, they often minimize or skip over financial wellness offerings that encompass potentially life- and legacy-changing benefits.

GISA administrators at all levels entertain the idea of financial freedom but rarely pursue it for themselves or those under their care. Analysis paralysis is largely to blame and will stifle the merits of a given offering by not pairing it with action. They simply don't believe a first-class experience is worth the investment.

The administrators weigh the risks against the return on investment based on their current frame of reference, which is likely to be different than the service provider's. More meetings are scheduled, inaction morphs into stagnation, and soon optimism is hobbled, souring the administrators' doubts about an empowerment opportunity for staff members and other key stakeholders.

They assume the costs to reach further are prohibitively more expensive than they're willing to pay. The status quo—contemplation overload—grounds them to a screeching halt.

This cursory explanation is offered to the service provider: "The timing for us just doesn't work right now. Perhaps we can explore a partnership of some kind in the future. Thank you for your time." The empowerment crusader is never contacted again. The rejection hurts, but he'll keep fighting to free the middle class from financial bondage they refuse to acknowledge. Their focus is on the next step in front of them. The future is not on their radar screen at the present moment. It's too far away.

Seniority

A seniority mindset is the foundation and framework used by the generationally and situationally wealthy, a multifaceted approach that runs their lives and guides offspring through the methods of legacy continuity. This modus operandi drives GAPAs' and SAPAs' schedule and time compression obsession. It compels them to keep steady watch on their personal and professional and social networks. It emboldens children and grandchildren to emulate key behavior patterns central to family traditions and established norms. It's a mindset about self-control over their emotions, attitudes, and economic destinies.

GAPAs meet periodically to discuss each family member's responsibilities as well as monitor the progress of stated goals and objectives. Like their strategy sessions, their Rolodexes are orderly and strategically labeled by context: family, personal, social, business, philanthropy, travel, entertainment, and leisure. If they recognize your number when you call, that mere fact speaks volumes about what they think of you.

CONDITIONED FOR THE EDUCATIONAL AND PROFESSIONAL JOURNEY

Educational conditioning is a hallmark of affluence. Children of affluent families know academic enrichment is a lifelong endeavor, a marathon they're conditioned to start running at an early age. GAPA and SAPA kids aren't academic sprinters but long-distance runners. Along the way, they grab each educational baton at measured paces from elementary school through college, while also keeping their eyes glued to the expected legacy set before them. It's always within their reach. Now, let's contrast this with how most poor children view their educational mindset.

In generational poverty, education is a 100-yard sprint. Kids stay engaged and are eager to learn from kindergarten to fourth or fifth grade as they build their intellectual stimulation and self-motivational skills. Out of nowhere, a drop in academic performance occurs for many between 10 and 13 years of age; they become disinterested and bored with school. They are at a crossroads and must decide to buckle down with academics or veer off course doing their own 'thang. The path of least resistance is often taken.

Many pre-teen and teenage girls seek attention from boys as a way to validate their self-worth. Feeling warm and accepted just so happens to be largely controlled by the parietal lobe. Several factors drive the reason why so many young girls in poverty feel they need affirmation from young boys ready to manipulate their emotions for personal gain and *faux orientation*, which I will cover later in the book. The breakdown of the nuclear family, or more specifically, the lack of involved fathers, is a primary cause.

Our nation's inner-city pre-teen and teenage males also lack positive role models. So instead, they are lured into the streets with promises of making easy money. Spending another seven or eight years in school before the first diploma is granted just doesn't feel right. Unfortunately, these academic casualties fall by the wayside, too exhausted to finish their educational race. They simply weren't conditioned, mentally and emotionally speaking, for the journey. Educational conditioning comes naturally to children living in affluent, privileged communities.

As Danny Levitt, a close friend and financial advisor, notes, "Wealthy children ask each other, 'Do you want to be a doctor, lawyer, executive at a large company, or entrepreneur?' This includes the world of finance, private equity, and hedge funds, places where their parents work or career paths of interest. By osmosis, affluent children gravitate to senior-level professions with super-high incomes that make it easier to build wealth-generating assets," he says. "These kids never talk about working at a grocery store or being a bank teller when they reach adulthood. These jobs aren't beneath them; they simply aren't on the career radar screen of the typical wealthy kid. Why would they be?"

GAPAs' and SAPAs' professional network fuels their children's career ambitions, along with high expectations that precede a successful outcome.

Mom's and dad's expansive networks push their children to the front of the line to attend prestigious East Coast universities. Those same networks help the kids secure internship opportunities in college that may lead to lucrative employment upon graduation. Extensive connections can even assist children who find themselves in a legal bind. It's not who you know, but who knows you.

Take a quick look around a courtroom the next time you're contesting a speeding ticket. What you will see is evidence of the glaring disparities among social classes. On one hand, the poor and lower middle classes attend in person because they can't afford to hire an attorney. They often lose out on pleading with the judge to reduce the fine or get the ticket expunged. On the other hand, the wealthy and well-connected won't be in attendance either, but their lawyers will.

AN EXCLUSIVE WORLD OF BUSINESS RELATIONSHIPS

Seniority is synonymous with exclusivity, particularly as it applies to the balance sheets of GAPAs and SAPAs. Their network is tightly regulated, and hasty decisions rarely happen when their reputation, resources, and respect are on the line. They know who to call for equity financing for investment opportunities. Money, expertise, and strategic networking alliances are three benefits that stakeholders will likely bring to a lucrative deal.

They also are incredibly patient, allowing potential partnerships to grow organically, but disdain getting pressured to make quick decisions about opportunities. They are methodical and deliberate.

Pushy tactics show desperation, and GAPAs will walk away from a deal without hesitation. Who in their right mind would want to invest millions of dollars under compulsion or duress? The generationally wealthy don't have to swing for the fences. They're content waiting for the perfect pitch to come over the plate.

Developing business relationships can take months or perhaps years to materialize. Due diligence is employed to evaluate a potential partner's character, credentials, and commitment level. Economic conditions are also weighed to determine how an investment opportunity will fit into a GAPA's overall wealth, asset allocation, and legacy game plan.

Speaking of legacy, business deals between super high net worth partners, as a byproduct, might even lead to introductions among their children. This is not coincidental. Part of the due diligence process includes learning about the offspring of a business partner. The rich get richer when GAPA children establish relationships with newfound peers, and in some cases, later get married. This is how their world mysteriously works, a self-perpetuating system of transgenerational connections.

A COMPLEX WEB OF GEOGRAPHICAL CONNECTIONS

You can tell a lot about a person's social class by asking two questions: Where has he visited? Does he have a passport?

The poor see the world through a compressed, local visual acuity lens. Life's options are limited, thus the prevalence of a myopic outlook. Desperation occurs when opportunities appear few and far between.

Many GEDAs don't go too far from where they live, and this predetermined sphere of travel limits their transportation options, where they shop, go to school, find entertainment, buy groceries, and so on.

This is why it's important to broaden the possibility filter of impoverished children, or what career and lifestyle options are achievable in the future based on their personal, educational, and financial development. Taking them beyond their travel orb, even if it's just on the other side of town to areas with thriving communities, diverse career paths, and safer neighborhoods, will go a long way in reshaping their economic frame of reference. It worked for me, thanks in large part to the hospitality of the Anthony family. I'm also incredibly grateful basketball gave me the opportunity to spend time overseas, a worldview far different than my GEDA upbringing.

Think of poverty as a bank, but one that doesn't hold any money. For those who live in poverty, the currencies exchanged are the relationships they have with peers, casual acquaintances, and sometimes, even total strangers. Credits and debits are traded and tabulated depending on who comes in or out of their lives, which often is a random occurrence. These are usually managed within the confines of the neighborhood.

Being in close quarters means others know a neighbor's personal and household business. Adjacent apartment walls are paper thin, letting you hear and smell what your neighbor is doing. Rumors spread quicker than wildfire among the poor, while perception and reality are not mutually exclusive terms; they're interpreted as interchangeable as circumstances and emotions dictate.

The middle class has a national or regional perspective of their personal and financial world. Their visual acuity lens is narrow, confined primarily to singularly focused tasks, work obligations, family, educational, social, and faith-based commitments. Most GISAs have traveled to multiple states to vacation, visit loved ones, meet for business, or to attend college.

SOCIOPSYCHONOMIC FILTER

Children born into generational wealth don't ask, "How do I get to middle management at a company?" They do ask this rhetorical question, "What's the path to senior management?"

Very few individuals or families I know from traditional, middle-class backgrounds, outside of military veterans, have ventured beyond the Atlantic or Pacific oceans. Outsourced jobs and stagnant wages have produced a heightened sense of nationalism among GISAs. Their America Dream is in big trouble. Seismic shifts are underway, but the middle class hasn't taken the time to combat them. One step they should take is upgrading their playbook to include some risk taking to build wealth beyond the traditional safety net: liquid assets, such as savings and checking accounts and certificates of deposit.

The visual acuity lens for GAPAs (and many SAPAs) is wide and encompasses travel to dozens of countries overseas. They do business internationally, invest globally, own multiple homes around the world, and have few restrictions on their travel sphere. Their orb is completely opposite of a GEDA's geographical framework and navigational proclivities.

WE'RE LOOKING FOR THE TURN

When it comes to educational and professional development, GAPAs and SAPAs congregate at some of the same venues, notably schooling for their children. In this setting, most of them don't have a problem with their children being around students who are new to the experience. However, inclusivity comes with one precondition: New students must eventually make "the turn," or conform to the school's ways and standards. It's an implicit agreement the super wealthy have with the highest-rated private schools, codified by their past donations and pledges of future gifts, a narrative never to be amended or altered by outside influences.

Entry barriers to elite-level private schools include tuition costs in the tens of thousands of dollars, limited openings, and academic rigor. These schools tend to be extremely liberal, cautiously generous (while awarding financial assistance on a case-by-case basis), and highly regimented. Students follow strict rules and codes of conduct.

Elite-level private schools place an emphasis on the turn for those kids, especially boys, entering this environment. It's about conformity and uniformity to how mega-wealthy children are groomed for higher-order, senior-level thinking in an educational settting with extensive networking and strategic ties. Welcome to the domain of the structured and sequential world of the frontal lobe, where planning, organizing, analyzing, weighing consequences, communicating, and regulating emotions takes center stage. Academic subjects, even art, are often taught from a linear and orderly perspective.

These frontal lobe characteristics play a large role in building and maintaining the seniority mindset. Students build upon previously held convictions that call for reason in a logical fashion with clearly defined outcomes and objectives. For this to happen, feelings are kept in check, corralling student demeanors into a stable where they typically share the common attribute of emotional regulation.

Let's consider the fictitious case of Shana, a single-parent mother who works as a grocery clerk trying to make ends meet. She and her son, Nicholas, live in the poorest part of their Midwest community. Nicholas is very smart and Shana wants something better for him. Based on an essay he wrote, Nicholas is awarded a needs-based scholarship to attend the elite-level private school on the other side of town where mostly GAPAs and SAPAs reside. Tuition exceeds $30,000 each year, most of which Shana can't afford.

Nicholas attended public school through the fourth grade and received a good education. Shana appreciates that but wants her son to reach his academic potential, which she doesn't believe is possible at his current school. As he enters into the fifth grade, Nicholas and Shana look forward to what they deem an opportunity of a lifetime. What does this mean for them?

He enters a world far different than anything he's experienced. Many of his new classmates have nannies, tutors, homes in gated communities, and can converse in French or Mandarin. While Nicholas was the brightest student at his former school, he's now in the middle of the pack. He also must get accustomed to public speaking, meeting CEOs and white-collar career professionals, wearing a school uniform, and having a lot of homework. Unless he and Shana move, Nicholas will encounter chiding from his neighborhood peers for attending an uppity, rich school, and tease him for speaking proper English or "acting white."

What the school doesn't know about are Nicholas's emotional challenges. He is an only child who has no relationship with his biological father and the sole student in class that has experienced parental abandonment. Does he open up and share his feelings with the school psychologist or keep them bottled up inside? Staying anchored to the ways of the GEDA community might hurt him in this new environment. On the other hand, exposure to affluence just might be enough to turn Nicholas's and Shana's possibility filter around. It did for me.

A RELATABLE INNER-CITY GEEK

I love educational movies in which poor students are given the opportunity to pursue academic excellence, in spite of the background noise from skeptics—friends and family members—who believe knowledge accumulation is a fruitless endeavor.

A movie that fascinated me was *Finding Forrester*, starring Sean Connery, who played William Forrester, and Robert Brown as Jamal Wallace. Jamal Wallace, a South Bronx native, is given a scholarship to attend a prestigious Manhattan prep school after his impressive score on a standardized test, though basketball is where he wants to concentrate all of his energies. William Forrester, a Pulitzer prize recluse and reluctant mentor, helps his protégé unlock a special gift for writing. His good deed comes full circle, the boomerang effect, as the teacher is also taught a few life lessons along the way, and breaks free from the emotional hang-ups that kept him bound for four decades.

I enjoyed this movie because as a child, my passion was education—especially math and language arts—not sports. I couldn't control my life circumstances, but with a religious fervor, I could control the knowledge placed in my brain. My love of learning is embedded in my DNA. Even as a poor kid, I dreamt about attending Harvard, Yale, Stanford, or Princeton, that is, until basketball powerhouses started recruiting me.

I had several conversations with Pete Carril, Princeton coaching legend and a former Sacramento Kings assistant coach, about my dream of attending a top-notch university with a stellar academic pedigree. The first time I told him this, he joked, "We wouldn't have been able to afford you. Your status as one of the country's top recruits was too expensive for our taste." I laughed, but wasn't quite sure how to take that comment, though I'm sure he didn't mean it as a slight.

Knowledge is power if it's leveraged effectively. An educational network tied to an Ivy League school, especially for impoverished students, can change their career prospects, standing in life, and legacy footprint. Gifted minds cover the socioeconomic spectrum, though I do find myself cheering for poor kids who get accepted to elite universities with impressive academic pedigrees.

After completing continuing education programs at Stanford and Columbia over a decade ago, a childhood dream was fulfilled, even if it didn't result in a four-year degree. This question was posed by one of my mentors and a key contributor for the book, Eric Seabrook: "Lawrence, do you think your life would be different had you attended an Ivy League school for academics instead of a basketball powerhouse for athletic reasons?" It's a hypothetical question that can never be answered.

Student-athletes are jokingly told to befriend the geeks in their college classes, because someday they'll turn into corporate superstars employing former college star athletes still clinging to their glory years. The geeks might not have been able to shoot a jump shot or catch a football, but they did hit the books hard.

Delayed gratification and goal planning, two benefits of frontal lobe reasoning, can pay huge dividends if more of our student-athletes at bigger universities focus on this area of the brain instead of being dominated by the sensory and athletic world of the parietal lobe. When star athletes' skills fade, and they will, what's next? Hopefully, something more than reminiscing about their time on the football field or basketball court or baseball diamond. Trust me, it's hard to let this former life go.

Former Chicago Bear and NFL Hall of Fame running back Gale Sayers said, "Athletes should think about the end of their careers at the beginning of their careers." Great advice but so hard to implement. A seniority mindset can help today's athletes plan for that fateful day and beyond.

I don't have any desire to be included in the rarified world of the generationally wealthy, an infinitesimally small number of families throughout the world. I have great admiration for their disciplined approach and tenacity to legacy continuity. I, too, am committed to lifelong learning and personal development until my last breath is taken on God's planet.

Order and structure make our lives more peaceful, which are prerequisites for the affluent. GAPAs have too much going on for any disruption that puts their lives in disorder. Imitating many of their traits and habits from afar is fine with me, because I enjoy being outside the gate in the presence of common folk who keep me grounded. My goal to help the poor and middle class build personal and financial assets would likely be a hard sell from inside the gate. I wouldn't have time for them, and they wouldn't have access to me.

CHAPTER

6

TIME

*How social classes manage or
manipulate their use of time*

Static

If you have more time than money, then you are probably poor or middle class. If you have more money than time, you're likely very wealthy or financially well off.

Outside of work and school, time flexibility is one of only a handful of intangible assets GEDAs have in abundance, the others being emotional expression and personality representation, such as style, humor, bravado, charisma, and magnetism. It is regarded as a renewable resource, a flexible commodity to adjust depending on the circumstance.

Some GEDAs don't appreciate or respect the generosity others extend to help the poor. I've painfully learned since leaving poverty that time compliant—the middle class—and time inflexible—the ultra wealthy—individuals were very frustrated with me when I failed to respect their time. I'm sure my actions were an inconvenience to their schedules and left them a bit frustrated.

Time insensitivity displays a lack of awareness of social decorum. Perpetual tardiness is a way of life in generational poverty.

WHERE DID THE TIME GO?

I attended a high school basketball game early in the 2016-2017 season with my son, Eli, to scout a couple of players who train with me. The game ended and I was on the court talking with folks I know through my basketball circles. At some point, I glanced over and noticed the school's athletic director gesturing and trying to coax fans from the gymnasium. It was past 9 p.m., but most of us didn't pay attention to his cues to leave even as he rightly invaded our space. Eli was standing right by my side the entire time and he kept pulling on my coat sleeve indicating it was time to go. On his final plea, he said, "Daddy, you talk too much." Message received and we left for the exit.

Parietal lobers, common among people who live or grew up in poverty, often lose track of time because they get ingratiated in the moment, giving bro hugs and phone numbers to just about anyone, and chit-chatting about a variety of topics. However, they don't realize that they've stayed well past their welcome. They are oblivious to the visual cues—like an athletic director trying to clear a gym—that tell them it's time to leave. My wife appreciates the growth I've achieved in this area, but I still have a long way to go.

GRACE AND THE GHETTO CARD

Time flexibility in the projects is a given. If it appears someone is home, visitors simply knock on the door or go right in. Showing up unannounced is rarely considered an etiquette breach.

My wife cautions me repeatedly that this is rude and impolite. She says I can't use my celebrity card to hide behind my ghetto card, adding that while I left the 'hood, it never left me. Monya's blue-collar, middle-class roots exude tact and a keen awareness of time compliance. She displays good manners and certainly has helped me improve in the etiquette department.

A GAME-TIME DECISION

For many in poverty, preferential treatment and latitude are given to feelings first and scheduled activities and tasks a distant second. This creates pressure for them, and pressure is a form of pain that can derail their best intentions to flee economic misery. The pressure to perform in pro sports is intense, as well.

Athletes know their bodies better than anyone. Even team doctors and trainers can't always bypass or overrule a player's self-diagnosis. Sometimes the decision to play or sit the game out must be made by the player just minutes from tipoff. Does team loyalty drive their decision, or does self-preservation prevail?

When I had to make a game-time decision like that, it created a sickening and gut-wrenching feeling in my stomach. Agony sets in as you waver between the choices, and sometimes, the body wins. When I really hurt, my body let me know sitting was the only option; the pain was unbearable. No amount of feel-good endorphins or pain-killers would change my mind. The poor similarly agonize and vacillate over the choices they must make in everyday living.

In partnership with other nonprofits, we've hosted dozens of pro bono workshops through the years to help residents in impoverished communities upgrade their personal and financial balance sheets—opening the choices available to them.

We knew going in that GEDAs' participation would be a game-time or last-minute decision for some of them. There were no-shows for sure, but I have no doubt that they had every intention of attending until their feelings took over, compelling a change in thinking when the deadline arrived. A cascading effect of emotions left them paralyzed and powerless to abandon their comfort zone; the path of least resistance has been taken. Even when transportation or childcare are not issues, GEDAs often pass on potentially life-altering opportunities that could have reshaped their frame of reference, turning them from spectators to active players in the wealth game.

Linear

For the traditional middle class, time is seen as a linear set of sequential steps. It follows a familiar and predictable pattern, and anything that disrupts this routine creates enormous stress in the lives of GISAs. The typical day for a GISA is fairly straightforward: Wake up. Work. Wind down. Weekend. Repeat sequence until retirement. They can see the sequential next step, but cannot anticipate steps 10, 15, or 20 as a chess grandmaster might. Longer-term goals are out of sight, and unfortunately, out of mind.

This back-burner mentality means items such as planning for the kids' college tuition needs or their own retirement are delayed. For many adults, retirement forecasting won't pop up on the radar screen until the end of the Third Quarter of Life comes into clearer focus, which is some time in their late 50s or early 60s. By then, most of the gains associated with compound interest will likely have gone to their wealthier peers who were comfortable taking more investment risks to meet future obligations, in particular, healthcare, nursing or long-term care, and asset distribution to beneficiaries upon death.

DRIVERS OF BLUE-COLLAR TIME COMPLIANCE

Time compliance is an intangible asset of the middle class because so much depends on it. Income and benefits are secured from their job, which provides GISAs and SISAs (middle-class transplants) with the lifestyles they enjoy, including homeownership in a decent neighborhood, moderate-to-above-average pay, and enough money to cover necessities and some luxuries.

However, fear also plays a huge role in their time-compliant nature. They don't want to lose what they've worked hard to earn. They expect fair treatment, and they view a paycheck with benefits as an equity measurement. Trepidation grips them when the line between them and poverty blurs and their social status is threatened. Indeed, wages have been relatively stagnant for nearly two decades as globalism fueled the exodus of many good-paying, domestic manufacturing jobs overseas.

Middle America's time-compliant nature also is shaped by their blue-collar reputation. They work very hard to wear labels denoting them dependable and trustworthy, but they fear being seen in an unflattering light and having people distrust them.

A FINANCIAL SOBRIETY CHECKPOINT

It's been said that time heals all wounds. Of course, it depends on the subject matter. Financial wounds and blind spots go away only when bad habits disappear. It's time to change, and GISAs can't afford to wait. They must look ahead and prevent staggering into retirement using what I term a *financial sobriety checkpoint*.

Two concepts that may provide context for GISAs single-minded focus, financial disequilibrium and economic vertigo, are best viewed through the lens of temporal lobers. We know that vertigo is a debilitating condition that occurs in the ears and causes people afflicted with it to feel as though objects are moving around them when they are stationary. Symptoms include nausea and dizziness when standing up, or turning or tilting the head.

My wife, a temporal lober to be sure, had a severe bout with vertigo in 2001. Monya's vestibular system, which is the body's balance center, malfunctioned. "It was impossible for me to walk straight," she says, "and I couldn't help veering off course." When she wasn't sleeping, she kept her eyes closed and head straight while sitting in a dark room without noise for two days until the symptoms disappeared. Bright lights were avoided since they contributed to her discomfort. She barely ate and kept interactions with others to a minimum, including with me.

Many GISAs are temporal lobers and prefer gradual change at a measured pace. Imagine how they might react getting stopped during a sobriety checkpoint law enforcement sets up to catch drunk drivers. Not a gradual change at all. Most people don't think about the checkpoints until it is too late, though the public gets a beforehand warning that checkpoints will be operating. The same holds true about financial planning among the middle class.

Holistic financial planning is little more than background noise to GISAs younger than 50, and lacking focus in this area contributes to their economic vertigo. What consumes their energy? The management of financial resources to meet life's pending demands only. They spend a great amount of time financially caring for their households and other immediate needs, with little room for anything else that complicates hectic schedules of single-minded tasks. Adding just one more activity would create incredible angst.

Too much motion or movement, financially speaking, can be a dizzying ordeal for GISAs. Financial planners who understand the premise behind economic vertigo might better comprehend why middle-class clients find it difficult implementing their planning suggestions. The more I work with the middle class, a clearer picture develops about how they want to receive and interpret financial information, and that's one step at a time.

Finite

For the ultra wealthy, time management is about order and structure. Time is a finite, nonrenewable resource. Once gone, it can't be replenished. Thus, time is spent wisely, efficiently, strategically, and tactfully. GAPAs are mindful not to waste their own time, and won't engage in activities that waste others' time, either.

Time allocation is their most prized intangible asset and a prerequisite of wealth accumulation. Activities not on the calendar don't attract their attention. That sounds harsh, but time inflexibility and embedded segmentation habits are never personal with GAPAs. It's about principles, which serve as foundational pillars for life and legacy continuity, passed down through ancestral lines. Principles stand the test of time as goodwill gestures, which is the reason why they hire the best lawyers, accountants, and financial advisors to manage their lives. GAPAs and SAPAs do not like to be inconvenienced.

The generationally and situationally wealthy compartmentalize their lives based on family, education, supplemental services (academic enrichment and athletic training for children), career and professional development, wealth accumulation and preservation strategies, wellness, social and intellectual capital, getaways, philanthropy, and legacy continuity.

SPEND MONEY, MANAGE TIME BETTER

A-list celebrities have very tight schedules when they travel and little time to accommodate fans' requests for autographs and photos. They willingly pay to ensure their time is not wasted due to unforeseen schedule disruptions because for them and GAPAs, time is money. Taking a page out of the GAPA playbook, some of our most recognizable celebrities invest in fractional jet ownership to manage their time more efficiently and effectively.

Children in our financial life skills summer camps get to see that world up-close during field trips to Columbus, Ohio-based NetJets, the world's top private air transport company and a subsidiary of Berkshire Hathaway, a publicly traded company.

This industry leader provides top-of-the-line travel and luxury service, access to an impressive fleet of private jets with an impeccable safety record, and the opportunity for clients to manage time with precision. Field trips to places like NetJets reinforce financial concepts that children learn in class, for example, equity investing or ownership interest in a

> Spending money to save time is a critical component of the GAPA and SAPA playbook.

business. An investment in Berkshire Hathaway is an investment in NetJets. This field trip does something else: It lets kids across the socioeconomic spectrum aim high in their imaginations of a world with unlimited possibilities available to them.

The children love sitting in a private jet in the company's massive hanger, soaking up the sights and sounds of the first-class amenities enjoyed by its clients. The company offers tiered pricing in fractional jet ownership to more than 6,000 clients worldwide. An entry-level fractional ownership for 50 hours of annual flight time over a period of five years can cost several million dollars or more. For 100 hours per year or a 1/8th share of an Embraer Phenom 300 with a five-year contract term, the acquisition cost of the jet, monthly management fee, hourly-occupied fee, and fuel for 500 hours of flight time, the estimated cost is over $3 million.

Jeff Talbert is a team manager at NetJets who oversees 26 employees and arranges the field trips and tours for our group. He also works with individuals and families representing various affluent mindsets, though time compression and operational efficiency are two luxuries enjoyed by all NetJets clients. Of course, not all wealthy people are cut from the same financial cloth. When the monthly invoice arrives, clients' reactions can usually be traced to their Sociopsychonomic filter—a vigilant cheapskate or thriftless spender. Money doesn't change you; it magnifies who you already are.

Jeff says, "Some clients spend seven figures on fractional jet ownership but are quick to raise an eyebrow on $50 charges, while others don't bother to question any line item on an invoice in the hundreds of thousands of dollars, racked up on a single trip." He adds, "Other clients pay management fees of $1 million per month before a minute of flying."

GAPAs and SAPAs fly NetJets because they've taken the necessary steps and ascended in their professions where they can afford the luxury. A GISA or GEDA might never fly on a private jet like the kind at NetJets, but they can take steps to improve their financial health and grow their assets. Maybe then they'll find it easier to manage time and enjoy life on their own terms, just like a GAPA or SAPA.

WHY DO THE WEALTHY ATTEND SYMPHONY CONCERTS?

I realize my 'hood card is in jeopardy of revocation for admitting that my fondness for classical music started way back when I was growing up in the ghetto. Not surprisingly, music genres were selected depending on my mood. I listened to gospel for spiritual growth, gangsta' rap for defiance, rock 'n' roll for energy, and classical for deep introspection. I spent many lonely days in my bedroom thinking about the life I would one day live. In a weird way, classical music helped me clarify my thoughts and fine-tune the rhythm of an orchestrated plan to escape poverty, the detail and big-picture side of it. Fortunately, the Lead Conductor—the Lord—got me back on track when I was out of sync with my life and music choices.

I surmise the wealthy attend symphony concerts and operas because they derive enjoyment from seeing and hearing the beauty of harmony in motion. I, too, appreciate the harmonic rhythm and timing of talented musicians who masterfully blend their geniuses together for one common goal.

Symmetry and balance are critical attributes of time management— beautiful music to a GAPA's ears—offering clarity of focus and tranquility in a fast-moving world that punishes the mismanagement of time, energy, and effort. Time disharmony occurs when GAPAs' schedules are disrupted, inconveniencing their personal, professional, and financial well-being.

Impromptu moments are rare occurrences in the world of legacy wealth. Spontaneity doesn't fit into their tightly knit calendars. For me, though, some of the happiest moments of my life have been times of spontaneity, which is a staple for those living in poverty but very seldom embraced by the generationally affluent. I can attest to it.

I stopped inviting my well-to-do friends over to watch sporting events during get-togethers, planned but a few days before the game. Their time is always accounted for in advance, so now I keep the guest invites to friends and family members with flexibility in their daily schedules.

7

ACADEMIC ENRICHMENT

The educational attainment level most representative of a social class's personal, professional, or intellectual pursuits

High School Diploma

The good news is that high school graduation rates are on the rise, even among low-income students. The bad news is that far too many poor students can't see beyond a high school diploma, dooming them to low-paying jobs with few benefits, while secondary education (and frontal lobe orientation in general) is often an abstract concept to them. Their struggles continue in adulthood as they race uphill, and always in the outside lane, toward economic advancement. Inevitably, the race exhausts them and they surrender, tripped by an unexpected financial crisis—a broken down car or family member needing a loan or money to pay a speeding ticket.

A large percentage of those who do pursue higher educational goals are first-generation college students entering unfamiliar territory. Members of their immediate family may have attended college, but none of them graduated with a degree. I was the first person in my family of five, three older sisters and a single-parent mother, to receive a college degree. I was determined to break the mold.

WHY ACADEMIC RULES ARE BROKEN

America's impoverished students disproportionally struggle more than their middle-class and affluent peers with reading, critical writing, and linear, or analytical, thinking. Why? I don't have all the reasons, although a lack of resources to afford intervention measures and little daily help from parents who might have had their own academic challenges in school could be two of them. Another supposition is linked to the clearly defined rules of grammar, where a subject and verb always agree, and mathematical reasoning, a discipline built around process and order like what one finds in solving a multistep algebra equation. For many poor students, school is a straitjacket and too boring, which these subjects point out to them.

The boredom with school may lead them to "check out" or misbehave. If the consequences for those actions come without severe repercussions, compliance is left solely to the individual's discretion. The street is one setting where rules and codes of conduct are followed by GEDAs, while they are optional in an academic environment. Learning that contradicts or corrects their way of speaking or thinking is seen as an unfair, baseless threat.

TOO MUCH LATITUDE CAN LEAD TO TOO LITTLE BEATITUDE

I'm not suggesting that we reinstitute corporal punishment, but when I was a child students could be disciplined in school for questionable behaviors. The more unrestricted latitude we give our children, the less empowered they become as feelings dominate their educational advancement filter.

I got paddled roughly four times throughout my elementary and middle school years for incidences that ranged from being disrespectful to teachers or principals, running in the hallway, or chewing gum in class. In other words, I didn't follow protocol or established orders.

Getting punished at school couldn't compare to the maternal discipline doled out by my mother who ensured her children "didn't act a fool in school." She disdained such nonsense. I was more fearful of 6-foot Ma Dukes than the wooden paddle administered by a school official. I also received a spanking— okay, a whoopin'—when I walked through the front door after being singled out at school for a breach in conduct. She'd give me a look of utter contempt when I returned home, and I would brace myself for what came next. She'd say, "Come over here right now Lawrence Damon!" I knew I was in big trouble whenever mom emphasized my first and middle names in the same sentence. Let's return to the severity of this subject.

If time is flexible to GEDAs, then the educational arena should also offer the same latitude extension. When you live in a world where time is static, how do you prepare and pace yourself when time is compressed? Time compression creates enormous stress, increases cortisol levels, and lowers concentration. For impoverished students, this leads to lackluster performance on standardized testing, among many other negative outcomes.

Poorer students typically struggle in math and language arts. It's not surprising that these are the same two content areas on the ACT, or American College Test, a popular entrance exam that is a barometer for a high school student's academic readiness for college. It's not an exact science—and neither is the Scholastic Aptitude Test or SAT for that matter—but it is fairly accurate.

> The street is one setting where rules and codes of conduct are followed, while they're an option in school.

An argument can be made that the ACT and SAT are inherently biased because they punish those in economic misery simply by virtue of the fact that the world of rules-based English and math aren't digested to the same extent as they are in middle and suburban America. Having said that, does this mean we should give poor kids an academic pass? Of course not. Capability is never the issue with impoverished children. Accessibility to college preparation and life planning from an aerial vantage point in earlier grades may very well be an equalizer.

A COGNITIVE HAND UP, NOT A CONSTANT HAND HOLD

Handholding is quite normal but entirely detrimental to kids in poverty. Although affirmation is critical to educational engagement, perhaps more important is weaning students off of it. Poor kids will either monopolize or disregard an educator's time. It's imperative that instruction and class participation be evenly spread to avoid the appearance of favoritism and intellectual bias, which children from economic distress can pick up on when a teacher heaps too much admiration toward a gifted student, for instance. I can assure you as an educator that it is an easy trap to fall into.

First, let's take a moment and revisit the four sensory processing responsibilities of the parietal lobe: taste, touch, temperature, and pain, of which pressure is a form. Sensory seekers attribute their dependency on internal or external touch to make sense of the world around them. They must feel something—a high five, a tender caress, a gut reaction, or inner warmth—in order to be led or lead themselves. Without an affirming sensation, they feel lost.

Handholding is about guidance, which speaks to students' inability to navigate the landscape of an academic assignment or intellectual experience. A shift from the physical to the intellectual, an uncomfortable feeling for many GEDA students since this isn't their preferred language, will lead many to seek the affirming touch of an educator to push or guide them along.

I've noticed interesting behaviors common among sensory-seeking students from poverty when they learn something new. They will grab me as I walk by, seeking validation and confirmation—call them affirmation surrogates—that they are doing a good job for whatever task or action is at hand.

Affirmation is a temperature gauge of judicious aptitude and navigational posturing, a warm, fuzzy feeling to keep the individual in the intellectual moment. The warmer or cozier poor students feel, the better the educational engagement. The danger occurs when a cold front enters and excitement dies down in lock step with their feelings. A shift from analytical thinking to instinctive reasoning has occurred. A lack of funds available in GEDAs' visuocognitive bank accounts is the cause, and it amplifies the cacophony of physical and verbal grumblings—hunger cravings caused by nutritional deficiencies, emotional thirst, peer pressure to check out, heightened disinterest, and other background noises.

This may explain why parietal lobe dominant poor students (and their families) use metaphors to explain how they feel on a physical or mental level. For example, phrases such as "that's sweet" or "that's salty" may not have anything to do with food. In reference to "that's sweet," this may describe a nice looking car. In the case of "that's salty," this may signal disapproval of something said about someone else. Taste, touch, temperature, and pain, in some word form, will often explain their frustration or satisfaction in the classroom and their lives. I'll revisit metaphors as key tools to use when presenting to the poor in Chapter 14, "Primary Sensory-Learning Drivers."

Internal leadership is a cognitive ability critical to escaping poverty, giving the individual a profound sense in seeing a better life. You live accordingly when you know your life has meaning, holding out hope through the virtues of faith and a divine mission to become a contented *Somebody*, though you're written off as a worthless nobody. A confident assurance barks that you won't settle for anything less, that your life of unending mistakes and mindless mishaps is over. Life gets better—you're sure of it. What else is there to lose when you feel on a subconscious level that you have everything to gain?

Being present in the moment and its impact on future outcomes is a concept that's gained traction over the last decade as teachers and students mitigate a stressful learning and living environment. Incremental steps taken today lead to giant strides in the future.

"Teacher Stress and Health: Effects on Teachers, Students, and Schools" is a 2016 report that looks at the impact of stress on teachers. According to its conclusions, nearly half of them don't believe the educational challenges are worth the emotional capital invested at their respective schools. Mark Greenberg, the report's co-author, notes that "between 30 and 40 percent of teachers leave the profession in their first five years."[14]

I don't find this shocking considering the expanded roles all teachers, particularly those working in the inner city, execute that weren't part of their original job description. It's an underpaid and overwhelming occupation for people who must prepare (and are blamed when student achievement falls short) our children for the demands of the twenty-first century.

Mental agility is an abstract concept that can't be quantified tangibly but helps lift children from generational poverty. First, though, they must take stock of their situation and chart a navigable course to follow. Second, they'll need a customized set of imaginative pom-poms to cheer themselves on when no one else will. A cheering section of one is more than enough inspiration to win this game, especially if they can avoid tripping themselves up.

Earlier in the book, I introduced the concept of economic vertigo to describe the middle class's difficulty to focus on other important financial matters—estate and retirement planning, for example—when they are preoccupied with a single-minded task, such as getting out of debt. Academic vertigo is the inability of a person to take intellectual risks for fear of falling, and it affects poor children trying to save face with their peers in a learning environment. Intellective disorientation is the inability to plug into the appropriate internal GPS coordinates to reach a destination far different than what's known and applies to many sensory-seeking poor students that struggle with academic focus. To them, it just doesn't make a whole lot of sense to stay locked in to an educational experience with delayed benefits.

The mental connection between time and space, and, thus, delayed gratification, is more real than what we can see and touch. This connection is the single most important factor to help poor students build a bridge between academic performance and a better life. Not new or updated schools. Not more technology. Not monetary gimmicks to keep students in school.

Mental dexterity overrides sensory stimuli if it's properly taught. It's how I made it out of the ghetto. So, how do you take poor kids somewhere they've never been physically? You consistently transport them in their minds to someplace different, a delicate and time-intensive process that involves all the emotive-driven learning modalities.

Amenities can certainly enhance the educational experience, but they don't define it. Cerebral enticements and mental agility with a long-term payoff are the keys to keeping poor students locked in to the rigors of academic calisthenics. *Sociopsychonomics* is a diagnostic tool used to contrast social class mindsets and financial habits. Workshops as well as this book's sequel will offer tools and suggestions in cognitive development to assist educators and social agencies who work with underserved populations.

Four-Year Degree

GISAs and SISAs make the assumption that educational competency beyond high school automatically equates to a better quality of life. Their linear framework follows a familiar pattern: More education leads to a better-paying job and a comfortable lifestyle, eventually. Maybe.

Eric Seabrook, my attorney friend, grew up in a traditional, middle-class Georgia family that placed a premium on the benefits of post-secondary education, but not on financial wellness. He says, "The middle class has very little appreciation of risk given their super-conservative nature. They place their trust in higher education degrees and institutional measures that show a track record of providing graduates with the intellectual skills to secure a safe job. But is the security mindset rational? I don't believe it is."

Many middle-class people have their undergraduate and graduate degrees and feel most comfortable with a job that ensures basic necessities and obligations are met monthly. Why should they rock the boat and drift farther away from their economic shoreline if it's not absolutely necessary? Besides, an island of financial bliss is too far away.

IS A COLLEGE DEGREE A SURE FINANCIAL BET?

Regardless where a middle-class person works, he should pursue a wealth-building mentality in asset acquisition beyond the confines of a safe job with benefits and homeownership in a decent neighborhood. This is the responsibility of the middle class, not their employer or the federal government. Most have no idea how punishing the future will be by keeping their eyes fixed on the next step in front of them, and we need the middle class to do well to keep our economy afloat. Their struggle is our struggle.

The middle class bases things on perceived value, and that certainly extends to a college education. However, many college graduates—and their co-signing parents—question whether the value of a four-year degree is worth the debt they've incurred, a figure that reaches well into the tens of thousands of dollars for the average student. This is one of the biggest fears college students share with me.

Millennials and Generation Z (also known as the iGeneration) might be the first generations in American history whose quality of life, as measured by health and wealth, fall short of their parents. They also have been told to pursue their passions, never mind the fact that passion degrees without lucrative paychecks won't finance their lifestyle or pay back their college debt.

Eric concurs, saying education won't be the economic catalyst the middle class believes. "I had a classmate, John, from high school, whose mother was a hairdresser. My folks placed a great emphasis on education, which is important, but John received a different kind of education that focused on building assets. He joined the Air Force and made a career of it. He owned three houses by the time I finished college," he says. "When he left the Air Force, he started a security business. John grew up in a home that emphasized business ownership. His parents didn't diminish post-secondary degrees, but they did place an inordinate amount of their focus on this: fundamental asset accumulation. They are categorically two very different types of learning."

The question, then, should be reframed to ask whether college degrees should be flexible and adaptable enough so that they benefit the end-user in good and bad economic times. Examples of flexible degrees include those in business, science, math, engineering, technology, law, entrepreneurship, and education. In today's economy, it is going to be a near impossible task to survive financially without flexibility.

Mark Cuban's candid response to an entrepreneur on a *Shark Tank* episode provides a nice capstone to this topic. He said, "If you follow your passion but can't monetize your efforts, what good will this do?"

BLUE-COLLAR JOB, WHITE-COLLAR MENTALITY

A four-year degree is worth the sticker shock if it is flexible and accompanied by a world-class financial education, and as long as those with blue-collar jobs employ a white-collar mentality to create wealth-generating and legacy assets. Again, one of the goals of this book is to help each social class improve their respective standing in life. We all have room for improvement in our financial survival skills.

I've been a guest lecturer on high school and college campuses for more than a decade. On one occasion I provided college students with a lesson in financial statement analyses and was shocked that nobody in that class could explain the foundational difference between an expense and a liability. Middle America is familiar with financial terms, but only a small percentage of them actually have a working financial plan. Most will outlive their money and very few of them have completed an estate plan. There are so many scenarios that beg for a financial planning strategy: Is there enough insurance to cover gaps if an emergency occurs? What effect would an illness, death, or drop from a two-income family have on your assets?

SOCIOPSYCHONOMIC FILTER
Middle America is familiar with financial terms, but only a small percentage of them actually have a working financial plan.

Suggestions to get their financial house in order can throw their vestibular sense of monetary balance out of whack. When GISAs are off balance economically, they hold on for dear life and focus on what can be controlled. It's not surprising to hear them express discomfort about adding more responsibilities to their plate when they don't have the stomach to digest another time-intensive task.

Most of the participants who attend our financial wellness workshops are decidedly middle class, and it's refreshing to see them take control of their financial destiny. Their trepidation is palpable as they hear a few rule-of-thumb averages for how much cash—three to six months—they should keep on hand for an emergency; how expensive a house they can buy—no more than 2.5 times their gross annual income; and the need to stow away 25 times the anticipated yearly expenses for retirement in today's dollars.

Lifelong-Learning Opportunities

In generational poverty, completing a high school diploma becomes a launching pad for individuals to enjoy life as an adult. This is the depth of the educational journey many poor students travel, and they breathe a sigh of relief after reaching the milestone. Post-secondary education is an abstract goal as the benefits of a college degree escape them. For the traditional middle class, completing a college degree or trade program kick-starts their life and family planning arrangements. The wealthy seek lifelong-learning opportunities at every level, not as the initiation of their lives, but as a requirement to complete their purpose and carry out the family's legacy manifesto.

For the informed wealthy, education is a conditioning routine for personal and professional growth, but this exercise regimen doesn't end as wealth levels reach certain milestones as it does for many GEDAs. The upper middle class and super wealthy often pursue similar undergraduate and advanced degrees. The key difference: GISAs move only toward a career path, while GAPAs move toward the fulfillment of their heritage or legacy mandate.

EDUCATION AND NETWORKING: A SYMBIOTIC RELATIONSHIP OF AFFLUENCE

It is true that our network has a direct effect on our net worth. For GAPAs and SAPAs, their network is exclusive and far-reaching. Entrance occurs by vote (not in the technical sense) or invitation only.

The poor have a haphazard network where friends hastily contact each other to fulfill an urgent and immediate request. I'm always hesitant to pass along my business card to a classmate or acquaintance who, like me, grew up in poverty, fearing a desperate plea for money or an employment referral. They've subsided the longer away I am from my NBA playing days, more than a decade ago. I take every call, but rarely honor the request; I have my own personal and financial brand to protect. My charitable side is evident, though influenced by neither guilt nor compulsion.

The middle class has a fragmented network, unless they've penetrated the wall of affluence and are given the chance to earn the trust of GAPAs and SAPAs. GISAs understand protocol, so they are less likely than GEDAs to squander a networking opportunity with the super wealthy.

Cecil Gouke has been a close friend for many years. An only child, he grew up in a blue-collar household with two nurturing parents. Mama Gouke's vibrant spirit is so amazing, a testament to her Louisiana roots. His father, now deceased, was an economics and black studies professor at Ohio State University for 25 years. As a former student of his, Professor Gouke's keen sense of classroom humor was memorable.

The Goukes lived in Berwick, a middle-class neighborhood on the east side of Columbus. Cecil's parents made a tremendous sacrifice to provide him with a first-rate education at Columbus Academy. The school is one of Ohio's most recognized and prestigious private schools, and Cecil is good friends with some of the richest and most successful families in the Columbus region who also send their kids there. We often discuss the power of an educational network, which Cecil says has served him well.

"What's interesting is that most of the parents who send their kids to Columbus Academy live in districts with very high property tax bases, for example, New Albany, Upper Arlington, Bexley, and Dublin. These suburban school districts, in their own right, have a pretty good academic reputation," he says. "Keep in mind that a large percentage of property

> Net worth and network are two sides of the same financial coin.

tax revenues are used to finance public schools in their respective districts. But many affluent parents still feel that an additional investment for their children on the academic and networking side is worth it."

The educational network supplied by schools like Columbus Academy and Columbus School for Girls and Wellington here in Central Ohio, where annual tuition exceeds $25,000, affords graduates chances to interact with highly successful alumni—the movers and shakers in the private and public sectors. These connections can last a lifetime.

Cecil worked for two years at an Atlanta consulting firm after graduate school at the University of Virginia where he earned an MBA. Returning to Columbus, he was able to leverage his Columbus Academy network to secure an employment position with a marketable upside at a Fortune 500 company. The significance of those ties does not escape him: "It's hard to say, but this job opportunity may not have happened had I not been in that Columbus Academy inner circle."

IN PURSUIT OF SUPPLEMENTAL SERVICES WITH LIFE-LONG BENEFITS

Lack of funds notwithstanding, purchasing supplemental services is rarely considered by the generationally poor because they don't recognize the long-term value attached to tutoring children or academic enrichment services from a holistic perspective.

To entice the middle class in the same endeavor, it's about making the supplemental services affordable and a justifiable extra expense. In other words, a deal they view as saving them money now or later, such as a service that might improve a child's chances of securing an athletic or academic scholarship.

GAPAs and SAPAs always view supplemental services for their kids as a long-term investment play. Cost is never the issue and they'll make time in their busy schedules if the benefits fit their narrative of personal growth and intellectual stimulation. Outcomes with little benefit are bypassed, while value-oriented outcomes with a track record of success are secured.

Lifelong learning follows a seamless continuum of educational and personal development experiences that are interconnected. Finding the time for and value attached to supplemental services are issues shared by affluent-minded subset classes to prepare their children for the journey ahead.

We offer financial education camps every summer for middle and high school students. Well-to-do households and middle-class families enroll their children to gain much-needed life skills that are covered throughout *Sociopsychonomics*. Participants enjoy a fun learning environment where they get introduced to entry- and advanced-level financial concepts, receive tutorials from industry professionals on field trips to local businesses, and consume healthy and nutritious foods each day.

FunderMax Fitness athletic training offers to help children develop their physical and mental skills. Kristin shares the effect training had on her son: "The opportunity for our child to train with a former pro athlete is priceless. As his parents, we don't have any illusion our son will play in the NBA. We are more impressed about the mental discipline and inner toughness he has gained from working out with you. These traits will help him decades down the road."

8

LIFE'S PURPOSE

The assignment for which an individual was placed on this earth to accomplish for the betterment of humanity

Shrouded in Mystery

For the male living in generational poverty, his life's purpose often hides behind an iridescent veil. Looking at the veil from one angle reveals a blinking, green-coded destiny to become a pro athlete or entertainer or social media star. He follows the light, oblivious that these dream jobs are mere occupations and not careers. However, they attract millions from impoverished communities who view these paths as their only ticket out. Ultimately, they are left disillusioned by the experience, unable to shake the disappointment when the dream fizzles. The veil reveals an ominous, much darker color from another angle. More disconcerting than the first, you're convinced your destiny is an early and tragic death. Your environment, your crew, your music, and even your internal dialogue orient you to the fulfillment of this prophecy. Perhaps someone or something—a family member, a teacher, a mentor, the Good Book, a funeral procession—can reroute your coordinates toward a different track before it's too late. Unfortunately, many GEDAs end up squandering their life assignment as they run headlong to an early and tragic death.

How someone dies and at what age offers telltale signs of one's social class, and the ability (or inability) of a person to carry out his or her life's purpose. Violent crime, premature death, or a drug overdose curtail one's aspirations and are simply more prevalent in poorer communities. The poor, middle class, and affluent often die from the same causes, such as cancer, heart disease, or cognitive decline, but the quality of life before death is where the similarities usually diverge. Suffering through a prolonged disease, illness, or health crisis before death without adequate resources would likely apply to GEDAs and GISAs rather than GAPAs.

The generationally affluent have the resources to afford supplemental care not covered by health insurance or Medicare, including customized meals and 24-hour medical assistance. GAPAs are also cognizant of not burdening family members with the responsibility.

The traditional middle class cares for the ongoing needs of a loved one by committee, taking turns based on family pecking order and availability. Older siblings, a child favorite, or a financially stable family member could be responsible for shouldering most of the burden. This theme will be covered extensively under estate planning in Chapter 34, "Inheritors' Inheritance."

A BANKABLE COMMODITY: THE CURRENCY OF REVENGE

Revenge can derail a life's purpose in the blink of an eye, especially for the poor, who often treat paying back the perpetrator as the pressing goal pushing their motivation. You might act on gut reaction or the impulse that has the loudest cadence, even when hearsay is the only proof. If you're wrong, you'll deal with the consequences later.

Jumping to conclusions is part of the normal ebb and flow of generational poverty. Minor transgressions are treated as major grievances that stoke your fatalistic attitude that others really are out to harm you. This corroborates your list of grievances that you hold responsible for your life of intense bitterness: police overstepping their boundaries; fathers not being held accountable when they abandon their parental responsibilities; the rich enjoying a carefree life of abundance with zero concern for the plight of the poor.

On the other hand, you feel trapped physically and mentally with limited opportunities to better yourself. The rage builds and waits for the right spark to set ablaze anything you touch, and acting as judge, jury, and executioner, you feel inclined to right the wrong. For evidence, look no further than the chaos in our inner cities and prisons where intense anger is expressed as revenge. It is currency in the land of economic distress and comes with little warning and a swift and severe punishment. The underlying rage lingers from one generation to the next until a link in the offspring chain screams, "Enough! It's time to break this curse."

SOCIOPSYCHONOMIC FILTER

Jumping to conclusions is part of the normal ebb and flow of generational poverty. Minor transgressions are treated as major grievances that stoke your fatalistic attitude that others really are out to harm you.

I had a right to be angry as a kid. Economic abuse, deplorable living conditions, and parental neglect by my father should have been enough to justify that anger. However, I did not have a right to execute judgment on someone who had nothing to do with my childhood pain. You may recall earlier in the book how I paid people back, mostly white men, for the pain I endured in being viewed as a second-class citizen, a nobody, during my childhood. Now a somebody as a sports figure, I just had to get revenge.

I felt like an invisible kid in poverty who no one cared about. I plotted and made good on my retribution pledge when sports stardom on a national level came my way. Confirming the payback method, there was absolutely no way I could forget how I was treated back then: "Now they want to take an interest in me simply because I can dunk a basketball for their enjoyment? Give me a break!"

I often displayed a laconic demeanor when white men stereotyped me, or so I thought, as a dumb-jock from a dysfunctional home life who could only talk about sports. Disgruntled adult black males in our housing project warned me as a kid never to trust white men because they harbored sinister or ulterior motives "to keep us down." They were adamant about drilling this mentality into me as a conditioning tactic aimed at shaping an elder's viewpoint as gospel.

My logic in those days made it entirely appropriate to mistreat a targeted group of people who accepted me as a physical specimen only and not an intellectual existing on an equal plane. My responses back then were, at times, distant and mean-spirited. Vengeance became the salve used to heal the scars of my bitterness. It didn't work.

In the 2016 ESPN documentary, *Rise Up*, black college and pro athletes take a stand on a variety of issues facing our African-African communities. A stark presentation, I was drawn to the segment featuring Taj Gibson, formerly of the Chicago Bulls and now with the Minnesota Timberwolves. This Brooklyn native did the best he could to hold back tears as he recited a list of friends and peers from his neighborhood fatally shot at a young age.

This gut-wrenching insight by Taj caught my attention. He said, "It's always something so small that just ticks off our [black] culture, something so small that we're so aggressive to the point, where [we say] 'I have to take him out. I gotta hurt him. I gotta kill him.'" Taj quickly looked down and gathered his next thought. "And then they [my friends] are never there anymore."[15]

What Taj alluded to was this: It's not a black issue, or even a gun problem, which is too myopic for observations. Violence in our poor, inner-city communities is a retribution problem, guided primarily by unrelenting sensations to depressurize the pain gauge and taste the sweetness of revenge. Recall that taste, touch, temperature, and pain receptors are processed in the parietal lobe. You pay back those who hurt you or someone else. With or without a weapon, you reason that revenge should be done posthaste, a task best completed before the emotions cool down and consequences are weighed.

"MY LIFE (OR THE SEMBLANCE OF IT) DOESN'T MATTER"

Fatalism is a huge stumbling block in generational poverty, where one becomes convinced tomorrow will be the same as it is today and as it was yesterday, while the future is unlikely to offer meaningful change. This narrative replays in your mind like a movie where you are the screenwriter, director, and star. The storyline, from start to finish, is entirely predictable. The star is born, has flashes of brilliance, and hangs out with the wrong people at the wrong time. He goes to jail or dies an early death. Stunned and despondent, you stay seated as the credits roll down the screen. If you are acquainted with ghetto life, you've seen this movie play out too many times. The world of poverty ain't no joke. It's truly a matter of life and death.

What's so perplexing about this rush to an early death for many GEDAs is its juxtaposition within their framework of time. As a static resource that can be replenished, time is seen as an elastic commodity, yet they feel their time on this earth is running out. How do you answer what your life's purpose is when you believe your fate is sealed? Enjoying the moment is what matters most for many who exist in economic distress, so attaching a purpose to their life doesn't matter. An educational goal doesn't matter. Hope doesn't matter, but it does disappoint. You believe life, an unrewarding voyage of unfair experiences, really doesn't matter. Generational poverty pursued me, but I wasn't going to be caught and submit to its devastating effects. I fought every single day for what mattered most to me, which was my sanity and human dignity as I committed myself to achieving a God-inspired life of purpose.

One of the most challenging tasks an educator faces today is convincing an impoverished child that education and purpose matter. School was seen as lame and a big waste of time by many of my neighborhood peers growing up. Unfortunately, this cumulative viewpoint still exists more than three decades later, and the academic disconnection among poor students has much to do with their inability to understand how capable they are to learn.

An identity crisis exists in impoverished communities. Social media and hip hop music have affected (and infected) our young people by creating a hyper-focused, image-conscious demographic. Indeed, many poor students in America place a heightened emphasis on outward features that make a loud statement instead of inward qualities that are foundational to one's life purpose. Here's what I mean.

We help teenagers identify their personal brand through our in-class developmental activities. Whether they realize it or not, this will play a large role in determining if a poor student graduates from high school, finds stable employment, and is able to survive financially in adulthood without public assistance. Poor kids typically highlight charisma, unique style, humor, athletic or rhyming skills, fashionable attributes, beauty, and physical traits—are they strong, tall, fast, or explosive—in the description of their personal brand statement. Boys open themselves to ridicule from their peers if they share their softer side, showing that they are kind-hearted, polite, or passionate about education. This apprehension doesn't usually occur with students from middle class or affluent households.

A personal brand statement communicates how an individual wants to be viewed and provides a glimpse into one's value system and success game plan. No one should expect children to comprehend their life's purpose at an early age, but the foundation is certainly laid during their formative years. Uncovering their individual gifts and talents is often a huge excavation project. I believe the benefits outweigh the short- and long-term costs.

I had an eye-opening conversation with several young men at a juvenile correction facility following my presentation on personal branding and emotional management. Most of these young men didn't just stumble into a life of criminal mischief. This is what happens when broken boys misidentify themselves and take on a persona that masks their internal fears and insecurities, surfacing later through the lens of outward or inward retaliation. One young man pulled me aside and said, "This is where I saw myself ending up, and I'm here."

"That may be true, but it doesn't have to define your future. You understand this?" I asked to which he nodded in agreement.

Juvenile correction facilities, in many respects, are miniature prisons for our most vulnerable males. When you go behind those gates and barbed-wire fences, your senses are on full alert. Some of the young men can be reached, holding on to your words of comfort. Others, tragically, have bought into the fatalistic narrative that accompanies a life devoid of meaning and purpose. If left to their own devices, prison becomes that self-fulfilling prophecy.

When trust is never taught, the individual trusts his instincts only, and this is especially dangerous for boys living in a highly stressed environment with no biological father or positive male guidance around. Who fills that void? Coaches and male teachers can fill the gap, but some will instead find personal validation in the streets from less scrupulous men eager to show them a grimier and nefarious side of existence. Negative role modeling carries immense consequences for young men teetering between right and wrong, and it costs society. Taxpayers are on the hook to fund juvenile correction facilities like the one where the young man predicted his incarceration.

Roger Blackwell was a professor of mine at The Ohio State University and remains a brilliant mind who knows business marketing inside and out. He spent time in a minimum-security prison for insider trading, a story that made national news. Although his ethnicity and life experiences were different, Roger became a stand-in father figure and counselor for many black inmates, and also helped them improve their writing and communication skills.

He says, "Of the hundreds of men who wrote essays about the person they respected most, only one African-American man wrote about his father. It was not unusual for the white men to write about their father. The African-American men sometimes wrote about their mothers or another family member who raised them, and sometimes about a sports hero, but not about their fathers."

It's hard to write about someone you don't know. Even young men with immense athletic talent from impoverished backgrounds and fatherless homes need guidance from dependable role models.

Thad Matta, the most successful men's basketball coach in Ohio State history, shared this with me at a practice before the 2016-2017 campaign, his last season with the Buckeyes: "It takes time to develop trust with some players who didn't grow up with a father. Down the road, I'd like to start an organization that addresses this issue, because I see its effects when young men come into our program and the distance between us is there. I eventually earn the trust, but it's not easy for them to let down their guard. My heart breaks for children who don't have a father figure in their lives."

> "It's about the journey—mine and yours—and the lives we can touch, the legacy we can leave, and the world we can change for the better."
> **–Tony Dungy**
> Former NFL Coach

If the generationally poor don't anticipate an early death or a life of crime, then another fatalistic destiny to guard against is perpetual dependency.

Perpetual dependency is not confined to government or nonprofit assistance to provide GEDAs with the basics of food, shelter, and clothing. Functional needs are symptomatic of a much deeper void. Actually, the roots of perpetual dependency might be the result of an over-reliance on sensory inputs to make someone feel appreciated, loved, or be accepted. The elements these sensory-seeking inputs share include the power of touch on a physical, relational, or emotional level.

Young ladies and single mothers living in poverty who want to feel loved on a deep emotional level set themselves up for continuous disappointment. They are susceptible to what I term *faux orientation*. Many females who haven't experienced genuine fatherly love will search for males who they believe can provide it. Literally, they try to feel their way to love. Males in search of physical love, and who possess the gift of faux orientation, a parietal lobe skill, can manipulate the emotions of females for personal gain and control, a tactic they use to validate their being and emit the impression of genuine interest. The two pursuers are destined to meet because it just feels like the right time. Never mind the fact that both are in need of authentic love, one that can only occur from a marital commitment and sealed by a lifelong covenant.

Faux orientation is a deeply troubling and dangerous skill. Manipulative males use humor or cleverly constructed words to access the sacred, emotional world of young females who can least afford to be hurt, which will happen again and again from one relationship to the next. Accepting brokenness as a permanent condition is at the heart of perpetual dependency.

Work in Progress

For GISAs who do know their life's purpose, the pursuit of it is a daily grind. The cares of this world often take precedence (unless a life assignment is directly tied to their occupation) in the lives of middle-class Americans trying to enjoy their economic pillars of comfort. They chip away at their life assignment when time permits. However, most of their focus is on the current task at hand—work, family, household obligations—an easier way to stay balanced in an unsettling world that is already too complicated to make it better.

Fulfilling their assignment in life is important, but GISAs always want to know the cost. If it appears too sacrificially expensive—time, energy, effort, emotional capital, or money—then life's purpose will be low on their priority list, pushed as far into the future as possible.

THE PURPOSE OF THE MATTER

I often get blank stares from people when I ask them, "What is your life's purpose, or the assignment on planet Earth for which you are here to accomplish for the betterment of others?"

Our life's purpose is tied to that unquenchable passion to do something, find something, build something, improve something, inspire someone, empower someone, reach someone, or equip someone. It's a burning desire to make the world a better place in which to live, work, or do business. Interestingly enough, it's not a capacity (mother, wife, etc.), job title, paycheck, or bank account. Inevitably, though, purpose comes down to people.

Purpose in life may change (but it doesn't necessarily have to) as we go through various milestones, seasons, or quarters of life. These will be instrumental in helping to fulfill our life's purpose. A brief description of each quarter follows.

In the First Quarter of Life, from birth to age 19, we uncover hidden talents and build foundational skills to succeed in life. From schooling to athletics to relationships to personal (and spiritual) development, the growth curve is steep. Life's purpose is often hidden in the first quarter, but the directional path is pre-set, or perhaps altered, based on the GPS coordinates that have been plugged in.

The Second Quarter of Life, ages 20 to 40, are spent improving on the foundational skills of the first quarter, for example, knowledge accumulation in college or the acquisition of a trade after high school. Settling into a career path, finding a suitable mate, and starting a family are likely to occur during this season of life. A spirit of youthfulness keeps us going in the face of career, relationship, parenting, and marital challenges. Optimism is usually still high in this stage of our lives, especially when walking in our assignment.

Halftime adjustments are typically made between the ages of 40 to 44. Like sports, it's a moment to pause and catch your breath. Players often contemplate on what was done right or wrong in the first half of the game. The opportunity exists to correct any bad habits in the first two quarters of life, including time and money management skills, relationship challenges and attitude problems that can derail career advancement goals or lead to marital discord, addictive behaviors, or emotional hang-ups.

The Third Quarter of Life, ages 45 to 64, is our highest salary earning years as retirement looms near. Some parents become grandparents during this span of time, while others look forward to the tranquility as empty nesters once children leave home for college. (In poverty, it's not unusual to become a grandparent before the age of 35.) Parents who co-sign for a child's college loan could experience financial shock from this act of generosity if *longevity risk*, or outliving their money in retirement, becomes a reality. The earnings window for third-quarter parents is limited.

The Fourth Quarter of Life, age 65 and beyond, should be a time of positive introspection as one looks back on the last three quarters of life. However, GEDAs who make it this far feel they are living on borrowed time, an extended warranty that is about to expire without warning. GISAs aren't as fatalistic, but many of them do behave in a rather cryptic fashion. They buy burial plots and pre-pay funeral costs as the game clock winds down. Instead of enjoying life and completing their purpose, they fret about the mistakes of the past. GISAs who did invest in their health and wealth for a 30-year retirement are likely to travel domestically or internationally, spend time with grandchildren, volunteer at church or pour their heart into a charitable endeavor, or pursue a life of purpose.

Overtime is where GAPAs excel. First, let's provide a quick snapshot of their progression through the four quarters, a deliberate and systematic process. These heritage markers are checked off along the way: graduation from a prestigious university; marriage, family planning, and the development of one's charitable footprint typically occur after the age of 30; career advancement in white-collar occupations, or mentoring the next generation to run their family business, with the succession plan likely occurring after the age of 40; a heightened sense of altruism in the third and fourth quarters of life, with children and grandchildren pledging to fulfill the legacy mandate.

Now to Overtime. For GEDAs, personality and outward features live on after death. GISAs' blue-collar attributes or inward features, notably their reliability and commitment to the welfare of others, are remembered. Heritage lives on for GAPAs decades or generations after their demise. Death is an extension of their legacy, not the conclusion of it. It's highly probable that the residual effects of GAPAs' former life of purpose are still paying dividends from the grave.

The traditional middle class may have an inclination of their life assignment, but the prospect of tackling it overwhelms them, or they believe the expiration date on it has passed. Nothing could be further from the truth.

To search for life's purpose, you must believe it has meaning, that it's not a mundane routine of uneventful experiences. Second, leave ulterior motives at the front door. Directly or indirectly, purpose is about people. Always keep this in mind.

> Too many people minimize the impact that they can have in the lives of hurting people.

Third, it's never too late to accomplish an extraordinary life and make a verifiable difference in the lives of others.

I see educators completing their life's purpose with zeal and inspiring students to new heights in the classroom. Others are there to collect a paycheck and can't wait for retirement where a pension awaits them. Compare them with inspirational teachers who care more about their life's calling than a paycheck or title. Great teachers are never forgotten. Which teachers from your childhood stand out? When it's about you and not about inspiring or empowering others, people can pick up on your self-centeredness and lack of enthusiasm to be an agent of comfort (or change) in the lives of hurting people.

Talents, abilities, and passions (TAP) can be used for a selfish or life-assignment purpose. TAPs must be uncovered, cultivated, or refined to complete a life assignment. The stakes are too high to squander them, and they must be used as a packaged deal.

Talent is a unique gift that you were born to do, though it must be given special attention and directional guidance to fully unravel it. Having an ability is a common skill learned or developed over time through repetition and practice. Passion is an intense desire to be, do, achieve, or enjoy something.

Change agents must commit to personal change before they become agents of change. This is unsettling at first for GISAs. We can grow into our purpose, but the catalyst for growth must be initiated before the assignment journey begins, otherwise jealousy takes root as we compare ourselves to others. Focus on you because nobody can be a better you than you.

My life's purpose is to help people reach their full potential. Is this assignment unique? Of course not. But my physical and spiritual DNA, upbringing, skills, passions, mindset, humor, and thought processes are unique to me, and my purpose-guided fingerprints can't be photocopied. Neither can yours.

Provision is often found in purpose. To accomplish life's purpose without letting life's distractions ensnare you, pay attention to the financial challenges you may encounter, character development, and contentment of circumstances. Be a person of principle and don't just talk about it. To be content, however, doesn't mean to settle for mediocrity, a mindset of indifference that neglects the

Breaches in character can be life-assignment killers.

fulfillment of one's personal, professional, educational, or financial potential. So many people hide under the status quo umbrella as they embark on their life's purpose. They become frustrated or give up when financial resources are not sufficient to cover monthly bills.

Let me leave you with this: The purpose of life is the Creator's gift to you. Life's purpose is your gift back to the Creator.

Preordained from Birth

Children in mega-affluent families are destined to be successful and carry out the duties of their life assignment. They are groomed for a life of purpose at a very early age, the result of a nurturing and expectation-centric environment. This is the difference maker.

From the time they can remember, children see a model of excellence through the behavior of their family, friends, and others within this aristocratic life and social circle. Elite private schools and country clubs are the norm, while money is never a problem. This lifestyle is expensive, but in GAPAs' minds, the alternative is even more costly—a heritage disrupted. They cannot afford to let this happen with so much on the line.

Children born into generational wealth are on a different track in life than their poor and middle-class peers. Their job is to maintain the legacy already in place. Creating a legacy is a lot different and harder than maintaining one.

Danny Levitt, a longtime friend and wealth management advisor with the Merrill Lynch affiliated Reichek Gladstein Group, is looking out the window in his office. He grapples with the economic dichotomy he can physically see from that window, especially considering the wealth-advisory group manages nearly $2 billion of assets for some of Houston's richest families.

His view from one of the top floors of the Lyondell Basell building provides Danny with a unique perspective. He can contrast two different worlds with a slight turn of his head, zeroing-in on a side-by-side comparison of abject poverty and mega wealth. Unlike the rolling hills topography in the Midwest, it's easy for Danny to point out different neighborhoods in Houston that are miles apart in life assignments, life experiences, and life expectancies. The third, fourth, and fifth wards comprise a community largely suffering from economic distress and never-ending despair. He then directs my attention to River Oaks, a suburb with multimillionaires and billionaires who follow a well-crafted script of legacy continuity.

The wealthy expect their life track to go a certain way, mostly good. The poor also expect life to go a certain way, mostly bad. Children from the poorer wards will travel a completely different path than those from River Oaks. However, what children from each community will undoubtedly share is the critical role their Sociopsychonomic filter will play in fulfilling or neglecting their life's purpose.

A TALE OF TWO WORLDS

An aerial view of the third, fourth, and fifth wards in Houston is not much different than any other economically distressed community in a major, metropolitan American city. Employment opportunities yield minimum-wage paychecks and jobs with few to no benefits. Housing accommodations in close quarters with limited space can lead to conflicts with neighbors. Cars are parked bumper to bumper in the streets since driveways may not exist to accommodate them. Fast food restaurants offer cheap and unhealthy alternatives to time-consuming, home-prepared meals. Convenient stores sell lottery tickets and high-margin items ripe for impulse buying. A consistently high and leery police presence frightens area residents, but truth be told, they are more fearful—and too afraid to admit it—of those on the inside, hell-bent on creating mayhem in the lives of decent folk who can't escape the web of despair.

These three wards offer very little foot traffic for area businesses and home values generally fall or remain flat. Crime seems a permanent fixture of life here, although hopelessness is perhaps just as (if not more) troubling. This is part of inner-city poverty, a punishing predicament in which to live.

Less than five miles from Wards 3, 4, and 5 sits River Oaks, a tight-knit community offering picturesque views of generational and situational wealth. The communities are close in proximity but galaxies apart in terms of amenities and opportunities. River Oaks boasts extravagant mansions with well-manicured lawns and domestic workers. Homes with less than 10,000 square feet are considered small. Tall walls and trees shield homeowners from gawkers hoping to get a peek at their stately residences. Huge gates and security guards provide additional protection. The police drive by in perfectly timed sequences, smiling and waving as they assure residents that their taxpayer dollars are being well spent. The subliminal message communicated by law enforcement: "We will protect the life affluence provides you."

It's the kind of place that if you must ask about pricing, then you don't belong in this well-connected part of Houston. "You either have what it takes to live here, or you don't," Danny says.

These two Houston communities show just how wide the wealth and opportunity gaps are in America, which aren't relegated to cities alone but also in rural areas. How the different classes view their life's purpose, driven largely by each class's representative mindset, speaks volumes about how they act on the day-to-day aspects of it. A baseball analogy demonstrates how each class collectively views their life's purpose.

The poor will step up to the plate with their eyes closed. If they feel lucky, they swing for the fences. They grope their way toward a life assignment, even if it's the wrong one. A few might smash one out of the park, but many will strike out, as do most home run hitters.

Middle-class crusaders will advance their life's purpose by grinding out bunts, squeeze plays, and sacrifice flies for the good of the team. It's a slow and steady slog that won't bring the same immediate elation a home run elicits.

The generationally wealthy start on third base, miraculously. Some have convinced themselves that they got there because of their own talent. Reaching home is a foregone conclusion with little worries of interruption by a pickoff or force out at third. The rules that apply to the poor and middle-class base runners are suspended for them. It's a run GAPAs usually score with ease.

> "The mega wealthy work hard but don't see life as a daily grind. They don't get to retirement and feel like they're going to fall over and collapse from exhaustion. They often go through life on a very comfortable cloud."
>
> **–Danny Levitt**
> Wealth Management Advisor

Danny, a diehard Houston Rockets fan, makes a brilliant observation along this line. He says, "A super wealthy teenager has sat courtside with his feet touching the floor of Houston Rockets games since the day he was in diapers. At the opposite end of the economic spectrum is a teenager from the Third Ward who lives in the shadow of the arena. Unlike the rich teenager, he has never been inside the Toyota Center to watch a live game. As luck would have it, though, he is selected to attend a Rockets game with several of his classmates. Their seats are in the nosebleed section of the arena. He is so happy to be there, and must pay careful attention to see the action on the court since he's so far away." Danny continues, "The teenager from the Third Ward can't believe he is in attendance to watch his favorite team. He looks down and notices the wealthy teenager sitting courtside, standing up and cheering wildly for the Rockets. He wants to sit courtside one day and slap high fives with his favorite players, too. That possibility exists, but the margin for error in his life is slim.

"Think about what this means. The super-rich kid has access to a life of opulence. His success track—a high-percentage shot—is basically a slam dunk. The super-poor kid has to shoot the ball from the three-point line under duress to escape his world of poverty. He can make it, but it's a low-percentage shot given the background noise and distractions he'll face in the arena of his challenging life. If he doesn't concentrate and hold his follow through—stay committed to the goal no matter what—the poor kid will miss his only shot to get out. That, my friend, is a lot of pressure."

9

FAMILY PLANNING

*The childbearing age range when a female
typically has her first and last child is 15 years*

15 to 30 Childbearing Age Range

Females living in poverty typically bear children between the ages of 15 and 30, or when their financial situation is most in flux. It is not unusual for an impoverished mother to give birth several times before she turns 21. The vicious cycle repeats as her children also become young parents ill-equipped to handle the responsibility. No education. No job security. No mindset change to see beyond their front door. Outside of social agencies and faith-based organizations, these young mothers and fathers often have very little support to prevent future pregnancies from happening.

There is a wide variety of reasons young mothers living in poverty offer for becoming pregnant. Some include that she and the young father got caught up in the heat of the moment; she believes a baby will keep the couple together; she's following in her mother's footsteps; and she'll access support from government and charitable sources should the father skip out.

The transient nature of poverty's residents makes it quite problematic because emotions often dictate actions, interactions, and reactions. For instance, if it feels right, pursue the relationship even though the suitor has other children that he doesn't support. But despite the warning signs, into his arms she goes, the casualty of another child born out of wedlock and a heartbroken young lady to boot. The father is skilled at faux orientation and manipulates feelings to meet his immediate desires, giving very little or no thought to the damage his actions create. The young mother also is complicit because she longs for love and thinks the relationship will fill the void in her spirit. It doesn't.

> "These young ladies don't move away from an unintended pregnancy; sometimes they even seek it."
>
> **–Dr. Augustus Parker**
> Infant Mortality Expert

There are far-reaching, residual effects for women who live in poverty and start having kids. On the front-end, mothers cope the best they can to care for their children with little assistance or positive influence from the fathers. At the back-end, taxpayers foot the bill for anti-poverty government programs while many parents abdicate their responsibility in a child's educational development to anyone but themselves. Disinterested students are the result, with blame laid at the feet of educators, though they often have their hands tied and struggle just to do their jobs. The young parents are repeating a dysfunction they likely experienced in their families for generations.

Exposed to such conditions, it is no surprise that such influencing factors contribute to infant mortality rates. Ohio is one of the worst in the country, ranking 46 out of the 50 states. Dr. Parker is not only a mentor of mine, but he also has extensive knowledge on the causality of infant mortality. He served as the senior medical director in the state for Molina Healthcare and on the boards for Columbus Board of Health, Ohio Better Birth Outcomes, and Infant Mortality for the State of Ohio. His insights follow:

"Nationwide, seven out of 1,000 births end in death. For African-Americans, the number of infant mortalities per 1,000 live births is roughly two times higher than the national average. Why is this? In the medical community, we use to think the disparity was attributable to access to healthcare. However, we found that social determinants, including poverty, lack of education, food deserts, lack of employment, lack of opportunities, and even racism explain the discrepancy. High-risk zip codes in inner-city communities have the highest rates of infant mortality. It's not surprising that these are the same areas where redlining, predatory lending, and foreclosures have been rampant through the years. We don't know to what degree, but a lifetime of racism, or the covert motives behind it, can certainly impact the development of a fetus."

Further, Dr. Parker shares an alarming forecast he says will be even more catastrophic for society. "The real scourge of the next two decades will be drug-addicted women and the babies born to them. This will be unbelievable as our young people succumb to an out-of-control drug problem. It's already bad, but it gets a whole lot worse," he says.

If Dr. Parker is proven correct, our public schools, traditional and charter, are ill-prepared to handle the impact poverty will play in the number of teen pregnancies as well as the number of children born to drug-addicted mothers. We have not given the educational community sufficient resources to deal with these complex problems. Educators aren't trained for most of these tasks, but by default, they must be social workers, crisis counselors, drug addiction intervention specialists, healthcare advocates, mentors, and role models.

REALITY DAZE OR REALITY DAYS?

Adjacent to the neighborhood where I grew up sits Franklinton. The demographics are a mix of Appalachian whites and inner-city blacks whose experiences with poverty are similar. Most parents think that tomorrow won't be any better than today for them or their kids. Some parents are more optimistic and pray their children get a chance to secure a substantive life. At one time, Franklinton had the highest incidence of teen pregnancies in Central Ohio. The reasons are multifaceted and have been highlighted throughout the book, but some of the likely causes are worth noting again: fatalism, academic neglect, parental abandonment, lack of purpose, cognitive dissonance, and the perpetuation of poverty, to name a few.

Teen pregnancies disproportionately impact poorer communities and lead some observers to conclude economic disparities among social classes are the underlying issue. Myopically, this would be true, but disparities are not confined to economics solely. They can be racial, or prejudice directed at the poor; emotional, or self-inflicted personal hang-ups; relational, or network limitations beyond the poor's core social circle; physiological, or poverty's impact on the body; and psychological, or poverty's impact on the brain, planning and decision-making in particular.

Olga Khazan, a staff writer with *The Atlantic*, wrote in 2014: "It's harder to plan when you're poor. People without college degrees tend to be poorer, and poverty has been shown to tax the brain's capacity for rational decision-making." She adds that poor "Americans tend to rotate in and out of cohabiting relationships as the years wear on. They have children with multiple different partners, creating complex webs of child obligations, stepparents, and half-siblings."[16]

To effectuate change in behavior, it's imperative children are exposed to a frame of reference far different than what they currently know. The sensory-driven experience must be fun and intellectually stimulating, with real-world interactions, illustrations, and consequences to keep them engaged. This is how to change a mindset, with appropriate behaviors following.

> "The poor, especially young mothers, are so many steps behind the money game. How do we help them move beyond a temporary mindset?"
>
> **–Toshia Safford, President and CEO**
> The Center for Healthy Families

My wife Monya believes our Reality Days game has helped dozens of teens, boys and girls, think twice about parenthood. Reality Days is an interactive simulation that mimics real-world decision-making. She says, "Poorer students will say, 'I'm not having babies; they're too expensive.' It's great for young ladies to go through this game because they get a firsthand glimpse on the work and costs involved in taking care of kids. Some, who already were teenage moms, said they would forego having another child until they were more financially and personally stable. Our Reality Days game forces poor kids to think about the consequences of bringing a child into this world without a plan."

Reality Days teaches young participants much-needed career navigational skills (parietal lobe), visuospatial skills (occipital lobe), internal dialogue skills (temporal lobe), and money management skills (frontal lobe). They are getting a preview of how difficult life might turn out for those lacking sufficient educational and financial skills. Here are a few of the game's lessons we impart:

> Participants gain a clearer understanding of the intersection between education, employment prospects, quality of life, lifetime earnings, network affiliations, and financial opportunities. They must evaluate the positive effect of abstinence, foregoing wants to take care of needs, as financial resources dwindle after each household expense. We get them to understand, for instance, that babysitting arrangements can't easily be pushed onto a grandmother, family member, or neighbor just because they've discovered childcare is expensive. We place poor students in situations where they make adult-oriented decisions. I often quote this statistic, which normally leaves them looking at me in stunned disbelief: Parents on average will spend $150,000 to $350,000 raising a child from birth to age 17, and the figure doesn't include the cost of college.

This game is ideal for children from middle-class and affluent backgrounds, too. They learn the same necessary skills as poor children do, and they get introduced to *empathy assimilation,* or being able to relate to the working poor. Some participants are given random occupations with low-paying jobs, limited skill-sets, and an educational achievement ceiling that includes a high school diploma or GED.

Toshia Safford, president and CEO for The Center for Healthy Families, assists pregnant and parenting teens in Central Ohio with the "resources to develop healthy, stable, and productive families," as its website says, and financial life skills are critical to the organization's holistic approach.

"We must look at the social and emotional side of poverty to help people escape the traps," she says. "In poverty, you're not taught what it means to have a checking account and establish a relationship with a financial institution. You may not know what a credit score is, let alone how to build a strong credit profile. But you do know how to make yourself feel better through frivolous consumption. Unfortunately, this could lead to financial chaos."

Toshia highlights a glaring mistake outsiders make in trying to understand teen pregnancy by attributing it to impulse-control issues. Having children at a very young age is symptomatic of family dysfunction, and sometimes, the wounds never heal.

"Imagine, a white teenage girl from Appalachian poverty, 15-years-old and living with her 19-year-old boyfriend and his family. There is more here than just a teen pregnancy issue. Why is this family allowing this relationship to happen?" she asks. "We need to back up and address why this young girl isn't at home with her family. Well, mom is in jail and dad's a truck driver. She stays with grandma, but is molested by a family member. The perpetrator goes to jail. He gets out and returns back to grandma's house. The young girl was abused and neglected in an unsafe, unstable environment. So, the teenage girl runs to safety, into the arms of a 19-year-old male who caught her at a vulnerable moment, never questioning the legality of this relationship. How does this happen? This situation is more common than you think."

"I WON'T LET YOU GO!"

My favorite movies are ones that depict human triumph in the face of insurmountable odds. The list includes films such as *Pursuit of Happyness*, *Life of a King*, *Finding Forrester*, *Coach Carter*, *Antwone Fisher*, *The Great Debaters*, *Akeelah and the Bee*, *Men of Honor*, and *The Blind Side*. I saw parts of my life story in each of these inspirational movies. In your life's movie, you must assume a completely different role and forget the script others write and believe applies to everyone living in economic distress or anchored by generational poverty.

Actors ad lib lines all the time, so be prepared to offend some cast members and screenwriters—family and friends—along the way when you choose to go off-script. They will view your life as attached to the same prophecy written for the poor regardless of how far you rise, and they won't let you forget it.

You'd think a neighborhood might celebrate an ambitious young mother from generational poverty who has graduated from high school and is pursing a college degree. Think again.

Poverty's vortex keeps others from leaving the ghetto, and few people who escape its clutches feel comfortable enough to shed light on what I label a last ditch effort to prevent someone's escape from the plantation of financial misery. Seeking a better life can be misconstrued as a premeditated, emotional assault by those left behind. They also misinterpret the progress of someone close to them as an indictment on their inability to achieve personal growth.

Economic distress creates many unwarranted fears and insecurities. You justify and juxtapose them to fit your narrative: Life has dealt you a bad hand.

You may recall my discussion of functional economically distressed Americans, or FEDAs, in the "Pre-Game" section of the book. They aren't technically poor, and, in fact, some are quite wealthy. But they keep a close association with financial hardship as a measure to maintain or regain an affinity connection with their former way of life. This connection is so strong to their community, their clique, or their cause—keepin' it real—that they are torn between staying or leaving. An abrupt or gradual departure from poverty won't go unnoticed either. You can't just walk away without at least one critical objection, sometimes from a close friend or revered family member.

"Young ladies," Toshia says, "without being disrespectful but forthright, have to be a bit selfish and tell their mothers, 'Mom, I'm going to finish high school and go to college. I love you, but I'm going to leave the projects. I have enough respect for myself that I can't stay here in this space with you and suffer. I'm sorry, but you don't see the knowledge and skill-set that I now have to move forward.'"

Those left behind may resent those who move forward. Conversely, those who press forward to achieve a better life might voice resentment toward those living on the government dole.

Saddled with guilt, FEDAs keep their kindred spirit at the street level to rebut criticism and silence those who label them a sellout. This word, *sellout*, has paralyzed more people in poverty than you can imagine. In their minds, it's okay to fantasize about a better life, but don't dare obtain it. If you do, you'll be shunned or vilified as a showoff, guilty of nothing but 'hood abandonment. Toshia and her staff coach and motivate young mothers to keep their eyes on the ultimate prize, to achieve something far better in the face of hostile support on the home front.

"Someone has to have the courage to leave and then go back and retrieve the others," she says. "Detractors have a very real hold on those who want to get out! They feel betrayed in the worst way. A sense of loss engulfs them, which they assume will be permanent. In psychology, this term is called *learned helplessness*."

Toshia, a woman who has worked in the trenches for a long time, says a change in thinking is the best way to reverse the helplessness. "It takes that one person to see things a little differently and convince another person to her way of thinking. This is how the cycle of generational poverty is broken. Learn and then apply the knowledge through skill-building, which speaks to one's value system. We can put the books and skills and structure in front of the poor, but the onus inevitably rests in what they want to do with their life. Something on the inside must drive them to achieve something on the outside. Change must be valued before it is administered." Amen sister.

20 to 35 Childbearing Age Range

The traditional middle-class couple typically has children when their financial situation is better, when they have job security and benefits, and when the relationship appears on solid footing. I'm no mind reader, but it is what I've heard from dozens of middle-class couples I have spoken with about family planning. A stable financial situation is enough for a couple to plan on having a child, which eventually jump starts the next leg in the family's middle-class journey that we call parenthood. Childrearing can be stressful, but the joys of parenthood make it manageable, memorable, and of course, malleable when a child's sad, puppy-dog eyes meet with yours.

Children provide middle-class parents with a nostalgia they associate with moments in their own lives from childhood memories to righting some past wrong to ruing about missed opportunities. More than any other social class perhaps, GISAs tend to have inflated opinions on how academically astute and athletically or musically gifted their children really are. It seems today's parents who label themselves middle class will spare no expense to cultivate their college-scholarship prodigies. Unfortunately, very few kids are full-scholarship material.

SOCIOPSYCHONOMIC FILTER
Obviously, there are pros and cons to weigh prior to the birth of a child, regardless of one's age or social status.

GISAs, on average, own a house in a decent neighborhood. In two-income households, ownership of two automobiles would be the standard. Most middle-class children enjoy a comfortable lifestyle where all needs are usually met. GISA parents want their children to be well-rounded, grounded, respectful, hardworking, compassionate, compliant, and kind-hearted in school while also engaged in extracurricular activities. These kids are such a joy to teach because the foundation in which to build upon is so strong. This makes my job so much easier.

IT'S ALL ABOUT THE KIDS

Family is such a sacred bond to the middle class. The entrenched poor and generationally wealthy care deeply about family, too, but the connection middle-class parents have with their children is special. I have a suspicion it might have something to do with their sacrificial nature. Let's explore a few presuppositions about each social class's expression of love for children.

For GEDAs, love for children is often expressed through emotions—fear, anger, sadness, disgust, surprise, and happiness. The poor are financially pressed to meet their children's needs, which creates enormous stress and unfair economic tradeoffs. Young parents receiving welfare or who have low-paying jobs feel paralyzed and trapped to stay the course. Personal growth is stunted and they remain stuck in neutral, even as their children get older.

> Most middle-class children enjoy a comfortable lifestyle where all needs are usually met.

GAPA parents and children express love through an expectation-centric mandate their legacy demands, an obligatory duty they are expected to keep. This agreement is not based on feelings but on an implicit oath or honor system. The lifestyle of generational affluence is a two-way, transactional re-lationship between parents and children. The super wealthy are not pressed financially, so unlike the poor, no economic tradeoffs or monetary stress inter-feres with caring for their children.

GISAs demonstrate love by making enormous time and financial sacrifices for their children, relinquishing their own peace of mind, marital harmony, social life, work routine, and retirement needs for them. The hectic schedules. The tutors and private lessons. Fuel to transport kids to and from activities. The groceries. The vacations and summer camps. The birthday parties and Christmas gifts. The co-signing on college loans.

These all take money, and though GISA parents may tell their kids finances are tight, miraculously, money appears in the nick of time to give children what they've grown accustomed to enjoying—a middle-class lifestyle that is becoming increasingly challenging for parents to maintain, although they'll continue trying. That's how sacrifical love is expressed.

30 to 45 Childbearing Age Range

For the wealthy, childbirth is more than a day to bring a precious life into the world. A pregnancy is not an accident, the result of an emotional moment without the consideration of attached consequences. No, it is a meticulously planned event to continue a legacy. It's always about the heritage script, the game plan they follow out of reverence for parents, grandparents, and their lineal descendants to have children at the appropriate time.

It's true that fertility rates or peak ovulation periods are higher for women in their 20s than in their 30s. This may explain why unplanned births occur more frequently in poverty. It's rare to find generationally affluent parents who are younger than 30. GAPA spouses fully understand that as a woman ages, her chances of conceiving decrease precipitously after 35. At that time, infertility treatments are likely to be sought and if pregnancy challenges occur. This scenario will not catch them off guard.

The mega wealthy are masters at the waiting (and weighing) game. To move too early on anything—a business deal, marriage, career change, or the birth of a child—could damage their personal and family brand. An integral part of proactive planning, they take great measures to avoid potential problems that may not surface for years. That's why legacy continuation, the birth of a child, is carefully planned in conjunction with the heritage script.

GAPA children in their mid-to-late 20s have a pretty good idea who and when they will marry, with their parents blessings of course, though the wedding is not likely to take place until the kids turn 30.

Thirty is an important age marker in some cultures. In Judaism, this milestone signifies that one, a male usually, is ready to embark on a mission to seek and serve God. It signifies that a person is ready for true wisdom in fulfilling a life assignment. For the generationally wealthy who are not Jewish, this age milestone also seems to be an integral part of their family planning playbook. GAPA offspring are now ready for parenthood, a rite of passage to continue their family heritage.

Regardless of the social class, though, children will usually mimic the same customs, habits, and traditions they witnessed growing up. It's true: The apple doesn't usually fall too far from the tree.

The circle of marital bliss for super wealthy children has a narrow diameter, which is by design to eliminate tainting their carefully selected gene pool. Make no mistake about it.

The generationally affluent are huge proponents of furthering a physical and financial genetic blueprint that creates a chasm between them and every other social class subset. So while a GAPA teenager may think a high school athlete she saw at the local mall or on social media is cute, that's as far as the admiration will go. If he comes from a household outside of generational wealth, even if he makes it to the professional ranks of his chosen sport, he can't choose her and she ovbviously can't choose him. The gulf is too wide for them to make a meaningful connection, and they must admire each other from afar only. Legacy fires are put out before a single spark is lit.

"WE CAN'T ALLOW THAT TO EVER HAPPEN!"

The script is already written in generational affluence. Danny Levitt, a financial advisor to dozens of affluent families, says, "If a mega-wealthy teenager has a child before she's married, this is seen as taboo. This is not allowed. Her parents are just not going to let this happen. No way."

The expectations for a GAPA child are ingrained at an early age, and the progression goes like this: Go to this college. Get this type of degree. Work for this firm in this particular industry for this amount of time. Marry this type of person from this family after the other tasks have been completed. By the way, here's a signet ring that binds you to keep this legacy oath.

Children are brought into the world once the first part of the script goes according to plan, which the GAPA legacy follows without fail, even as it pertains to the birth of the next child in their carefully crafted ancestral line. There are no unexpected childbirths in generational wealth.

Some people living in economic distress are astonished by couples who choose to have children after the age of 30. The poor often don't think in terms of career aspirations, financial stability, childcare arrangements, maturation development, or emotional readiness when bringing a child into the world— the checklist items for GAPAs. These factors take time, energy, and effort to complete. GEDAs feel part of their lives would be lost by waiting to have children beyond age 30.

The generationally wealthy, meanwhile, take the opposite view. Here's what I mean.

Foundational skills are developed during formative years—critical thinking and personality expression, interpersonal and intrapersonal communication abilities, relational and social development, and career forecasting. Effective parenting skills cannot begin until foundational skills are set and the brain crosses a certain maturity threshold. Waiting to have children later in life (but not too late)—as fully functioning adults—can be beneficial to parents, their offspring, and society at large.

> "Kids from mega-wealthy families can't make their parents grandparents in their 40s. You are not going to go to high school pregnant. Not in the world they operate in."
>
> **–Danny Levitt**
> Wealth Management Advisor

A WAITING GAME PLAYED BY OTHER SOCIAL CLASS SUBSETS, TOO

Look around the soccer field on a Saturday afternoon in an affluent part of town and you'll see plenty of fathers with gray hair cheering for their children. Some observers might assume the dads are the granddads by their appearance. Now contrast this with an impoverished community on the other side of town. A father watching his son play little league football in the inner city will likely not have any gray hair in his beard. In many cases, the father from the poor community will be younger than 30, while the affluent fathers will likely be well in their 40s and early 50s.

For many women, a ticking biological clock isn't the litmus test for bearing a child. They just weren't ready earlier to make the sacrifice professionally, personally, emotionally, or financially. Many women, and not just those from mega-affluent backgrounds, wait until their careers and life experiences reach a certain level before starting a family.

The intentionality of family planning at a later age can have a noticeable financial benefit, writes Ellie Kincaid in the September 2015 issue of *Business Insider:* "For women between ages 40-45 with professional degrees and full-time jobs, those who gave birth to their first child at age 35 made more than $50,000 more per year than women who had their first child at 20, on average. Even waiting to start a family just five more years, at 35 instead of 30, made a difference of $16,000 per year, on average."[17]

Having a child shouldn't be based on economics solely. Financial stability is an important consideration, but so too is emotional stability.

We know that poor young mothers must often care for their kids on a limited income, and in many instances, without help from the fathers. That is not an easy job and my heart breaks for them, because I remember my mom's frustrations seeping out as she kept track and cared for her four kids. On numerous occasions, I've watched impoverished mothers berate or punish their children in public for what appeared to be minor offenses.

I could not imagine becoming a father as a teenager or even as a young adult. Heck, I wasn't ready for the rigors of fatherhood even after graduating college and starting a pro basketball career that provided me financial stability. Still reeling from a dysfunctional childhood less than a decade earlier, it would have been a disaster. Showering a child with gifts can't replace the genuine love and affirmation that an involved and emotionally stable father provides. I understand divorce, and parents who quibble about child-sharing arrangements, but children need and deserve involved mothers and fathers. My mom did the best she could, but the other half of my DNA shortchanged me. In some ways, I'm still paying for the loss.

FINANCIAL MANAGEMENT AND WELLNESS

CHAPTER

10

FINANCIAL COACHING BUY-IN

The thematic message(s) or method of delivery that best suits a social class to increase the likelihood of contemplating and implementing information to achieve or maintain economic success

Personality Driven

"Maestro Factor"

You're drenched in sweat, emotional capital exhausted from keeping the poor engaged throughout your hour-long presentation. You used humor, allegories, hand gestures, life experiences and challenging moments, entertainment, charisma, cadence, and stage presence to make a heartfelt connection with your audience. They fed off your antics and artistry, a sensory and visually stimulating performance that kept their attention spans high and discomfort levels low. You left an indelible impression in their minds. They will never forget your timely message. You made it out of economic misery; they can, too.

Outward appeal to make an inward connection is the language of poverty. It must be authentic and believable, and animated if necessary. This connection does come with a pre-set time limit, though. If it's not made within the first few minutes, credibility in your message, regardless of the content, will be lost. You'll know it because boredom will be demonstrated as they yawn, stretch, and fidget in their seats to fight through your presentation. You will be viewed by GEDAs as a performer who didn't deliver when the lights came on, a game show contestant ready to be gonged and escorted off stage. Your nerves got the best of you, or perhaps you simply weren't prepared for the task at hand. You weren't ready for prime time, at least not on this occasion. If you're passionate about making a difference in the lives of the poor, you'll get another chance.

> Just because a connection is made with the poor, this doesn't guarantee they will move toward or away from a given behavior.

The raw emotion and intensity to provide the poor with a memorable experience can drain you while it uplifts them. It's worth it, even if only one person is touched.

I have done hundreds of presentations for disadvantaged communities over the past two decades. Every time I made it about a number—how many were in attendance—I left heartbroken, ready to throw in the towel and tell God, "Please use someone else for my life assignment. I've had enough."

Much of the disappointment wasn't egocentric, but related to the effort and energy it took to prepare. This preparation is akin to a coach getting ready to play a big game. The team is pumped. Their adrenaline is so high that the coach literally has to calm them down. A game plan exists, but latitude is given to make tactical adjustments. Underserved populations need an extension of grace when working with them because things rarely go as planned.

The game plan to connect with impoverished communities includes the *sensory* (or maestro) *connection*, the *participatory* (or inclusion) *connection*, and the *transitory* (or movement) *connection*. For the most part, these are based on the magnetism and likability of the presenter.

THE MAESTRO CONNECTION: LET IT FLOW

The maestro factor is about making a rhythmic, sensory connection with GEDAs. They have to feel your message. Presenters will be judged on their wardrobe, emotionalism, and harmonic command of the English language. This is required to solidify educational or financial coaching buy-in from underserved communities.

I'm always very cognizant of my attire when speaking to kids from the inner city. They stare me up and down to see if my style is cool (dress-down casual), techie (business casual), or stuffy (business formal). Obviously, the setting will dictate my wardrobe selection. My attire for an awards ceremony will be different than an impromptu classroom visit. It's superficial, but the "look test" is a real phenomenon in poverty.

A suit and tie or preppie look can send mixed signals until they hear my story. I see them lean in when the connection is made, that I truly do understand (and have made it through) the financial and psychological torment of generational poverty. I'm quick to point out, "Don't let these fancy clothes fool you. I'm straight ghetto." My wife cringes when I admit this.

An emotional connection is an unfiltered, unscripted, and sometimes unsophisticated message. Passion, pain, and pace must be woven into it. The deeper one goes, the more interested GEDAs become in a speaker who can't contain a transparent story, even if it's embarrassing or intensely sad.

The connection may elicit laughter from some, although the intended emotion is one of sadness. Some will employ the tactic to deflect attention from their own pain, while others will reflect on a difficult situation with a similar storyline and emotional profile. Whatever their response, the message should stay true and get delivered without a hint of phoniness. Audiences have a keen sense of smell for fake people. Poverty buzz words can't replace an authentic poverty experience.

So, what if you didn't grow up disadvantaged but want to assist the poor? They'll be skeptical at first, but tell them, without feeling guilty, that this life wasn't your reality. Don't beat around the bush. Honesty is always appreciated from outsiders looking to get in.

It'll take time perhaps for you to craft a compelling message that resonates with GEDAs, and trust won't materialize overnight, either. Rest assured, though, your good heart will go a long way to soften or mend theirs. Don't be alarmed by their facade of toughness. Poverty hurts so much, no matter the gender.

THE INCLUSION CONNECTION: LET THEM JOIN

Generational poverty is very participatory. Dialogue at home, work, or school is viewed from an open microphone mentality. You participate in a conversation based on feelings and opportunities to speak, not an orderly system of conversational etiquette. The inclinations to chime in should turn off when leaving an informal setting. Place the chatter switch on mute when going into a more structured setting with clearly defined rules and standards of conduct.

Whether it's initiated or not, poor children are likely to interject, interact, or intercept the speaker, or some aspect of the presentation. Even if they're given specific instructions to raise their hands before blurting out a thought, some take the liberty anyway to satisfy a spontaneous urge. Here are a few participatory examples that stand out in my mind when presenting to impoverished communities:

Interjection Connection

A young boy named Michael catches my eye. I hadn't completed my thought yet, but he can't wait to share his comment. He's waving his hand frantically. I signal to him that it won't be long before I give him the floor. He shouts out, "Mr. Fundy, my mom grew up in the same housing projects as you. She said it was rough because …"

He wants to continue his comment, but I cut him off because he was getting ready to share a private comment in a public forum that might have led to his peers ridiculing or humiliating him. Protecting children from themselves is a necessity when the audience consists primarily of other poor students.

Interjecting with a speaker lets students, particularly those from impoverished backgrounds, drive part of the experience. Movement or navigating through any activity in which they feel in control of is extremely beneficial for their buy-in and retention of the information shared. Stay in control, but give them latitude to express themselves.

Interaction Connection

Humor is a big part of my presentation. It often develops organically without much prompting since I'm not quite certain what will make an audience laugh. No stand-up comedy routine is needed. Growing up in poverty is a good enough story.

Two participants in our workshop were laughing about decisions made in a financial game, totally oblivious that their conversation was being heard by the rest of class. One of them joked, "I ain't paying for no babysitter. My grandma will watch my kids while I'm at work." The other kid nodded his head in agreement and added, "Now that's what I'm talking about."

Laughter is critically important when stuck in a perpetual, economic rut. You don't have money, but you do have plenty of laugh capital to make light of a dismal situation, from telling stories about borrowing a cup of sugar or a few slices of bread from neighbors to adding water to an empty ketchup bottle, praying that you can get one more serving out of it. Humorous (and painful) memories can be retrieved instantly.

Interception Connection

This last example can be good or bad depending on the situation. I remember one child took part of what I said and added his special touch to it. He shared this amazing truth: "I get it now Mr. Fundy. The goal isn't a degree; it's what the degree stands for, someone who can finish what he starts." This young man was spot on correct, because we, the educational community, push kids to graduate but we don't communicate nearly enough that the real benefit is the journey. Yes, this is an abstract concept, but it needs to be repeated over and over to poor students, many of whom aren't fond of conceptual thinking.

The interception connection also has a troubling side. Some participants want to interfere with your presentation in spite of your goodwill gesture to help them. For some strange reason, they feel indicted or indifferent before even one word is spoken. They will sabotage your presentation if given the opportunity, convincing others to join them in tuning you out. Their disinterest is palpable, a toxic gas that will contaminate anyone who breathes its vapors. Of course, you can't take a chance on your message getting diluted. They will get to the others before you do. If it comes to removing them from the presentation, so be it, especially if they are admired by peers. Don't be emotional about it; be intentional.

In a respectable manner, I politely asked a young man during a presentation to leave the room. He didn't object and left quietly. He didn't want to be there, so why make the entire group suffer from receiving a good message because of this one person?

Getting dismissed from a classroom or sport's team can be the catalyst for a person to see the error in his ways. I speak from experience. I got kicked off my high school basketball team for being disrespectful to our head coach, Chuck Kemper, in front of my teammates. What did it cost me? A likely state player of the year award and a spot in the McDonald's All-American Game as a senior, and of course, bad publicity on a local and national level. What did

I gain? A newfound appreciation to respect elders—take the high road, even if a gripe is legitimate.

THE MOVEMENT CONNECTION: BE ACCESSIBLE

Physical movement is visually stimulating, a key facet when presenting to GEDAs. When you feel trapped in an environment of despair, motion is welcomed. In affluence, people are not constrained and move seamlessly through their world of opulence. Navigational aptitude is not limited by money, transportation, or imagination. Physical and mental movement is needed to keep poor students locked in to hope—life offers boundless opportunities.

GAPAs may interpret too much movement by a speaker as intentionally distracting, a measure to divert attention from the message. It may be seen as a cover-up to hide behind a speech devoid of substance. (Could this explain why Tedx Talks, a relatively new forum catering to local audiences with an affinity for intellectual topics, requires speakers to stay inside a small red circle? As a past Tedx speaker, this was difficult for me initially. The title of my first Tedx Talks was "The Emotional World of Poverty: An Inside Look.")

Keeping a child's attention span is hard enough in our instant gratification society. Now, it is doubly challenging to inspire children from economic distress whose bodies may lack adequate sleep and proper nutrition. Presenters must step up their game to keep poor students engaged. The process is exhausting, but worth it.

The presenter may do so by constantly moving among them, as if asking the students to take a journey with him and persuading them to follow. This idea of movement can reinforce important points crucial to navigating a difficult landscape and provide a roadmap to avoid dead ends where people inevitably get hurt or killed for being in the wrong place at the wrong time with the wrong friends.

Poverty is a construction zone; those who are fortunate enough to make it out have the battle scars to prove it.

The Mr. Fundy's Math Basketball Jam is an interactive presentation to help students make a connection between this subject and the game I love. To date, more than 10,000 students in Ohio and California have participated in this campaign.

Math is fun and shouldn't be feared. Without a solid foundation of math skills, poor kids will fall farther behind their middle-class and affluent peers in school and the race to educational success. Further, a lack of math skills will impact their future economic livelihood as well. Basic math skills are needed to manage money, understand the pros and cons of economic decisions, and assist young children with their homework. In short, math is critical to escaping the poverty trap.

Sports fans marvel at the exploits of their favorite pro athletes, who can make NBA three-pointers 30 feet from the basket with ease as the shot clock winds down, or catch passes from an NFL quarterback while running perfectly timed routes under duress. How are they able to do this? Math. A long-distance shot must have the perfect arc and rotation to go in. A wide receiver must run a certain distance at a certain speed to catch a football traveling 60-mile-per-hour in the air. In fact, sports and life and finances are all about math—geometry, algebra, and statistics. Those who don't respect or get math are punished accordingly.

What's fascinating is that poorer students predominantly, as I move around the gym demonstrating the connection between math and athletics, will go to great lengths to share hugs and high-fives with me. They do so voluntarily. As noted, physical and emotional touch are an integral part of generational poverty. Without establishing a kindred connection, where life experiences and cultural ties are the common bond, it is very challenging (although not impossible) to reach poor students through an encouraging and timely message. So many kids today are yearning to move toward authentic love and away from their world of excruciating pain.

I love all kids, who truly are gifts from God, and deserve our best regardless of their economic situation. They touch my heart just as much, if not more, than I'm fortunate enough to touch theirs. (For more information on the Mr. Fundy's Math Basketball Jam, please visit www.MathBasketball.org.)

Problem-Solving Driven

"Micro Factor"

Delayed gratification and basic financial planning habits used to be hallmarks of the traditional middle class. In days gone by, GISAs would save religiously. Back then, a 20 percent (or more) down payment on a home was the norm, not the exception. They didn't spend future money to buy things today. Layaway was for suckers. If the cash wasn't in their bank account, then the item in question didn't get bought. Also, it wasn't unusual for GISAs to purchase a car with little to no financing needed. A steady job and a simpler life made things more predictable. How appropriate to describe that timeframe with a back-in-the-day sitcom. Edith and Archie Bunker's (the two main characters in *All in the Family*) hit theme song rings true in our modern world: "Those were the days." Those days are likely not coming back.

Lax lending standards and the proliferation of easy credit in the 1990s and beyond enticed GISAs to live above their means. Many got caught up in the consumerism trap to keep up with the Joneses by spending a lot right now and attempting to pay the huge debt later. Record low interest rates made the debt-financing facade look like a great deal. A crisis not seen since the Great Depression woke them (and the world) up.

Savings levels prior to the Great Recession were negative for many Americans. It's hard to save when you have debt up to your eyeballs. The 2008 economic meltdown did a number on the middle class. They are now trying to get back to who they were: meticulous savers, frantic planners, and optimistic worriers—an oxymoron, I know.

I got mad love for the middle class, but they do frustrate me at times. They dream about financial freedom, but many are afraid of the costs involved to achieve it.

> ### SOCIOPSYCHONOMIC FILTER
> Financial freedom is a goal for the middle class, but the psychological costs involved to achieve it are more than they're willing to pay.

They know job security and Social Security may not be the guarantee they once were. College costs are rising faster than inflation. Many GISAs make too much money for their children to qualify for need-based tuition assistance, Pell Grants for example, which primarily go to students from really, really, really poor families. Full scholarships, academic or athletic, are hard to come by. Super talented or super smart kids are somewhat rare.

Health insurance for a family of four is through the roof. The Affordable Care Act (ACA), also known as Obamacare, has had its challenges in making health insurance more cost effective. It appears to be on life support under this new, no-holds-barred administration. Additional concerns are credit card debt, retirement shortfalls, and the 800-pound gorilla stuck in the corner of the room no one sees: long-term (or elderly) care, which Medicare doesn't cover but Medicaid does. Most GISAs would have to liquidate or draw down assets to near poverty levels, including the likely selling of their house, a cherished possession, to qualify for Medicaid. Homeownership is the holy grail for the traditional middle class. A lot of them would be quite hesitant to move a revered and valuable asset off their balance sheet—their home.

GISAs can't kick the financial planning can down the road any longer. Something must be done right now on their end to avert future disaster. A new (or updated) playbook is needed to get them back in the center of the economic track. It's time to shape up.

If the poor respond to feelings, then the middle class is likely to be moved by words, the more eye-opening the better. Auditory processing occurs in the ears or the temporal lobe region of the brain. Equilibrium, or balance, is handled here, too. Financial distress can wreak havoc on GISAs' vestibular system, economically speaking.

Their playbook is typically focused on a specific strategy, such as getting out of debt, saving more money, or sending a child to college. Very seldom do they ask themselves, "What's needed from a holistic perspective to achieve long-lasting, financial freedom?" If they have the framework of a comprehensive life and financial plan, the difficulty occurs in getting them to implement one, which also requires periodic monitoring and updating.

These do-it-yourselfers retain the responsibility of their plan but don't want to do the work to complete it. It's really simple. Hire an expert or handle it yourself. Again, don't lose sight of my love for middle America. I owe a great deal of gratitude to them. My wife. The families who welcomed me in to their home as a kid—the Johnsons, Scifreses, Wilsons, and Coopers—and taught me the ways of the middle class. My current friendships and reconfigured value system as a FISA transplant. That's why delivering this message hurts so much.

A SHAKY FOUNDATION

Financial harmony, based on their definition of the term, is what the traditional middle class cherishes, a state of being they want to achieve when their money is acting funny. Monetary disruptions that often are self-inflicted create internal stress and compel GISAs to act before these problems get worse. Multiple financial fires may be burning simultaneously, but energies outside of daily responsibilities are deployed to put out one fire at a time. Never mind that the financial fire could spread to other areas of their personal or family economy. GISAs realize this, but proceed ahead with their problem-solving strategy nonetheless. If a strategy doesn't exist, they will find one.

> The poor feel the moment, but have little regard for the future, as foretold by a punishing past.

> The middle class operates in the moment, but are often very fearful of an unknown future.

> The informed wealthy are mindful of the moment, but very cognizant of the future's impact on their overall well-being and plan accordingly.

GISAs see the trees but not the forest. Their attention span is typically focused on saving money, paying off a particular debt (credit card, mortgage, student loan, etc.), sending a child to college, keeping their job or finding a new one, private tutoring for a child, or dealing with retirement. These are legitimate worries but they can be tackled as part of a broader game plan. It's hard to get GISAs to understand the value in a process that demands a long-term outlook against the backdrop of day-to-day decisions. They feel their plate is full enough, so why add anything else to it?

Our financial workshops are attended largely by the middle class, who are looking for answers. Unfortunately, the presentation of The Mr. Fundy's Life and Financial Planning Playbook,™ a detailed synopsis of the key areas of a comprehensive plan, raises more questions in their minds than answers. The depth of the information is overwhelming—giving GISAs their money's worth—and analysis paralysis sets in. My wife notes, "It's too much informa-tion for them to digest at once. They need to be spoon fed one topic at a time." She adds, "Fear and anxiety set in because they now realize how far they're behind financially. Also, their faith is shaken, because what they envision about their future just might be totally different from reality. It can be very deflating for the middle class. Their body language says it all." Middle-class angst in digesting large quantities of financial information in an educational setting is very apparent. This will be covered in greater detail in the chapter "Primary Sensory-Learning Drivers."

A do-it-yourself attitude that pushes important financial decisions into the future—insurance and estate planning matters, along with longevity risk, or the likely reality of outliving their money in retirement—will create even more economic disharmony in GISAs' lives. It's not too late to turn things around. They need to get going now, though. It'll be an uncomfortable process, but the benefits are worth it.

THE UNCOMFORTABLE NATURE OF FINANCIAL CHANGE

Change is uncomfortable. Financial change is even more discomforting. When you have done things the same way for so long with your money, it is difficult to change course. Gradual change may be the preferred course, but that may not be an option if finances are in disarray.

Monetary behavioral changes are unsettling for GISAs. Monya's insights shed light on this issue. She says, "Fear of not being certain on how things are going to turn out is demoralizing for the middle class. Every dollar is allocated and stretched thin already, and they aren't willing to make sacrifices elsewhere to reach their financial goals. They do not want to cut back in certain areas, or else their middle-class lifestyle gets exposed as a fraud."

My wife's blue-collar upbringing and astute observations point to a very telling and troubling problem for the middle class. They are behind the change curveball, a wicked sinker dropped from the sky coming right at their head. She adds, "It's very difficult for them to embrace financial change. The implementation of it frightens them to death. Let's take investing, for example. This is so foreign for many people in the middle class. They are terrified to take ownership of their financial future. It's okay if someone else handles this responsibility, but God forbid, if it ends up being theirs. With no pension, coupled with potential Social Security payout challenges beyond 2030, the middle class must face a retirement future that is unpredictable. My parents were so fortunate to have a pension and Social Security. The middle class yearns for certainty, a life that is known from one day to the next. Our world is constantly changing, which overwhelms them. They want to walk when they should be sprinting."

In the past, a pension or credited retirement account based on an employee's years of service with a company could be used as an effective retirement planning tool. Today, very few companies offer guaranteed pensions or defined benefit plans because the costs to fund them are prohibitively high. A paycheck, health insurance, and a predictable work schedule were handled by their employer. All the employee had to do was show up. Now, that role is flipped today with defined contribution plans—for example, 401(k) and 403(b) retirement accounts—being the responsibility of the employee to manage. Job layoffs and outsourcing are part of the economic landscape in the twenty-first century. Part of, if not all of the health insurance premiums, have to be paid by workers at some companies. GISAs have to own their financial well-being. Again, this is a frightening proposition for the middle class.

The poor deal with transiency quite often, moving from one apartment or relationship to the next, but they are resistant to financial change. They feel it's too painful to implement. During one of our pro bono financial planning workshops nearly a decade ago for disadvantaged families, a single mom on a limited income told me as I was explaining the topics, "That all sounds good, but I can barely feed my kids right now. I'll have to pass on the opportunity."

GAPAs and SAPAs take pre-emptive measures to deal with economic changes. They are rarely caught off guard or surprised by them.

The traditional middle class, generally speaking, are hesitant to financial change. They see it coming, but are late adopters in taking the necessary steps ahead of time to deal with a future problem.

I had a discussion with a Jamaican-born limo driver, a self-described, middle-class worker, about the difficulties he was experiencing. His industry was undergoing seismic changes. Of course, he was not a fan of ride-sharing services. Our conversation follows:

> **Me:** What is going on in your industry?
>
> **Limo Driver:** Uber is taking our customers.
>
> **Me:** So, do you mean that they are forcing many limo drivers in your industry out of business?
>
> **Limo Driver:** Yeah man, that's correct.
>
> **Me:** It's really hard to compete against them on price. To pay half of what it would cost to use a taxi or limo service is very enticing for customers. What are you going to do about this?
>
> **Limo Driver:** I dunno. Hopefully, I can figure something out.

This limo driver is the classic case of a GISA hesitant to make a needed financial change but won't, at least not yet. Working harder without a different approach won't matter. Our modern world rewards those who are willing to adapt to change. Uber, Amazon, Netflix, and other disruptors force GISAs to update their job skills, reinvent themselves, or start their own business after getting laid off. No administration or political party can guarantee the middle-class job security.

The squeeze is on for GISAs. Make a change or get run over by an economic steamroller when movement is too slow.

Playbook Driven

"Macro Focus"

It was the 2002 Western Conference Finals, the Sacramento Kings versus the defending NBA Champions, the Los Angeles Lakers. I played sparingly in this series, but I had to study the playbook as if I were Chris Webber, our team's best player. I was his backup.

It came down to Game Seven, a nail-biter, just like most of the other games. Our team wasn't respected by the Lakers or their fans. We had a good game plan, but came up short. Why?

Our game plan was strong. We knew the Lakers' triangle offense inside and out. We were even given a two-inch thick notebook before the series as a supplement to our playbook, which highlighted every Lakers'—superstar or reserve—strengths, weaknesses, and tendencies.

Before each game in that series, one of our coaches would lay out our game plan on a very large whiteboard in the locker room. Statistics, strategies, and statements were written to reinforce what we already knew. Of course, we knew what was on the line if we won Game Seven—a trip to the NBA Finals against the New Jersey Nets and a likely NBA Championship.

It wasn't a secret who the Lakers' go-to players were. We doubled Shaquille O'Neal when he received the basketball in the post, and pushed the other dynamic duo, Kobe Bryant, to help side defense. The goal was simple: Make the other players, Robert Horry, Brian Shaw, Rick Fox, Derek Fisher, Devean George, and Samaki Walker beat us.

Coaches create the playbook, but players have to execute and make shots. We lost Game Seven at the free throw line, a sign of nerves perhaps more than anything else. The Lakers were in familiar territory as the defending NBA

Champion, even though this last game was played on our home court, a right we had earned by having the best record in the regular season that year. Our odds in winning Game Seven, based on previous series, was over 70 percent. Obviously, our chances of a successful outcome were very high. Our opponent played calm down the stretch, and we got a bit rattled.

Game Seven in the NBA playoffs that year was quite different than playing a regular season game. We had a really good playbook to win the Western Conference Finals; the Lakers had one a little bit better. Phil Jackson had coached Michael Jordan and the Chicago Bulls through six NBA Championships. His playbook with the Bulls and Lakers, although not foolproof, was battle-tested. His methods were a bit unorthodox, given his use of mind games on his own players, opponents, and referees. Psychology is as much a part of winning as a well-constructed playbook is.

The GAPA playbook, as Danny Levitt notes, is already scripted. They know winning is about preparation, positioning every player on the team—children, grandchildren, and advisors—to stay true to character, a calm assurance to remain focused on the legacy mandate. Economic downturn? Don't sweat it and stay true to character. Geopolitical tensions? Don't get distracted and stay true to character. The death of a family patriarch or matriarch? Grieve as the occasion warrants, but stay true to character.

Character is about being calm under pressure, no matter the circumstance. The big picture, a legacy play, is always in focus. Character tests always show up, oftentimes unannounced, to see how committed an individual, family, or team is to their playbook.

The generationally and situationally wealthy see the big picture and make plans years before it actually appears. This macro focus sets them apart from the middle class and poor, who often believe a lucky break or grind-it-out work ethic puts someone over the top financially. Waiting for a fortunate outcome to randomly show up without intentionally planning for it is a fruitless endeavor.

Luck is not something I believe exists, but I am an advocate of creating an environment that leads to favorable, financial outcomes.

I understand why some wealthy people who've experienced success may attribute a positive outcome to luck. Some of them go out of their way to convey genuine humility in the face of massive wealth inequalities among the social classes. They want to show their humanness, without coming across as arrogant or insensitive to those in a different net worth bracket. I get it.

Humility is a virtue that is palatable when economic inequality is discussed. It's much easier to demonize the über wealthy and their life of privilege than families struggling to make it on fixed incomes. Many GAPAs won't even try to defend a baseless critique that casts a spotlight on their financial situation. In the court of public opinion, no one will feel sorry for the super rich. However, no one should apologize for having the right financial playbook, and those having the wrong playbook shouldn't be castigated, either.

CLEAR FOCUS, MADE SHOT

When you are blessed to have access to a winning playbook and a team of seasoned pros, successful outcomes—personal, educational, professional, and financial—appear to be slam dunks. What a privilege it is to play every game on your home court in front of fans who provide constant support. You won't hear a lot of boos or cheering gimmicks in this arena.

The GAPA playbook sets children and grandchildren up to make the legacy shot before they even step on the court. They are well-conditioned players who usually execute the game plan with precision. Skills and abilities are developed through adulthood. Elite-private schooling. First-class amenities and gated communities. Professional mentors and legacy consultants. Timeless family values. Tradition of excellence.

When the opportunity to make the legacy shot is presented, GAPA offspring are ready to knock it down. They're not nervous at all. Actually, they appear to have a calm, confident disposition. It looks like they have their game face on, a laser-like focus to complete their life's mission. Vision will play a huge role in this.

Values are the guiding principles that shape daily decisions, actions, and activities. Mission is one's life purpose, the assignment on planet earth he or she must complete for the benefit and betterment of humanity. Vision, the ability to peer into the future and predict how it will unfold, is perhaps the most important attribute of affluence. Many people confuse sight, what we see with our natural eyes, with vision, what we see with our imaginative or creative eyes.

For GAPA progenitors, vision is the footprint or impression they leave behind for others to follow. Vision is about stepping into the future to plan your legacy, then retracing the necessary steps back to today to complete it.

CHAPTER

11

ECONOMIC SUCCESS

*The psychological state that a socioeconomic
class may operate or function in once a favorable
financial condition is achieved or maintained*

Retaliation

"Pay Back"

If you're over the age of 30, you know the phrase, "Sticks and stones may break my bones but words will never hurt me." That might work for some, but for the person who has climbed out of poverty, the jokes and name-calling do hurt and reverberate into the future as you mask the pain. Whether innocent or intentional, you've probably replayed these hurtful words dozens of times in your head.

Economic success is an opportunity to show up and show out for those fortunate enough to escape generational poverty. When you've been beaten and kept down for so long, how do you justify a fortuitous or anticipated economic gain? In the world of poverty, you make a statement: words (loud and somewhat obnoxious), watches (to show the haters what time it is), whips (it's about styling and profiling in your car with only one hand on the steering wheel), weaves (as in beautiful hair extensions), and wares (the shinier, the better). As the slang vernacular goes, "Do your thang; I'm checking you out!" It's all about validation.

"IT'S SHOWTIME!"

My favorite NBA team growing up was the Los Angeles Lakers. Led by Earvin "Magic" Johnson, their brand of basketball was in your face. The behind-the-back, no-look passes on the fast break. Alley-oop slam dunks, high fives, frenetic crowds, and chest bumps. Famous celebrities sitting courtside wearing sunglasses. High scoring games. Opponents were beaten before introductions.

The Lakers had it going on. Coach Pat Riley, Magic, Kareem, Byron Scott, James Worthy, A.C. Green, Michael Cooper, and Kurt Rambis, a grind-it-out fan favorite who never seemed to smile. They knew they were really good. They had an air of invincibility that you either loved or hated, but you couldn't be neutral. As a kid from the Midwest, I chose the Lakers over the Philadelphia 76ers and Julius "Dr. J" Erving. Pennsylvania is next door to Ohio, but California had the Lakers. The glitz and glamour of Showtime, a moniker given the team of that era, was instrumental in lighting my basketball fire. I was hooked.

Showing off or showing out or showing a lack in conversational etiquette is part of the poverty game, and I am guilty of all three. Here are a few vignettes of which I'm not proud but illustrate how the poor or people who've escaped economic distress feel the need to assert themselves by making personal statements:

> As a 14-year-old Cooper Stadium vendor, I had a few choice words for a chest-thumping fan before the start of a game one evening. He didn't appreciate my innocent "Hi, how are you doing?" introduction to his teenage daughter. Come to find out, the fan was a high-ranking law enforcement official and had the badge to prove it. Of course, he showed it to me after the fact. My boss sent me home over the incident, though I hadn't broken any code of coduct rules, and it was the only time I ever left the stadium without making any money.

> As a rising high-school prep star, I'd dunk on an opponent and say, "Sit down clown." Bob Ghiloni, then the head basketball coach

at Bishop Ready and the current coach at Dennison University, warned me in an open gym at his school that if I said this to one of his player's again, he'd kick me out. He did, in front of everyone.

On my official basketball recruiting visit to Florida State University during my senior year in high school, I had the distinct honor of meeting Seminole football legend and movie star Burt Reynolds during halftime of their game against East Carolina. I was elated and told him that as a kid I watched all his movies. A few minutes after shaking his hand, I blurted out, "Mr. Reynolds, you seem so much shorter in person than on TV."

I talked mad trash on the court in high school, college, and in the NBA when given the chance. I even had a few choice words for Michael Jordan my rookie year playing for the Sacramento Kings. Of course, MJ quickly put me in my place and gave me that look, indicating I had overstepped my boundaries. I can't share the entirety of his remarks here, just the gist of his timely advice: "Lawrence, you gotta bring it every day to make it in this league." I'll revisit more of my enlightening encounter with MJ in Chapter 12, "Financial Topography."

Whatever you lack in financial resources or opportunities or even genuine love, in generational poverty, you often try to make up for the loss in other ways, making boisterous statements, dressing provocatively, strutting in the presence of others to get attention, being a comedian in school to get a reputation, or riding through the 'hood with a gangsta lean. But if you peel back the top layers, what you're likely to see are insecurities buried underneath. We all have them, but they appear to be more pronounced and glaringly obvious in poverty when analyzed from one's Sociopsychonomic perspective.

You feel the need to overcompensate for the pain or loss associated with poverty, often an unfair predicament for a family, especially children, to be burdened and harassed by it each day. You are bitten by bed bugs or have roaches crawling on your body at night. You go to bed hungry and wake up starving. You open the refrigerator and not much is there to give your body the nutrition and sustained energy levels it needs to stay awake in class. You're afraid to walk outside of your home for fear of being robbed, assaulted, shot, or wrongly accused by the cops. You are mentally exhausted, a mind on a collision course with depression if your situation doesn't drastically improve.

In many cases, the circumstances surrounding poverty are intrinsically unfair—abuse, neglect, suffering. But when we look or respond entirely from the lens of fairness, this can lead to very troubling and misguided outcomes. Life is inherently unfair, but do we quit the race just because we're running in the outside lane? Of course not.

ECONOMIC PILLARS OF POVERTY

It's fitting to integrate economic pillars in any discussion concerning economic success. For the poor, these are critical to their survival and dignity. Poverty's three biggest needs in the construction of their financial foundation are job opportunities, reliable transportation, and a safe environment.

Economic pillars are embedded in the framework of financial freedom, a four-tiered platform. At the base, personal development must be addressed before or in concert with job prospecting. We're talking personal brand management 101 for the poor and it encompasses taking proactive steps to demonstrate your seriousness. How does one go about that? He or she can build rudimentary math and communication skills, have a clean (or improved) record, pay any outstanding fees to reinstate a driver's license, write a basic resumé, manage emotions, treat an addiction, and eliminate toxic relationships. Ownership of financial assets starts first with an upgrade in intangible, personal assets.

> ### SOCIOPSYCHONOMIC FILTER
> The circumstances surrounding poverty are intrinsically unfair—abuse, neglect, suffering. Life is inherenly unfair, but do we quit the race just because we're running in the outside lane?

Upgrading their personal assets will move the poor from perpetual dependency to self-sufficiency as they find employment, and thus, rely less on government assistance, nonprofit organizations, and lucky breaks to survive. This timely enhancement of GEDAs' Sociopsychonomic filter makes them ready to advance up the second rung of the financial freedom ladder.

Transforming one's image, literally and cognitively, provides a catalyst for the third platform and level of growth, which is financial stability as an employee or business owner. Reliable transportation to and from work is very important. As a kid, I remember on two occasions that our hooptie, a high-mileage car with maintenance problems, wouldn't start after we left the grocery store. It was so embarrassing, and the frigid temperatures did little except leave us to shiver in the cold.

Car trouble is a recurring theme in poverty, one that is often an impediment to getting or keeping a job. It's also symptomatic of a much deeper, underlying problem—the lack of sound planning. Instead of saving to buy a reliable car, the poor move too quickly in their purchase of a cheaper, more affordable automobile. Of course, the law of unintended consequences will appear when they least expect.

Older, high mileage vehicles cost less and are more economical, but extended maintenance issues will rack up expenses that disproportionately punish the poor more than any other social class. The poor know this, but the chance to snag a can't-miss deal outweighs the potential problems of used vehicles. They are quite skilled in absorbing previous owners' vehicle headaches. Just drive through any poor neighborhood and you'll see dealerships in strategic locations on busy intersections selling reasonably priced cars "as is" with above-average miles. You can get a good deal, but how long will it last?

A predictably safe living situation is another component of financial stability. It's hard to get to work when your living arrangements aren't stable. A dangerous neighborhood with high rates of drug abuse, crime, and threats to personal safety can impair one's ability (and motivation) to work, and getting there may be the least of their problems. Forget about clocking in on time; they might have to worry more about stray bullets and assaults that come with the territory of inner-city poverty.

The economic ladder's fourth rung is economic empowerment, or the establishment of liquid accounts and other assets that have the potential to increase in value. In its simplest form, we're talking about a relationship with a bank or credit union.

For the middle class and rich, these relationships are slam dunks. But for the poor, as a percentage, very few of them have an ongoing relationship with a credit union or traditional bank. Unfortunately, as de factor members of the unbanked community, they are likely to engage in transactional arrangements with check-cashing establishments, pawn shops, and creative-financing options offered by loan sharks to "premium customers" in the neighborhood. These come with high interest rates or penalties, the kind that are incurred when a cash advance is made before a check clears. The law of unintended consequences in motion again.

A checking or savings account can segue into securing a home mortgage. For many people, a house is their largest and most valuable asset. Homeownership is not for everyone, and people should be well-versed in personal or family finance before house hunting. However, it can kick-start an asset acquisition mindset for the poor instead of them building equity and wealth for someone else. As consumers, they do not envision or see themselves ever being investors, either. Why?

The poor believe a force field surrounds the world of investing, and they are not welcomed. However, GEDAs spend money on goods and services offered by publicly traded companies that make shareholders and CEOs richer. I see poor kids wearing designer clothes from head to toe. Some have iPhones and other expensive gadgets. Fights break out in stores over the last pair of $200 sneakers

> If it takes a village to raise a child, then it takes a nation to save a legacy.

for sale. Why not own moderately priced stocks that show a high probability of appreciating instead of looking cute wearing an outfit that will decrease in value once it leaves the store? There are hundreds of stocks that are priced well under $100. Statement assets may make a person feel good, but very little else. Image-conscious people fail to realize this.

Legacy continuity is the top rung of financial freedom. On the positive side, it is the hallmark of generational affluence. It's certainly not a pressure-free pursuit, but the confident assurance GAPA families have in transitioning their children and grandchildren for the responsibilities that follow can be duplicated by GEDAs and GISAs, too.

The wealthy don't have a monopoly on creating a positive heritage that follows a predictable pattern, but their passion pursuing it does monopolize a great deal of their time. You may recall that they don't like to waste time and avoid anything that doesn't produce an immediate or deferred benefit.

GAPAs care as much about their legacy (if not more so) as they do about their net worth. That's why so many families from multigenerational wealth are giving much of their money away to charity, which I highlighted in the "Pre-Game" section of the book. I may not agree with some of the causes they support, but their aim is purely a legacy play.

Any family can make money if they have intellectual capital and an investor's mentality. That's the easy part. The challenge is to position direct and extended family members so that they will fulfill their potential, civic duty, and life's purpose. Sounds simple, but it's challenging. If it were easy, wouldn't more families be collectively tuned in to their legacy mandate?

Remuneration

"Pay Up"

Quid pro quo **is a term I fell in love with** when I first heard it in high school, although I didn't know what it meant exactly. However, its context was discernible enough that I knew it had to do with an obligation, what each party owed the other.

The poor often operate on the *payback principle* of a quid pro quo interaction. Economic success is usually retaliatory in nature, driven by a sensory connection to right a wrong through the big four: taste (execute sweet revenge), touch (purchase tangible assets), temperature (feel inner warmth), and pain (gauge internal pressure). This is the domain of the parietal lobe.

The generationally wealthy are guided by the *pay-it-forward principle*. As economic success dictates, the obligatory exchange compels them even more to carry out a life assignment. Mission, vision, and values also soothe and reinvigorate the soul. The intentionality behind their life's purpose is an obsession. They see its culmination in vivid imagery, though it may take years before the seeds produce any fruit. GAPAs know that a life of purpose must mature and develop organically; it can't be forced.

The quid pro quo arrangement of a job well done for GISAs is grounded in the *paycheck principle*. Work performed equates to a paycheck with satisfactory benefits earned, notably health insurance and an employer-sponsored retirement account. Employment income allows the middle class to maintain a comfortable lifestyle, though it is constantly under attack. Health insurance premiums and deductibles are through the roof, regardless of a family's medical trend line or propensity to visit the doctor each year. According to a shocking 2016 report by the Economic Policy Institute (EPI), "The State of American Retirement," the median retirement savings for an American family is $5,000 only. What's even more mind-boggling is that roughly half of all American families, regardless of race or ethnicity, have nothing saved for retirement. (For more information on this study, please visit http://www.epi.org/publication/retirement-in-america/#charts.)

The middle class, and Americans in general who owe a debt of gratitude to them, took a lot for granted back in the day when wages and benefits were more plentiful. Blue-collar workers could take comfort in knowing that their jobs couldn't be lost unless they did something terribly wrong and got fired, and the unions enjoyed more leverage to fight for their members.

Life was simpler and predictable back then. You knew what channel your favorite TV show was on. Basically, there were just three from which to choose. You knew how to allocate your time among work, family, and leisure activities. You knew how much money would be needed throughout the year to cover monthly living expenses, summer vacations, and back-to-school shopping for kids. You knew what college or trade school your kids would attend and how much it would cost. You knew at what age you could retire and how much money it was going to take to live modestly during your golden years, thanks to a generous company pension and Social Security benefits.

That was then and times have changed today for GISAs. They are in a state of flux, though few would care to admit it. Financial stress is largely to blame and the culprits are job instability, stagnant wages, rising debt levels, and lack of financial planning.

QUID PRO QUO AT A CROSSROADS

While researching various words, phrases, and sentences that aptly described a given social class's characteristics, habits, customs, traditions, and mindsets around financial matters, remuneration was the perfect (or most obvious) choice to describe GISAs. Hard work should translate into a meaningful financial benefit. Not so fast.

We see remuneration in action in our grocery shopping habits and agreements with service-based companies. Coupons in the mail and annual insurance multi-line discounts are extended in exchange for customer loyalty. These reward or incentive programs create a powerful dynamic between two parties where both, whether implicitly or explicitly, are expected to keep their side of the deal. When grocery store customers' behavior patterns change unexpectedly, the store sends them coupons to win back their loyalty. For the middle class, their work ethic elevates and they work harder when their jobs are threatened. The quid pro quo arrangement GISA employees have with their companies isn't always reciprocated by some employers whose primary goal is maximizing shareholder value. Working harder won't matter if your job is destined to get shipped elsewhere or one day be replaced by technological advances. Here come the robots, and there goes your job. Take notice.

Sascha Burns is a well-known Democratic consultant and advocate of pay equity. Her analysis on the subject is foreboding in terms of the wage struggles of Middle Americans. She appears to be pretty level headed in her party's ideological beliefs. I don't recall the network, but her chilling words to a national audience as the 2016 presidential race was heating up echoed what many of us already know: The high-paying, blue-collar jobs our parents and grandparents enjoyed pre-1995, with and without college degrees, are rare in our world today. What Sascha Burns was really saying is that a hardworking person in America should receive an honest day's wage for work performed and effort given. This is true, but I guess this depends on how the word *honest* is interpreted. Job well done doesn't always mean job well paid.

GISAs resent being thought of as a charity case. They show up for work, don't cause any trouble, or complain unless their foundation is collapsing. Fair compensation for on-the-job sacrifices made on behalf of their employer is their primary wish. They feel like they're getting the short end of the pay equity stick. Many of them are!

SOCIOPSYCHONOMIC FILTER

The middle class operates by the *paycheck principle*. But a job well done today doesn't automatically equate to a job well paid like it did in the past.

Job insecurity is a frightening issue for GISAs. Presidential elections are won or lost on calming middle-class fears since employment income is the foundation of their economic platform. No job. No income. No homeownership. No middle-class lifestyle. No financial equilibrium.

They're not looking for an economic savior, but want an economic system that lets them enjoy their lifestyle without interruptions. I'm afraid that future economic shocks will test the middle class's three economic pillars—a stable job with benefits, homeownership, and a secure retirement—like never before.

An interconnected world, despite calls for protectionism and tighter border security, almost guarantees it.

Reinvigoration

"Pay It Forward"

Wealth without being encumbered by trappings of materialism or an outdo-thy-neighbor, score-keeper's mentality is reinvigorating to the generationally affluent. This doesn't mean that their lives are problem-free. No, they are mindful of lawsuits, economic downturns, geopolitical tensions, and other unpredictable risks that might impact their balance sheets or net worth statements. GAPAs deal with a different kind of stress than GEDAs and GISAs, who must concentrate their energies and efforts on economic survival and financial stability. Monetary freedom allows GAPAs to avoid the pay-back (the poor) or pay-up (the middle class) mindset. The generationally affluent have mastered the pay-it-forward mentality. It's seen in everything they do, from parenting to investing to legacy building.

When I speak to impoverished communities from inner-city backgrounds, I tell them success in life isn't about being white or selling out but about buying in to the process that works regardless of the color of one's skin or social status. If it works in sports, why wouldn't it work at school, on the home front, or in the world of business? It has worked for me. If you work it without giving up, it'll work for you, too.

> ## SOCIOPSYCHONOMIC FILTER
> It's not about selling out; it's about buying in to the process of success, which takes consistency of character to pull off.

GAPAs find economic success exhilarating, rejuvenating, refreshing, transforming, and reaffirming because it confirms the playbook works, though it may take time for all of the moving parts to come together.

They are incredibly patient when it comes to achieving economic success, and it's the process of achieving success that excites their souls. GAPAs are more attached to the intangible nature of a completed goal versus the end result of it, on which GEDAs and GISAs are prone to focus. The super wealthy already have plenty of stuff, so the reward factor of economic success must be centered on something completely different. Attaining a successful outcome is their reward. GAPAs seek intellectual pleasure through procedural tasks, charitable endeavors, and legacy continuity.

Most people applaud physical skills more than mental aptitude. That's why the middle class is given the euphemistic blue-collar worker label that they proudly wear. When a single-parent mother escapes poverty, she is celebrated, revered in fact, and rightly so. Economic success, whether through physical or mental labor, shouldn't be minimized.

ECONOMIC SETBACKS IN DISGUISE FOR PERSONAL OR PERSONNEL IMPROVEMENT

You can't discuss economic success without mentioning economic setbacks, which are unavoidable. How each social class is likely to deal with these challenges follows.

Financial obstacles are paralyzing for the poor, whose incessant thoughts of unfairness dominate their minds. It's easy for GEDAs to come to this fatalistic conclusion, "This is my lot in life, so what's unusual about having financial difficulties at every turn?" They feel immobile and powerless to change their circumstances or navigate a different course.

The middle class is overwhelmed by financial challenges. Some look for specific strategies or tools to overcome or deal with a difficult situation. Other GISAs tend to push the problem far into the future with no timetable to rectify the situation. Postponement becomes their default coping strategy.

The informed wealthy approach such difficulties differently. They realize setbacks are symbolic growth markers to initiate a personal or personnel change (if necessary). They can be empowering moments to build character, gain focus, increase skills, and alleviate future problems.

Setbacks should be setups to shed the extra baggage for the long journey, a race that demands discipline, endurance, and an impeccable attention to detail. That's why startup businesses that fail are celebrated in Silicon Valley. Wrong execution or game plan? Time to press reboot.

Dave Houze, a close friend and very wealthy businessman, shared his insights with me on this topic. Our conversation follows:

Me: Do you look at economic setbacks as opportunities for personal growth?

Dave: Yes, I do. We would all rather avoid setbacks, but when they inevitably occur, I want to know the lessons, hidden or otherwise, that need to be learned. I don't want to repeat the same mistakes again.

Me: Very interesting. What lessons have you learned in the past?

Dave: Well, the list is long. But a few of the lessons include waiting too late to exit an investment deal, chasing a bad problem with more money—which usually ends in an even bigger disaster—and keeping a key participant or advisor in place who should have been let go much sooner. Each of these lessons falls into the due diligence category, a process that requires constant attention.

Me: Has an economic setback ever paralyzed you?

Dave: Oh no, a financial challenge in the past has never stopped me from wanting to take risk in the future. Investment risk requires the implementation of sound risk management techniques. Setbacks, especially major ones, can easily pose paralysis unless you are mentally and structurally prepared. Procrastination is clearly a direct path to failure.

In the NBA, the acronym K.Y.P. means knowing your personnel, and it's used quite a bit. For example, a good point guard won't set his teammates up for failure. He will play to their strengths. He won't expect a center, for instance, to be a shooting guard. Nor is he likely to pass the basketball to a post player running down the court on a fast break when a three-point shot is needed to tie the game. Point guards must understand the strengths and weaknesses of their teammates. The effects of K.Y.P. can mean the difference between winning or losing in sports, business, or life.

As they analyze economic setbacks, GAPAs look outward once an inward assessment or personal inventory is made. They realize that a change in personnel is never personal; it's business. Dave added, "You can't know everything, so you want to have the best players on your team in business. Sometimes this may mean letting someone go."

With so much on the line, the ultra wealthy need a well-crafted game plan. This may require a personnel change or tactical adjustment to avoid further damage. The decision to take this step won't be made in haste, but it will be right on time.

A RITZY LIFESTYLE ... IF ONLY FOR A DAY

Life as a former NBA player afforded me many luxuries and amenities I never could have imagined. Chartered planes and five-star accommodations, travel outside North America, meeting famous celebrities and billionaires. I'm a simple guy who got labeled in the NBA as a penny-pincher. Didn't bother me one bit. Frugality has always been a part of my financial DNA. Earning a high income back then didn't change who I was and still am. I mow the lawn and take care of the pool, clip coupons, and try to save a dollar at every chance. However, regardless of my financial condition today, it's impossible for me to forget the struggles of poverty.

Even now, I can't believe that a poor kid from the projects would have the opportunity to provide such a good life for his family, though my kids are quick to call me a cheapskate.

Two areas I won't cut corners financially when it comes to their well-being, however, are what food is placed in their bellies (nutrition) and what memories are stored in their brain (experiences). I'll cover nutrition in Chapter 15, "Wellness."

My son and I traveled to Cleveland one weekend to watch the Cavaliers play the Oklahoma City Thunder. Eli saw it as a cool road trip, and I viewed it as a bonding investment to strengthen our relationship. Given our life standing as functioning members of the middle class, it was also good for him to see the world of luxury up close with his usually El Cheapo dad, which included dinner at Morton's Steakhouse and an overnight stay on the Club Level at the Ritz Carlton.

This hotel offers five-star amenities, excellent service, and impeccable hospitality. Its Ritz Club Level benefits are amazing. There's never a mad dash to raid the exquisite supply of appetizers, desserts, and beverages. These guests don't live in scarcity, and they're not big fans of marinating in the lounge area. In other words, they're not out to get their money's worth. These folks are few in number, but stand out like a sore thumb in the lounge area.

The Ritz Club Level is a well-oiled machine where guests come and go, even with more than five selections of food options strategically displayed throughout the day to accommodate all of the guests. No room vacancy on this floor existed, probably due in large part to the showdown of two of the NBA's biggest stars, LeBron James and Kevin Durant, now a member of the Golden State Warriors.

If every Club Level guest had shown up at once for a meal, there would not have been enough seating. But in this world of exclusivity, it's as though guests intuitively know when to arrive, how long to stay and eat, and who will arrive next.

I was struck more by the rituals of the people sitting across from me who had an air or look of affluence. They exuded a confidence that this life was theirs; they owned it.

The newspapers placed in the hotel's common area caught my eye and were further signs that announced wealth was in abundance. Appearing in order were the *Financial Times, Wall Street Journal, New York Times, USA Today,* and the *Cleveland Plain Dealer.* It told me that the wealthy stay informed and abreast of world events to maintain their economic advantage, no matter their geographic location.

On our two-hour drive back to Columbus, we had just left the Cleveland city limits and my son shared that it was the best weekend of his life. The hotel was awesome and he got to take pictures and meet his favorite NBA players after the game. He thanked me for the trip and said, "I love you dad!" I looked at him in the rearview mirror before cracking a proud papa smile, holding back a few tears in the process while reflecting on his touching words. I then flashed back to my childhood when my father only took me to a corner store on the periphery of my neighborhood, and never did he express his love for me. It was an unintended contrast in life experiences.

ECONOMIC PILLARS OF AFFLUENCE

The three primary economic pillars of generational affluence are comprehensive planning, luxury accoutrements, and legacy continuity, and they serve as foundational anchors in which nearly every aspect of their life is attached. If it's not connected, then it's probably not important. These pillars are non-negotiable expectations and top-of-the-line benefits that mega-wealthy people enjoy daily. They don't know (or expect) anything different.

Their lives are meticulously organized in such a way that most problems are averted before they even surface. GAPAs take pre-emptive and precautionary measures to ensure that future generations follow the script. Little room exists for children and grandchildren to deviate from the flight path. It's on autopilot, so why would they?

12

FINANCIAL TOPOGRAPHY

*The illustrative approach used to connect
with a given social class when explaining key
economic concepts, terms, and phrases*

Aerial View

If you listen closely to the word choice of those stuck in generational poverty, you will hear a familiar theme of feeling trapped with no way out. Misery and heartache are just around the corner, with companions too eager to pile on to a situation that's already bad enough. There are plenty of co-signers as well who will vouch for your dismal situation, fraught with a lack of opportunities, parental neglect, community violence, and systemic abuses that take advantage of the poor. It's a great analysis, but absent from the list is toxic thinking, which suffocates personal responsibility and paralyzes hope that tomorrow can be better (or brighter) than today.

My last name, Funderburke, has its etymological roots in coming up, or rising out of a difficult situation. Monya and I were in Atlanta several years ago to present a financial life skills workshop to disadvantaged kids at a local Boys and Girls Club. Our goal? Help them escape the poverty trap.

While having breakfast that morning in the hotel restaurant, our waiter couldn't contain his excitement to share something with us. Initially, I thought he was a basketball groupie, someone who was a fan of mine back when I played in the NBA. He had no clue who I was, but was struck by my last name. The waiter, a Dutch and U.S. citizen, asked if we knew what my last name meant in his native tongue. We did not.

He said that "Fun" or "Vun" means "from." "Der" is translated as "the." "Burke" means "mountaintop." My wife and I looked at each other in stunned disbelief. We knew this was a moment to look heavenward and thank the Good Lord up above.

This revelation by an unlikely source confirmed a suspicion I had as a kid that poverty wouldn't be my permanent abode. I knew my rocky journey would one day, by God's grace, take me to the top of the mountain. My come-up would be a mental and physical struggle in which I would prevail through endurance. Time to reach down in the valley below and pull others up. The poor have a right, if they so choose to exercise it, to be up here, too. (My first name Lawrence is of Latin origin and derived from the word *laurel*. *Victor* and *competitor*, in the context of a crowning ceremony, are often used to describe people who share this name, or a variant thereof.)

SOCIOPSYCHONOMIC FILTER
A view from the air provides the poor with a clear roadmap or navigational path to achieve a desired result.

A financial come-up is so appealing to the poor because it allows them to jump over or bypass the traditional process of success, for example, going to college or working their way up the corporate ladder.

Pastors, musicians, and motivational speakers use descriptive words that align with the poor's come-up doctrine, including jump, fly, bounce, explode, catapult, reach, rise up, move up, and go up. A back-in-the day sitcom like *The Jeffersons* or the animated movie *Shark Tale* also offer rags-to-riches, feel-good entertainment. These come-up metaphors denote economic success, something GEDAs desperately want. An elevator ride up from the depths of despair isn't too much to ask, is it?

THE TRAMPOLINE SYNDROME

Patrick Dent, a former Ohio State University gymnast, worked at the Sullivant Gardens Recreation Center adjacent to our neighborhood back in the 1980s when I was a kid. He taught us how to tumble and roll, do handstands and cartwheels, and jump on a mini trampoline. Of course, the mini trampoline garnered the most enthusiasm from the group, because with the right momentum, timing, and foot positioning, we could propel ourselves far into the air while landing on the outskirts of the large blue mat. Most of us tried to jump beyond the mat, which Patrick always cautioned us not to do to avoid hurting ourselves. We were having so much fun and never considered getting hurt. It was about the jump.

Michael "Air" Jordan is considered the greatest basketball player of all time. I was fortunate enough to play against MJ in the NBA for several years. I even made a point to talk trash to him one fateful day. As you can imagine, he quickly put me in my place.

My rookie year in the NBA with the Sacramento Kings was my most productive season. I felt pretty good about myself, having led our team in preseason scoring that year. Before my shoulder injury, I was averaging nearly 13 points in 22 minutes through the first 19 games. I finished the season averaging nearly 10 points and almost five rebounds per contest. I was given the nickname "Instant Offense" by my coaches and teammates. One assistant coach told me, "Lawrence, you never saw a shot you didn't like." This is so true about me on the basketball court. One shot that I'd like to have back, still today, was a snide remark directed at Air Jordan.

We played the Chicago Bulls in the preseason at the United Center. I started the game and was naturally quite nervous. I scored 11 points that game and stopped MJ courtside when the contest ended. The cameras were still rolling. Our announcer, Gary Gerould, joked, "Lawrence is telling Michael that he's his hero." I did mention to MJ that I met him back in high school, which he acknowledged.

We played the Bulls again early in the regular season at Arco Arena, our home court. The atmosphere was electric. Fans were evenly split between Kings and Bulls fans. My moment to show that I had indeed made it to the pinnacle of sport's success occurred after getting fouled on a shot attempt.

On my way to the foul line, just as I walked past MJ, I blurted out, "Nobody out here can stop me." He was bending over with his hands on his shorts and quickly rose to share these words with me, "Lawrence, this is not Ohio State." After concluding that I had made a monumental mistake, I thought to myself, "Wow, MJ watched me play back in college?" MJ then levied a sobering wake-up call. He said, "You're on a whole 'nother level now. You gotta bring it every day if you want to stay in this league." I made my two free throws, but scored a few points below my game average.

Our team got blown out. To make matters worse, I even asked MJ to autograph a pair of sneakers for me after the game in the visitor's locker room. He then chided me in front of the rest of his teammates, "Look how old these shoes are that Lawrence wants me to sign." They broke out in laughter. Back to life, back to reality for a hotshot rookie who was rebuked in front of peers on the biggest basketball stage by the game's biggest superstar.

Here were a few takeaway lessons from my wake-up call moment with MJ, a seasoned veteran and six-time NBA Champion. First, don't talk trash when you haven't yet earned the right to do so. Rookies are called rookies for a reason. Talk more with your ears and less with your mouth. Chew on words of wisdom and swallow accordingly. Second, be careful how you want your humility medication

> Talk more with your ears and less with your mouth when in the presence of wise counsel.

to come. In some instances, the dosage will catch you off guard and shock your system. Third, absorb the nuggets of truth that come with constructive criticism and discard the rest. MJ had a few other choice words for me, but I made a personal vow not to share them in public.

MJ means a great deal to people in poverty, especially African-Americans, even those who weren't born during his heyday. Symbolically, MJ represents the ultimate come-up for GEDAs, though he was reared in a blue-collar home in Wilmington, North Carolina. Doesn't matter. His "Air Jordan" logo on clothes, shoes, and hats is a status symbol for the poor. GEDAs buy statement assets to feel better and to show up the haters. In poverty, image or outward projection means everything. I will cover this in greater detail in the next chapter, "Asset Acquisition Habits."

Like MJ's spectacular moves on the court, GEDAs often gravitate to the ultimate economic opportunity for themselves or their children. Their financial come-up through an extraordinary circumstance is usually concentrated on three low-probability outcomes: winning the lottery (or gambling), becoming a pro athlete, or making it in the entertainment industry as a singer or rapper or social media star.

I cringe whenever I ask inner-city kids how many of them want to become a pro athlete or entertainer because the response is the same no matter where I am at the time. Most of the males believe such a goal is within their reach. I never crush their dreams, but they have a better chance of earning a great living as a doctor, lawyer, business owner, investment advisor, or middle manager than as either an athlete or entertainer.

Far too many poor students believe they can bypass the process of hard work by dropping out of school to focus exclusively on a physical talent as their ticket to success. Some of them will find out later that their fallback plan is going on welfare when they turn 18.

Success inside or outside sports involves a process, and this can't be bypassed. No trampoline has enough springs on it to propel a person to this platform independent of sweat equity, talent, and favorable circumstances occurring simultaneously. Success doesn't happen by accident or a lucky bounce of good fortune. It is a planned event.

THE PROCESS CONUNDRUM

Rules-based school subjects can be incredibly challenging for many poor students. They are often torn between how their world of disorder operates and one that is foreign to their way of thinking and speaking—the orderly world of math and English.

We have tutored dozens of kids in math from impoverished backgrounds. Most of them struggled with the order of operations in algebraic equations. Like many children introduced to algebra, they ask a lot of questions because they just don't get it. My standard reply instructs them to follow the rules of math, where order and structure are key to success. I tell them, "Don't try to figure the 'why,' just trust and work the process."

The poor's difficulty adopting the process of success as opposed to the result may very well be attributable to the challenge they have in grabbing, feeling, or seeing a concept that is intangible in its origin.

Our daughter Nyah is a parietal lober. Regardless of social standing, parietal lobers share many of the same characteristics. She is an amazing athlete and sports come naturally to her. She is sociable and image conscious, preferring style over substance in the majority of cases. Friendliness is one of her most admired traits. As a sensory seeker, though, her internal GPS looks for opportunities to feel the moment, which may not bode well when time management is most needed. Parietal lobers must work to suppress transitory sensations that can be distraction traps. If not, they can be punished for losing track of time, skipping steps, or wishful thinking.

Nyah at one time also struggled with the order of operations in algebraic equations. Multiple step problems used to give her fits, for example, $2x + 5 = 20$. To solve for x, the order of operations requires that you subtract both sides of the mathematical expression by five and then divide by two. Our daughter would try to feel her way through these problems, but would run into one roadblock after another. Her navigational strategies left her frustrated and even more fearful of this subject. Fortunately, she has two parents who enjoy math and refused to let her wallow in doubt and self-pity.

> Certain things must be completed in certain ways to make success in life a certainty.

My wife shared with Nyah during a tutoring session: "This is how the order goes. It may not make sense now, but eventually it'll register. Trust the process." Order can't be felt; it must be followed regardless of feelings. Certain things must be completed in certain ways to make success in life a certainty.

Many poor students will often bypass adherence to rules where the consequences aren't severe enough to trigger intense emotional or physical pain. Math and English in a school setting, as noted in the "Academic Enrichment" chapter, are two such examples. A bad grade doesn't strike fear in them. For those who disdain school, and more specifically, the agony of frontal lobe development in sequential reasoning, they don't see the correlation between academic performance and quality of life in adulthood. They don't think walking away from a high school diploma or college degree is a big deal. They will voice displeasure in working minimum-wage jobs, but fail to take ownership of the cumulative effects that have led them to their life standing. There's plenty of blame to go around, but taking personal responsibility must be at the top of the list.

The best way to help poor students has little to do with modifications to their schools and everything to do with upgrades to their mental bank account. Poor kids deserve modern schools, but these visual aids will do little to improve their short- and long-term financial frame of reference if they are not accompanied by process buy-in and educational endurance.

Horizontal View

The traditional middle class seeks safety in being grounded. The phrase "keep your feet on the ground" is a financial commandment they take seriously. They seek economic harmony in a life that is sequential, simple, and sensible. When GISAs get out of character—spending money that they don't have—their center of gravity lets them know that financial equilibrium needs restored, sometimes quickly.

Financial advisors who work with the middle class must communicate a game plan that's achievable through a sequence of orderly steps on a horizontal plane. This roadmap might show detours, but the terrain should be clear of steep inclines or free-falling declines. The mere mention of these possibilities at the first meeting can be paralyzing to GISAs. They might be so afraid that a second meeting with a financial consultant is not scheduled.

The middle class often misjudges temporary and otherwise normal disruptions that occur in an economic cycle, which typically span three to five years. During economic peaks and valleys people make money or lose assets. GISAs prefer only one outcome—a sure bet, which doesn't exist in the world of investing.

Action steps to assist the middle class in meeting their goals should include these descriptive words: walk (on pace financially), jog (pick up the pace financially), run (move quicker because you're behind financially), or sprint (far behind financially and above-average investment risk must be taken to catch up). I'd say it's safe to conclude that most GISAs need to be sprinting right now if financial freedom is a pressing, lifelong goal.

Explosive words used by planners to motivate the middle class toward a financial goal can be unsettling, especially when GISAs are asked to push past their comfort zone once analysis paralysis sets in.

You may recall that analysis paralysis involves thinking about getting financial advice but never acting on it. A GISA can't seem to make up her mind to move forward, for instance. She wants to stay the present course that is most comfortable and bearable. Unfortunately, she will have to live with the con-sequences, preferring to walk when she really needs to sprint toward a secure financial tomorrow. She may need to find a secondary income source outside of her full-time job or delay buying a home. Each scenario creates enormous discomfort, but the latter will require more emotional capital to pull off. She might not feel that it's worth it.

ON THE GROUND, BUT IN THEIR ELEMENT

Anytime you persuade GISAs to shift their center of gravity, discomfort may follow. In the interim, economic vertigo will worsen for those suffering from it and cause them to give up on a financial goal. The rewards of a monetary goal are simply not worth the aggravation and effort that precede them. They feel overwhelmed by the process.

Let's look at a couple of hypothetical GISA examples that fit those descriptions as well as the real-world implications of their decisions.

Michael is 52, divorced, and an independent contractor who does handyman work. Whatever needs fixed around the house, he has the skills to do it. In good and bad economic times, he has enjoyed steady work. Michael knows Social Security won't be enough for him, and he has pledged, in retirement, not to burden his two adult children. He knows they have their own families to care for and their incomes are limited.

> **SOCIOPSYCHONOMIC FILTER**
> A sudden or even gradual shift in their financial center of gravity is very unsettling to the traditional middle class.

He consulted four times with a financial planner online. Much of the advice centered on retirement planning. An individual retirement account (or IRA) was recommended based on available savings. Michael can see that time is running out to meet his goal of retiring at age 62. He contributed to the IRA for two years only. Goal aborted.

Stacey and her husband Eric are thirty-something school teachers. They teach at a private school with no health or retirement benefits. With four children under the age of 10, finances are tight in this household of six. However, they have been able to save $12,000, which they've set aside in a rainy-day fund. Eric's brother-in-law, Mason, is a financial advisor. He told the couple to consider life insurance and a basic estate plan as protective measures.

Mason has nothing to gain financially by suggesting the implementation of these two pillars, key components of a comprehensive financial plan. Mason is not licensed to sell insurance or draw up legal documents. He just wants Stacey and Eric to protect their four beautiful daughters as well as several cherished assets in the event of death: a house, modest savings, and two reliable income streams as teachers. The couple doesn't believe the protection, at this time, is worth the expense. Big mistake.

THE TIGHTROPE PHENOMENON

I am not ashamed to admit this, but I am afraid of heights. I consider myself a pretty fearless person, but I do get that queasy feeling in my stomach when I'm up high in the air looking over a ledge with short guardrails. You'd think that someone just a few inches short of seven-feet-tall and used to the "how's the air up there" jokes wouldn't be such a scaredy-cat of heights, which a lot of tall people are for some strange reason. I'd never walk on a tightrope that wasn't more than five feet off the ground.

My fear of heights is comparable to what I call the tightrope phenomenon that describes GISAs' cautious financial approach. Walking along a path, their eyes are fixed downward at the next step to stay firmly in line with an ongoing goal, instead of looking ahead to accomplish a longer-term objective. It's about the next step for GISAs, a methodical process to avoid a potentially disastrous misstep on a tightrope that demands their undivided attention. They are perfectly comfortable moving at their current pace.

The middle class is terrified of the financial tightrope, cognizant of the danger of being suspended midair, which is an uncomfortable place for them if finances are shaky.

Nik Wallenda is a world-renowned tightrope performer. He doesn't like using a harness or safety belt for any of his stunts. Obviously, he must keep his center of mass firm, directly over the rope. Failure to do this with each calculated step and his rope will sway back and forth like a pendulum. For a tightrope walker without a harness or safety belt, this could be the difference between life and death.

GISAs fear for their financial lives, and rightly so in some cases, at the mere whisper of a potential job layoff or economic downturn. God forbid if something unexpected shows up—car breaking down or household repair costing thousands to fix—to deplete their savings.

Rigidity, measured acceleration, and weight distribution are essential to controlling your balance on a tightrope. Let's dissect each of these from a financial perspective.

A rigid body is resistant to rotation, especially head movements. This may explain why GISAs are so hesitant to focus on anything outside of their financial comfort zone, such as starting a side business to supplement employment income or hiring an attorney to complete an estate plan. They continue their course in a straight line while cautiously looking down, totally oblivious to the hazards that lie ahead.

GISAs rarely deviate from what they know. We know that objects in motion want to go in the same direction. Middle-class comforts want to be enjoyed. Nothing more. Nothing less.

A tightrope walker feels friction as his body's weight is distributed on the next step forward. GISAs don't mind taking that next step forward. They can see it, but the challenge comes when they must look ahead to step 30. Economic friction can't be avoided, but a balancing pole—a financial game plan—can supply GISAs with needed stability in an unstable world.

Microscopic hairs filled with a liquid substance reside in the semicircular canals of the inner ear. They act as a motion sensor to alert the brain on the body's current state of balance, especially upon tilting of the head. As human beings functioning in a three-dimensional world, our vestibular system is trying to keep us balanced while interpreting our vertical, horizontal, or forward or backward head movements. The body can get used to being out of balance. When this occurs for long periods of time, though, stress, pain, illness, or disease invade our bodies and balance sheets.

On the cognitive side, neuroscience hasn't quite caught up with the physical side in gauging our sense of financial balance, a function of the vestibular system. This isn't pseudoscience; it just hasn't been studied to the degree as the tangible aspects of other behavioral forms, thus any findings are theoretical but not necessarily wrong. We just need some willing candidates, scientists, and test subjects to measure how neural pathways in the brain can explain a given social class's likely behavioral norms around *Sociopsychonomics*.

Neuroscientists tend to study areas where the research dollars get distributed, which doesn't include studying social class differences. Who knows, maybe this will change. However, along that front, neuroplasticity is garnering a lot of press these days. The term was first used in 1975 to discuss the idea that our brain has the capacity to develop and change for better (or worse) throughout one's lifetime. More and more neuroscientists are leaning in this direction, which is a position that was taboo just a few decades ago. I will revisit this phenomenon in the chapter on wellness.

I am convinced that how we process our lives through our mental or financial senses will have a profound effect on just how likely we are to move forward, backward, or stay stuck in neutral. The brain will always fight to keep its current neural connections—what we as the programmers believe is normal since our brains don't have independent motherboards—until a new activity or frame of reference shows up to change or supplant our thinking. The brain is always beholden to the programmer, though at times we are inclined to think that it controls us. Not so, but the "second brain" (or GI tract) can.

Conceptual View

For the generationally affluent, their financial topography is seen from a theoretical context. Their world is abstract, full of intangible values and fundamental beliefs that guide their actions, activities, attitudes, and aspirations.

GAPAs see the end from the beginning. The big picture is in full view, as well the sequential steps to accomplish stated goals. Visual acuity or clarity of focus is the catalyst and driving force behind their legacy mandate.

They have an uncanny ability to bring thoughts into reality, thanks in large part to research, resources, and an unshakeable resolve. Plans come to fruition in the right timing and sequence. Concepts come to life as the construction process to develop them unfolds. Any of us can use this same template and achieve better results. Like GAPAs, it is always within our reach, waiting patiently to be uncovered.

> For GAPAs, the model of a successful playbook is predicated on an uncanny ability to bring images and concepts into reality.

As we know, success is a process. The generationally wealthy don't create a new playbook for success, but follow what's already in place. That's why you'll never see GAPAs chase after a financial guru promising newfound riches. There's no secret formula to making money, though trap doors concealing ill-conceived ventures and far-fetched ideas abound to help them lose money.

GAPAs do lose money in investment deals. What's different is that they are meticulous about doing due diligence before capital is deployed. The risks and rewards are understood in their proper context. What is the saving grace for GAPAs? Holding onto their convictions and principles that bypass emotionalism when the economic landscape is spiraling out of control. These attributes are based on logic, not feelings. Emotions can be deceptive.

GAPAs have a mentality that is completely different from GEDAs or GISAs. Danny Levitt, a financial advisor to dozens of affluent clients, says, "The wealthy seek shelter in a process, which, at times, can capitalize on out-of-control fears caused by economic uncertainty. Both money and fear can cloud judgment. The super wealthy do not let their money get into the way of good judgment.

"Policies and procedures often prevent decision-making blunders that could prove catastrophic. The super wealthy are principle-oriented people. This is a defining characteristic that can protect investors when the stock market is acting irrationally."

THE TIME MACHINE EFFECT

I've never been a huge fan of science-fiction movies. *Back to the Future*, starring Michael J. Fox as Marty McFly, was a blockbuster movie series during my teenage years.

The DeLorean time machine that transported Marty McFly between the past and the future was a cool looking car. It did resemble a miniature space ship, with doors that lifted upward but not outward to open. A teammate of mine my freshman year at Worthington Christian drove a DeLorean to school when the first *Back to the Future* hit the big screens in 1985. The generationally affluent don't make a distinction between the past, present, and future. They see time markers as extensions of each other versus segmented moments. They hold to a code of principles outlined in their family constitution, a document that is followed from one generation to the next with few modifications.

The GAPA time machine is adept at going backward so their offspring can appreciate the foundational pillars of a family's beginning, and forward so children and grandchildren can see their contributions to legacy continuity.

Time management is a task GAPAs typically delegate to others who coordinate the daily aspects of a life where every second matters, and is a critical component of GAPAs' terrain. How do they make it work?

You may recall my introduction of Jeff Talbert back in the chapter on time. Jeff is a NetJets team manager. His company provides luxury air travel for the wealthy. He says, "The traditional definition of a time machine can transport a person backward or forward in time. Our definition of a time machine at NetJets is that we create and save our clients time through the efficiency of our product."

> ## SOCIOPSYCHONOMIC FILTER
> Destiny, a component of legacy continuity, is not something you can run from or bump into by accident. Either you'll fulfill it or let it waste away as time passes by.

NetJets clients have access to hundreds of small, private facilities across the U.S. In many of these places, the nearest commercial airport is several hours away. What NetJets offers clients is peace of mind. There's no hassle with long lines at check-in, no security pat downs, no lengthy walks to the terminal gate, and no lost bags. They are transported quickly to their destination of choice. Time has been compressed.

Time is more valuable than money to the generationally wealthy. Time compression can unite a family. Jeff says, "The investment manager on Wall Street can leave the office and head to Teterboro airport in New Jersey where his family will be waiting. They board the plane and reach their destination to enjoy the weekend at their vacation home in Florida. There's no loss of time sitting in an airport. They immediately get to spend more precious hours with their loved ones. To them, no price tag exists to make up for time spent with family. If you can't spend valuable time with your spouse and children, what good is a lot of money?"

CHAPTER

13

ASSET ACQUISITION HABITS

The asset-generating strategies that a social class is likely to pursue, attain, enjoy, and pass on to heirs or charities

Statement Assets

"Showstopper Possessions"

The poor acquire assets that make them feel and look good, items that provide enjoyment despite their unfortunate predicament. They hold on to them as motivation to keep going. Energies are exhausted one day at a time. It's about today; tomorrow and beyond will be dealt with when they arrive. Some GEDAs live, others just exist.

A GEDA's economic doctrine is the same for the jobless man in Appalachia as it is for the single-parent mother in the inner city who yearns to earn a dignified wage: Financial opportunities, it is assumed, are beyond their reach. Why do the poor feel this way? Lack of opportunities. Lack of mentors. Lack of education. Lack of parental support. Lack of endurance to complete a challenging goal. These add up to a lack of hope. Thus, it's natural for them to see their world from the lens of perpetual lack. Unfortunately, most GEDAs don't know any different.

The trampoline syndrome, which I highlighted in the last chapter, can help a small percentage of GEDAs bounce over their economic pain and land in a better place through a fortuitous event or "lucky break." However, most poor people cannot bypass the normal process of financial success. As any middle-class and situationally wealthy person can attest, this success path requires a tremendous amount of sweat equity, patience, and self-reflection to achieve.

How the poor use their assets speaks volumes about their gravitational pull toward consumption. The larger narrative, however, goes much deeper. The "why" behind an acquired asset is significantly more important than what was purchased.

A financial balance sheet is a mere reflection of one's personal net worth statement. Net worth denotes the difference between assets and liabilities. Assets are things owned, while liabilities are debts owed. Three asset categories exist: cash and cash equivalents, investable, and use.

> Intangible assets are the key drivers behind wealth-building assets.

Liabilities are typically defined as short- (less than a year), intermediate- (between one and five years), and long-term debts (greater than five years).

It's true that having too few resources usually spurs out-of-control emotions that result in quick-trigger spending habits. Impulse buying reigns among the poor. Let's go even deeper.

GEDAs tend to hide the fact that life has beaten them down, their spirits embattled by liquidating their cash to buy material goods that are presumed to be absolute necessities. What they can't control in life shows up in loosely gripped consumption habits, and while these feel-good assets lift their spirits, the euphoria is fleeting. In the meantime, they may delay paying their bills, postpone a car repair, or not have enough cash to bury a loved one in a timely manner. It's priority disengagement.

The consumption mentality often masquerades as an urgent need, hence the propensity toward impulse buying. The poor rarely see beyond the moment. Now, frivolous spending can happen at any income level, but it's more common in a scarcity environment dominated by real and imagery fears. Anticipated financial problems often become self-fulfilling prophecies.

"CLEANER THAN THE BOARD OF HEALTH"

A teammate of mine at Ohio State, Mark "Shake and Bake" Baker, was our point guard and point of contact to keep us in line with our fashion. You always thought twice about what you were going to wear in his presence. When your attire wasn't up to par, you braced yourself for the jokes that would follow.

Mark grew up in the ghetto, as I did, in the Arlington Courts housing project in Dayton, an hour's drive west of Columbus. As our team's comedian and wardrobe consultant, Mark judged each player's threads as we entered the locker room before home games. On one occasion, I had a suit on that was pretty spiffy. I'll never forget what he said, "Fundy, I see you baby. You are cleaner than the board of health today." This meant that I passed his wardrobe inspection and wouldn't be ridiculed for wearing something that should have stayed in my closet. Mark told one teammate, Rickey Dudley, a freshman at the time who went on to become an NFL star, "Slick, you have that after-hour joint on. You can only wear that kind of suit after 3 a.m. in the nightclub." Rickey's suit was shiny and dark green with pinstripes. The entire team couldn't help but laugh.

> ### SOCIOPSYCHONOMIC FILTER
> Sneakers may make a statement, but your financial balance sheet walks the talk.

Statement assets also serve as a buffer for GEDAs to keep from being clowned by their peers. Outward appearance in poverty is about manufacturing an image that communicates this message: "I may not have it going on financially, but it looks like I do."

Sure, middle-class and affluent kids are image conscious, too. But when you and your family lack basic economic survival resources, you may take heightened measures to blend in or stand out with the in-crowd. Being on the outside looking in is a terrible predicament for a poor teenager wanting to feel good among her peers. In poverty, wardrobe selection is viewed as pain deflection.

I've bought my share of designer suits and clothes through the years, but neither fashion nor making a wardrobe statement has ever been an endearing trait of mine. However, I do go overboard when it comes to televisions and cars.

We all have our non-negotiable items we want and will spend money on regardless of the economic climate. Cars and TVs are mine. As a certified financial planner, I think latitude should be given to clients in the non-negotiable area if it does not hinder the outcome of a financial goal. Sometimes to win the war, you inevitably lose a few battles along the way.

I wouldn't classify myself today as a sucker for high-end automobiles, but having a nice looking car free of maintenance issues is important to me.

The embarrassment I felt when our car sat stranded on the side of the road or in the parking lot of a nearby shopping center as well as the humiliation of riding in a hooptie emitting smoke as it puttered down the road are unforgettable. The memories would resurface every time I entered the showroom at an auto dealership.

When I turned pro, driving a nice car gave the appearance, or so I thought, that I had arrived. I bought a Mercedes Benz immediately after leaving Ohio State, though I told others that a Honda Accord would be my automobile of choice even in the pros. It was easy to say this when I had no money in my pocket.

Two years after college I bought a Porsche 911 convertible from former Ohio State great and NBA player, Dennis Hopson. This car was the ultimate financial come-up for me. My license plate read "I Get Up" as a sign of my jumping ability on the court. The audio system was off the hook. It was deafening loud and added to my come-up posturing: "Check me out; I've arrived."

I added aftermarket accessories to nearly every car I bought during my NBA days. Sure, I did save and invest a sizable amount from each and every paycheck, but still I wonder what was the point of my accessory obsession? Ego and image, I'm sure, topped the list.

The generationally wealthy, although they can more than afford to do this, don't waste money upgrading a high-end car. This is a fundamental difference in mentalities between the poor, or those still holding on to an impoverished mindset, and the super wealthy. Fortunately, I've outgrown the car accessory trap, but not since my housing project days have I felt ashamed to ride in a car that should have been buried in a junkyard somewhere.

You may recall my reference to using a coat hanger as an antenna for our television back in the ghetto days. My mother or oldest sister Adele controlled what we watched on the one small TV in the house. Mom loved soap operas (I couldn't stand them), and Adele watched *Gilligan's Island* reruns (I absolutely loved them). Her nickname is Ginger, so named after the glamour queen of the show.

In addition to the antenna, the knobs on the TV would get stripped, forcing us to improvise and use pliers to turn the channel. You can probably relate to this if you are acquainted with poverty.

I feel embarrassed to admit this, but I went overboard with televisions as a pro athlete, and at one time we had 20 televisions in our home. Most of them collected dust, but this was immaterial. I wanted the assurance of knowing that I didn't have to wait to watch television or squint to make out what I saw on TV. This definitely was excessive, but you do some questionable things when you leave behind the scarcity world of poverty. Indeed, many of the same habits and behaviors will follow you to your next destination.

> The effects of poverty leave behind a trail of heartache long after its victims have left the plantation of economic misery.

They were invited by your memory to come along. We often go to great lengths to make amends for something that we lacked when times were hard. Economic deprivation can do a number on your psyche.

For our family today, small is the new big. We live a life of simplicity, but are focused on wealth accumulation to meet our future needs, wants, and charitable endeavors: college planning for Nyah and Eli, making a difference in the community, and affording the retirement lifestyle my wife and I desire. We won't actually retire from our life's purpose, but you get the point.

Stability Assets

"Shelter Possessions"

Generational income-stability Americans want protection from the financial elements that rain down on their economic world. I've mentioned them throughout the book, though most of them can be summarized by this fact: Seismic shifts are happening politically, geopolitically, corporately, and financially around the globe. Abrupt or gradual, change unsettles GISAs.

Stability assets provide cover, peace of mind, and security for the middle class. Without financial harmony, their world sways and they look to restore their state of balance.

GISAs rarely venture outside of their financial lane. A good job with benefits is central to their stability narrative. All is good when paycheck security and the status quo are maintained. However, cause for concern looms.

Most GISAs are one paycheck away from slipping into financial ruin. They don't have adequate savings in the event of a job loss, which breeds a play-it-safe mentality. Risks are usually avoided when their money is at stake, even if they are far behind in building meaningful wealth and accomplishing an important financial goal. GISAs' balance sheet is reflective of their cautious nature, and this statement is indicative of their mindset: "Financial opportunities are within my reach." The middle class must pay a price when they're taken out of their comfort zone, and it's unavoidable if financial freedom is their ultimate goal.

SOCIOPSYCHONOMIC FILTER

Most GISAs are one paycheck away from slipping into financial ruin, which breeds a hyper, play-it-safe mentality.

Whenever you are in a position of instability—taking a long step or stretching to grab something overhead—your core, or center of gravity, gets impacted. To stabilize the rest of the body, the core needs tightened, and this requires a conscious effort to pull off.

In high-level sports participation, core strengthening is key to performance and success. Athletes often find their bodies in compromised positions, and those with weaker cores, abdominal and lower back muscles, tend to struggle more. The same can be said about individuals on shaky financial ground.

GISAs don't want to take a step backward into poverty, and most of them are terrified to gravitate toward affluence. They instead want to stay the course—an inner core that is hesitant to financial change.

Given the economic road ahead, Americans must strengthen their monetary cores by incorporating more risk taking and overcoming their fears if they look to bulk up and meet their financial goals. In many respects, that time is now; just look at our country's unsustainable national debt. The GISA challenge, meanwhile, is deciding between maintaining the status quo or pursuing financial freedom. They can make the jump, but only when they abandon the comfortableness that their present financial condition provides.

GEDAs may not know that the cliff of abundance exists, and for the poor who have thought about it, only a few are able to make it to the other side. GAPAs and SAPAs, on the other hand, aren't paying attention to those contemplating the jump over to their side of the mountain. They're preoccupied and already have permanent reservations.

A PREDICTABLE BALANCE SHEET

After the Great Recession in 2008, the wealth gap grew wider between the mega wealthy and the middle class. The stock market not only recovered, but it reached one new high after another. Many GISAs were standing on the sidelines fearing another crisis. Economic booms and busts come and go. Unfortunately, middle-class angst amplifies during the economic lows.

The rich disproportionately profit during good economic times as a percentage of wealth. They can absorb the shock of a downturn because of their flexible asset profile. If cash is needed, they have liquid accounts, marketable securities, and lines of credit at their disposal.

A balance sheet is a snapshot in time of an individual's or family's financial condition. For GISAs, it follows a predictable and general pattern that includes two cars, one house, an assortment of personal property, and a retirement account that's well short of what they'll need to meet future needs. Absent are adequate savings that should contain at least three to six months of living expenses; a game plan to pay for a child's college expenses; a taxable investment account independent of a retirement account; and other income-stream assets that have upside profit potential.

> Wealth has to start in your mind before it manifests in your wallet or bank account.

On the liability side of GISAs' balance sheet are the usual suspects: credit card debt, home mortgage, student debt, and a business loan for some, as their debt loads fluctuate. Debt often rises during periods of economic growth, lax lending standards by the banks, or after a loan is secured to attend college. Many middle-class parents are absorbing too much student debt on behalf of a child and do not have time to make up for a retirement shortfall, considering it could take 20 years to pay off the loan. They are in for a rude awakening.

Debt loads decrease for GISAs when easy access to credit is tightened. They get back on track when financial disequilibrium becomes too unbearable. Now they must target particular, high-interest debts as available cash dictates.

Here are five tips to help the middle class strengthen their personal and financial balance sheets:

Tip #1

Think like a millionaire or billionaire. GISAs must shift their mind-set from four-digit monthly income earners to five-or-more-digit wealth creators. GISAs tend to make this big mistake: They cap their income potential.

Tip #2

GISAs must embrace the concept of making money while they sleep. The stock market has inherent risks, but so does driving a car. Mr. Market also is irrational at times, but this doesn't mean a portfolio can't be protected during turbulent economic times. It can, to a certain degree.

Tip #3

GISAs must find ways to monetize their skill-set to supplement employment income. Identifying passions and interests are good starting points to generate additional cash. Economic survival in the future will require at least three income streams.

Tip #4

GISAs must create a game plan to combat economic vertigo and analysis paralysis. They must find a well-respected, fee-only certified financial planner in their area to assist them in reaching their goals. Accountability is needed when personal responsibility in money matters falls short.

Tip #5

GISAs must check and immediately correct their internal dialogue filter on a daily basis when it turns negative. If not, tips 1 through 4 won't matter.

Stewardship Assets

"Shareholder Possessions"

The generationally affluent take stewardship seriously and don't spend money recklessly. It's easy to lump them in with SAPAs and FAPAs, who can be suckered into the spendthrift and image trap.

GAPAs do not give money away to needy charities simply because a request is made. The request, however laudable the organization's mission is, must align with GAPAs' benevolent playbook and protocol. There's intent behind nearly every dollar that leaves GAPAs' hand.

Stewardship is the coordinated effort to manage and maximize an asset, talent, or skill. GAPAs steward their time with religious fervor. They steward their children to fulfill their potential and carry the family's legacy forward. GAPAs steward financial assets with clarity and conviction.

Good stewards protect financial assets from their own personal devices. In other words, it's imperative to cast emotionalism aside and block insatiable appetites from becoming disruptive forces. Oftentimes, the greatest factor in wealth dissipation is internal in origin.

It is not surprising that most people miss the mark to maximize their wealth by ignoring advice from unbiased observers with professional credentials. GAPAs understand that and follow the suggestions of trusted representatives. The poor and middle classes typically don't have this luxury at their disposal. GEDAs and GISAs can't afford the advice or feel the benefits don't exceed the costs.

Asset growth is a key feature of GAPAs' legacy and charitable footprint. The best wealth advisors are hired after an arduous vetting process, or kept as holdovers when a parent or grandparent dies. These advisors are paid handsomely for their expertise and rightly so, because they must always be on top of their game. GAPAs don't think twice about the compensation arrangement with professionals. As long as they deliver, it's all good. But make no mistake about it. The mega wealthy will fire an investment advisor who falls short in the character department or struggles to protect assets from the effects of inflation and taxes. It's strictly business.

The generationally affluent and many SAPAs live by this economic mindset: Financial opportunities are an extension of their reach. Now, contrast this with GEDAs who believe that financial opportunities are beyond their reach, while GISAs are aware that opportunities are within their reach, but few have the risk appetite to pursue them.

AN ENVIABLE BALANCE SHEET

The generationally wealthy purchase tangible assets, as do the middle class and working poor. GAPAs can buy big homes in multiple locations, designer clothing, and six-figure automobiles on a whim. However, the construction of their balance sheet is executed with precision.

Let's start with cash and cash equivalents. Liquid assets are viewed as an *opportunity fund* by GAPAs, an *emergency fund* by GISAs, and a *crisis fund* by GEDAs. Each social class's characterization of savings has profound implications on their well-being and emotional state.

The poor live in crisis mode with little relief in sight, while the traditional middle class employs a mindset that anticipates financial problems but does little to address them until there is an emergency. The generationally affluent use their available savings to capitalize on exclusive opportunities that are presented only to accredited investors with significant assets and favorable risk-appetite profiles. There always are strategic opportunities for GAPAs to allocate capital.

Cash and cash equivalents for GAPAs include multiple savings and checking accounts, life insurance policies, certificates of deposit, money market accounts, and short-term Treasury securities. Some wealthy people spread their cash and investment assets among various institutions since the FDIC only offers guaranteed protection on certain accounts up to specified limits.

Use assets on the typical GAPA balance sheet, which they are great tacticians at protecting, include multiple high-end automobiles, homes in gated communities, a yacht or private plane (or ownership interest in a luxury jet service), custom home furnishings, and expensive jewelry.

Stocks and bonds, mutual funds with a global focus, business interests, private equity, hedge funds, real estate, precious metals, and commodities are part of their extensive investable assets. Diversification and asset allocation are key drivers of their investment portfolios. We'll cover these concepts in greater detail in the "Investment Planning" section.

The generationally affluent are masterfully diligent in protecting both sides of the balance sheet. Their wealth affords them access to the most lucrative financing options, though they have the liquidity to self-fund most deals. They understand the power of leverage: Long-term success is predicated on bringing other business partners and credit relationships to the table. Network inclusion is a key factor in net worth expansion.

Assets and liabilities are scrutinized to mitigate lawsuit exposures and other disruptive forces to their wealth picture. Protecting their possessions and insulating the family brand from external threats are unavoidable considerations for GAPAs. These will be highlighted in the insurance and estate planning sections. For the generationally affluent, protecting wealth may be more important than the methods used to accumulate it.

A GAPA steward or shareholder does things quite differently. They plan obsessively and take intentional measures to protect their heritage and family identity. Board meetings are scheduled months or (likely years) in advance, while third and fourth generation mentors are hired to coach legacy recipients in the ways of wealth and groom them for family governance positions. These outside consultants are brought in to help offspring clarify their dreams, visions, aspirations, charitable interests, and passions in life, which of course, must merge seamlessly into their family's overarching framework—regardless of their biological connection. No exceptions exist in this meritorious system of checks and balances.

14

PRIMARY SENSORY-LEARNING DRIVERS

*The dual approached used to reach a
social class through their senses*

Sight and Taste

How do you get the poor to see and taste a different kind of success? First, movement toward or away from a behavior will often be contemplated based on the stimulation of somatosensory inputs of the parietal lobe: taste (palatable connection), touch (kindred connection), temperature (emotional connection), and pain (pressure-gauge connection). However, the primary sensory-learning drivers to move GEDAs through the process of change are sight and taste.

Superstars never shy away from taking game-winning shots. They relish the moment on the big stage and are followed by millions of adoring fans on social media. Even after they've retired, their exploits are never forgotten. Why? Superstars provide salient emotional experiences that are witnessed and enjoyed by mesmerized spectators who want to associate with a proven winner. No sports fan will ever forget Michael Jordan's game-winning shot against the Utah Jazz in the 1998 NBA Finals, or Tom Brady's heroic efforts to lead his team to victory in Super Bowl LI.

The poor's path to success must be shown to them and filled with neon lights, flashy signs, and timely messages from inspirational coaches that keep them engaged. Without that type of emotional support, GEDAs are apt to return to their land of lack and unfulfilled

> To change a fatalistic mindset, you must meet the poor where their sensory-learning drivers are.

dreams quicker than a New York minute. Such giant goals come with their share of giant obstacles. Visual stimulation keeps them focused on the goal ahead. Distractions must be viewed as background noise that doesn't deserve their attention.

Not everyone will become a professional athlete or entertainer, but there are hundreds of career paths that over the long haul are just as, if not more, rewarding in terms of personal satisfaction and cumulative benefits. More importantly, they show GEDAs the way out. The choice to leave won't be easy. If the escape route is taken, others might find it easier to follow.

If seeing is believing, then tasting is achieving. The poor know how to taste bitterness and disappointment, but what about the taste of success? They deserve this opportunity. Now, we can argue about how it should be administered or who should pay for it, but they need be given access to favorable outcomes that can change the trajectory of their flight path. They deserve a seat at the legacy table, too.

Speak the language that appeals to GEDAs' sensory experiences, which is the use of metaphors. Metaphors matter a great deal when economic survival and social class mobility are on the line.

Financial semantics also matter when the issue of capability is discussed or implied. Slight changes in word choices can be key drivers in getting people to reshape their economic frame of reference, a requirement before advancing up the social class ladder.

I cringe hearing someone use the term *financial literacy*. Literacy is the ability or competency one has in a field of study. For literacy to follow the word *financial*, it conveys a lack of financial knowledge in economic matters and implies the inability to learn as well. By its nature, this term offers a codified meaning of inadequacy or inferiority in intellectual thinking, processing, and decision-making—the domain of the executive command or prefrontal cortex.

Poverty does tax the brain, but new neural pathways can reverse the damage done from chaotic toxicity that often accompanies a life of economic misery. The brain of a GEDA child can learn high-level financial concepts to the same degree as the brain of a GAPA child. I don't water down what is taught to impoverished populations. If anything, they need constant exposure to wealth-building concepts that arouse their possibility filter.

Financial illiteracy is primarily used to describe underserved populations, GEDAs and GISAs with less than stellar balance sheets or net worth statements.

It's never an issue about capability; it has everything to do with accessibility. The poor and middle class are punished for not knowing the language and ways of wealth. That's why I find it highly offensive given my impoverished roots and transplanted middle-class ways to mention the term *financial literacy*. It pains me to even say it. My word choice: financial education.

CONFESSIONS OF A FORMER JUNK-FOOD ADDICT

From the front of the tongue to the back, the five distinctive tastes include salty (tip and front sides), sweet (tip and top front), savory (tip and top front), sour (middle sides) and bitter (back middle).

Addictive foods have distinct flavor profiles and do a number on our taste buds, according to scientific studies. Basically, they keep us coming back for more, going to great lengths to duplicate that ecstatic feeling to satisfy our fix again and again.

The reward center, repetitive actions that trigger deep pleasure from an activity, are the result of processes that join forces in the frontal and temporal lobes of our cerebral cortex and gastrointestinal tract to form a wicked, addicted response. The thought is retrieved from memory to satisfy a craving, which we entertain incessantly in our mind and gut, or "second brain." (A significant portion of dopamine, a reward neurotransmitter, and serotonin, a feel-good neurotransmitter, are produced in the gut.)

Arousal, a crescendo effect, begins in anticipation of the actual reward. Our pupils dilate to show our level of excitement, but we still aren't satisfied. We plot the steps required to pull off the fix, which in this case is food. We arrive at our destination—the grocery store, drive-thru line, refrigerator, or kitchen cabinet—for our reward. The euphoric feeling takes hold as we ingratiate ourselves in the experience. Nothing else but the sensation matters at that moment. We get what we want as the food is consumed. Our taste buds are satisfied. Goal completed, that is, until that compulsive feeling churns inside and we are once again held captive to the unrelenting devices of our addictive food behavior.

As a former junk-food addict, I remember the struggles quite well. For someone with a naturally slender body type, a fast metabolism, and a few extra dollars in his pocket, a junk-food addiction can be dangerous.

The 1998 NBA lockout that precipitated an abbreviated season of 50 games left players with a lot of time on their hands. I picked up, or should I say returned to, a bad habit. Too much time on my hands culminated in long drives from the suburbs to a less desirable area of Columbus to fetch some potato chips.

The potato chips that I pursued weren't sold in big-box grocery stores, which were much closer to our home. Had this been the case, I would have saved a lot of gas money. Also, my wife wouldn't have been so worried about me heading into a crime-infested area.

I pulled up to the convenient store in my high-end sports car. A few customers recognized me, while others gave me a strange look. I wasn't a neighborhood fixture. They didn't know I was coming to get my fix, and it didn't matter what anyone thought. The folks who typically shop at these types of stores tend to know each other. Strangers stand out like a sore thumb.

I bought half a dozen large bags of Grippos Bar-B-Q potato chips. I got in my car and immediately opened one of them before the key was in the ignition. The bag was gone before I made it to the freeway. The second bag was opened as I pulled into our garage.

These potato chips, the company's bestseller, certainly had a grip on me. The taste, texture, temperature, and tang of each chip excited my taste buds. I haven't had them in more than a decade, but the aroma of an opened bag of Grippo's would make me think twice. I wouldn't want to put myself in that situation.

CAN YOU TASTE SUCCESS?

Why do the poor associate life events or experiences with the sensation of taste? Reasons may vary, but consider this. Their diet is high glycemic (think junk food), low in nutritional value (think processed food), and limited in variability (think empty carbs and bad fats). With limited resources, quantity is more important than quality. Scarcity forces them to make predictable choices. I will expand on this in the next chapter, but in short, the typical GEDA diet is high in sugars and starches and additives. Absent are antioxidants, phytonutrients, vitamins, minerals, and probiotic-rich superfoods. These nutrients can help the brain, body, and gut flora ward off illness and disease and stay focused in a classroom setting.

The poor tend to consume pick-me-up foods and sugary drinks at bargain prices that provide temporary jolts of energy. Unfortunately, the residual effects are hazardous to their health and concentration efforts. Staying alive is what's on their mind. Staying healthy or attentive in an academic environment isn't their most pressing concern.

In terms of positive behaviors and responses, it's important to validate the poor from the perspective of their taste buds.

Taste, a sensory receptor processed in the parietal lobe, serves as an anchor for the poor to accept the bitterness of life's cruel fate. It helps them cope with the pain of misery and despair through their consumption of food. It can drive them to execute sweet revenge when an injustice occurs. It may even help some poor and middle-class people savor the palatable nature of a successful life.

Meeting with a nonprofit representative from New York, I discussed sensory-learning drivers for the poor, the methodology and tactics to reach them, taste in particular, and the phrase "That's sweet." All the while, I'm watching as he smiles and licks his lips as I take him into a virtual and sensory-filled world using descriptive words equating a successful behavior with taste and conjuring up images of delightful foods. His actions appeared to be unconscious, conditional responses that excited his palate, memories, and emotions. In other words, he couldn't help it.

Metaphors can be important tools to use when presenting to poor communities. Here are several taste metaphors that do not refer to food: "That's sweet," an explanation or response given that something is cool, nice, or good; "that's salty," given to show disapproval of something said or an action taken by someone else; "that's a lemon," references a car or asset in bad condition; and "that's butter" describes a person's talent, skill, or physical feature.

The metaphor most often used by me in the presence of inner-city children from impoverished backgrounds is "That's sweet." This phrase affirms their ability to learn as well as their capability to achieve any worthwhile goal that takes patience, discipline, and refinement of character to achieve. I want them to activate their taste receptors in such a way that success becomes attainable and automatic. They can taste, touch, and see it with their mental senses.

My goal with the poor is simple: I want them to become addicted to the process of success, knowing that the rewards will follow in time. I want them to transfer their food addiction for a success addiction, which I believe they can.

I learned how to do this early on as a poor kid. The insatiable benefit that couldn't sustain me from food or a sugary beverage was found in a success addiction. I am not a fan of any addictive behavior that can lead to a troubling outcome, but this was a coping mechanism I used to keep my sanity amid economic chaos and neighborhood dysfunction. Sure, I had other outlet choices, but this is the one that worked for me.

One last thing. Life lessons are plentiful in sports participation. You don't celebrate the sweetness of a victory until the horn sounds and the game ends, so keep going until you hear it. Cockiness, not confidence, is a magnet for a humility wake-up call. I should know.

CHANGE YOUR IMAGE, CHANGE YOUR LIFE

For the generationally poor, what they see largely determines what they think is economically possible. Their landscape—despair, dysfunction, and despondency in dehumanizing conditions—doesn't offer them much hope in crafting a positive image of success.

Image consultants are needed to inspire and accessorize the poor in the finest visuocognitive and accomplishment threads. They must help clients clothe themselves in colorful goals with vibrant apparel that make this statement, "I'm coming up, check me out!"

Getting dressed for the success journey isn't just a catchphrase; it also may define the difference between floundering in a sea of economic hardship or getting rescued from it.

Nonprofit organizations across the country—Dress for Success, Clothes That Work, Image and Attitude, Bridge to Success, Jackets and Jobs, and Suited for Change—empower their constituents to upgrade their tangible and intangible wardrobes. In other words, the poor are learning much-needed financial life skills.

For GEDAs, this transformation starts inward and moves outward. Single moms struggling to make ends meet and men who spent time incarcerated are now feeling good about themselves. A positive self-image is half the battle to reaching the self-sufficiency mountaintop, and the poor must paint a portrait of their future selves that is far different than their current image. (For more information on organizations that provide disadvantaged communities with job skills training, please visit www.jailstojobs.org.)

> ### SOCIOPSYCHONOMIC FILTER
> An outwardly distraught countenance could be a mirror image of an inwardly bleak success picture.

In one of our summer camp activities, children spend two days creating their future life and financial portrait. They use paint, magazine cutouts, markers, construction paper, excitement and animation, and a boundless imagination to complete this task.

Health, wealth, family, relationships, education, charity, and career-aspiration themes force students to envision their future, a world with invigorating hues. Color theory is introduced during this lesson, which holds that colors stimulate certain emotions or disseminate various attributes. For example, blue is said to communicate trust, strength, and dependability. Perhaps, this is why middle-class employees are aptly described as being blue-collar workers.

At the end of the week, career professionals, including doctors, lawyers, accountants, business owners, investment advisors, financial planners, and marketing executives, are brought in. This gathering provides a venue in which students can network and describe their artistic designs to white-collar professionals. Parents are also invited to support their children in this life-changing experience.

I'm always struck by the countenance of impoverished participants, especially teenagers, who take part in our life and financial empowerment workshops. Some embrace the moment, while others slouch down in their chairs, giving the initial appearance they aren't interested in anything I might have to say. Most of the students have somber looks on their faces, as if they're not sure what to make of me or the opportunity presented to them.

Body language has never deterred me from carrying out my purpose. In fact, I step up my game to another level. I'm exhausted afterward to keep them engaged, but so be it.

To change the countenance of those suffering in poverty, you must change their circumstances, if only visually. You must transport them, in their mind, to a world that is full of possibilities, even if the excursion is temporary or fleeting in nature. The generationally wealthy have a success time machine. Why can't the poor have one also?

If something like a success time machine existed, GEDAs wouldn't likely use it because they'd consider the cost too prohibitive. They would then bail on the entire idea given the demands and process involved to complete long-term goals.

We help poor children metaphorically build their individual success time machines by immersing them in the three E's: experience, excitement, and eats. The experience must be salient on the positive side or it will quickly be forgotten. Participants are reeled in to the financial apps that we've created for their personal enjoyment, but the takeaway lessons are the real fruit. These should last a lifetime depending on the duration and length of our engagement with them.

A change in poor students' countenance comes as excitement builds inside of them, that feeling of warmth. Great teachers in our nation's schools do this every day. To those who do, I salute you.

SOCIOPSYCHONOMIC FILTER
Seeing and tasting success, even for a brief moment, can go a long way in changing a life and legacy.

Seeing their peers look happy and become more animated instills a collective hope among participants, creating a ripple effect throughout the room. They grasp the correlation between education, formal and financial, and a better quality of life in the future. For that moment, they can see, touch, and taste a successful life. It's not as daunting as they originally thought.

The experience and excitement must be combined with eating. Good food that tastes great has a synergistic effect on the mind and body. Healthy food and It's All Good Cookies,™ a company my wife started that makes delicious and nutritious cookies with real ingredients, satisfy their palates. We never cut corners on what we place in their minds and bodies for their educational, financial, personal, and nutritional development.

A DESTINATION TO REACH

I bumped heads on the basketball court in college with former Michigan basketball star Chris Webber. But we joined our hearts together as NBA teammates to save inner-city youth in Sacramento from 1999 to 2003.

Webber, our team's superstar, was sitting alone on the plane ride from Sacramento for one of our long, East Coast trips. We had a discussion on helping kids escape poverty. The gist of our conversation follows:

> **Me:** Monya and I recently started a nonprofit to help inner-city kids make it in life. What are you passionate about?
>
> **Webber:** Fundy, my heart breaks for those kids who will have a hard time in life without the right guidance and direction. My mom and dad were always there for me and my siblings. We were very fortunate. What do you two got in mind?
>
> **Me:** We're providing educational programs and field trips to enlarge their vision. We take poor kids out of their environment and show them what's possible, what success looks like, and that the world is much bigger than their neighborhood.
>
> **Webber:** Man, you're so right! It's important to get them to see success up close and have a good time experiencing it. Look, I just started a limo company and I want you to use our bus to transport your kids on those trips. It's laid out inside with leather seats, cool lighting, and a killer sound system.
>
> **Me:** C-Webb, this is unbelievable and will go a long way in supporting our belief that just a few minutes out of the 'hood can jumpstart a person's dream.
>
> **Webber:** Also, I want to plant a financial seed, my brother. I love what you and Monya are doing. Here's a check.

I declined but he grabbed my right arm and forced a check into my hand. When I looked at it, the amount was for $12,000, which left me speechless. C-Webb's generosity was the largest check ever written by any single donor to LFYO.

On the first field trip in C-Webb's limousine bus, we took the kids ice skating and treated them to a five-course dinner at the upscale Firehouse Restaurant in Old Sacramento. Owner Lloyd Harvego hosted us for the evening, a wonderful man who has used his affluence and influence to make a difference in the community. A participant named Stephen said something that I'll never forget after being the last kid to be dropped off that night. He shared, "Mr. and Mrs. Fundy, I never want this day to end."

Years later, we were fortunate enough to purchase the LFYO Mercedes Cruiser, complete with satellite TV, PlayStation, and 12 leather seats. Thanks, C-Webb, for your inspiration to transport children in style. They deserve it.

Movement is a necessity for parietal lobers, a group that includes many poor students. Public schools and nonprofit organizations make a big mistake by not including imagination boosters or success trips throughout the year into the educational experience. These should be non-negotiable, line-item expenses. Regular success trips, even just to the other side of town, could go a long way in broadening poorer students' outlook on life and improve their academic performance. They need to see what success looks like before they are willing to taste it.

Smell and Hear

In comparison to the middle class, I've often said that it is easier for the poor to achieve financial success because their mindset proffers a what-do-I-have-to-lose attitude. The middle-class mindset, however, is the complete opposite. GISAs think they have everything to lose, so when economic disruptions erupt, they become their own worst enemy. They are quick to rifle through their Rolodex—the hippocampus that helps form, store, and process memory—and retrieve historical outcomes that provide context for the current situation. They worry more about what could go wrong instead of what they are doing right.

A GISA's vestibular system that is experiencing financial distress sends out urgent signals to control what can be controlled even more: working harder on the job, saving money, and paying close attention to discretionary expenditures. They anchor down even more in the things that provide them balance.

Outside of these factors, GISAs give little attention to financial decisions that don't appear vital to the preservation of their middle-class lifestyle. I've outlined several of them in earlier chapters, but a few are worth noting again. They include incapacity planning, income replacement, and legacy continuation.

It shouldn't come as a surprise that smelling and hearing are the two primary sensory-learning drivers for the middle class that play a large role in their sense of economic balance.

A discussion of each of these follows.

A KEEN SENSE OF SMELL

Our bodies are a creative miracle. We may isolate the vestibular system from the central nervous and digestive systems, but they work together as one integrated unit.

It boggles my mind how a scent can trigger a physiological chain of events that cause us to lose our balance, send our nerves on high alert, and tie our stomachs in knots. The body senses danger and will take measures to protect itself.

Think about a situation in which you jumped to a faulty conclusion that was manufactured in your mind, not someone else's. I can think of dozens of examples in my life when I got my body worked up in a stress-induced state based on an illogical assumption. The body doesn't differentiate between faux or authentic triggers.

A positive comment from a boss, colleague, friend, or coach can have long-lasting effects. In those examples, a pleasant aroma is emitted, causing the opposite reaction in the body. We feel balanced, our nerves are calm, and our breathing, as measured by the expansion and contraction of our diaphragm, is not gasping for air.

Temporal lobers are greatly affected by words and smells that make them feel secure or vulnerable, and none more than when their financial equilibrium is on the line.

Our olfaction system (aka smelling center) can differentiate thousands of odors in a split second. But the physiological reaction generated, or how the body feels, often responds to real and perceived odors the same, though the intensity level of the smell may vary from pleasing to putrid. However, the deep-rooted feelings of being overwhelmed, distraught, agitated, or grief stricken produce chemical responses that alert us to deal with a problem—right now!

These feelings drive our state of indifference or dissatisfaction with a financial outcome or experience.

Imagine GISAs surveying the current economic landscape. Their keen sense of smell is on high alert. Something is not right. The playing field and opportunities are not equal as the forces of globalism, fanaticism, capitalism, recidivism, fatalism, and emotionalism squeeze them.

The connection between the vestibular system of the temporal lobe and the proprioception center in the parietal lobe is profound. The vestibular system controls our balance, while proprioception helps us understand where we are in relation to our environment. If we feel out of balance, we will have a difficult time navigating our financial landscape to reach an intended destination, such as paying for a child's college expenditures, retiring with enough money, or leaving a financial legacy for others to enjoy.

GISAs smell a foul, paralyzing odor in the air. They know movement toward financial freedom should be taken but feel stuck in a deep rut. How are they going to get out without being pushed?

Their keen sense of smell can cause them to question the intentions of financial representatives who really do want to help. Of course, professional advice isn't free and GISAs tend to deliberate indefinitely on whether to seek the services of a financial consultant. A discount, or the accumulation of benefits that far exceed the costs, just might be the catalyst to move them to act.

SWEET MUSIC TO THEIR EARS

The value proposition in attending a financial workshop is tough to sell to GISAs when the basics of life are on solid footing: a stable job, adequate savings, and homeownership. Even when the foundation is shaky, it's still a challenge to get GISAs in the door. Without gimmicks or pushy tactics, how do you convince them to act? Give them a great deal that they can't afford to pass up.

A great deal is sweet music to the ears of GISAs, and they listen for buzzwords to trigger a reaction: markdown, price reduction, discount, rollback, bargain, closeout sale, budget price, rebate, and cost savings. Their ears perk up even more when a good deal becomes a can't-miss steal.

Groupon, Target, Costco, Southwest, and Amazon appeal to the consumer who is cost conscious, which encompasses the middle class, the bedrock of the U.S. economy. Deals are persuasive gestures to move people to action. GISAs do not know how good of a deal they are really getting until they attend a life-changing seminar or work with a seasoned professional who, as a fiduciary, really does have their best interests at heart. Most workshops, the kind you see advertised on TV, draw participants in to sell them a residual product or service after the event. GISAs are leery of salespeople disguised as financial mentors or coaches. As an educator and fee-only certified financial planner, I make a clear distinction between my profession and that of commission-based salespeople.

BODY LANGUAGE: WHAT GISAs ARE COMMUNICATING

It's hard to determine what percentage of communication is nonverbal, but our bodies can do a lot more talking than our mouths, especially when the subject of personal finance is discussed.

Money is intensely personal, and people will unconsciously affirm or contradict what they are saying through their body language, which must be viewed in context. The venue could be cold or hot. The chairs may be hard or soft. The audience might be hungry or well fed. The time of the day could be early morning or mid-afternoon. These are additional factors to take into consideration in monitoring behavioral cues.

I pay close attention to hand gestures, body positioning, and eye movements whenever I am presenting to large and small audiences alike.

Planners, educators, and executives need to be mindful of their body language and quite adept at interpreting what others may be communicating with theirs.

Body language is not native to a social class, but GISAs have displayed some rather noticeable behaviors in my presence. Here are a few of them:

Pulling on an Ear
- what has been said is a threat to their economic frame of reference, or unsettling to hear.
- left ear pull could also be interpreted as the retrieval of an auditory detail, and a right ear pull to retrieve an auditory outline.

Rubbing the Nose
- the aroma of what has been said doesn't pass their smell test, or is too convicting.
- this gesture may also be used to signal that a deep breath is needed to calm their nerves.

Scratching the Side of the Head with Eye Squinting

- head scratch near the left ear is the comprehension and visualization of a detail, and a head scratch near the right ear is the processing and visualization of big-picture information.

Nervous Energy or Being Fidgety

- subtle gestures and eye contact with their partner that communicate, "Hey, this is where we are coming up short financially." (Couples do not sit together at our financial workshops. This prevents undue influence. Also, spouses need to make independent decisions in case the other spouse becomes incapacitated or dies.)

Deflated Body

- sink down in their chair, stunned and dejected, after estimating their retirement living projections based on current expenses (rule of thumb calculation for retirement money need is 25 times current living costs).

Paralyzed Bodies

- an in-depth discussion of our nation's fiscal situation often renders them immobile and despondent.

Enlarged Eyes

- gaps in areas of their financial situation that are revealed during the Mr. Fundy's Life and Financial Planning Playbook for Adults™ are eye-opening and shocking.

Touch and Faith

Touch, a physical or emotional sensation, is critically important while connecting with those in generational poverty. They must feel a sensory or kindred association with your message, but taste and sight are the primary sensory-learning drivers needed to upgrade the poor's frame of reference and pessimistic mindset.

The sense of touch through mental or cognitive measures is an absolute necessity when working with the generationally wealthy. Their world is conceptual, full of symbolism and tradition that make a statement without uttering a single word.

Persuasive speech and elegant words may make you look smart, but these don't automatically endear you to GAPAs. They respect knowledge but aren't captivated by it or someone who brags about his impressive credentials.

In the past, I've tried to move GAPAs through intellectual stimulation by seasoning it with a rhetorical bent. It's their language, but it may not excite their soul when deciding to support a laundry list of charitable suitors who are in desperate need of financial assistance. GAPAs rarely deviate from their benevolence script, no matter how urgent the request.

My pleas for the super wealthy who attend our fundraising events to do more in assisting the poor are contemplated, but may not move them to action. Emotionalism is a physical sensation; GAPAs prefer cognitive orientation that moves a legacy forward. The generationally affluent start with the end in mind first, which solidifies the continuation of their heritage.

For GAPAs, life's purpose serves as the foundation to their playbook. Food, shelter, clothing, and transportation are important, but these do not drive and only supplement their sense of self. The who, why, where, what, and when questions that shape GAPAs' purpose in life are: Who am I? Why am I here? Where am I going? What are my contributions to the world and our family's heritage? When can I reasonably expect to fulfill the legacy mandate for which I am personally liable?

Abraham Maslow's theory, Hierarchy of Needs, is often used to provide context in explaining human motivation. At the most basic level are physiological needs, which include food, water, oxygen, and sleep. Moving up the order of needs next comes safety (employment, shelter, and health), belonging or love (friendships and family support), and esteem (confidence and respect). At the top is self-actualization (creativity, morality, and purpose).

I don't believe Abraham Maslow's Hierarchy of Needs follows such a smooth, progression pattern, which certainly wasn't my experience as a child. In poverty, lower-order needs are just as important as higher-order needs. In fact, compression of needs into one scaffolding level is required to escape economic hardship. Time is of the essence. You can't sit around and wait for the next leg up to appear before the light bulb turns on to fulfill your potential. You'd never get out if you followed, in lock step, Abraham Maslow's sequential script.

I was fortunate to see beyond my present circumstances as a poor kid from the projects even when my lower- and middle-order needs were being questionably fulfilled. I knew there was something more to life than a dismal environment. How I envisioned my place in the world back then as a teenager isn't that much different than today. Only time has changed.

I never bought into the belief, pervasive in poverty, that says there is a nothingness to life. Life has purpose, and this message is embedded into every speech I offer to those stuck in economic hardship. Life's purpose is an abstract concept to the poor, who experience mild to severe dysfunction and random chaos on a daily basis. Getting them to wrap their arms around an intangible notion is tough. Those who do grab a hold of it are able to get out. Unfortunately, very few do.

HIDDEN EVIDENCE WAITING TO BE REVEALED

Philosophy intrigues me as a way to explain the deeper things of life, though without the God of the Bible being included in the discussion, this field of study has serious shortcomings. However, some things can only be understood through faith, especially laws and principles that exist in the invisible realm.

Faith is hidden evidence waiting to be revealed. Most of us need documented proof that a challenging goal will materialize before we take the first step to achieve it. This is human nature, but it's based on a faulty assumption that discomfort is a sure sign problems exist. In the unseen realm, that queasy feeling in our stomachs may show up to compel us to trust our physical senses less, and push us to rely on our mental (or spiritual) senses more. This is counterintuitive to our normal way of thinking.

> Most of us need documented proof that a challenging goal will materialize before we take the first step to achieve it.

The generationally wealthy understand that success is a process of planting and harvesting. It takes faith to wait for a goal to show signs of life. When efforts aren't immediately rewarded, most people turn back.

GAPAs know that in order to touch a future goal, they must let go of their doubts, fears, and the roadblocks they can physically see. As a preacher once said, "Fear is not the opposite of faith, sight is."

The capitalization of intangible attributes—clear thinking, deductive reasoning, navigational prospecting, and future planning—is a distinguishing trait of generational affluence, albeit with a big-picture purpose in mind. GAPAs are guided by an unswerving faith to grab, grasp, take hold of, or carry their legacy mantle forward. As you know by now, the responsibility of legacy continuity isn't optional for GAPA offspring. It's mandatory.

A CAUSE FOR ALARM

I had a meeting with Steve (not his real name) regarding legacy continuity. It took months to arrange a meeting time conducive to our respective schedules. Even then, his calendar was booked. He squeezed me in given the serious topic at hand. Of course, my schedule, unlike his, was clear three months out.

Steve and his family are generationally wealthy, with an estimated net worth that most of us can only dream about. They play the real-life version of Monopoly, while the rest of us are relegated to the board game.

Steve does emit a confident disposition, free of arrogance but full of stately class befitting a person of royalty. If you make it a point to brag about your wealth all the time, then you are foolishly being controlled by it. GAPAs don't do this. Class is an enduring quality that is always on display.

Steve exudes, like most GAPAs, that "it" factor. A lifestyle that can afford any experience, product, service, or desire does offer them a cherished and enviable place in our society.

After a few customary pleasantries, Steve and I turn our attention to the three big E's that GAPA parents have for their children: education, experiences, and expectations. Each play a major role in legacy continuity.

After showing several of our financial education apps, Steve shares that he is worried about whether his children will have the ambition to earn their own wealth. It's a conversation that needs to take place at the appropriate time. I provided a few insights and talking points to broach this subject with his children, which he took to heart.

Money is a taboo subject among the generationally affluent. Kids know they are privileged, but parents typically do not discuss finances with them. Most often, they learn important financial terms and investment concepts through second-hand knowledge.

Kids are sent to camps or attend secretive, closed-door workshops with other affluent peers to learn about financial management and wealth accumulation. GAPA parents do want their children to be financially savvy. It's part of a child's educational development and personal brand. However, I think mega-wealthy parents should take more ownership in teaching their children about money, the good and bad side of it.

Prior to our meeting, Steve vetted me to get an idea of my value proposition. He didn't want to waste time on the nonessentials and agreed to meet after I touched his *legacy nerve*.

This legacy nerve gives GAPAs cause for alarm, and may explain why so many of them are giving away the bulk of their wealth to charity instead of their children. They are keenly aware that handouts can do more harm than good, especially for those children wearing the trust-fund baby label as fully functioning adults, perfectly capable of earning their own keep after the age of 30, an accountability marker for them to start building meaningful wealth.

GAPA parents know their children, but they also know the fickle nature of the human spirit. Their children are given a head start in life, but eventually they must run their own race.

I make it a point to touch the mind, heart, or soul of GAPAs through their faith lens. They have extensive knowledge and experience in bringing ideas into reality. In many respects, this is what separates the generationally wealthy from every other socioeconomic subset. They're not magicians, just people who operate using the laws of physics and compound interest. GAPAs also live in the world of possibilities. If you offer a suggestion that will augment some aspect of their lives, you will be viewed as an asset.

Nonverbal communication that works well with GAPAs and other social class subsets include the following:

Mind

I often point to the side of my forehead to reinforce a plan or problem-solving strategy that will enhance their playbook.

Heart

A hand over my heart conveys the sacredness of something special that needs to be cherished and protected: a child, a marriage, a reputation, a cause, or a carefully crafted legacy.

Soul

Using an index finger, I place it in the center of my opposite hand to emphasis the sanctity of a creed, value, or guiding principle.

15

WELLNESS

The proactive or default strategy deployed by a social class when emotional or physical well-being is on the line

Disclaimer

I've been providing physical fitness training for over 12 years and it's a huge part of my life. But I am not a physician, so you should check with a qualified healthcare practitioner before starting any exercise or nutrition program.

Symptomatic

Poverty is home to millions of Americans who often tough it out and push through various health and emotional challenges. They continue to fight or disregard painful symptoms until their bodies can't take the suffering any more. A visit to the dentist, doctor, or emergency room is truly an urgent matter in many instances. Let's step inside this world to get an up-close look of their environment, a danger zone that carries enormous health risks.

Drive through the impoverished areas within rural and inner-city communities, and what will you find? Vandalized and boarded up windows, houses that ooze sanitary problems, and faulty ventilation systems that breed allergy and mold problems, wreaking havoc on the respiratory systems of the occupants. Couple that with a chaotic living arrangement and crime-infested neighborhoods, and it shouldn't come as a surprise that the end result will be a bunch of stressed-out bodies.

These health challenges are accentuated for adults and kids alike when family members smoke in the home, abodes face ongoing infestations of bedbugs or roaches, and by the growing number of poor people who are homeless living in a shelter or on the streets with their kids.

In a 2015 *Scientific American* article titled "Poverty Disturbs Children's Brain Development and Academic Performance," Diana Kwon writes about an interesting study conducted by Seth Pollak and his colleagues from the University of Wisconsin-Madison. They found that the gray matter in the temporal lobes and frontal lobes, key areas of the brain that are critical to memory and learning, were roughly 10 percent below normal development in poor children when compared to their middle-class and affluent peers. That's significant and carries immense implications.

Toss in poor nutrition and sleep deprivation, and it shouldn't come as a surprise that so many of our nation's poorer students struggle in school. In fact, school may be the only place where they can get a reprieve from the disorder, which is often the routine they find at home or in the neighborhood. But instead of learning, it's not uncommon to see kids fall asleep at their desks, using arms and hands to prop up their heads. We must do more to help the poor. Of course, they must help as well.

Our heavy hearts are overwhelmed every time we drop a group of poor kids off at their front door after they participate in one of our LFYO programs. The yard is usually unkempt, and the neighborhood is littered with trash. My wife never ventures inside their house or apartment with me. She stays back and waves at the kids from the limousine or van. I am quite familiar with the sights, sounds, and smells of poverty; Monya is not. As I'm walking up to the door, I tell the kids not to feel embarrassed by my presence in their home. However, once inside, the memories return and I am back to my humble roots, but there is a difference. This time I don't have to spend the night in poverty after saying my goodbyes.

I make no distinction between poor and rich kids, though I do provide im-poverished children with more care and attention since their emotional state is often more fragile than their affluent peers. They receive hugs and high-fives in abundance. Tavis Smiley, a prominent and influential advocate for the poor, once shared with a Columbus audience his typical introduction to disenfranchised communities: "I got a lotta love for you, and there's nothing you can do about it." Love is a very powerful word and motivational tool, but it shouldn't be used lightly in the presence of GEDAs.

Tavis's words aptly describe how I feel about the poor, though I will hold them accountable for what they can reasonably control, especially in the area of their thought life. Toxic thinking is one of the main contributors to poor health and their fatalistic outlook on life.

A TRUE EMERGENCY

In terms of physical and emotional wellness, the poor typically have a symptomatic outlook and behavioral response. Unfortunately, this follows a familiar pattern in other areas of their lives where symptoms are addressed but the root causes are not.

GEDAs visit a doctor when symptoms of an illness cause such intense pain that they can no longer avoid it. Type II diabetes, a preventable condition, is a perfect example. Loss of sight or loss of a limb just might be the last attempt to change course with their lifestyle choices, but most poor people don't.

It has been said that 20 percent of the people in America consume 80 percent of the healthcare services. I don't know if this statement is true, but it sounds plausible from this standpoint: Our overcrowded emergency rooms are the option of choice for the poor to receive a doctor's care.

Dr. LaMont Clay, a personal friend and emergency room physician in Columbus, grew up on Chicago's South Side, a community that for decades has been riddled by crime, poverty, and hopelessness. His family later moved to Oak Park, an affluent suburb in the western part of the city. He sheds light on why the generationally poor wait until a potentially life-threatening health crisis shows up before they visit an ER doctor.

"I believe the poor live on a day-to-day basis, and as such, they do not worry about what tomorrow brings. This includes their health. They are consumed in a survival mode, forced to think of the next meal. The next day, week, or year is never a sure thing, so planning is not a priority. The poor fear getting sick, but they don't trust the medical profession, so to them, it is easier to avoid interacting with doctors until they have no choice and a trip to the emergency room occurs," he says.

With no established connection with a family physician, many GEDAs' only encounter with a doctor is in the ER, where the doctors come and go and are unfamiliar with the patients or their health backgrounds. Opportunities and relationships come and go, too. This is the transient nature of poverty, which GEDAs accept.

GEDAs are taught to be leery of doctors because they pry into their business or make an existing condition worse through medical diagnoses the poor construe as judgmental or belittling. Obesity and drug addiction top this back-off-from-judging-me list. To them, lifestyle suggestions from outsiders should stay on mute.

THE PERCEPTION OF PAIN: MORE DEBILITATING THAN THE REALITY OF IT

As a kid, I hated going to the dentist, dreading the pain of having a tooth pulled or cavity filled. The thought of it sent chills up and down my spine, and the sound of the dentist's drill created knots in my stomach. The good news: I don't recall our family going to see the dentist but a handful of times. Oral health never tops the priority list in households of resource scarcity.

The pain I associated with visiting the dentist was imagined and conjured up all sorts of scary scenarios in my head, but it didn't match the outcome. Something similar happens to GEDAs. The anticipation of pain is more debilitating than the reality, but it creates stressors for the generationally poor. Pain paralyzes the poor and delays them from dealing with health problems, so they avoid pain at all costs. This type of paralysis is a sensory processing responsibility of the parietal lobe.

A story told by my friend Maria, a dental hygienist, illustrates how the poor often get punished because they don't know how to care for themselves or the children they carry in the womb.

One of Maria's patients, Jeremy, was a 17-year-old white male who never took care of his teeth in his adolescent and teenage years and ended up having them all pulled. He now has a full set of dentures and comes into the dentist's office on a regular basis to have them relined. Let's look at a second story that sheds light on a familiar problem seen in generational poverty, this being willful or unintentional prenatal neglect.

Jeremy's mother was a heroin addict. She got clean, but the damage to her son had already been set in motion. What the mom ingested, smoked, drank, or shot into her body was transported through the placenta into her innocent son. The antibiotic tetracycline was prescribed to fight the infections that resulted from the mother using unclean needles and other pathogens that entered her body. As a side casualty, the onslaught of antibiotics compromised her son's fragile gut flora or good bacteria, which are vital to ward off illness and disease. Little room for error was present for this child to avoid a life of health complications.

This family was fortunate to have government-provided dental insurance to pay for the surgery. The cost to sedate a patient, extract his bad teeth, and provide him with a pair of dentures can range from $3,000 to $5,000.

Maria does more educational coaching than teeth cleaning and sometimes she shocks her patients to be proactive with their oral health. Fear-based commands are a language the poor understand quite well if the consequences produce unrelenting pain.

> "With the underclass, it's all about appearance. 'Hey, what can you do to make my teeth look whiter?'"
>
> **–Maria**
> Dental Hygienist

"If I don't tell them in a threatening way, 'Look, you're going to lose your teeth if you don't brush or floss, or at the very least, swish around some mouthwash,' they won't take my suggestions seriously. I let them know that they're going to get cavities or decalcification on their enamel unless they make some drastic changes," Maria says. "Not all of them, but many come back in six months and I notice a complete change in their oral health. They want others to notice their teeth, too."

Unfortunately, Maria also says a large percentage of poorer patients that do come back in six months have periodontal disease, a gum infection that decreases bone levels in the mouth. Eventually, the teeth become mobile and many of them will fall out or need pulled.

Maria, who's African-American grew up middle class in Portsmouth, a river town decimated over the last few decades by poverty and a hopelessness that pervades this Appalachian region. Like many other small towns in the Rust Belt, where manufacturing centers with plenty of blue-collar jobs once thrived, the residents of this Southern Ohio community have seen their way of life change as has their employment landscape.

"Poverty is a lot different than my life experiences," Maria says, "but I appreciate the opportunity to help the poor. My first job was downtown seeing patients who were lawyers and other white-collar professionals. The atmosphere downtown compared to West Columbus, where I am now, was like night and day. I'm grateful for the change in scenery because not only have I helped my poorer patients, but I've grown as well. I have a different perspective on life now."

Big-city and small-town poverty are similar. Both populations think they won't make it out, that tomorrow will be the same as today. They may not like it, but they endure the circumstances economic distress has dealt them. They may dream about a better life, better health, or a better future, but won't take the steps to reach any of them.

The poor don't often hide how they feel. Their body language reflects their emotional state when pain is agonizing. Maria says they aren't interested in hearing about practicing good oral health or interacting with her beyond normal small talk.

"Some are extremely aggressive and hostile, or flat out rude," she says. "They're like, 'Listen, my tooth hurts. Give me some pills to make the pain go away,' which I can't do. On the upside are the kids who come in and are excited to get their teeth cleaned. Some children are afraid, but it's important for me to ease their fears so they'll come back. I love helping them."

THE GROWING HEALTH DIVIDE IN AMERICA

In many respects, this country's health divide reflects our nation's wealth divide. We know the poor consume lower-quality foods than do their middle-class or wealthy counterparts based on anecdotal and scientific research. Lack of money, a key factor, is but one reason to explain the discrepancy. Other factors include food deserts, lack of planning, lack of transportation, and family instability in poorer communities.

As the name implies, food deserts represent areas of a city without substantive food choices that are healthy, abundant, and reasonably priced for lower-income consumers. The poor, by default, are left with corner or convenient stores to do most of their grocery shopping.

These stores carry impulse items with high margins and low nutritional benefits. Potato chips, frozen pizzas, candy bars, and sugary drinks may provide a temporary lift to the spirit until the body realizes it lacks adequate nutrition to sustain energy reserves beyond 30 to 60 minutes. A barrage of sugars wreak havoc on the bloodstream and pancreas, which can lead to a wicked insulin-resistant response. Think diabetes-related complications. Sugars that aren't used as fuel by the body are stored as fat. Combine a daily supply of fast food into the mix, and the chances of being diagnosed with obesity or cardiovascular disease increase greatly.

Discussing food deserts often fails to mention the necessity of drinking plenty of water, which is an important factor for good health. Without adequate hydration, the body and brain suffer.

When you think about a desert, a lack of water should come to mind first, though the subject often doesn't make the cut when talking about food insecurity challenges the poor encounter. However, water comprises more than 75 percent of the brain, making it obvious that an adequate daily supply is needed for optimum performance. Proper hydration is critical for memory, energy, learning, mood, and restfulness at night.

Water is important for brain, nerve, and digestive functions, as well as assisting the body in many other important tasks. According to a shocking study by the Centers for Disease Control and Prevention, "[43] percent of adults [in America] drink less than four cups of water a day. That includes 36 percent who drink one to three cups, and 7 percent who drink none."[18] For you soda drinkers, I would not bank on getting your daily water supply from this American beverage of choice. In fact, caffeine—think soda, coffee, tea—and alcohol can act as diuretics or sweeping agents in the body. This means water is excreted from the kidneys at a faster rate when these liquids are consumed.

Water hydration was a vital part of our son's cognitive improvement. Not only did he have an irritable gut, but he also had a brain that was dehydrated. Increasing a child's water intake, especially if behavior problems, depression, or autism-spectrum disorders are an issue, just might go a long way in helping the brain detoxify and stay focused.

Not all water is created equal. The order goes as follows: alkaline water, distilled or reverse-osmosis water, spring water, and tap water is last. Many nutritionists and fitness instructors suggest that adults drink 50 to 70 percent of their body weight in ounces of water each day. Obviously, high-level athletes will likely need more water than non-athletes would. For example, a man weighing 200 pounds should drink between 100 to 140 ounces per day. Children under 100 pounds but over 80 pounds should aim for 48 to 64 ounces. (It's best to consume all of your water needs before 6 p.m. to prevent frequent trips at night to the bathroom. Also, drink water throughout the day naturally, not forcefully.)

Weighing consequences of food choices is rarely considered in generational poverty. Items are purchased to satisfy a physical need, not a wellness goal. A grocery shopping and nutritional plan can help the poor achieve a healthy lifestyle. Planning is about taking control of one's future. Sadly, most GEDAs feel life is beyond their control, and that includes what goes inside their bellies.

A positive outlook on life has a major impact on our sense of well-being. We want to live and extend the shot clock before our time on earth is up. We tend to make better plans with our health and wealth when we're passionate about what the future holds.

Included in grocery shopping and nutritional planning is the knowledge to make wise food choices. Most people know what foods they should eat and avoid. However, few people understand the roles specific foods play in the body; how they should be prepared or cooked; what time of the day they should be consumed; and why certain foods should be paired with other nutritional goodies. It's called

> Welfare, at times, may lead to being well fed, but this is a far cry from being well nourished.

food science, which a good chef or registered dietician knows well. I'm no expert on this subject, but over the last three decades as a pro athlete and health advocate, I concluded the body desperately needs the right fuel sources to function properly and keep disease at bay: water, healthy foods, and supplements (where needed) that pass strict safety standards.

Chef Jim Warner, whom I introduced in an earlier chapter, is program director of food and nutrition at The Ohio State University Wexner Medical Center, one of the leading healthcare providers in the country. As you'll see, I am proud to call him my friend.

Jim is not only a gifted chef, but he also provides 100 healthy cooking tutorials and grocery store tours each year to disadvantaged populations here in Central Ohio to help the poor make better decisions on what they eat and drink. He is helping to bridge the health divide.

This wasn't a part of Jim's initial job description, but he insisted on the community outreach part because this is what he wants to do. Besides, there's such a huge need for his compassionate line of work. Not enough chefs in the Columbus area go into the community and give back to the less fortunate through cooking demonstrations. One national organization, Cooking Matters, helps low-income families shop, prepare, and eat healthy meals on a tight budget. (For more information, please visit www.cookingmatters.org.)

Jim's classes are experiential, which keep participants engaged and go a long way in helping the poor develop needed life skills. Cooking, as he points out, is one of the few tasks where all five senses are being used. Sensory learning is the best form of learning for at-risk communities. Knowledge immersion can lead to application conversion. A mindset change usually translates into a behavior change.

> "This is not about race, gender, or even socioeconomic status. Giving people good food to eat is about humanity."
>
> **–Chef Jim Warner**

I interviewed him about the health crisis in our country. "Our bodies, notably our digestive system, have not changed over the last 5,000 years, though our food choices unfortunately have. Our bodies were not designed to digest foods with preservatives and man-made chemicals in them. These additives do weird things to our bodies and brains when we ingest them," Jim says. "Poor dietary choices lead to predictable health outcomes. It breaks my heart to see so many sick and unhealthy people in our society. It's imperative to help the poor who are most affected."

According to Chef Jim, most adult Americans eat the same 200 foods throughout their entire lives. The poor are quite reluctant to try food that is foreign to their palate. Chef Jim's culinary brilliance and ability to explain challenging concepts simply break through their fears. First, he shows them how to prepare healthy meals that fall within their palate boundaries and satiety needs, which are key for those in poverty.

"We tailor meals to the target audience and the foods they typically buy," Chef Jim says. "Also, they may not have an ample supply of pots and pans in the home. So, we often prepare one-pot meals for this very reason. This takes a bit of creativity, but it's not too difficult to create stews and soups that pack a nice healthy punch that fill the belly."

After earning their trust, Jim says they are ready to try different foods like spaghetti squash and fried vegetables cooked in olive oil. He and his team showed a group of Hispanic attendees how to make greens in 10 minutes, which Jim says they absolutely loved. Sometimes bigger lessons are learned, and Jim tells the story about a young girl who made several food requests during one demonstration.

"We were making sweet potatoes but without sugar or butter," Chef Jim says. "However, participants could add nuts, dried fruit, or other naturally sweet toppings. She comes up and asks, 'Can I have another sweet potato for my mother?' I said, 'Sure, no problem.' Moments later she asks, 'Can I have another one for my dad?' I respond, 'Of course.' Within minutes she returns a third time, and asks, 'Can I get one for my bus driver?' I reply, 'Wait a minute. No one gets food for their bus driver.' We both laughed, but the seriousness of this story is that this little girl grabbed three sweet potatoes because she knew the food would feed her hungry family back home."

How do healthy living programs like Chef Jim's gain traction? It's an uphill battle to get the poor to invest in their health when they perpetually live in survival mode. The short answer is demonstrating a consistency showing up, showing that you care, and keeping your promises. The poor need to know that you can be trusted with their fragile emotional state.

"As a white guy, if I come into these minority communities only one time and tell them to eat certain types of food and you'll have better health, they are not going to listen to me. All they are going to do is grab the free food and leave," Chef Jim says. "But if they see me come back consistently, then trust develops; they know I truly care about their well-being. My involvement in their lives lifts me up just as much as it helps them. I'm so thrilled to do this—you just don't know!"

A body under a barrage of stress depletes key nutrients at a faster rate than one that's not. Any athlete who has trained at a high level sees precious vitamin and mineral reserves (and critical water levels) leave the body through perspiration from intense, pressure-filled competition. The poor are in a battle for their emotional and psychological lives as they deal with daily stressors that most middle-class and wealthy people freely avoid. The game of life, many GEDAs believe, is not worth fighting for because the outcome has been predetermined and little can be done to change it. Of course, I disagree with this fatalistic assessment.

Lack of transportation is another contributing factor in the health divide. Most poor communities in the inner city don't have grocery stores in their neighborhoods, and residents must drive several miles to reach one or a shopping center. Convenient stores, however, are in abundance and strategically placed on corners of high foot-traffic areas in a community. Convenient stores may serve a purpose, but grocery shopping shouldn't be one of them to satisfy their hunger and taste buds. Frankly, they are anything but convenient.

Think about the vicious cycle created when the poor are forced to shop at these stores where goods are more expensive than the same items at a traditional grocery store. Depleting necessities like milk and eggs means another trip to the corner store. While the milk and eggs get bought, so are comfort foods—pizza, colas, and chips—often devoid of any nutritional benefit.

Household instability is another factor in the health divide. An unstable home typically results in an overstressed body. Precious energy reserves are depleted, leading to bad food choices that are made to lift the spirit and help people cope with stress. Just to be clear, stress makes all of us susceptible to eating the wrong foods and drinking the wrong beverages when it shows up in our lives. However, imagine all that plus the toxic stress created for a person without a good job, safe neighborhood, or relatively stable home life. Welcome to the world of poverty, where instability and transience are part of the daily landscape.

Unexpected change is taxing to a poor family just as they are getting settled in to their current living arrangements. Monya shares a story from her growing up days. "I remember this poor family in Chillicothe that moved from one apartment to the next in the same housing project. I'm not sure what was going on in the home, but this had to be traumatic and stressful for the kids because they could never get too comfortable. Time to pack up and move to the next spot was probably in the back of their mind," she says.

It's not uncommon for a poor family to move three or four times during a school year. Thus, it is a nearly impossible task for an impoverished student to thrive academically when faced with this predicament. It's hard to eat nutritiously, digest food properly, and sleep peacefully in an environment of chaos and instability. Paying attention in class the next morning might be the furthest thing from his mind. Poverty is full of surprises, most of which aren't good for a growing or fully developed body.

A HEALTHY GUT FOR A HEALTHY MIND AND BODY

Leaky gut syndrome, an inflammatory condition I suffered with for several months three years ago, sends the immune system into panic mode as food particles seep through the intestinal wall and enter the bloodstream. By and large, the medical community does not yet acknowledge it; in fact, many label this condition as pseudoscience. Nonetheless, many Americans have undiagnosed leaky guts and inflamed bodies. Inflammation is at the root of most illnesses and diseases—cognitive disorders in particular.

Alternative healthcare practitioners and some researchers approximate that 70 to 80 percent of our immune system resides in the intestines, or gut. If that is true, then our intestines, excluding our skin, serve as the first line of defense to protect our bodies from harmful bacteria, viruses, and other pathogens. Eating bad foods—pre-packaged, fast, and processed foods—in abundance creates havoc in the body, setting us up for a life of sickness. The poor are disproportionately affected since they typically gravitate to unhealthy food options.

Poor nutritional habits, though, aren't based solely on financial resources. Mike Uckele, a close friend of mine, certified nutritionist, and CEO of a very successful company that bears his name, says, "The poor may buy more processed foods for convenience instead of health reasons. But there are plenty of people who have money and still choose to eat an overabundance of unhealthy foods, because they don't know or simply don't care."

Functional economically distressed Americans (or FEDAs) may have wealth, but still duplicate the same negligent habits of poor health that were present in their lives growing up in an impoverished environment. As highlighted in the "Pre-Game" section of the book, an impressive income statement or balance sheet does not automatically move people out of a social class, but an upgraded mindset does.

The gut is called the *second brain* because it has a profound effect on how we feel and respond emotionally. Dysbiosis, or an imbalanced gut flora in the gastrointestinal tract, often leads to a lot of emotional distresses.

"I even see this in my kids. If they eat foods that they're sensitive or intolerant to, they will get extremely emotional. If my six-year-old ate dairy for three or four days, he would be an emotional train wreck. He would be defiant and moody and agitated the entire time until we removed dairy products from his diet," Mike says. "Now imagine if parents aren't cognizant of the effects of poor nutrition on a stressed-out body. What happens to their children? They continue to suffer with no relief in sight."

Behavior problems in school may simply be mirroring what is happening with the gut. An irritable gut devoid of beneficial probiotics or good bacteria could trigger irritable behaviors. We knew this was the case with our son, Eli. He was diagnosed at the age of seven with *Candida albicans* overgrowth, an out-of-control fungus in his gut. Just enough of it is okay, but too much *Candida albicans* in the gut is not good. No doubt, Eli was acting funky in school, and we dreaded those too frequent calls from his teachers. As parents, it was a nightmare for us on so many fronts.

DID YOU KNOW?

The gut has been called the *second brain*. Our gastrointestinal tract, with an ample supply of neurons, has a direct line of communication with the brain since bacteria in the gut produces a large percentage of dopamine and serotonin, our reward and feel-good hormones, respectively.

He craved simple carbohydrates and man-made sugars. He would get sick like clockwork at least once per month and miss several days of school. Antibiotics were prescribed to fight recurring respiratory infections, which were likely caused by food intolerances to such things as dairy, eggs, mustard, and the chief culprit, gluten. He loved these foods, though his gut ecosystem treated them as harmful substances. Our son's body and brain were overburdened with inflammation. He'd have emotional meltdowns, one after the other, for seemingly trivial reasons.

Carbohydrates, sugars, antibiotics, and stress have been identified as prominent triggers for the overgrowth of *Candida albicans*. Bad bacteria thrive in a compromised gut, while good bacteria is kept in check. We have the financial resources to seek alternative treatments for Eli that improve his health through natural options, but poor parents don't. Their kids suffer and likely carry the gut agitation to school each day.

A parent without adequate financial and emotional resources receiving government support may take her child to the clinic, but the doctor, as Mike points out, is unlikely to prescribe a food allergy or food sensitivity test to identify the potential catalyst of a behavior problem. However, the child will likely be given a prescription to cope with the mood disorder from a chemical perspective while no dietary recommendations or nutritional changes are made to improve his gut health.

At the time, Eli's teachers said he got agitated easily and would be aggressive and hostile toward other students. Sound familiar? Unfortunately, this describes many kids in America across the socioeconomic spectrum.

We are quick to attach labels to poor students who have behavior challenges, when the culprits may lie with gut health abnormalities and nutritional deficiencies from the overconsumption of gluten, bad foods, and a lack of adequate hydration.

LET'S MAKE A CHANGE

Monya and I were invited to tour KIPP Academy, a charter school in Columbus, several years ago. I was struck not by this state-of-the-art facility, though it is impressive, but by the foods these kids, most of whom were poor, had access to each day. In-house chefs prepared breakfast, lunch, and a healthy end-of-the-day snack for the kids.

Obviously, millions of dollars from donors are needed to build and maintain schools like our local KIPP Academy. Most traditional public schools, however, aren't as fortunate. Their budgets get squeezed continually and food upgrades probably are low on the priority list.

"I don't think it would cost any more money for public schools to change how they feed our children. They elect to serve children convenient foods that may be palatable to the taste buds, but are not beneficial to the body. They will stick tater tots on a plate and call them vegetables," Mike Uckele says. "You can make the case that fresh green beans could be substituted for the tater tots and perhaps be less expensive on a comparative basis. And it's certainly easier to heat frozen meals up in an oven, rather than cook fresh food on the stove."

Poor kids in America deserve good food at school. Children may turn their noses up to vegetables like carrots, Brussels sprouts, cauliflower, zucchini, spinach, broccoli, and asparagus until they try them cooked in a good source of oil, such as olive or avocado. Remember, seeing and tasting are key sensory-learning drivers to change behaviors when working with the poor.

We've presented cooking demonstrations to kids who try these types of foods for the first time. Their typical reaction: "I don't like vegetables, but these ones taste awesome! It was so exciting to watch them sizzle in the pan!" The law of familiarity for the poor paints healthy eating as too much work, too much money, and too distasteful to the palate. This defeatist outlook must change one person, one family, one school, and one community at a time.

A practice I've witnessed in wealthy private schools is certainly worth exploring for poor public institutions. Some private schools let students retrieve healthy snacks from the cafeteria between class periods. Of course, these kids don't live in a world of lack, so they're unlikely to take more than what they need. Shouldn't their poorer peers at the inner-city schools have the same or a better setup to replenish their energy reserves and provide their minds with the fuel to stay alert and help them concentrate through the day?

SOCIOPSYCHONOMIC FILTER
The law of familiarity for the poor paints healthy eating as too much work, too much money, and too distasteful to the palate.

Improving education for poor kids is more than just providing them with updated schools and better technology. We must invest in their health as well. This shouldn't be debatable considering the widening opportunity gap between poor and rich students. Economically distressed students need good food to thrive academically. We must revamp what our most vulnerable children are eating at school each day to include foods with substantive nutritional value.

I believe a healthy breakfast, lunch, and afternoon snack made with real ingredients should be provided to poor students who attend public schools. Our nation's wealthiest taxpayers may grumble about another burdensome federal government expense they must pay. However, poor nutrition is a factor in the academic and cognitive gap, although most people pay little attention to this subject. The bottom line is that high-stress foods loaded with empty calories and fake ingredients are irreparably harming the impressionable minds and growing bodies of underserved children.

Attached to how a child learns are nutritional, psychological, emotional, parental, and educational components, and each contributes to the child's overall wellness. Having said that, children from impoverished and challenging environments, especially those not getting sufficient nutrients in their diets, also will need mental fortitude and discipline to reach their highest level of success at school. The brain has enormous influence over a tired and even nutrient-depleted body.

"SAY WHAT?"

A terrible prediction has been made about our children: This will be the first generation in American history that won't live as long as their parents. Not just the duration of life, but the quality of life toward the end of their lives will also suffer if this dire prophecy holds true. Keep in mind, there's a big difference between living and existing.

Chef Jim says children as young as 10 years old are being admitted to his hospital for hardening of the arteries and Type II diabetes, conditions once seen only in adult populations. He adds, "A lot of kids think they have time to make up for poor nutritional habits. This just isn't true."

Several years ago, I watched a grandmother place soda in her grandson's baby bottle at the Ohio State Fair. Unfortunately, this was a common practice back in my housing project, too. In rural communities, this is called *Mountain Dew mouth* (or tooth decay from excessive soda consumption), a term echoed by J.D. Vance in his best-selling book, *Hillbilly Elegy*.

At the time, I thought that if this grandmother is providing her infant grandson sugary drinks in a public setting, what in the world is the child getting behind closed doors? That was the last time I visited the fair with my family, a place where I worked as a teenager for two years. This experience left such a bad taste in my mouth (no pun intended) because I couldn't stop thinking about how the grandmother's actions would impact the child's health and quality of life. I felt like going up to her and

> For the poor, positive health outcomes can (and should) lead to positive life outcomes, and more importantly, a positive-slopping legacy trajectory.

saying, "What are you doing? You are going to send your grandson to an early grave?" I'm not sure what stopped me, because I am not afraid to intervene when a blatant injustice occurs right before my eyes and victims are too paralyzed or too young to defend themselves.

Health is a sensitive topic to discuss in America, already split politically and culturally, because everyone has his or her own interpretation. We should at the least be able to unite and bridge the health gap that also divides the country.

A discourse on health and wellness must start at the grassroots level. If we don't change course, our children will suffer the consequences of lifelong illness and disease, and those from impoverished backgrounds will suffer most.

Diagnostic

The traditional middle class takes a diagnostic approach to wellness. They often wait until a triggering event occurs—a doctor's recommendation or painful symptom or threat to their finances—before implementing change.

They receive routine checkups from their doctors, and rarely question a physician's insights. The wealthy respect doctors, but will seek a second opinion for a diagnosis and explore alternative methods of care to remedy a health challenge. The poor, as noted earlier, are suspicious and view doctors as too intrusive, prying eyes who want more information than GEDAs are willing to provide.

GISAs are hesitant to adopt a holistic approach to better health that includes consistent exercise, financial and emotional wellness, nutritional supplementation, alternative care options, and targeted grocery shopping for foods that prevent illness and disease. Sacrifice is something that GISAs do for their employer and children, but many of them fail to take the pre-emptive steps required for a healthy lifestyle.

They have a basic understanding of health, but most GISAs know little about food synergy and its effect on the human body, including the GI tract to improve energy and concentration levels, and curtail inflammation. They are keenly aware of nutritional habits that form a foundation of good health, such as eating a variety of fruits and vegetables and lean meats, but accumulated knowledge is quite different than applied knowledge.

GISAs think long and hard about spending money on optional expenses like wellness offerings, so they see paying for an exercise program or gym membership as low on their priority list. They're focused on taking care of the basics: house payment, food and utilities, and other fixed expenditures that fit into their mindset of comfort.

TURNING OFF BAD GENES

GEDAs tend to display a fatalistic attitude toward health, preferring to live for the moment. They will do whatever is needed to extend their existence one more day. GEDAs generally don't give much thought to what types of foods they put into their bodies and the potential problems that can result from nutritional neglect.

GAPAs incorporate an altruistic attitude regarding wellness, believing a healthy mind and body are critical to fulfilling their life's purpose, family legacy, and philanthropic pursuits. A holistic approach to healthy living helps accomplish these objectives.

GISAs lean toward the fatalistic side from this perspective: Their diagnostic filter is quick to accept a disease or illness that runs in their bloodline as a precursor, at some point, to poor health, and eventually, death. Some even own life insurance policies that cover cancer, heart disease, and other life-threatening conditions.

Genetic weaknesses can make a person susceptible to a specific illness or disease, but one field of study shows that we are not automatically doomed by our bad genes if measures are taken to keep them turned off.

Researchers are discovering through *epigenetics* that our genes do turn on or turn off an illness or disease for several reasons. That's the good news. But to ward off illness, our health comes down to lifestyle choices and environmental factors. Toxic thoughts, toxic foods, toxic environments, toxic relationships, and toxic metal exposure can turn the bad genes on.

"WHAT'S WRONG WITH MY KID?"

When it comes to their kids—struggling to fit in with peers, spending hours in front of the TV, or falling short in their sports aspirations—many middle-class parents are worried. Today's children are far less active than previous generations and don't get outside as much because of ample distractions like the Internet, social media, and their smartphones that keep them preoccupied.

As a child, I was always outside and came back inside our apartment to eat and sleep. Mom would advise me to get home before dark, and when I stayed out too late, she'd yell, "Lawrence Damon, get your tail in here right now!" No matter where I was in the neighborhood, I usually made it through the front door just before a second command could turn into a threat.

Life was simpler and safer back then, even in the ghetto. Parents are not as trusting as they once were when their children played outside for hours at a time without adult supervision.

Today, a growing number of children are inactive by choice or force. The former often prefer to sit around the house playing video games or watching television instead of honing their skills getting in shape. The latter are relegated to a sedentary lifestyle because they have tremendous difficulty getting their bodies to sync up with their brain. I see so many kids, boys primarily, who struggle in their athletic skills or get unusually tired very easily while participating in sports. Most of these kids have vestibular, proprioceptive, ocular, and digestive systems that need fine-tuning adjustments.

Though many go undiagnosed, more children are being affected by sensory integration disorder, which kids on the autism spectrum also have, and they are easy to spot. They may struggle socially since they can't excel in rhythm sports, basketball and soccer in particular. Those who do compete in improvisational sports feel lost as more skilled players dominate the competition, which places middle-income parents looking to help their child(ren) in a quandary. They can pay for training sessions or occupational therapists, or watch their kid lose confidence and find solace inside the home, a solitary figure parked behind a game console or remote control.

A BODY IN NEED OF MOTION

Our bodies are meant to move. Dysfunction brought about by cognitive or physical challenges occurs when the body is out of rhythm. Whether it's sports or finances or health, the body needs a state of equilibrium to function normally or it opens itself to ailments.

It's so convenient for busy parents to give their child a smart device, which acts as a stand-in babysitting tool.

Video games affect kids from every socioeconomic class. As Katie Morton, an exercise and sensory movement specialist with Brain Balance Achievement Centers, shares:

> "The left hemisphere in the brain handles the dopamine centric attention network. Video games are left-brain stimulating, a repetitive process that feeds off the high these addictive activities provide players. Kids can't get enough of them and prefer to sit around the house and play video games all day. Muscle tone weakness in kids is often attributed to a sensory motor feedback loop malfunction. When kids don't have strong muscle tone, they don't feel their world. They're physically disconnected from their bodies. Thus, their brain doesn't get messages that are driven by muscle tone stimulation or exercise. Therefore, the brain doesn't send messages back to muscle tone to build even more muscle tone. When you strengthen this

process, both by working on the muscle tone and the brain at the same time, the feedback loop is reset and then the brain and the body come into sync with each other."

Motor skills and exercises on the left side of the body build the right side of the brain (and vice versa). If we as parents don't make our children move, they don't build the right or big-picture side of the brain effectively. We think a smartphone app, or a prescription drug will magically improve a hemispheric weakness or cognitive dysfunction. These may temporarily support where a child's current struggles are, but movement is needed to correct severe, brain-muscle imbalances.

YOU ARE WHAT YOU EAT

A middle-class mom and I discussed grocery shopping one day. Tracy couldn't believe that we spent so much money on groceries each month for a family of four, saying she spent 25 percent less for her family of six and thought us wasteful. I concluded that she was not taking into consideration the health benefits of consuming foods rich in nutrients that may cost more than processed or nutrient-challenged foods. As budget-conscious as she sounded, the supposition that you can pay now so you can play later didn't register with Tracy. Whether it's food or empowerment programs, we are proponents of paying more at the front end so that the burden will be less at the back end. Bad habits—nutritional or financial—are cumulative and tend to show up later in life. Change is much harder to implement as each year or decade passes by.

> "Every time you sit down to eat, you are making life or death decisions."
>
> **–Dr. Don Colbert**
> Best-Selling Author and Health Expert

Mike Uckele sheds light on an assumption made by many grocery shoppers who think that even eating moderately healthy is too expensive. He says, "In some cost-versus-benefits grocery shopping studies, research indicates the poor and middle class do not save as much money as they anticipated when compared with some healthier options. Going to the grocery store and purchasing non-organic fruits and vegetables is, in many cases, less expensive than buying packaged foods with little to no nutritional value. This misconception could be more of an educational issue rather than purely a socioeconomic issue."

You can tell a lot about people's health outlook by observing what food choices they have in their shopping carts. I had a conversation with Teresa, a checkout clerk, about the shopping habits of customers. It's customary for me to toss out an open-ended question to see what info a clerk is willing to share. She said, "I find it amazing that shoppers will buy a lot of healthy items—all natural or organic—to justify the purchase of so much junk food buried at the bottom of the cart. This is baffling to me."

"Everything in moderation" is how some would describe it. I'm not so sure I agree with this trite expression given that our food ecosystem (and depleting nutritional benefits) has changed drastically over the years and decades. It's incredibly difficult for the average consumer to decipher what's real and what's fake because they often look the same. The eye can be easily fooled, but the body can't.

HEALTH KOOKS BY A DIFFERENT NAME

Family members and close friends think Monya and I are crazy. They think it's pointless to spend money on organic and all-natural foods. They will sniff foods my wife prepares to see if these edible goodies pass their smell test. They quickly realize that the food not only tastes good, but it is great for their mind and body. Eating super healthy isn't cheap, but the alternative down the road on your body, if not already, will be even more costly.

We shopped at a Whole Foods and spent $710.38 while vacationing in Florida, and it was the largest grocery bill we've ever had. Organic meats and body care products were the big drivers. As someone who monitors each expense, I wasn't the least bit upset about this amount. Most American families don't spend this much on groceries in an entire month. Monya and I don't want to save money now to lose on our health later.

> If you think healthy eating is costly now, just wait until the results of poor nutritional choices catch up with you or your children later on.

We make it a priority to feed our two children real food. We refuse to put anything fake in or on their bodies. If a food option has been altered, manipulated, enhanced, or modified, our kids don't eat it regardless of how appealing it looks. We do this because it's incumbent upon parents to provide an atmosphere where children have the best opportunity to succeed. Nutrition and adequate hydration play a huge role in a child's success journey.

Nyah and Eli understand, though temptations still exist for them to eat the wrong things, that healthy food is preventative medicine for their growing bodies. Benefit comes first, with taste a secondary (or ancillary) consideration. This is something they've learned early on, which will not only pay huge dividends for them now, but also decades into the future. This has been one of the best investments we have made in their young lives.

A short conversation I had with Nyah, a too-cool-for-you high school teenager who won't cave under peer pressure to eat bad foods, about the importance of healthy living follows:

> **Nyah:** Daddy, how long do you plan to live?
>
> **Me:** Lord willing, well past 100. I don't think anyone on either side of our family has lived beyond the century mark.
>
> **Nyah:** Wow, you haven't even made it to age 50 yet. That's a huge goal.
>
> **Me:** Yes, it is. But if you treat the body right, longevity should be the rule not the exception.
>
> **Nyah:** What do you mean?
>
> **Me:** Eating right, thinking right, and praying right do the body good. As you age, the body doesn't necessarily have to break down. It can be just as strong at 80 as it was at 50. It's a mindset that translates into a healthy lifestyle, not the other way around.
>
> **Nyah:** I see.

This opportunity proved to be a timely moment to enlarge my daughter's frame of reference on keeping illness and disease at bay, regardless of one's age. Nyah and Eli have a solid foundation of healthy eating habits to build upon. They are not the food police and have never confronted their peers' lunch choices in the school cafeteria. However, they will stand firm on what goes inside their bellies.

Here are five tips to help budget-conscious parents make healthy eating a regular lifestyle choice:

1. **Prepare snacks and meals in advance.** Hectic schedules often lead to poor food options and bad snacking choices when outside the home. This takes work. We pack healthy snacks and light meals before heading out on long road trips or when our children compete in all-day sporting events. Money is not wasted on buying junk food, fast food, or processed food, impulsive options that can harm their bodies.

2. **Prepare a weekly meal plan to eliminate impulse shopping.** Most people tend to spend more at the grocery store without a comprehensive shopping list.

3. **Make healthy stews and soups that can last for several days.** Our two favorites: organic chicken tortilla soup and organic turkey chili.

4. **Pack your children's lunch for school each day.** You can't control what is served in the school cafeteria, but you can regulate what goes inside the bodies of your most cherished assets and stewardship responsibilities before they walk out the door.

5. **Buy organic meats, fruits, and vegetables.** It's tough on a tight budget, but I'd recommend cutting back on entertainment or another variable expenditure and dedicate those savings toward buying healthy food and beverage options (kombucha drinks, for example).

Holistic

Most GAPAs place limits on what they consume. Recklessness threatens their modus operandi, so they guard against overindulgences that are likely to jeopardize their health, wealth, image, and social standing. Self-control is an endearing quality they employ in every aspect of life.

A term that intrigued me during my undergraduate studies in college at Ohio State was *social loafing*, which describes a group member who fails to contribute his proportionate share to complete a team goal. Social loafers in sports have ample talent to get the job done but assume others will pick up the slack, like a basketball center not boxing out on defense at crunch time, or offensive linemen who shirk their responsibility to protect the quarterback and then point fingers at their teammates when he's sacked.

Social loafing in generational affluence is forbidden. It's much easier to pull off in generational poverty or the traditional middle class when a family member checks out on the responsibility to fulfill his or her potential.

The generationally wealthy don't leave anything up for chance, especially health, which plays a critical role in their overall legacy game plan. Only the best healthcare providers and wellness practitioners, including doctors, dentists, nutritionists, trainers, and therapists, are hired by GAPAs. Affluence affords many luxuries. Without good health, though, the lifestyle to which they are accustomed couldn't be enjoyed or duplicated by offspring.

SOCIOPSYCHONOMIC FILTER

Emotional wellness, financial wellness, physical wellness, and spiritual wellness are pivotal to heritage continuity.

Wellness is taken seriously by the generationally wealthy. They understand how foolish it is to gamble with their health. Precautionary measures in the form of a health mitigation playbook for a middle-age GAPA might look something like the abbreviated diagram that follows:

ANTICIPATED LIFESPAN: 100+

Health Goals
- Exercise four days a week for 45 minutes with a private trainer.
- Increase phytonutrient profile of each meal.
- Strengthen gut flora with probiotics (good bacteria) and prebiotics (food that feeds good bacteria) before traveling overseas.

Exercise and Fitness Routines
- Weight, core, and endurance training three days per week.
- Body lengthening and isometric resistance training once weekly.

Meal Planning and Nutrition
- Sit-down and on-the-go chef-prepared meals with a healthy balance of good carbs, fatty acids, fiber, vitamins, minerals, antioxidants, and protein.

- Eat three healthy snacks in between meals each day.

- Drink 60 percent of your body weight in ounces of water each day.

Medical Care and Emotional Wellness

- Consult with primary healthcare practitioner or psychologist once per month.

- Receive therapeutic massage or spa treatment once per week.

AN INVESTMENT IN HEALTH DOESN'T TAKE A VACATION

Wellness involves stress decompression. Part of health is decompressing from the stressors of life. Regardless of our socioeconomic status, we all deal with stress. A planned getaway may be the remedy needed to *relax*, a timely destination to step away from job and household responsibilities; *rewind*, a chance to discover areas needing improvement; and *reboot*, an opportunity to press restart and change what isn't working. Inevitably, wellness is about continuous improvement. It doesn't take time off for the generationally affluent, or anyone for that matter, even while on vacation.

Monya notes, "The poor can't take a vacation. The financial resources just aren't there. The middle class will take one vacation a year, usually in the summer or during their children's school spring break. The wealthy take vacations as often as their schedule dictates."

The informed wealthy and middle-class people who invest in their health find time to exercise while on vacation, rising early before scheduled family activities commence. They might jog or lift weights. They understand the importance of healthy eating and exercise; it's a way of life for them.

If you want to reach your health goals, changes must occur.

Your body will respond to the mental image that's given to it by the mind. What you see will shape how you live your life. The foods you buy, the beverages you drink, the grocery stores you frequent, and the exercise regimen you employ (or neglect) at home and on vacation are framed by your wellness filter. Have you checked it lately?

FOOD SYNERGY IS LIFE SYNERGY

The ultra wealthy live a synergistic life. All the pieces seem to fit neatly together, with wellness being an integral piece of the legacy template that offspring tend to replicate. Every aspect of GAPAs' lives must be in harmony with each other, including the interactions of a well-nourished body. It's hard to enjoy a prosperous life if you're constantly sick.

You don't have to be rich to achieve a healthy lifestyle, but you do need to be diligent. You must adopt a wealth-building mentality where you look at life from an investment lens. Whether it's your kids, your job, your business, your community, your retirement portfolio, or your health, you don't say, "I'm going to neglect this area so that I can dedicate more time and resources in another area."

A body in rhythm is nutritionally sound. You digest your food better. You absorb key nutrients better. You think better. You learn better. You feel better. You move better. You sleep better. All told, you function better.

Our bodies store key nutrients from foods, beverages, and supplements that we ingest. When these reserves run out, nutrients are pulled from organs, muscles, bones, and cells where the supply is perhaps more plentiful. A body deficient in key nutrients will eventually break down, paving the way for illness and disease to ravage that individual. "Whether the food consumed is abundant or minimal in nutrients, the body is doing everything that it can to absorb and utilize these nutrients to the best of its ability," Mike Uckele says. "There are primary storage sites in the body for every vitamin and mineral. Let's take calcium for example. About 90 percent of it is stored in the bones. The other 10 percent serves hundreds of functions throughout the body."

> "Even the best foods today often don't provide in nutrient values what they did 50 or 100 years ago. Soil depletion from aggressive farming practices is largely to blame."
>
> **–Mike Uckele**
> Certified Nutritionist

If an individual has deficiencies in copper, Mike says she may run into all sorts of health problems depending on where this mineral is most void in her body. She could have issues with arthritis since copper is important for the formation of cartilage tissue and the reduction of inflammation. She could lose pigment in her hair. Her immune system may be affected from the copper deficiency because this mineral has tremendous antibacterial properties. Her body needs adequate amounts of this mineral as well as many other key nutrients to achieve optimal health. Having a well-functioning gut is imperative to nutrient absorption.

A broad spectrum of vegetables and low-glycemic fruits should be consumed to create a powerful effect in the body. Plant-based meals full of color provide phytonutrients beyond vitamins and minerals, which send positive messages to the genes so they can express themselves in a positive way.

We generalize what foods people should eat, but a food sensitivity test is recommended to ensure that the body doesn't negatively react to a certain item. A food could be very healthy and still make a person feel sick, with inflammation being a key response to let that individual know that the body reacts to it. Most meals contain several ingredients, making it nearly impossible to isolate a food intolerance, which is different from a food allergy. I have a moderate intolerance to chicken, but I'm not allergic to it. Though I wouldn't break out in hives, I do feel a bit off when I eat chicken, rice, chili peppers, and a few other foods that my body does not like. Mike suggests rotating foods throughout the week since most people generally eat the same 25 to 50 foods. (For more information on Uckele Nutrition, please visit www.uckele.com.)

> Real foods contribute to life. Fake foods disrupt the quality and quantity of life.

As parents of two finicky eaters, we realize how challenging it can be to get our kids to eat vegetables. One of their favorite vegetable dishes follows: olive oil, sliced onions, Brussels sprouts, broccoli, cauliflower, carrots, and minced garlic with a pinch of Celtic sea salt. Nyah and Eli have a more sophisticated palate than we did as children. I can't explain why they like this sautéed dish, but I do know the benefits it provides their bodies: immune system support and eye health, digestive support and a properly functioning gut, a cardiovascular system capitalizing on beneficial fats and phytonutrients, and a healthy body conducive to achieving peaceful sleep through the night.

Parents, take your kids grocery shopping at least once a month with you and let them prepare part of the meal. It'll go a long way toward familiarizing them about what goes in their stomachs. Don't allow your children to treat their bodies like trash cans. You must set a good example, because they will always emulate what you do, not what you say. This is especially true when it comes to their health.

The informed wealthy are not superhuman, but they understand the value of consuming superfoods that are packed with abundant nutrients to promote well-being in the body and mind. I've mentioned several of them that our kids enjoy.

Another superfood favorite of ours is pistachios. They are full of nutritional goodies, including vitamins, minerals, antioxidants, fiber, and healthy fats. (Tree nut allergies are on the rise, especially in children. Do not consume pistachios if you are allergic to tree nuts. In most instances, allergies and food intolerances are signs of an inflamed or poorly performing GI tract; the culprits behind illness, disease, cognitive disorders, and abnormal bodily reactions can usely be traced to the gut. Always start here if good health is your goal, because absorption of key nutrients is, well, the key.)

I am so enamored by healthy eating that a rather peculiar habit has developed over the last several years. I will periodically walk in the kitchen and open the refrigerator. I'm not hungry or thirsty. I stare at the wholesome foods on the shelves and in the temperature-controlled storage bins: wild-caught salmon and halibut, organic meat (turkey, beef, lamb, and chicken), colorful vegetables in abundance and low-glycemic fruits, cage-free eggs, kombucha drinks, fermented sauerkraut, and organic almond butter. The vow I made as a kid to provide my future family with good food has come true. It's so surreal that I need to see it repeatedly to make sure I'm not dreaming.

What you place in your body has profound implications on your overall health and legacy footprint. To know that good food can enhance the quality and longevity of life is a liberating feeling. I am not a big fan of counting calories, but I advocate counting the consumption of nutritious foods each day. Make sure your meals are balanced with a good protein source, healthy carbs, and other key nutrients. Eat three healthy meals every day and several strategically timed nutritious snacks in between. Vitaminfingerprint.com is a great resource to help you identify your nutritional blueprint, or the specific foods you need to eat (or avoid) to enjoy better health.

The Good Book says that we reap what we sow. Ask yourself, "What's my rationale for eating this food or drinking this beverage?" The more conscious you are about what goes in (or on) your body, the better health outcomes you're likely to have, as well as for your children who are watching and emulating everything you do.

INVESTMENT PLANNING

Disclaimer

Investing involves risk, including the loss of principal. The information high-lighted in the "Investment Planning" section is for educational purposes only. Investment decisions should not be made without first consulting a licensed financial advisor and after thorough research and due diligence of available offerings that align with an investor's goals, risk capacity, principal and profit expectations, and time horizon.

CHAPTER

16

BUSINESS AND
INVESTMENT OPPORTUNITIES

*Income or wealth-generating options that are
hidden, contemplated, or accessed
by a representative social class*

*Business and investment opportunities were briefly covered earlier in the book.
However, a more in-depth discussion is needed to highlight the growing economic gap
between social classes when viewed from the lens of wealth accumulation.*

Pass By

Discount stores such as Walmart, Dollar General, and Big Lots are frequented by lower-income and middle-class consumers on a regular basis.
However, few of them ever think of becoming shareholders in these companies. They are intimately acquainted with the products and services of publicly traded companies. Everyday items that the stores supply and the poor
acquire include cell phones, clothes, food, toiletries, and laundry materials.

They'll spend money on toys and electronics for Christmas gifts, which
certainly was the happiest time of the year for me as a kid. But a share of
a company's stock would make a nice stocking stuffer and empowerment

gesture for any impoverished child. Hundreds of stocks can be purchased for less than $75 per share. The poor know reality consumerism but not equity ownership.

GEDAs regularly pass by wealth-building opportunities to become investors or business owners while conducting their day-to-day affairs. Strategies with upside potential aren't considered by them. You can't see what you're not looking for, even when it's right in front of you.

WEALTH CREATION: HOW THE POOR CAN TAKE MATTERS INTO THEIR OWN HANDS

I met Beth Sparks, a certified financial planner and investment advisor with Raymond James, at a continuing education seminar several years ago. I was struck by her passion for financial education, a key component to bridging the wealth gap in our country.

At the heart of wealth creation, Beth says, is capital formation. By and large, we don't teach in our schools how our free enterprise system can work for anyone who will work it, though it has embedded flaws. Children need to learn at an early age how a company is built and financed, and how publicly traded companies affect them on a consumer or investor level.

"Les Wexner, founder of L Brands and a key figure in our Central Ohio community, received seed money from his mother to start his company," she says. "Other avenues to finance and grow the business were secured early on, which eventually led to a public offering. As shareholders, investors or equity owners have benefitted from the upside of his company. But more importantly, Les has provided thousands of jobs to area residents over the years and helped countless people who bought shares in his company become wealthier—significantly, in some cases—along the way.

"If I have an idea, how do I raise money to build my business? Payment on a loan to a bank or bondholders must be made as the business gets going, though it might be short on money. Now, an equity infusion or investment from shareholders can give a company breathing room to grow as the business becomes more profitable. And maybe later, a dividend from profits could be paid out if the bottom line increases and can be reasonably predicted," Beth says.

Sweat equity in a private business and shareholder equity in publicly traded companies are two possible pathways out of poverty. Rep. Joyce Beatty, a member of the U.S. House of Representatives, once told me something that rings so true: "We—minorities and the working poor—need to be on both sides of the cash register."

There are a lot of incredibly talented people living in poverty. I've worked with thousands of GEDAs over the years who have unique gifts and remarkable abilities, but their skills often go unnoticed. Talent cultivation outside of sports, entertainment, or as a social media sensation is rarely considered as a viable income stream and career path by GEDAs. In their minds, they feel it's better to strike out swinging for a home run, rather than being satisfied with a single. First base isn't home, but one must start somewhere to reach his intended destination. It's time for the poor to enter the wealth game.

Their focus remains centered around immediacy of needs and financial survival. The moment is what matters most to the poor, a constant struggle to get to the next day. Economic benefits with a future payout are too abstract and not worth the energy expended—or so many GEDAs assume.

The poor can monetize their skills by creating touch businesses as caterers, caregivers, artists and painters, motivational speakers, or authors, to name a few. But first a person will need to conquer the marginalization and humiliation that oftentimes those living in poverty experience. If she can't, one of two outcomes typically result: She becomes embittered and reflects her pain outward onto others or inwardly on her skills. In other words, she sabotages and minimizes her unique talents and abilities. Either way, she has shortchanged herself and her contributions to the world. Tough times make you bitter or better. How you respond to those challenges is left up to you.

Feel-good stories invigorate the human spirit, regardless of a person's socioeconomic background. When you overcome a setback in the face of enormous odds, you'll be amazed how many lives can be touched.

The poor are too quick to discount their stories of triumph, which they must see before even the first offshoot of it buds. They believe the journey is too far for them to travel. It's not, but many can't be convinced otherwise.

A young lady I met a couple of years ago has a special gift. Monica's ability to articulate internal pain is extraordinary. I told her that she could help so many women who've been in abusive relationships but don't know how to move forward. I urged her to first, write down her story, and second, to gather the courage to share it with others. These tasks, I said, required Monica to get out of her own way.

Unfortunately, Monica found tremendous difficulty managing the mental image and negative internal dialogue she communicated to herself. She shared in agony, "My life has been a big mess. Emotionally, I am spent." She also didn't think her story was worthy of being heard.

How can the poor get started in business? First, they must devise a business plan that should include a mission statement defining the business's purpose; an outline of its values and guiding principles; and a marketing plan that identifies the objectives of the business, plus a strategy to achieve them.

Second, a tax identification number is assigned to every limited liability corporation (LLC), which establishes a legal footprint for the business and offers some liability protection. A sole proprietorship, or *sole prop* for short, does not need a tax identification number. The business and the owner are one and the same. Obviously, there are pros and cons to each that you should discuss with a financial planner or attorney to determine what will serve your interests best.

Third, a social media page or website adds further credibility to your business. Most customers will not take you seriously unless your business has an Internet presence.

Fourth, the poor need ongoing coaching and guidance throughout the business structure process. Nonprofits and social agencies around the country offer free entrepreneurship classes for disadvantaged populations.

I waited until now to mention money. Yes, business start-ups need it. However, a lack of financial resources shouldn't be the sole reason why the poor pass up a business opportunity. The blueprint for economic empowerment starts with the decision to change the trajectory of a legacy, which attracts seed financing from individuals and organizations ready to provide a hand up but not a handout.

IN IT TO WIN IT LIKE BENNETT

The poor understand that playing the lottery is gambling, though they rarely (if ever) consider the overwhelming odds of losing and remain blinded by an anticipated payout. That's what keeps them coming back and has such a hold on them that's hard to explain. Playing the lottery is a recurring outflow with no turnoff switch. It's something for which the poor pay even at the expense of more pressing matters that need an immediate cash lifeline. They can't help it.

Regular people do win the lottery. Sudden riches, however, will bring out the best or worst in a person who is unacquainted with opulence and wealth. It's easy to develop an affinity connection with someone whose life experiences are like yours. Seeing them win a big payout is a powerful, gravitational hook that lets the poor fantasize and anticipate their date with financial destiny as they plop down their next investment in the lottery. Signs and symbols are used to confirm their good luck. They reason, "It's bound to happen; I can feel it."

Those who can least afford to gamble are captivated by the chase, as they expect to turn misfortune in the other direction. It costs but a few dollars to chase the dream. Of course, a few dollars turns into tens of thousands of squandered dollars, which otherwise might have bought a reliable automobile to get them to work, get out of debt, fund a child's college expenses, start a side business, or invest in the stock market.

Time insensitivity is a bad habit of mine. My wife repeatedly warns me not to bother contractors while they work at our home. Rarely do I take her advice since this provides an opportunity for me to delve into their Sociopsychonomic filter. Their life story keeps me tied to my humble roots as I watch them grind it out doing backbreaking work.

One of the contractors is Bennett (not his real name), whose life experiences I find fascinating. He's a personable guy with a keen sense of humor. He's a gifted and hardworking painter in his early 50s with two adult children. He has been married for 30 years. Bennett asked me one day if I kept up with sports now that I was retired from the pros. I told him no and that outside of going to church and spending time with my family, my interests are twofold—health and wealth.

I asked Bennett, who was thrilled to be interviewed for this book (although I took the liberty to protect his identity), if he was invested in the stock market. He said, "I have no idea or understanding what the stock market is about. A few people in the past have told me the market is a good way to make money. But it was so foreign to me that my mind was closed off to learning about it. I do play the lottery every day, though."

Unlike those who play the lottery to get ahead financially, Bennett is not pressed to pay a bill or strike it rich. He and his wife earn a good living. So why does he play the lottery?

His actions offer an up-close view into the serious and comical world of behavioral finance. You may recall Kioshi Smith's story in Chapter 3, "I Did What?" Kioshi experienced a whirlwind of emotions and financial setbacks as his investment in a classic car became a never-ending money pit. More than 20 years later he's still scarred by the setup, which he painfully admits is mostly his own doing.

Bennett grew up in the streets, and the streets grew up in him. "I come from a family of gamblers—bingo, horse racing, playing cards, street craps. You name it, and we played it. Unfortunately, I took on the identity of my father's hustling ways early on, though I didn't see much of him after he and my mom divorced," he shares with a downcast look on his face.

Many see the lottery as an easy way to make money, and it is a natural fit with Bennett's Sociopsychonomic filter as it magnifies gains on a relatively small wager. Bennett says, "I played my birthday for 10 years. It never came out straight. Now, I hit it several times throughout the year playing it in a box. Each time I win roughly $800. Just a few days before I met you it came out straight. I was shocked! The payout was $5,800."

> "I didn't have a reliable father figure. I had to figure things out on my own. The streets and hustling were my mindset. No one could tell me any different."
>
> **–Bennett**

Bennett spent $8 a day, seven days a week playing the Pick 4. He has pledged to cut back this vice that he admits is hard to shake. He doesn't waste time playing the Pick 3. A winning boxed number nets only $42.50. "That won't fill up the gas tank in my work truck. At least if I hit the Pick 4, a boxed number will pay me $600. Now, that will pay a bill, but $42.50 won't do much," he reasons.

Winning a lottery is random, and Bennett says his path to playing is sometimes guided by hunches, all the better if those hunches lead to a winning ticket. "I'll be riding down the street and pull alongside another car. The license plate attracts my attention because I may have seen it twice in a day. This must mean something and I put a little money on it. But I know it absolutely, positively means nothing that I've seen my birthday on two separate license plates. I still can't explain why I play the lottery."

Let's calculate how much Bennett has conservatively spent on lottery tickets over the last 10 years. Using 52 weeks in a calendar year, his lottery outflows were $29,120. Now, he wins on average $2,400 each year. Cumulative winnings were approximately $24,000 over this same period. Up until his big payoff occurred, he was in the hole $5,000 and this doesn't include the times when he spent triple or quadruple his daily outlay playing the lottery.

The allure and realization of winning provide a euphoric boost. It's the same feeling I experienced playing basketball in front of a live audience on national TV. The applause is captivating and addicting. It's a feeling rarely found navigating the mundane, day-to-day routine of a life without purpose. I don't chase that high anymore now that I'm walking in my God-given life assignment, but I do understand how a lottery win

> Misperception has kept more people poor than either a lack of education or job opportunities could ever do.

does a number on your emotions. Lottery players are drawn to the money, but many also gravitate to a warm, euphoric sensation throughout their entire being—body and mind. State lotteries understand this and behavioral finance perfectly well.

Bennett has played the lottery for so long that he was afraid not to play every day. "I was so invested that I couldn't back out." This behavioral phenomenon is called *anchoring*—you stay the course despite changing circumstances. Hindsight bias also plays a role.

Hindsight bias, or the erroneous assumption one holds that a recent event could have been predicted all along, is something Bennett guards against. The fear of his Pick 4 number being selected ensures that he'll play his birthday every day of the week throughout the year.

Even when you lose, Bennett says, you can still win. "Your losing lottery tickets aren't losing lottery tickets. You can keep them and earn points to win prizes by scanning old tickets in the Ohio lottery app, MyLotto Rewards.™" Consolation prizes include appliances, cell phone accessories, electronics, video games, and gift cards.

As a beneficiary of public education at the elementary and middle school level, though my children attend private schools for religious reasons, I can't knock how our state pays its bills to educate children. What does bother me is that the poor spend a significant portion of their income playing the lottery than do the middle class or wealthy. They can least afford to subsidize public education given their financial situation. Bennett adds, "I have a family member who plays the lottery religiously. She can't afford it, because she's constantly asking to borrow money. Really, I'm done playing the lottery when I can't afford it."

Bennett knows only five people who invest in the stock market—I'm one of them—and roughly 80 people who play the lottery on a consistent basis.

He has a son who works at Chase Bank, which employs thousands of Central Ohioans. I mentioned to him that from its 2009 low of $1 per share, Huntington Bank, a competitor headquartered in Columbus, is up nearly 1,500 percent or $15.

Huntington is a regional bank with a solid standing and extensive community outreach. I said to Bennett that the stock would likely rise in value if it were acquired by a bigger bank, which typically is the case, while the stock of an acquirer usually goes down.

Keep in mind that banks lead us into and out of recessions. Picking stocks is risky, thus mutual funds that hold a collection of stocks may be a better option for you to get exposure to the equity markets. A competent investment advisor can help you get started after assessing your financial goals, risk capacity, expected rate of return, and time horizon.

Lottery players may not follow what goes on in our economy and stock market, but they should. Success in the stock market isn't guaranteed, but it does offer people better odds to build incremental wealth if they remain committed to the process. Bennett says, "I'm out here walking around with blinders on. You just woke me up to a world that I had no clue about. You broke it down—the stock market and other investment options—in rich dummy terms. Here's what I now know: Making legit money outside of a job is not as hard as I previously thought."

Wealthy people don't typically play the lottery. The primary reason isn't because they already have too much money; that's too simplistic. GAPAs and SAPAs understand, respect, and operate their lives by the laws of probability and compound interest. Financial opportunities with razor-thin odds are simply avoided. They take risks and some of their investments undoubtedly lose money, but they avoid schemes that bypass normal due diligence. Why throw good money after bad?

Pass Up

The traditional middle class sees business and investment opportunities, but they wait too long to move on them, ultimately, because of their risk averse disposition and hyper-focus on stable employment. Their security mindset wouldn't have it any other way.

A public school teacher once sought my advice on creating a supplemental income stream because she was finding it difficult to manage monthly cash flow, especially as more money was taken from her paycheck for healthcare and funding her retirement. I asked if she ever thought of starting a side business tutoring children in math, which was her specialty and something she did quite well. I even offered to put her in touch with other teachers who tutored on the side to get information about how they started. However, she wasn't sure if giving up weekends and summer for a few more dollars was worth it.

It's customary for a GISA to talk herself out of a financial opportunity by answering rhetorical questions. What if this goes wrong? How would I recover? Can I squeeze this into my overcrowded schedule? GISAs will spend more time contemplating what could go wrong instead of marinating on what's likely to go right. Thus, the window to act closes. Pivotal intersection points must be taken when the light turns green.

Tyler Cook, a close friend of mine and a certified financial planner with John E. Sestina and Co., encourages people to consider starting a side business if they need extra income. "It's a great way to supplement income without impacting your primary work or job responsibilities. A hobby can segue into a reliable and much-needed income stream."

Business ownership is not for everybody. It's tough work. In fact, most businesses fail within the first three years of operation. It requires a whole lot more than a great idea and positive attitude to run a profitable business. It takes heart.

NOT FOR THE FAINT OF HEART

Kenny Crump is the proud owner of Gym Skills, where kids learn basic and advanced gymnastic techniques. It also is a popular venue for birthday parties.

I met Kenny several years ago while our children participated in Gym Skills. Our friendship has blossomed through the years. We've collaborated on joint programs to assist children in their financial and physical development. He's also one of It's All Good Cookies™ biggest fans, providing each child during Parent Watch Week with a delicious cookie that also doubles as a healthier snack option.

Kenny is the middle child of five. He grew up in a blue-collar home with two hardworking parents, each of whom retired from jobs with Columbus

City Schools. His father was a teacher; his mother, an administrative secretary who now works part-time at Gym Skills.

Kenny's work ethic is a testament to his parent role models, who practiced what they preached. He says, "They told and showed us that you get what you work for and that you can't sit around and be lazy. We didn't know anything different."

He is the only child among his siblings who has ventured into the entrepreneurship arena, an environment with little fanfare and a whole lot of pressure to earn an income. Nevertheless, Kenny wanted to take matters into his own hands despite the challenges that come with business ownership.

His first job was at a grocery store, and he credits Jim Oberla with being a mentor and an instrumental force in developing his stewardship skills. "He must of saw something in me that I didn't see in myself at the time. I was the first male to manage a cash register at this IGA location, though I was only 14 years old. Mr. Oberla owned and managed the grocery store as well as the shopping center where it was located. He taught me leadership skills, from owning real estate to interacting with customers to managing and massaging employee egos."

Kenny's journey has had its share of twists and turns along the way, despite the tutoring he received from his mentor. "I didn't understand all of the risks associated with running a business. I got started right out of high school. Had I waited until my early 20s, I, too, would have settled into a comfortable job like my other siblings."

> "Great entrepreneurs understand that failure is part of the success path."
>
> **–Kevin "Mr. Wonderful" O'Leary**
> *Shark Tank*

At the age of 18, Kenny and a friend started Trueline, a clothing company. First, they attended a clothing trade show in Las Vegas. Upon returning to Columbus, the duo hit the ground running. Unfortunately, the business closed 18 months later. As he notes, "We had no idea what we were doing. Good thought but poor execution led to a predictable outcome." Kenny says, "It was a great thing that it failed. My father suggested that I get back into gymnastics, so I worked part-time at a recreation center. I started a mobile gym a year later, which eventually birthed what I'm doing today."

Prior to Gym Skills, and right before Trueline, Kenny and a cousin started Uplift, an energy drink and T-shirt line. They went to Los Angeles without any legal guidance or understanding of the sports beverage market. Kenny laughs now, but he and his business partner paid a heavy price for their lack of knowledge. They lost thousands of dollars and once again, another venture failed. He adds, "Though it didn't end well, this was one of the best experiences of my life because I learned so much. First, do your homework before getting started in business. Second, don't fall in love with an idea that isn't really that special. Third, hire professionals to protect your downside risks."

> "Owning a business is no jacuzzi. The water is a little cold at first but you get use to it."
>
> **–Dr. Scott Paton**
> Chiropractor and Entrepreneur

A business mentor of mine and Kenny's, Ron Stokes, a former Ohio State basketball star and CEO of Three Leaf Productions, told him to find a good attorney and accountant, have a great relationship with a banker, and seek wise counsel from a trusted confidant. Ron's timely advice has served Kenny well.

He started Gym Skills in 2005 as a mobile gym. Kenny opened his brick-and-mortar location in 2008, which coincided with the Great Recession. He says, "Being naive, I didn't even know what a recession was. Also, I had just gotten married and had two business failures staring at me through my rear-view window."

Fortunately, his wife Christina, who owns a hair salon, was there pushing Kenny past his comfort zone.

Realistic goals were set when the facility opened. He says, "We wanted to have 12 kids per month at $60 per kid. Then my next goal was 60 kids, which grew from there to several hundred participants each month." Initially, Kenny taught all the classes for the first two years. As business grew exponentially, he hired several coaches to meet the demand. He says, "It took five years to develop the model before we expanded into a larger space. We recently purchased our own building and opened a second location in Cincinnati."

GISAs that take the entrepreneurial plunge return to the surety of having a steady job when their new business flops. They make good on a vow never to be suspended midair without a safety net under their feet. However, failure doesn't mean fatal if important lessons are learned along the way, including pressing the reset button and starting over. As Kenny says, "Fix what's broken and keep moving forward."

Pass Down (Or To)

The generationally wealthy transfer knowledge or investment opportunities to family members and close associates within their tightly regulated network. However, they won't turn over a business without ensuring the recipient knows the responsibilities that go along with it.

A GISA or SAPA may trust a child or family member to carry on a business because of the blood connection. However, that individual may lack the same work ethic or CEO DNA as the previous owner, and thus the business may falter because stewardship principles weren't developed in the successor. Handouts to children without legacy conditioning often do more harm than good. It's hard to appreciate an opportunity in which you expended no sweat equity.

"I saw this working as a server at Muirfield Country Club, where the Memorial Tournament is played each year in Dublin, Ohio," says Tyler Cook, a certified financial planner. "This suburban kid grows up in a pampered environment and is handed a business with little personal investment. He runs the business into the ground, mismanaging capital and treating customers with contempt. Succession may have been planned, but the recipient wasn't groomed for the responsibility."

Outliers exist of course, but this scenario is more common in situational affluence rather than generational affluence. A business rich in heritage will not automatically be passed along to a blood relative who failed (or didn't take) the stewardship test. He or she must learn the business and the importance of treating customers and employees with respect. Legacy continuation—the commitment to personal growth and professional development, simultaneously—is always on the mind of the GAPA steward passing the baton to the next family member.

GUT-CHECK TIME

Mike Uckele and Derek Sharp are two friends who share an affluent mindset, though they each grew up in humble circumstances. Mike was reared in a traditional middle-class home with an intact family structure, while Derek's upbringing was a bit more challenging. He grew up lower middle class with separated parents, hand-me-down clothes, and severe financial struggles as a child.

Derek's father, Louis Dale Sharp, played football at Florida A&M under legendary coach Jake Gaither and was the first African-American Ohio State Highway Patrolman.

Mike and Derek both have a voracious work ethic, an inherited trait from their respective parents. However, they were determined to break free from the contentment-of-needs attitude that is pervasive among GISA households. Fulfillment of their economic potential was a gradual process, but the catalyst began, as both men pointed out to me, the moment they became equity business owners. To do so, a different perspective relating to financial empowerment was required, one that would challenge conventional thinking of a barely enough mindset.

SOCIOPSYCHONOMIC FILTER

A barely enough mindset can be a catalyst or crutch for the typical middle-class person. It'll drive him to pursue an entrepreneurial opportunity or stay parked at a dead-end job with no career advancement or income mobility.

Derek's parents stressed education as the way to get ahead.

"I was fortunate to go to some pretty good schools in childhood," he says. "When Princeton and Dartmouth were recruiting me to play basketball, I thought that there was no way I could pay for my education at these schools since Ivy League universities don't give out athletic scholarships. So that option was off the table for me, or so I assumed. The realization escaped me that I could have taken out loans to pay for school. I missed the larger point that an Ivy League education carries immense benefits beyond a degree. The network and connections made with peers at these schools can lead to profitable job and financial opportunities that could have pushed me far ahead. It likely would have allowed me to pay off school loans at a faster clip, too."

After college Derek worked at Accenture, a publicly traded company. He says, "What I found out was the founders and early investors, before the company, then Andersen Consulting, went public, walked away with a windfall of cash as their shares became more valuable with the transaction. This got me thinking, 'How I could I put myself in a lucrative position to collect a financial windfall as an early-entry equity owner in a company before it goes public or is acquired?'"

That opportunity, which Derek couldn't pass up, presented itself when former Andersen colleague Dave Schoettmer asked him to come on board as an equity stakeholder at Navigator Management Partners, a management and IT consulting firm that assists large organizations with back office tasks, including payroll, employee benefits, and software.

Derek is one of five equity partners. Although he had ample business experience, leadership training, and networking skills, Derek did have to address a common fear GISAs ask themselves: "Do I pursue a business opportunity without a guaranteed path to financial success, or stay put in a stable job with excellent benefits?"

He took a hard look at what Dave Schoettmer built and calculated the likelihood of him selling comparable services at Navigator. Liking what he deduced, Derek trusted his gut and accepted the offer without any lingering reservations. "I'd rather have a larger piece of a smaller deal, than a smaller piece of a bigger deal. At Accenture, my upside was somewhat limited. At Navigator, I have a bigger influence on developing employees and growing our company."

Navigator Management Partners is attracting interest from private equity groups as its portfolio of major clients expands across the country. If a strategic acquisition or major capital infusion from investors materializes, Derek will have taken a huge leap toward his financial windfall.

Mike Uckele has been president and owner of Uckele Nutrition since 2005, buying out his father and uncle before taking over. At the time, annual sales were $4 million. Not bad, but it should have been better.

"The company was leaving a lot of money on the table," he says. "It was cruising along, but had so much more room to grow." Today, Uckele Nutrition has sales of $36 million, an 800 percent improvement in 12 years.

Mike grew the company, as he says, "by getting rid of bad business, whether it was perpetually late-paying customers or unfavorable accounts receivable ratios and inventory drains on products that weren't being sold in an efficient and timely manner." His methods sound counterintuitive since this led to a $500,000 drop in sales. However, bad customers were let go along with several unprofitable products. This improved Uckele Nutrition's cash flow and let the company focus on growth-oriented objectives.

However, unavoidable headaches often accompany business growth pains.

"When you move from a $4 million to a $10 million company, it is completely different. The expectations and demand on human and intellectual capital are more intense," Mike says. "Operationally, we had to revamp our processes. Sometimes, you can't simply work your way out of a tough situation; you must work smarter within the situation.

"We had to build systems and processes and procedures to deal with the growing pains. This doesn't mean that we do everything great, but we're certainly moving in that direction. If we didn't grow at all, then every employee at our company would be perfect at what they do."

As a continuous improvement organization, Mike adds, "We're committed to being the best we can be as a company when one workday ends and a new one begins. The ride thus far has been rewarding, but we know there's still so much room for growth."

This was Michael Jordan's timely advice to me as a trash-talking rookie: Greatness demands that you bring it every day. Like sports, you can't take a day off in a competitive business environment.

Mike Uckele offers encouraging words to entrepreneurs who take financial matters into their own hands: "If you focus on doing all the right things in business, success and money will follow. Be diligent on getting better every day, cultivating long-term partnerships with your suppliers, customers, employees, and community stakeholders."

His and Derek's stories illustrate an important theme of this book: It's not so much about a social class as it is a mindset upgrade. Whether we're running a business or household, or trying to improve our health, it comes down to processes that require sticking to a successful game plan. We'll stumble at some point, but falling is not always a bad thing if lessons (subtle or glaringly obvious) are learned along the way.

17

STOCK MARKET FILTER

*The view or opinion held by a social class
regarding the intricate world of
publicly traded stocks*

Slot Machine

Children born into generationally affluent families are up 20 points in the wealth game from the get-go, with a victorious end assured if they avoid taking quick shots or playing recklessly. Newborn middle-class children start the game tied and, like their parents, will shy away from taking risks to win the wealth game. Children born into poverty start the game down 20 points. Most of them dig a deeper hole by taking low-percentage shots early in life, which continues into young adulthood. Now they're down 30 or 40 points and feel it's pointless to try winning at the wealth game—so why bother learning about the stock market?

The poor know about the stock market but not how it works, perceiving it as a game of luck where only a select group of investors win. Inside information, superstition, serendipity, and "tall paper"—investors with deep pockets—improve one's odds of beating the house, skeptics assume.

In the "Pre-Game" section of the book, I discussed the phenomenon of street craps in Chapter 2, "Outside In," a game with clever sayings and superstitious rituals as participants place bets on a roll of the dice.

The poor throw good money after bad playing the lottery, gambling at a casino, or getting involved in get-rich-quick schemes. Conversely, they also fail to view the stock market as a viable path, and one with better odds, to improving their wealth. If they bothered to check out the stock market, they would find that publicly traded stocks have consistent-

> "The poor feel like it takes a lot of money to invest, which they say they don't have."
>
> **–Monya Funderburke**

ly outperformed bonds, precious metals, real estate, and savings accounts over many decades. Of course, like any investment offering, inherent risks do apply and the market does experience periods of extreme volatility.

However, the poor, in general, think the stock market is an opportunity beyond their reach, especially when they discover there is no guarantee their investments will earn sizable returns.

Statement assets, although hindrances to building legacy wealth, are always viable options for GEDAs because they manufacture inward feelings of personal self-worth and generate outward perceptions of social acceptance. These include cell phones, clothes, cruisers (or shoes), and cars. Accessorizing their cars, even when they don't have the money, is a sacrifice the poor are willing to make. Looking the part instead of being the part is about styling and profiling. Doesn't matter if the sideshow is detrimental to their financial well-being. Remember, pretense is always more important than substance in generational poverty.

LaMont Hardiman, a friend of mine and financial advisor for more than 25 years, has a firm grasp on social class dynamics. He says, "The poor invest in depreciating assets. They spend money on things that don't build wealth or create a legacy. Why is Rim Tyme, an offshoot of Rent-A-Center, in existence? I stopped by one of the locations here in Columbus to see this business in operation. You lease rims to place on a hooptie. If a payment is not made, the rims will be repossessed and the car is left on blocks."

Back in the 1980s as a child, my familiarity with the stock market was relegated to a 10-second blurb on the local news that day. A reporter would say by how much the Dow Jones went up or down in value. Nothing more or less. Since no one in my immediate circle was invested in the stock market, I didn't pay much attention to what was said. Besides, it didn't affect our welfare benefits, or how we survived financially as a family. Why would we care? Equity investing wasn't taught in middle or high school back then either. How could I learn about a subject to which I was never personally exposed?

Most teachers in America come from middle-class backgrounds. They may be well-versed in cash flow management, but this is quite different than wealth accumulation. Tyler Cook says, "Schools should be the ideal place for children to learn about financial matters, especially the stock market. However, most teachers can't educate students on a subject they may struggle with themselves." If financial wellness is not taught before college, Tyler maintains, then the wealth gap in America is likely never to be closed outside of self-education and empowerment programs.

Until I went to college as a business finance major, I didn't realize the stock market impacted the rich, middle class, and poor in different ways. It's a forward barometer of our U.S. economy. A rising or falling stock market affects consumer confidence and our willingness to spend money. When it rises, consumers purchase goods, and when it's falling consumers are hesitant or unwilling to spend money. Remember the stock market downturn of 2008 and its impact on the American psyche? I do.

FINANCIAL TERMS

A stock represents an ownership interest in a company, whereas a bond is a loan made to a company or the government for a set period of time with a predetermined interest rate and predictable income stream paid in the form of a coupon payment.

The stock market is not gambling, which is based strictly on odds. In the case of the lottery, mysticism or a lucky hunch supposedly improves a player's chances of winning. Evidence-based research and data are at an investor's disposal with the stock market, and very well may improve an investor's selection of winning stocks.

A stock's value rises and falls for any number of reasons, including an analyst's upgrade, economic data, good or bad publicity, political instability, the weather, or a shift in consumer tastes. Investors can only estimate how a stock will perform based on historical price movements and fundamental information. Past performance doesn't guarantee future performance, but it can serve as a baseline.

In general, the economic cycle lasts between three to five years. Healthcare, consumer staples, and utilities are sectors that typically do well during a downturn because companies in these sectors usually have stable earnings and offer attractive dividends. As value stocks, they tend to fluctuate less often than growth stocks.

Investors buy stocks in the financial, technology, and transportation sectors during a recovering or expanding economy. Consumers spend money and take out loans when economic prospects are favorable. Big-ticket items, also known as consumer discretionary expenditures, are often purchased in a rising interest-rate, wage, and disposable-income environment. These include cars, appliances, flat-screen TVs, designer handbags, and jewelry, to name a few. Home renovations and vacation splurges shine brightest when consumers have more money to spend and the economy is on solid footing.

Companies hire or lay off employees depending on customer demand and our economy's trend line. Optimism is good; pessimism is bad. In a pessimistic trend line, interest rates fall and are intended to stimulate economic growth. Interest rates and prices often move in tandem. In a deflationary environment, prices on goods and services fall. In an inflationary environment, they go up and necessities such as food and fuel cost more.

SOCIOPSYCHONOMIC FILTER

The rent-a-depreciating-asset mentality punishes the poor, as well as their reliance on convenience stores, payday loans, check-cashing places, and the lottery to survive in the land of economic hardship.

Savers are punished in an environment of low interest rates. Interest-bearing accounts, although guaranteed in many instances, can't keep up with inflation. More risk must be taken to stay ahead of inflation. Those with a wealth-accumulation mindset understand this.

The affluent invest in the stock market. On the other hand, the poor and lower middle class often look to the lottery to strike a fortune. The stock market has made the rich richer. The lottery has made the poor poorer.

My mom played the lottery on occasion, especially when the palm of her hand itched, a superstitious sign that an unexpected monetary blessing would soon appear. She'd open her book of lottery numbers to confirm her inclination. Ma Dukes would play the recommended three-digit numbers straight and boxed, the latter giving her the best opportunity to win if any combination of the numbers was selected. From personal experience, an itching palm could be a sign of intestinal discomfort—a food intolerance.

Rigged System

Institutional traders use algorithms, or computer-generated calculations, on the buy- and sell-side of the stock market transaction equation as they execute an investment position. Emotion is bypassed since the operation is computer generated. Obviously, their actions can move the market in either direction within milliseconds.

Beth Sparks, a financial advisor with more than two decades of experience, says the stock market is more efficient today than when she first entered this profession, but with one caveat: "Keep in mind that algorithms are designed to manage risk, and volatility may be an inevitable byproduct if transactions to liquidate a position are made simultaneously by an untold number of market participants. As such, though, algorithms can work for or against us. I believe the middle class has a difficult time with the ups and downs of a gyrating stock market, thus most of them are apt to avoid it altogether."

Retail investors—middle America—don't believe they have a chance against the wolves on Wall Street. To a certain extent, they're correct. Institutional investors have a decided advantage based on the tools and knowledge at their disposal. However, money can still be made by retail investors.

Many people in the middle class assume they'll reach their financial goals solely by saving money, not by investing in the stock market. In fact, they see savings and money market accounts and certificates of deposit as viable investing vehicles in which they'll achieve their financial goals. It's an assumption built around an FDIC-insured guarantee.

GISAs also try to hedge their bets through their employer. However, loyalty to employees isn't what it used to be, and job and retirement insecurities are worrisome. Company pensions, or defined benefit plans, have been dwindling since the 1990s.

If a retirement plan is offered by their employer, employees today have the difficult task of managing a 401(k) or 403(b) account through a fear-based filter. Many GISAs believe the stock market is inherently rigged, thus they tend to gravitate to investment selections with low-risk, low-return profiles.

LaMont, himself a product of a blue-collar upbringing, says, "The middle class often looks at a 401(k) or 403(b) account as a savings vehicle, regardless of the employer match. What they fail to realize is that it should be viewed as an investment multiplier or wealth generator."

The traditional middle class wants an annuity stream indexed to inflation without the possibility of loss of principal, guaranteed income for the rest of their lives, which Social Security and pensions were set up to be. The preservation of their middle-class lifestyle must be protected at all costs. They don't believe the benefits of stock investing outweigh the risks. Let's go a little deeper to understand what's driving their apprehension toward the stock market.

> One of the best hedges against an uncertain financial future is physical, emotional, nutritional, and spiritual health.

Stock ownership is a difficult concept for many to grasp. The intangibility associated with a paper transaction is controlled electronically. Unlike a bank, you can't physically access your money. Beth says, "People have been conditioned to trust the bank because of the safety this institution provides. We inherit most of our financial IQ from our parents. Back in my parents' generation, the bank was where they parked their money, not the stock market."

Income is tangible; stocks are not, unless you sell them, which may be at a higher or lower price than what was initially paid. It's easy for us to visualize how we can use or spend money. An investment vehicle in which we have no familiarity is somewhat of an abstract concept. This level of familiarity with wealth-accumulating assets is often commensurate with one's level of affluence. But this needs to change.

Stocks offer *marketability*, or a system of buyers and sellers, while savings and checking accounts offer *liquidity*, where you access your money on a whim from a bank or credit union without losing your principal.

By and large, the middle class is fearful of the stock market. They're afraid to tie up their money for any length of time when loss of principal is a distinct possibility on paper. Even temporary illiquidity is a terrifying predicament for them to be in. That's why they replay what-if emergency scenarios for their money, ad nauseam. Granted, these potential concerns are legitimate but still somewhat contrived. They convince themselves that investing in the stock market, under any circumstances, is the wrong thing to do. Guess what? Many don't.

Another aspect that trips GISAs up about stocks is fractional ownership. Affluent investors, on the other hand, welcome fractional ownership, whether it's a stock, business relationships with multiple partners, or interest in a luxury jet service. With all its flaws, equity investing isn't a perfect system. But this doesn't spook GAPAs and SAPAs. They trust the process. They know it works. They are conditioned to stay committed to the wealth playbook through good and bad economic times when equity markets are gyrating. But they do take profits off the table when necessary and won't hesitate to make a substitution to their portfolios when referees (or Central Bankers) are calling a tight or loose game. GAPAs, and their advisors, pay close attention but won't act hastily.

Equity interest in a company is based on the number of shares owned. If a company has 100,000 shares outstanding and you own 1,000 shares of common stock, then your fractional ownership is 1 percent. Your stock will rise and fall in value depending on how the company performs. With such a low equity interest, you're not likely to have much influence in how the company operates unless you also happen to be a key employee.

An outside shareholder who owns, say, 40 percent of the company's stock, could potentially wield incredible influence. He or she is likely to have a seat on the board and make recommendations to hire or fire top executives. It's not a perfect system, but this aspect of the world of publicly traded stocks frightens people. Combined with risk aversion, it's no surprise why many GISAs stay out of the stock market. Too many moving parts can affect their monetary equilibrium.

Most GISAs are scared to get out of their financial lane, and aren't comfortable unless they're driving in the lane marked, "middle-income drivers only." They are terrified to venture in the lane for affluent-minded drivers, and God forbid, don't let them swerve into the lane where the poor drive. They don't want to drift to the left, the lane of plenty, or to the right, the lane of lack. They are perfectly content where they are until the moment arrives, as LaMont points out, that GISAs realize they don't have $250,000 to pay for health insurance and long-term care in retirement. They don't have sustainable assets to last them from age 65 to 95. The middle class takes great measures to prepare weekly or monthly for upcoming bills, but fails to plan for the costs that will cripple them financially in the future.

Wealth Generator

The informed wealthy—transplants into affluence and those born in it—embrace the stock market. As Beth notes, they see the subtle and obvious value of this compounding machine. They understand the formation of wealth creation and the responsibilities that come with it. As you'll read in upcoming chapters, the equity markets play a pivotal role in GAPAs' and SAPAs' investment philosophy.

It is one of many avenues used by high net worth individuals and families to boost and protect their income statements and balance sheets. Dividend-paying stocks receive favorable tax treatment, tend to rise in value, and provide a recurring income stream for investors, though most wealthy people are likely to reinvest quarterly dividends.

Growth stocks are riskier than dividend-paying stocks because profits are usually reinvested back into the company to acquire a competitor, expand a product line, or pay down debt. Growth stocks tend to provide capital appreciation. Hybrid stocks offer the best of both worlds because they offer a growth and an income-oriented component.

The stock market is often viewed as a hedge against inflation for the affluent-minded investor, which comes in handy if we reasonably conclude that future costs associated with our standard of living on goods and services will likely rise.

The 2008 meltdown often is the context for middle-class fears. The wealthy shrugged it off since they weren't emotionally scarred by this historic event. Financial advisor Danny Levitt says, "When you mention 2008 to some clients, they want nothing to do with the equity markets. But if we look at the last decade, inclusive of 2008, the stock market was up close to 10 percent per year. The image in their mind is that the S&P 500 index was down 37 percent that year. That's all they want to remember."

This scared-straight mentality forced many investors to the sidelines (permanently in some cases), where they huddle with their apprehensions, patiently waiting for the markets to correct themselves. The next proverbial shoe to drop is just over the horizon, they think. This is a very real and troubling stumbling block for GISAs.

Affluent investors silence runaway emotions. They have experience, seasoned professionals, and perpetuity conditioning metrics on their side. This is how generationally and situationally wealthy investors doubled or tripled their money post-2008, while the middle class lost money in the stock market and left the scene psychologically scarred.

The rich did blink when the stock market dropped in 2008 and continued its downward plunge until early 2009. Danny says, "Then they got a little twinkle in their eye and asked, 'How can I make money in a market downturn? How can I invest in something at a discount? How can I dollar-cost average or deploy incremental capital into an investment position?'"

A CORPORATE HOUSEHOLD STRUCTURE

It's a natural fit for GAPAs and SAPAs to run their households with the same attention to detail as the publicly traded corporations in which they invest. Organizational management is a critical component of wealth accumulation and preservation strategies.

The mega wealthy also are accountable for what makes it onto their financial statements. In some respects, they are even more meticulous in the operational aspects of wealth creation.

"The middle class hasn't quite grasped this concept yet," LaMont says. "When they leave work, they leave work. When they shut down, they shut down. It's time for happy hour after work or watching their favorite shows on TV instead of taking a few hours per week to build or monitor a wealth creation game plan, and for them, the stock market should play an instrumental part of it. The working class is entitled to spend leisure time as they see fit, but it won't change their financial condition one bit."

Tyler's blue-collar roots and concern for the middle class are seen in his heartfelt assessment. He says, "I think it goes back to this storyline of what the traditional middle-class life should look like. However, our world has drastically changed. Middle America is afraid to veer from the script. Also, they don't want to think about any wealth-building opportunities—the stock market in particular—that tax their brain when the workday ends. They decompress from the entanglements of money at the end of a long day on their jobs. The wealthy, however, wind down after work watching CNBC, Bloomberg, or Fox Business, or reading the *Wall Street Journal* to recap the day's news on the equity markets. Their mindsets are polar opposites."

LaMont adds, "The wealthy look at their profitability on a quarterly basis. They may even have a bad month financially, but not a bad quarter. Unlike the poor or middle class, they're not stressing about things on a weekly or monthly basis."

Emotions get the best of you when you're pressed financially over short periods of time. Changing how you see things weekly to monthly and then to quarterly starts with planning. Soon your perspective will change and your mental and financial wealth will grow.

18

MULTIPLE INCOME STREAMS

*The cash inflows from monetization
opportunities that are required to
achieve financial freedom*

Fantasy

To survive in the future with or without government support, active and passive income streams will be needed. The working poor, often content with reaching for and securing just one, have a hard time grasping multiple income streams, a sentiment echoed by financial advisor Beth Sparks.

Beth highlights a truth that haunts many GEDAs and GISAs: "They work hard and never get ahead financially," she says. "If I'm working at an hourly wage job, I'm never going to get ahead. Somehow, I've got to have my money working hard for me. Since the working poor can't typically see wealth-building opportunities, they unfortunately cannot benefit from them. They're also afraid of the risks associated with these opportunities."

To realize an income stream, it must first start with the mental picture of one. This is a cognitive skill that comes naturally to GAPAs and SAPAs, but is a struggle for GEDAs. They feel ill-equipped to handle the task of economic emancipation, a liberating state in which every financial need is met, and per-haps, a few luxuries, too.

Helping the poor achieve financial freedom they may wrongly think is beyond their reach starts by never placing them in a box, which limits their potential and life's purpose. The box suffocates, marginalizes, and debilitates the poor, making them feel like caged animals, enraged that someone would have the audacity to belittle their capability as human beings.

> ## SOCIOPSYCHONOMIC FILTER
> You must see the income-stream potential in others before it can manifest in your own life.

If you look at the poor from a limitation perspective, you not only limit what they can do, but you also limit what they're willing to do, a far more devastating consequence of low expectations.

Working with a GEDA to help him grasp that his capability is extraordi-nary—personally, intellectually, educationally, or economically—is the key to unlocking his potential. Remind him that he is limited only by the limitations that he places on himself. Blaming others for what you can control is the ulti-mate self-inflicted limitation. Difficulties in life happen to everyone.

Next, help the poor see the income-stream potential in others before it reveals itself in their lives, a journey that requires discipline and mental stamina to stay the course. Take them high above their landscape, metaphorically speaking, and let them observe how to navigate the terrain below, including which paths to take and obstacles to avoid. From a financial perspective, aerial topography helps GEDAs plot an escape route out of poverty.

CROSSING THE FIRST BARRIER TO REACH THE POOR

In the chapter "Financial Coaching Buy-In," I discussed three primary meth-ods that connect with impoverished communities: the sensory connection, the participatory connection, and the transitory connection. These strategies set the mood for the poor to consider the merits of a value proposition at an introductory level. Inevitably, though, finding the motivation to change rests with the individual.

An emotional appeal is made through the sensory connection. The target audience is drawn in through humor, pain, triumph, or some other inspirational factor. A former life of hardship, as measured by authenticity and credibility, is also needed by the speaker to generate buy-in. Whatever the message, if it doesn't connect with GEDAs' experiences, it will get dismissed.

I hold onto a food stamp as a constant reminder of poverty's shackles and pull it from my pocket when presenting before GEDAs to demonstrate unrestrained transparency. You can't fake economic hardship and government dependency in front of the poor, or anyone for that matter. Most people can spot a phony in a heartbeat and recognize that something just doesn't line up with the person's alleged experiences.

Once a personal connection is made on a sensory, participatory, or transitory level, attention should turn to this urgent plea: convincing GEDAs to implement life-transforming information. As trust is earned and they're locked into your message, the virtues of perseverance to complete a challenging goal must be colorfully and tastefully packaged to excite their senses.

Securing wealth is a gradual process, but many people (not just the poor) employ a trampoline mentality toward financial wellness, thinking a few bounces here and there will get them to that goal. However, you can't bypass the grunt work and character-building tests that precede wealth creation. It takes time to land in a better financial situation.

ROLE PLAY AND EXPERIENTIAL LEARNING ARE KEY TO PERSONAL AND FINANCIAL GROWTH

Interactive simulations with real-world scenarios, such as our Multiple Income Stream Game, help GEDAs reframe their possibility filter from exasperation to motivation. Once they play, you can physically see the excitement in their eyes and pep in their step as they grasp that life's voyage has an upside. They come up with creative suggestions for the hypothetical game contestant to build wealth—writing a book, starting a side business, or investing in the stock market—all while learning key attributes and skills that can be used by GEDAs to jumpstart the wealth-accumulation playbook in their own lives.

Touch-and-feel experiences bring abstract concepts to life, which is a critical first step in reshaping their economic frame of reference.

We create apps specifically designed to assist participants in the development of their personal and financial potential. Complex terms are explained in a format that is easy to understand. Language demystification can lead to a viable navigational path in which poor and middle-class communities take the first steps to acquire legacy assets.

Four general categories comprise multiple income-stream vehicles: employment, a for-profit business, investing generators, and intellectual property. (Starting a nonprofit organization could technically be considered an income-stream vehicle. However, it's not advisable to enter this world for monetary gain. Obviously, no one should expect you to provide an ongoing service to disadvantaged populations without being compensated, however laudable your efforts.)

Income drivers fall into three primary categories: physical labor, financial labor, and intellectual labor.

Physical labor, or ordinary income, describes income generated from a job or business that requires your time, attention, and diligence each day. Income from real estate can be either ordinary or passive depending on the amount of work required by the owner to generate monthly rent payments.

Financial labor, also known as portfolio income, is the income generated from stocks, bonds, mutual funds, exchange-traded funds (or ETFs) and index funds, private equity, hedge funds, and other investment classes that are not related to rental and commercial real estate.

SOCIOPSYCHONOMIC FILTER
Financial role play through interactive simulations is an effective tool in helping the poor start the process of building meaningful wealth, personally and economically.

Intellectual labor is passive income from royalties generated through the creation of residual monetary inflows, such as writing a song or book, or establishing a licensing agreement with a vendor of copyrighted material. More on passive income later.

Income from any labor source is derived from our TAP—talents, abilities, and passions. Talent is an innate skill that comes naturally to you and is confirmed by others. An ability is a skill or skill-set that you learn, develop, and refine over time. Passion drives you to be something, do something, create something, change something, or improve something. It's an intense desire often tied to your life's purpose. The distinguishing traits of your TAP will often determine what level of wealth accumulation you reach.

A ONE-SIDED, WEALTH-BUILDING RELATIONSHIP

Consumers buy a lot of products from publicly traded companies, whether it's food, toiletries, clothes, or entertainment gadgets, and regardless of their socioeconomic spectrum, most Americans are viewed as consumers. However, a glaring irony exists in the dynamic relationship the social classes—consumers, workers, and investors—have with multibillion-dollar companies.

A one-sided relationship typically exists between publicly traded companies and GEDAs. The poor, as U.S. Rep. Joyce Beatty notes, are on one side of the cash register. GEDAs exhaust their financial resources purchasing necessities, impulse items, and statement assets.

Among the middle class, GISAs share a give-and-take and employee-employer relationship with publicly traded companies. They do receive a paycheck from these companies, but far too many of them stand on the sidelines fearing the next Lehman Brothers or Enron. Holding stock in your company is one thing. Having one concentrated position of company stock as your entire portfolio is something else. Single-stock investors get crushed when economic headwinds shift directions suddenly. That's why mutual funds (and index funds and exchange-traded funds) may make sense for most investors. Instead of outright ownership, they can still capitalize on a stock's upside potential while limiting their downside exposure if the price drops.

> The poor provide free advertisement and generate multiple income streams for others, but not themselves.

Publicly traded companies share a multifaceted relationship with GAPAs and SAPAs. They certainly purchase products and use services offered by them, but many high net worth individuals also are shareholders and white-collar executives at these organizations. The rich get richer because they take calculated risks in their career- and wealth-building pursuits.

Publicly traded companies strategically place their stores in pockets of American cities and rural areas where consumption is high but resources are scarce. Within these geographic footprints, companies know the poor's shopping habits, tastes, preferences, and daily schedules. Scary, right? It's not so much that Big Brother is watching—he is—but what consumers are doing that is quite revealing. They know how much GEDAs and the working poor spend, when they're likely to buy, and what drives them to spend money they don't have. If you think multinational, publicly traded companies don't un-derstand *Sociopsychonomics*, you would be making a huge mistake. They know it very well.

The consumer profile of the poor is relatively straightforward: An appeal must be made to GEDAs' immediacy of needs and the fulfillment of sensory desires that excite the soul and enhance their social image, and most impor-tantly, assuage the pain, albeit temporarily, of a life shackled by unrelenting economic heartache and perpetual dysfunction.

When given hypothetical money to invest, GEDAs usually purchase publicly traded stocks based on their level of familiarity with products or services. This isn't a bad strategy, by the way. In fact, many investment profes-sionals advocate this strategy as an entry point for beginning investors. GEDA selections include stocks of affinity companies in these five bucket areas:

The Food Bucket

The poor often prefer quantity over quality in what they put in their body. Cheap, filling, and low nutritious foods are staples of the high-caloric GEDA diet.

The Shelter Bucket

The poor make tradeoffs each month for housing accommodations and personal comforts. These include rent payment, utilities, and even some big-ticket purchases.

The Clothing Bucket

The poor often prefer quality over quantity in what they put on their body. Name-brand apparel is often purchased over lesser known brands. Saving face is sometimes more important than saving money. Statement assets are purchased by GEDAs to make them feel better and be accept-ed by peers.

The Entertainment Bucket

GEDAs make incredible financial sacrifices, oftentimes to their own detriment, to deal with the challenges of a difficult life. Movies, music, video games, and other enjoyable experiences are used to deflect or cope with their pain.

The Transportation Bucket

Using "bucket" and "transportation" in the same sentence can be com-ical. In the ghetto, bucket is another name for a car with perpetual maintenance problems. Fuel, mechanic shops and auto parts stores, public transportation or taxi service, bureau of motor vehicle requirements, and basic auto insurance coverages capture much of the focus for this expense bucket.

SOCIOPSYCHONOMIC FILTER

I may not personally like some of the products and services offered by many of the companies, on the poor's bucket list, but this shouldn't stop GEDAs from flipping the script; they need to get rich off the companies, instead of just making these companies and their shareholders rich.

I find it fascinating that many GEDAs in our empowerment workshops will bypass company stocks they feel take advantage of the poor, including banks and financial services, utilities, and oil and gas companies. Politics may play a part in their make-believe investment decisions when multibillion-dollar companies "don't pay their fair share of taxes," but the primary reason could be the boring nature of companies in these respective industries. They might be boring, but most of them do pay a decent dividend.

Here's a proposition for publicly traded companies that target the poor as customers: Partner with nonprofit organizations around the country that assist the poor in building personal and financial assets. Further, allocate shares of company stock to GEDAs and the working poor who complete empowerment programs. This would enhance your public relations image and profile on two fronts. First, the poor often spend what little money they have on the products and services offered by your company, and stock ownership could turn into a wealth-building legacy play for GEDAs. Second, it shows that your company values the poor as customers and investors, which is what others would see as an economic mobility and fairness play.

Possibility

The pursuit of multiple income streams paralyzes the poor, overwhelms the middle class, and energizes the affluent.

Middle America is very resilient maintaining their lifestyle, but apprehension rules the day when risk aversion and caution stop them from pursuing multiple income streams. Here, capability paralysis can affect GEDAs and GISAs alike.

Most of our financial DNA is inherited from our parents, and Monya sheds light on how an unfamiliarity with the concept of multiple income streams impacted her wealth-building filter.

"I saw my mom and dad go to work every day to provide for me and my siblings. We never struggled financially, and lived the typical, middle-class lifestyle. This was my baseline. I didn't know anything different until I was exposed to this other world of wealth," she says. "For me, generating multiple income streams goes against my conservative nature. Although you pushed me to fulfill my economic potential, I still don't feel like I measure up. Being aggressive, networking, selling my personal brand, and dealing with rejection—aspects of wealth building that can't be avoided—are still very uncomfortable. It's hard to shake a play-it-safe upbringing."

> Most of our financial DNA is inherited from our parents, which can serve us well or serve us notice.

In basketball, you can miss three shot attempts in a row, but make your next five. One thing is certain: You will miss 100 percent of the shots you don't take. The same is true if you're a business owner. Five potential customers may say they're not interested, but the sixth, seventh, and eighth customers could be the catalysts to catapult your sales to the next level. Pursuing financial opportunities and building generational wealth take a certain amount of optimism and tempered realism. It also takes time when an individual's learning curve is steep.

The middle class wants as close to a sure thing as possible before they let go of their money, which doesn't exist in the world of investing. Opportunity costs and financial sacrifices must be weighed. Investment advisor LaMont Hardiman says, "They use their savings to cover emergencies and their next major purchase, such as a household appliance or automobile. The pursuit of a secondary income stream isn't on their mind, unless of course, it comes with that guarantee."

Multiple income-stream opportunities are often shunned by GISAs because they view risks in relation to losses. They also can short-circuit their sense of personal and financial harmony if they become overwhelmed when multiple income streams are contemplated. The information is just too much to handle.

Tyler Cook, a fee-only certified financial planner, offers some cautionary advice: "At John Sestina and Co., we are obviously big fans of multiple income streams, but they shouldn't interfere or become a detriment in a person's capacity to earn them." I wholeheartedly agree.

What wealth-accumulating avenues are available to the middle class? Earlier, we talked about four multiple income streams that exist for GISAs: working as an independent contractor arrangement with their employer; starting a side business; investing in bonds, dividend-paying stocks, mutual funds, exchange-traded funds, and index funds; and acquiring an outright or fractional interest in rental real estate.

> ## SOCIOPSYCHONOMIC FILTER
> If you are not going to take the time to learn about investments with higher-risk-and-return profiles, then don't invest in them.

One of Tyler's clients moved from India to the U.S. 20 years ago. He and his wife landed at LaGuardia Airport with only $49 to start their American dream. Today, they are millionaires. The husband worked for IBM, his core income stream, but started a side business to take the couple's financial goals to the next level.

Perhaps the stock market, the third income-stream opportunity, causes the most trepidation for GISAs. It's risky, no one can deny this fact. However, some stocks are less risky than other stocks. Value stocks tend to be less volatile than growth stocks. Companies with proven track records in paying quarterly dividends to shareholders are usually safer stock choices than those who don't pay dividends.

A laddered dividend-income strategy, now or in retirement, is appealing to GISAs because of the cash flow this provides. Dividend income from various publicly traded companies can be laddered or timed to cover monthly obligations. Stock dividends are paid to shareholders every three months.

Beth Sparks says, "It comes down to covering whatever you need to meet your lifestyle obligations. The middle class can relate to income since they're good at keeping and earning a paycheck. Stock dividends could be a viable income stream to help pay monthly bills."

Real estate investing is an income stream that appeals to the middle class on four fronts. First, it's tangible. A house, duplex, or apartment complex can be accessed and touched, just like the money in their bank accounts. Second, real estate is perceived by GISAs as a safer investment choice than the stock market (though it's not) since people always need somewhere to live. Third, rent payments offer a consistent or residual income stream. Fourth, real estate owners can tap into the property's equity—the difference between the home's current value and the loan balance, if there is one—when cash is needed.

There are inherent drawbacks to investing in real estate, though late-night television infomercials lead you to believe otherwise.

"Clients will approach us and bring up flipping houses to generate another income stream," Tyler says. "When we sit them down and go through an exercise on a spreadsheet to evaluate the merits of this potential opportunity, their euphoria quickly dissipates. Most of the time, it's not as lucrative as they think. If you don't know what you're doing in the real estate game, you're likely to lose a lot of money and time.

"Our clients have us as filters to weigh the pros and cons of various wealth-building options, but let's stop and think about the people who pursue opportunities without an advisor in their corner. What are their evaluation metrics, other than an emotional whim?" he says.

A MULTIFACETED APPROACH TO GOOD BALANCE

The ears not only play a major role in hearing, but they also send out distress signals to the brain when our equilibrium is compromised. The connection among the cochlea (verbal and nonverbal hearing), vestibular system (balance and spatial orientation), and semicircular canals (communication channels that relay our body position in three-dimensional space to the brain) is fascinating.

I believe GISAs find difficulty moving vertically pursuing financial freedom because the costs to reach this goal rattle their monetary balance, which is largely influenced by the horizontal canal in the inner ear. Gravity's effects on financial well-being for the middle class, mentally speaking, can be a dizzying ordeal. My assumption may be supported by the following commentary from the Healthline Medical Team. They write, "The vestibulocochlear nerve is responsible for both hearing and balance and brings information from the inner ear to the brain. A human's sense of equilibrium is determined by this nerve."[19]

Whether an auditory sound is heard or felt, our sense of balance on a physical, financial, emotional, or even spiritual level could be affected.

Monetary disequilibrium, or economic vertigo, for the middle class is a debilitating condition. It can show up when they step out of the box to pursue something new. As we know, GISAs rarely venture outside of their lane, even as the financial sirens blare and signal to them to devise a wealth-improvement game plan. They are terrified by the prospects that their investments will fail and they'll join the underclass. As a result, most GISAs don't attempt to move up the wealth ladder. They're perfectly fine balancing on the horizontal plane of comfort: contentment of needs.

SOCIOPSYCHONOMIC FILTER

Discomfort must be embraced when financial freedom is being pursued, which can create enormous instability in our thought life and emotional state.

THE FOUR PILLARS OF GOOD BALANCE

Four factors contribute to a person's good balance, an important facet of good health that declines as we age and gravitate to a more sedentary lifestyle. They include strength training, visual dexterity, proprioceptive skills, and a properly functioning vestibular system. A deficit in any one of these areas may impair our state of equilibrium.

Let's compare the physical and mental attributes of balance to cast a spotlight on the social classes' monetary vestibular system.

Strength training, specifically core building of the abdominal area and lower back, includes exercises to strengthen the hips, quadriceps, and hamstrings. The ankles also play a huge role in keeping the body stable, and without a firm foundation, the body will teeter uncontrollably on unstable surfaces. The frontal lobe oversees the planning and coordinating of strength training for large and small muscle groups.

The occipital lobe handles everything related to the eyes. Depth perception, color clarity, and eye tracking—visual dexterity—are critical to balance. Without these, we would bump into walls, skip entire paragraphs when reading, or not be able to coordinate body movements with objects in motion. This was the area where our son Eli struggled the most with sensory integration disorder. Thank God, he no longer suffers from this condition.

The body's positioning in relation to the environment is called *proprio-ception*, an important parietal lobe task. Sensation, what the body feels, and perception, how the body interprets what it feels, impact our sense of balance. Our personal orientation will keep us stuck in a financial rut or propel us to get out of it.

The vestibular system houses the temporal lobe, a balance component that garners a lot of the attention. Along with several others, tinnitus (ringing in the ears) and vertigo (dizziness and nausea) are two debilitating conditions of an inner ear malfunction.

Okay, here's the possible connection between mental and financial balance, or for many Americans, economic disharmony.

GISAs rely too much on the basic building blocks of their financial core without realizing that overall core strength improves with calculated risk taking. Resistance training builds physical and financial muscles.

Financial atrophy occurs when their fear of failure—which applies to GEDAs and GISAs—prevents them from fulfilling their economic potential. The brain doesn't grow without new neural networks getting established as our experiences broaden.

The development of our visual acuity lens expands our wealth-generating possibility filter. On the other hand, a compressed focus can be self-sabotaging or limiting in scope. Of course, we only pursue what we feel is possible to grasp. Taking a page from the GAPA playbook, it's time to widen our vantage point of what's economically possible and permissible.

Our financial filter is shaped by factors within and outside of our control. Our actual and perceived standing in life will largely determine the destination path and GPS coordinates we plug in to reach, or drift away from, economic freedom. The voyage is usually uneventful for GEDAs, unnerving for GISAs, and unshakable for GAPAs.

A STORAGE WAR (OR WASTE) CHEST

The hit reality television show "Storage Wars" leaves me scratching my head at the lengths people go through in hopes of securing and holding on to a so-called treasure chest. Unfortunately, the highest bidder is often suckered into the ego-driven bid and left with a storage full of junk. I have used storage facilities and boy, did I hate paying that monthly storage fee.

I once asked a manager at a local facility how long was the average length of stay for storage customers. He said a little more than four years, and I replied that most of the units probably hold things that aren't worth a year's worth of storage costs, let alone four years. He agreed and added, "People work hard to buy stuff and hate to get rid of it. It's amazing how a family buys new furniture and then places the old furniture in storage, hoping that their 14-year-old son will gladly use it when he goes off to college. Nine times out of 10, he'll decline the outdated furniture and the parents will have wasted thousands of dollars in storage costs. Now these parents must buy new furniture for their son, plus pay for his college tuition and related expenses. It doesn't make common or financial sense."

The storage facility manager didn't know it, but selling possessions that are taking up space in a residence is a fifth income stream for GISAs. Call it the garage-sale option if you want, but consider that the average household has more than $2,000 worth of sellable items laying around. Sentimental value is largely to blame for a person's reluctance to let go of cherished possessions, but that isn't a wise way to think. It might be in your best interest to sell them outright on the Internet or give the possessions to a tax-exempt charity and take a charitable deduction on your tax return, such as Goodwill.

> Make a statement with your heart or compassion for others, not your bank account.

As a distancing hoarder (poverty attribute) and former storer (middle-class attribute), I've learned that trying to justify keeping a possession that hasn't been used for years—even if it cost thousands of dollars—isn't worth the aggravation, and it's liberating letting go of my emotional attachments and financial justifications to keep certain things. What's out of sight is out of mind. It certainly rings true in this instance.

Before moving on, let's clarify a few things about pursuing multiple income streams. I've seen many people chase riches and wealth as a scorekeeping measure, surely a sign of our outdo-thy-neighbor society. This is distasteful and shows a lack of class. Trust me, I've had my moments making a fool of myself in this area. I've shared many of them throughout *Sociopsychonomics*, and I'm not proud of any of them.

People show off their financial wares for a myriad of reasons. For manipulation. For prestige. For applause and praise. For attention. For a false sense of security, or to cover up internal pain. Truthfully, your guess is as good as mine, and I don't judge anyone's motives.

I leave you with this advice: Make a statement with your heart, not your bank account. Be generous in your good deeds to a hurting world. Besides, not everyone will be a fan of your financial success. In fact, some people just might be plotting your demise. Jealousy doesn't always come with a snarly facial expression. Envious people can simultaneously smile outwardly and inwardly grit their teeth, staring you up and down as if you're a sideshow character who doesn't deserve financial blessings.

Reality

The poor often are too impatient for wealth principles to work, while the middle class ponders the costs of implementing them into their daily lives. The mega affluent, meanwhile, already know wealth principles work because they trust the process and reason they'll work because they worked for their parents and grandparents. This is their reality.

For the generationally and situationally affluent, wealth-accumulating opportunities extend their reach, while attaining multiple income streams are a natural byproduct of their frame of reference.

> ### SOCIOPSYCHONOMIC FILTER
> Emotional IQ is a must-have for anyone desiring to build legacy wealth.

GAPAs and SAPAs are optimistic and believe due diligence and professional advice increase their odds of success when financial opportunities appear. Multiple income-stream opportunities for GAPAs and SAPAs tend to appear at the right place and time, letting them capitalize on lucrative partnerships, investing opportunities, and business dealings with other high net worth individuals. Unlike GEDAs and GISAs, they understand the correlation between risk and reward and weigh each side of the investment coin before making a decision.

Using the half-empty, half-full glass analogy, the informed wealthy's glass is overflowing. This mindset spills over into nearly every aspect of their world. Meanwhile, the poor see the glass half-empty and believe few legitimate opportunities exist in which to amass a fortune. The middle class sees a half-full glass, where possibilities for multiple income streams exist, but the opportunity costs don't gel with their taste buds and aromatic risk filter. Instead, the middle class prefers maintaining a comfortable lifestyle.

The mega affluent have a different philosophy and want to grow or preserve their legacy. See the difference? Rich people with a legacy mindset may have nice things, but they're not driven or defined by the accumulation of tangible assets.

"The informed wealthy, as you call them, spare no expense investing in the growth of their children's financial fitness. They acclimate kids and grandkids to this subject at an early age by sending them to camps and legacy continuation workshops, where other wealthy children will be in attendance," Monya says. "Think about our summer camps, which are probably one of the most expensive weeklong programs in Central Ohio. The wealthy don't blink an eye at the cost, because they gladly pay for the value proposition. They're all about giving their kids an advantage, or preserving the head start that has already been set in motion since birth."

GAPA and SAPA children run the race at a measured pace they're conditioned to complete at the appropriate time. Even with tightly regulated schedules, the informed wealthy don't feel like they must exhaust themselves to generate multiple income streams, which is in stark contrast to the GEDA and GISA return on investment (ROI) brain. More on this later.

Wealth-building opportunities can be birthed from character tests. Difficulties shouldn't always mean surrender. When people see hazard signs and detours, they become terrified and turn back. They misinterpret challenges along the way as roadblocks instead of as signals to find a new route.

GAPAs and SAPAs understand that problems are amplified when the growth process is bypassed or rushed. Organic farmers also understand this idea. Each year they sow fields in the spring and harvest crops in the fall. If they plant too early or too late, crops can die with an early frost or because they aren't mature enough in time to harvest. Along the way, they make adjustments for severe weather, pests (without chemical use), and environmental challenges, for instance. It's a process that relies as much on patience and perserverance as it does good weather. Organic farming is a character builder.

The laws of sowing and harvesting must be followed in finances as well. People don't fully grasp that money brings out the best or worst in our character. Having a lot or just enough or a little of it is not a basis for good or bad character. Money, or the lack thereof, will however magnify who we are at the core, our inner countenance.

THE SCAFFOLDING MINDSET OF WEALTH CREATION

Three primary income classifications exist—ordinary, portfolio, and passive—and an important distinction must be made in how an income stream is earned and obtained.

Most people benefit only from a single income driver: their job or business. This is fine if a significant portion of their income is saved or invested, but most Americans live paycheck to paycheck and don't have $500 in a liquid account to cover an emergency, this according to a shocking Bankrate report.[20] This portends an uncertain financial future.

The informed wealthy make money from anywhere they sit in the wealth-creation arena. They initially have their primary income-stream driver, and from that single source births multiple drivers. That initial driver eventually is used for new investments—you've heard the expression "putting your money to work for you"—that ultimately increases their net worth and leads them into more wealth-building, scaffolding opportunities.

> "The working poor and middle class want to touch and smell the aroma of their hard-earned cash. They deposit their paycheck in the bank every two weeks like clockwork. The wealthy want their money working for them."
>
> **–Danny Levitt**
> Wealth Management Advisor

The hit television show *Shark Tank* illustrates this technique. Most of the Sharks created a company, which they then sold for hundreds of millions or billions of dollars. This segued into other business opportunities, creating a multiplier effect on their wealth. They were handpicked to be equity investors for *Shark Tank*, which first aired in August 2009. I'm not certain how much money each Shark has made investing in various contestant businesses, but whatever that number, it's safe to say that show mainstays Mark Cuban, Daymond John, Kevin O'Leary, Barbara Corcoran, Lori Greiner, and Robert Herjavec are richer today than when the episodes began.

Some equity partnerships will fail no matter the due diligence performed to limit risk. That's the nature of high-risk investment offerings. But a flop doesn't stop GAPAs and SAPAs dead in their tracks. They remain optimistic but cautiously vigilant not to jump into an enticing opportunity.

PASSIVE INCOME: THE WEALTH COLLECTOR

As a financial advisor, Danny Levitt is well acquainted with ordinary and portfolio income, assisting hundreds of clients and their families with their financial goals. Passive income intrigues him. Once it's set in motion, energy usually doesn't have to be expended to keep it going. A few of his wealthier clients collect what's known as "mailbox money," or recurring income that's directly deposited into their cash accounts.

This doesn't mean you're not fully employed. In fact, you're likely to have a really good job that allows you to invest in a passive income stream and let your money work for you. We call this a compounding wealth machine. For instance, you collect monthly payments from tenants in your rental properties, receive royalties from a book deal, or are paid residual fees on sitcom reruns. Keep reading to learn about a few other passive income-stream options.

Danny lives in Houston where a lot of people get rich from leasing their land to oil drillers. Whatever you think about this industry, it's huge in Texas and drives a significant part of their state and local economies. "Many über-wealthy Houstonians have made a fortune on recurring passive income streams," he says. "They walk to their mailbox, figuratively speaking, and collect five- and six-digit checks every month."

Here are a few tips and suggestions to generate passive income without the responsibilities of owning land or a rental property:

Write an eBook or Workbook

- It's been said that a book is inside each of us. If you've overcome a difficult situation or have an interesting story to share, there are plenty of people who will pay money to hear it. Self-publishing isn't as costly as one might assume.

Create an Online Membership of Paying Customers

- We've become addicted to free information over the Internet. But if you offer a service or knowledge booster that separates you from the masses, why not monetize it? Be sure to keep the information fresh and relevant. If you do, on-the-fence customers will turn into loyal customers. Cha ching!

Create an App

- This is a viable income stream for those who are tech savvy. App design templates have come way down in price, thanks in large part to an oversaturated market. Nevertheless, the demand for apps will continue to be strong. Most of us can't live without our smart devices.

License Your Creative Content

- A licensing arrangement of your innovative techniques to solve a nagging problem is an income stream that may take more time and start-up capital to pull off, but the long-term benefits can be lucrative. Word will spread quickly if your methods have staying power. An online series of experts and professionals can provide a boost to your service. Of course, they will need to be compensated for their efforts.

19

INVESTMENT PHILOSOPHY

*The strategies, tools, or default system used
by a social class to achieve an investment
or monetary result*

Dependability

Whether we realize it or not, we all have an investment philosophy. It doesn't matter if we play the lottery or invest in the stock market or hide our money under the mattress, the actions we take are driven by our financial acuity lens. This is shaped by our upbringing, life experiences, and possibility (or impossibility) filter.

The poor rely on favorable circumstances to survive economically or when they come into an unexpected windfall. Dependability catch-alls include government or nonprofit support, financial assistance from family members and friends, fortuitous job opportunities, "lucky breaks," modest inheritances or death benefit proceeds, and gambling earnings.

Talented kids in poor neighborhoods often are viewed as a family meal ticket. The prodigy is expected to take care of immediate and extended family members, some who have postponed their own lives to invest in the child's development, a monetizing skill-set they assume will improve their financial lot and social standing in life, too. After all, they're invested in the payoff just as much as he is.

Family members and friends fantasize about a boost in their wealth status thanks to the prodigy, envisioning homes in gated communities and exotic cars. The wunderkind will improve their situation, they expect, and the clan goes to great lengths to shower the child with praise for his athletic or artistic abilities. Enormous pressure is placed on him to maximize his gift.

What they fear is getting excommunicated if they offend the talented superstar. They will bend over backward to accommodate him until the truth is revealed: His talent wasn't good enough to generate a financial windfall. He knew it all along, but unfortunately, his family and friends did not.

My NBA experience was a test of character on two fronts. First, the expectations—and the accompanying scrutiny—to perform at a high level is intense. Even the bad teams had great players, so you could never take the night off. There were a few games in which I played poorly and missed every shot I took. Did those mishaps stop me from taking shots the next game? Of course not. Second, it was incredibly difficult to shift my mindset from being a former high school and college star to a role player who received little attention. The transition was more mentally daunting than physically demanding.

Likewise, a string of bad days or years of financial hardships don't doom the individual to a life of perpetual economic hardship. In poverty, fatalism takes its cues from life's unfortunate predicaments, and there are many.

SOCIOPSYCHONOMIC FILTER
The poor often interpret challenges and setbacks as proof that success in life is a fantasy.

Too many GEDAs find it easier to depend on others for a financial breakthrough rather than take the necessary steps to craft one themselves. A belief that life is inherently unfair keeps them pinned down, and it fuels their skepticism.

This generational mindset is pervasive among the poor, guided by a compass of unwavering feelings that validate their belief. A perceived emotional injustice by an individual is self-sabotaging in nature and causes more damage than the economic and social injustice grievances that precede it could ever do.

It's easy to reach this conclusion if you exist day-to-day in deplorable living conditions, broken homes, violent communities, low-paying jobs, and high-stress environments. Poverty is taxing, and I should know because I've lived it. These aggregate filters affect how the poor view investment and monetary opportunities.

A sign, symbol, or gut feeling is often needed by the poor before they'll pursue a financial breakthrough. Chance encounters with people of financial means might spur GEDAs to seek an escape route out of their challenged environments. However, devising a game plan for their escape must first start in the mind. If it doesn't, the poor will never physically or emotionally get out.

If you're like me then you've had chance encounters with people who grew up in the same neighborhood as you. You both exchange pleasantries, which in my case includes talking about the economic hardships we faced living in our poverty-stricken area. However, there comes a point when the acquaintance starts asking for a favor. For instance, a neighborhood friend sought a loan from me to start a business. He had no business plan for me to review and determine whether the idea was sound, but I felt pressured to make a decision that was largely driven by guilt and an affinity connection. I should have rejected his request outright, but I didn't; he continued pursuing my help until I eventually shut that door.

GEDAs feel like it's make or break when a chance encounter presents itself and could ultimately pave the way out of a financial rut with a loan, a job referral, or cash. The fortuitous meeting must mean something, right? Well, not necessarily.

SOCIOPSYCHONOMIC FILTER

Financial breakthroughs without an updated frame of reference and mindset do little good to counteract the dysfunctional living conditions of generational poverty.

Their sense of urgency can repel the person who hasn't forgotten his humble roots or the pain of poverty, but instead has moved on from the debilitating mindsets that keep most GEDAs tethered to their past. He's willing to help them, but they must first help themselves. Successful outcomes are driven and sustained by internal stimuli to do what's right independent of personal feelings, though the poor often believe the reversal is true.

"TOO GOOD TO BE TRUE"

The poor and middle class are quick to call out unscrupulous characters like company executives that walk away with golden parachute packages in the tens of millions of dollars, who contributed to the housing market collapse and Great Recession in 2008. Their reckless behavior was indefensible, but despite the untoward and illegal actions taken by some market participants, this shouldn't sideline spectators—permanently—from investing in stocks.

One of our signature financial life skills apps is The Portfolio Management Game, which provides a real-world setting for participants to gain a better understanding of investing.

In the 90-minute game, participants invest and manage a hypothetical $1 million, placing $200,000 each in five different investment choices. The following concepts are covered: assessing risk tolerance; arranging financial goals in order of importance and time horizon; evaluating investment options based on fees and expenses, performance over a one-, three-, and five-year period, and each option's risk and liquidity profile; and understanding how macroeconomic forces affect our domestic equity markets, and thus an investment portfolio.

A prospectus supplements the cursory introduction given to describe the 20 investment selections and eight asset classes, including cash and cash equivalents (certificates of deposit), stocks, bonds, mutual funds, index funds, exchange-traded funds, private equity, and hedge funds. Not surprising, very few people take the time to read the modified prospectus while constructing their investment portfolio, though they are encouraged to do so at the onset of the game.

Each asset class is explained in detail or an abbreviated fashion, depending on the audience and their likely Sociopsychonomic filter. As I move up the risk continuum to introduce more advanced asset classes, hedge funds and private equity for example, their association can carry political ramifications. I will mention public figures in the world of high-structured finance who, fairly or unfairly, are associated with a political party.

Mitt Romney, a former presidential candidate who ran against Barack Obama in the 2012 election, was branded an out-of-touch 1 Percenter. He made millions as a hedge fund investor with Bain Capital. The mere mention of Mitt Romney's name propels some to remove hedge funds and private equity from participants' list of viable game choices. He is often negatively associated with these two investment classes.

The game's private equity and hedge fund options by design, unlike the other investment choices, don't disclose past performance. However, it is highlighted that each type of firm has an excellent track record producing superior returns for investors. Transaction expenses and management fees for the two choices are significantly higher, which some participants believe are excessive and a trap.

More than 1,100 participants across the socioeconomic spectrum have played the game. We document their selections and the range of emotions from trepidation to euphoria that are expressed throughout The Portfolio Management Game. Monya says watching people play elucidates pertinent information about how they approach financial management.

"You can tell a lot about a person's social class by his or her body language, interactions with other participants, and ability to process financial information with several moving parts," she says.

GEDAs playing the game expect something bad will happen and deplete their hypothetical investment portfolio. It's a common response among those participants. Life's unfortunate experiences have conditioned them to anticipate punishing financial setbacks, and in this game, they are convinced a market pullback lurks over the horizon.

They are either super aggressive or extremely cautious in their investment choices, and they'll employ the same extremes when taking a risk. One middle-aged man with GEDA roots said, "I'm taking a gamble here with this hedge fund." He later commented, "My portfolio is up after year three; now I can go to the casino!" His optimism changed when his investment portfolio dropped precipitously. "This is too risky. That's why I keep my money in a jar!" He wasn't joking.

This gentleman, like many GEDAs, distrusts the stock market, which to him is worse than gambling. It will take some time and participation in a few more investment games, perhaps, before he alters his mindset.

Our investment games provide economically and functionally distressed individuals with a new frame of reference about financial opportunities that don't involve luck or gimmicks. In most of the investment games, participants cannot change selections after their portfolio is constructed; only the value changes. This prevents them from trying to anticipate or manipulate favorable circumstances that result from superstitious feelings and not intellectual analysis. It's a losing proposition for investors who try to time a rationally irrational market. Financial advisor Danny Levitt says, "Getting out and getting back in the stock market is a bad strategy. In any given year when it's up, roughly 10 to 20 days are likely to move the market to the upside. Sideline investors miss this upside time after time."

To the Portfolio Management Game, we add humor, entertainment, and emotion to accentuate the experience. We find that by empowering people through their language filter, or how they process information, the amount of knowledge shared and recommendations an instructor makes dramatically increase. Financial knowledge and experiential learning enhance quality of life for the poor and middle class. These empowerment tools help GEDAs break vicious cycles that perpetuate poverty.

Liquidity

Cash accessed through savings and checking accounts, certificates of deposit (CDs), and money market accounts brings the traditional middle class peace of mind. Their down-to-earth, conservative nature relies heavily upon FDIC-insured assets that are easily accessible for lifestyle expenses and emergency situations.

Perpetual safe havens such as savings or checking accounts protect cash, but they may very well be detrimental to GISAs' financial well-being, especially if they ignore investment opportunities.

Beth Sparks says there are three legal ways to generate money. You can work for it. You can inherit it, but how many people have a wealthy parent or grandparent who will leave behind a fortune? Or you can invest it. Your money can work hard for you, or you can continue to work too hard for your money.

When GISAs reluctantly move up the risk-and-reward continuum and invest, they typically gravitate to bonds, dividend-paying equities, and real estate, perhaps because of the tangible nature of this asset class. What they might not realize is that owning real estate for investment purposes can be incredibly risky. If the 2008 housing market collapse taught us anything, it was that real estate is cyclical in nature and its value doesn't always increase.

A 2012 study designed by Primerica and the Consumer Federation of America titled "The Financial Status and Decision-Making of the American Middle Class" highlights the struggles of middle-income Americans in basic and advanced financial subjects. Middle incomes were between $30,000 and $100,000 per year.

The middle class gave themselves high marks in basic financial education: cash flow, credit card management, and auto insurance purchases. However, they weren't as confident as the upper-income group about saving for retirement, understanding the stock market, and purchasing life insurance.

Perhaps most troubling about this study is that many of the middle-class respondents took less investment risk with higher increments of hypothetical dollars. The findings noted:

> "One striking difference between the financial decision-making of upper- and middle-income Americans is their confidence in stocks and bonds. Nearly half of the upper-income group (48 percent) said they would invest most of $1 million in stocks or bonds while little more than 21 percent of the middle-income group said they would do so. While the differences for lesser amounts invested were not as great, they were still significant."[21]

When GISAs choose to invest, they seek shelter in investments with lower-risk and low-return characteristics, which matches up with their comfort zone. Actions taken by the majority of middle-class participants in our financial workshops mirror the findings of the study.

SOCIOPSYCHONOMIC FILTER
For GISAs, the correlation that having more money leads to taking greater investment risks is a fallacy.

The proliferation of instant news has done a number on GEDA and GISA fears to avoid a stock market and investment environment that punish the faint at heart. People know what they see on TV or read on social media, but this is not enough to make a good decision about investing in the stock market, much less any other financial decision. It's human nature to fear the unknown and seek information from sources that appear to be trustworthy.

The reality is that creating wealth takes work and time. It's sad because there are very few people who'll go through the necessary measures to produce a better financial result for themselves and their families.

The subject of behavioral finance fascinates Tyler Cook, as it does me. He believes the stock market was way oversold and went down much lower than it should have during the Great Recession. Granted, we had the subprime mortgage crisis, liquidity challenges of major banks, and the bankruptcies of century-old companies, so justification for a sizable correction existed. But Tyler says the recession went far deeper and wider than necessary because of the cascading fears of investors who left the market in droves, causing an even bigger sell-off of equities.

Behavioral finance is clearly on display in The Portfolio Management Game, where they choose stocks to invest but can't change selections once they're made. You'll find participants start questioning their judgment and strategy when their "investments" falter. One middle-class man was visibly distraught that his portfolio shrunk by more than $200,000 in a single year. He blurted out, "I'm so depressed right now. This is killing me inside."

Tyler, a former athlete and huge sports fan, helps middle-class clients overcome their investing fears by sharing this analogy. He says, "It's like basketball, when you're struggling with your shot, you go back to the fundamentals of shooting mechanics: square up to the rim, keep your elbow straight, and hold your follow through. Same is true helping clients overcome their investment fears. This involves a great amount of excavating. First, you must find the pain, and it's likely to show up in how much or how little money they're spending, or their lack of knowledge about the world of investing. Once you identify the pain in a client's financial life, then it often leads you to the path that solves the problem. I can explain what stock ownership means, what a bond is, and what rates of return are probable for a given level of risk, but for most people, these terms are over their head. They often have one question in mind: 'How will the knowledge that is shared impact my specific situation financially?'"

GISAs playing The Portfolio Management Game view liquidity and accessibility as important considerations. Safety and security are embedded principles that come into play when money is discussed at the beginning of the game. By the game's end, a disconnect is clear and glaringly obvious: The risk tolerance many participants selected at the onset didn't line up with the risk profile of their overall investment portfolio four macroeconomic cycles later.

Any wealth advisor will say it takes time getting clients to embrace investment risk instead of fearing it.

"Today in our world of instant gratification, everybody expects everything right away," Tyler says. "Financial planners must get clients to understand investing in terms of decades and not days. Like in sports, there are gut-check moments. Clients must assess how much risk they're willing to take to reach their financial goals. Also, the portfolio needs to be reviewed on a consistent basis, but this does not mean daily. Clients need to recognize where they are and where they're going, and always keep moving the ball forward. Sometimes, though, you must move the ball backward to go forward. Some clients understand this, while others panic when they see a down period."

> "The discounted pricing of stocks in early 2009 when the market bottomed may very well have been the buying opportunity of a lifetime for those investors who weren't scared or scarred by the meltdown."
>
> **–Tyler Cook**
> Certified Financial Planner

The Portfolio Management Game benefits middle-class players on several fronts. First, they are forced to face their legitimate and illegitimate fears about investing. Second, they must quickly transition in and out of a wide range of emotions as macroeconomic conditions dictate. Third, participants gain a better understanding of domestic and global events, and how they can affect GISAs' personal and family economy. Fourth, they can upgrade their Sociopsychonomic frame of reference, erasing preconceived notions about the benefits of wealth creation and how GISAs get left out. They're also introduced to financial concepts that were foreign to them before. Fifth, they are now better informed about taking control of their financial future. Sixth, they see the urgency in taking necessary steps to reach financial freedom and discuss the process with their children and grandchildren.

Here are seven general findings I've discovered about the middle class in the area of investment planning during my 10 years as a financial planner and workshop presenter:

- Even losses in hypothetical games cause GISAs to exhibit the same emotional reactions that result from real life financial decisions.

- The middle class has a basic understanding of economic events, such as how war in the Middle East can impact oil prices or the Fed's discussion (or decision) to lower interest rates can have a positive effect on the mortgage market. However, most GISAs don't truly understand how macroeconomic events impact the precious dollars they have in their bank accounts and investment portfolios.

- Investing is the most feared and biggest area of concern for GISAs. However, cash flow management, estate (or end-of-life) planning, and life insurance coverages are their most pressing needs.

- They understand basic investment terms but struggle with asset allocation and diversification.

- They entertain the idea of financial freedom but fear the conceptual, sequential, and actual steps required to achieve it.

- Most admit their failure in setting a good example for their children and grandchildren in economic empowerment, where future survival will require a wealth-building mindset.

- Many first-time workshop participants don't believe they'll ever be able to retire unless they make drastic changes and generate multiple income streams.

MILLENNIALS' ANGST

It will be interesting how Millennials, youngsters back during the Great Recession, prepare for their financial future. A lot of them have a jaded view of the stock market, and to a certain extent, whether the American Dream is fact or fiction. They have serious doubts about success in life, previously thought to have no ceiling for the ambitious go-getter. However, a confluence of factors—a lack of purpose, a toxic political climate, and college debt—has dampened their spirit.

Most people's thoughts about money, Tyler says, solidify during their teenage years. If they had a good experience with money, their outlook about investing is likely to be favorable. The opposite would likely be the case if they grew up watching their parents fight over money.

The social media generation is also quick to call out the super rich, especially the profligate types who distastefully flaunt their fortunes in the face of glaring wealth inequalities. Affluence has lost its mystique for many young

Americans, perhaps because they equate a life of privilege with affluenza and guilt. This is a very troubling sentiment.

A number of Millennials also believe the greed of Wall Street fat cats and dishonest bankers brought our country to the precipice of economic collapse. Surprisingly, they are silent about the poor decisions many Americans made buying homes they knew were unaffordable and who threw money at an over-valued stock market without the slightest hint of due diligence. The lure of easy riches can be intoxicating.

Tough times inevitability lead to hard lessons for all to learn. Might we fall victim to these unfortunate mistakes again? Only time will tell. But it's often said that history has a funny way of repeating itself.

Perpetuity

Most middle-class, do-it-yourself investors use a 10-year backdrop when charting their investment course. What's fresh in their mind are events that occurred within this window of time. They forget about the days of double-digit inflation, higher than normal tax rates, oil shortages, or massive unemployment in decades gone by. The generationally and situationally affluent consider a stock's historical performance over many decades in their strategic and tactical assessment of equity markets, key attributes of an investment philosophy. An unknown future will be influenced by an undisciplined past, one that punishes investors who do not learn from their mistakes and irrational exuberance. A poorly constructed investment portfolio is largely to blame.

A clear distinction exists between an investment philosophy and an investment strategy. For GAPAs, their investment philosophy is based on guiding principles that determine how they invest, where they invest, when they invest (or deploy capital), who they invest with, and why they invest. This philosophy is shaped by their carefully crafted legacy, life filter, family values, and circles of influence.

An investment strategy is a tactical or behavioral position that, on the surface, appears closely linked to an investment philosophy, and that may well be the case. However, semantics matter a great deal here. The whims of emotions can heavily influence an investment strategy, but are less likely to affect an investment philosophy.

Legacy continuation through asset allocation and diversification is a hallmark of the GAPA investment philosophy. We've all been told, never put all your eggs in one basket. Countless studies correlate a reduction in investment risk with asset allocation, a concept that comes naturally to the wealthy, but one the poor and middle class struggle to grasp.

> "The rule book for wealth creation is the same for all of us, except most people refuse to read it."
> —**Danny Levitt**
> Wealth Management Advisor

"GAPAs and SAPAs," says LaMont Hardiman, a wealth advisor, "have well-balanced investment portfolios with non-correlated assets, or assets that don't move in lockstep with each other, generating impressive returns whether the market goes up, down, or sideways."

Mixing asset classes will account for roughly 90 percent of an investment portfolio's success or failure, financial advisors say. Diversifying assets spreads the risk within an investment class. The challenging part is positioning and rebalancing a portfolio to capitalize on the ebbs and flows of investment offerings. Unless you have the time, this job is best left to the professionals.

Here's a more simplified illustration to better understand these investment terms. Think of asset allocation as 24 hours. Our time each day is spread out among several categories: sleep, work, extracurricular activities, responsibilities, and leisure. Within each category, we break down time commitments into segmented tasks. As parents, our responsibilities include taking care of kids, preparing meals, and helping children with homework. High net worth individuals go to great lengths to allocate both their time and capital in an efficient manner. GAPAs and SAPAs have a thorough rendering of every second spent each day, and every dollar invested in a portfolio that aligns with their risk profile, time horizon, financial goals, and return projections.

A THREE-PHASED APPROACH TO WEALTH

Through good and bad economic times, the generationally affluent stick to the script. They do not deviate from their wealth playbook, which follows a three-phased approach: wealth accumulation, capital preservation, and asset liquidation.

Wealth Accumulation Phase

Part of this phase probably occurred before most generationally wealthy people were born. Accumulating legacy assets is not attributable to children's efforts per se, but something that their parents and grandparents did long before the kids became a reality. Danny Levitt says, "When you're born on third base, your job is to go to an elite-level college and get prepared for the responsibilities that follow after age 30. From there, the child just needs to keep the wealth machine going."

The affluent want to collect interest, not pay interest. In fact, as Danny notes, many of them reinvest dividends, interest, and bond coupon payments. This investment philosophy of capitalizing on compound interest is done over generations, which is how über wealth is created. Gains from any investment, regardless of the risk profile, needn't be used to supplement a Social Security check, pension, or savings just to cover lifestyle obligations.

This wealth machine of legacy assets includes intellectual property, domestic and global equities, U.S. and international bonds, cash and its equivalent (savings and checking accounts, money market accounts, certificates of deposit, cash values in life insurance policies), real estate, master limited partnerships, precious metals and commodities, private equity, hedge funds, and art and collectibles.

Capital Preservation Phase

You're sitting on this empire of wealth and don't need to go to Vegas to roll the dice. You just need to keep the money ball in place. How do you preserve and keep it safe?

> "My job as a financial advisor is not to make people wealthy. They're already wealthy; it's to keep them wealthy."
>
> **–Danny Levitt**
> Wealth Management Advisor

As noted, the mega wealthy have buffers built into their portfolios through their asset allocation and diversification mix. In effect, risk goes down as the portfolio is hedged or protected against market turbulence.

The affluent have a diverse investment risk palate that prevents them from taking undue risks, as might be the case for those terrified they'll run out of money in retirement because they didn't plan in their younger years.

You may recall my baseball analogy in an earlier chapter. The mega wealthy don't have to step up to the plate and swing for the fences. They can wait for the perfect investment pitch to come across the plate. Some even choose to switch their lineup around once their net worth crosses a threshold.

The sophistication of one's investment palate can sway back and forth between stocks and tangible assets. Tyler Cook maintains that when the wealth of some of his SAPA clients surpassed $50 million, they reverted to touch-and-feel investments, such as cash, real estate, land, and artwork, which limits exposure to the stock market while providing additional layers of portfolio diversification. He says, "Once accumulated wealth reaches a certain point, they place an even bigger focus on the preservation of appreciated assets."

Asset Liquidation Phase

GAPAs understand that removing certain assets from their investment portfolios is a decision designed to continue a legacy. Say what? Indeed, weaving the solidification of a heritage into the fabric of their charitable footprint, which in theory should continue long after they are gone. They set up estate trusts to support organizations with mission-focused directives. These organizations are expected to outlive their affluent donors, and serve as an extension of a GAPA's philanthropic reach.

SOCIOPSYCHONOMIC FILTER
True wealth is not measured by a financial balance sheet; it's based on the number of lives we invest in to make our world a better place, now and upon our death.

The wealthy will often donate appreciated stock and other investments to their favorite charities. Now, a GAPA grandfather may have bought a stock for $3 a share. Today, each share is worth $125 and the underlying security may have split 15 times since it was first purchased. The grandfather can do one of two things: He can sell the stock for millions of dollars and incur a huge tax bill. Or he—through the estate trust set up for this reason—can donate the stock to charity and potentially reduce his estate tax liability by a significant amount. More importantly, this transaction helps a nonprofit organization fulfill its mission.

In effect, the wealthy donor becomes a philanthropist even if he did live on the dividend income for years before donating the shares. Danny says, "We get calls at our Merrill Lynch office here in Houston all the time from affluent clients who want to give away highly appreciated stock to a charity."

As you'll later read in the "Tax Planning" section, the wealthy have conversations with their CPAs and investment advisors seeking guidance on how much they can give to their kids and grandkids for future college tuition costs without incurring a tax liability.

Keep in mind, there are no taxes, fees, or penalties connected to this type of wealth-transfer arrangement that provides GAPA and SAPA offspring with a head start in life.

Tax minimization strategies—not double-digit annual investment returns—are first and foremost on the minds of the super wealthy when they invest. While the wealthy can't avoid paying taxes, they certainly can delay that moment.

Some people are quick to cry foul when the effective and marginal tax rates are vastly different for many super wealthy investors. What they fail to realize is that not all income is taxed equally, and nor should it be.

An individual's or couple's annual gross income from a job, before allowable deductions and exemptions and credits are included, will fall within a marginal tax bracket from 10 percent to 39.6 percent, as of late 2017. After deductions, exemptions, and credits are included, the amount of taxes paid divided by their annual gross income becomes their effective tax rate. For some people, this can be quite different than their marginal tax rate.

The mega wealthy may pay a lower effective tax rate because capital gains income from some investments are taxed at a lower rate than employment income. Deploying income that has already been taxed at the highest marginal tax rate of 39.6 percent to a non-guaranteed investment should receive some type of favorable tax break. Thus, long-term capital gain income for those in the highest marginal tax bracket is currently 20 percent, not including an additional 3.8 percent surtax on investment income for some wealthy earners as part of the Affordable Care Act. (Under the GOP's proposed tax plan for 2018 and beyond, marginal brackets would fall from seven down to four.)

The wealthy are obvious targets to pay more taxes because this is how our country pays its bills. They have more, but should the rules on capital gains be changed just to make them pay a higher tax rate on the same favorable investment tax rates of offerings that were designed to benefit risk-takers? These types of discussions are why we have elections.

Danny Levitt says the money of high net worth individuals and families is quite mobile.

"Even in the consideration of death, their investment philosophy comes into play. They realize the nature and drawbacks that highly appreciated investments can have on their estate tax liability, assuming no changes are made at the federal level to eliminate the death tax. They are asked often about how to pay the least amount of taxes when they die. How would the death of a parent affect a child's overall tax bill?" he says. This is where GAPAs' and SAPAs' team of advisors earn their keep.

> ## SOCIOPSYCHONOMIC FILTER
> The wealthy take advantage of the unlimited charitable deduction by donating money or other valuable assets without paying taxes on them. Once an individual relinquishes total control of an asset to a tax-exempt charity, it is permanently removed from his or her estate, and thus can't be taxed.

The super affluent don't need to understand all the rules surrounding taxes, because GAPAs and SAPAs have investment professionals with track records building and preserving the wealth of their clients through boom and bust market cycles. These advisors have longevity and stay abreast of changes in the law. It's too risky for affluent-positioned Americans to allow unseasoned investment representatives to handle their money. Decades of experience managing assets for other high net worth families is a requirement. You can't penetrate their world without this time-tested credential.

"YOU GET WHAT YOU PAY FOR"

I employ frugality in my life but I won't cut corners when it comes to seeking and securing professional advice from people with impressive work-related pedigrees. Danny says people might have to spend a little money to find the right advisors to guide them through good and bad (and even sideways) investment environments and other important financial matters.

The informed wealthy know their strengths and weaknesses and understand the importance of delegating responsibilities to professionals when they reach a certain net worth.

It also pays to get good advice from an expert. Data show the benefits of working with a financial planner instead of handling this task alone, which GAPAs and SAPAs understand and appreciate. Beth Sparks says, "Very few individuals or couples are disciplined enough to accomplish financial goals without some type of outside accountability."

That's why it's important for the middle class to work with a financial professional to help guide them through the process. The problem for GISAs is that most of them know they need assistance, but don't want to pay for the service. In their minds, costly advice exceeds the value of the benefits.

AN EXCLUSIVE WEALTH LADDER

Most people are too afraid to climb the wealth ladder, held back by insecurities and personal hang-ups that prevent them from taking that first rung upward. However, it's also true that access beyond a certain rung on that ladder is closed to 99.9 percent of people in America. Without a qualified accreditation label, which gives wealthier clients exposure to investments with greater profit potential, most investors are denied access to more sophisticated offerings. Access to some alternative investment classes is granted to qualified investors with investable assets of at least $1,000,000 and who are willing to tie up their money for extended periods of time.

As LaMont Hardiman says, "The mega wealthy are flexing that Heisman trophy pose or stiff arm to distance themselves even more from the middle class, which is becoming a vanishing class."

High net worth investors understand illiquidity and thrive on it. Liquidity drives the emotional state of the typical investor who panics when the stock market is acting like a spoiled brat. The unseasoned investor is prone to check the price of his equity account on an hourly basis, barking at his financial advisor when the value decreases, and claiming the advisor didn't give him any forewarning. If the nervous investor gets out, he's likely to stay out permanently and miss the upside of the stock market when the cycle reverses and value increases.

What happens when you're invested in an illiquid product, or an asset hard to convert to cash, that you can't sell? Well, for GAPAs and SAPAs, they won big when the market rebounded post-2008. Danny says, "The super-wealthy person who invested in a private equity offering is sitting on his yacht, taking a few days to depressurize from work. He's on vacation with his family. He's reading quarterly reports on several of his investments, but he's not flustered or frustrated when the equity markets are in a state of flux over a short period of time. He, along with his super-wealthy counterparts, respond differently to market turbulence. They stay calm amid economic storms."

With private equity and hedge funds, an illiquidity premium exists. Investors holding these asset classes must subdue their emotions. GAPAs and SAPAs are not tossed by a schizophrenic stock market and seek investment offerings where they can't get out on an emotional whim.

They gravitate to market corrections when retail investors make a mad dash to the safe haven of cash. Granted, this can work if sideline investors are open to getting back in when market turbulence has subsided. For the informed wealthy, though, available funds sitting idle in a cash account for an extended period is a waste of time, especially in an environment where risk is handsomely rewarded. The mega affluent want yield. They want income. They want protection. Their investment philosophy provides them all three.

CENTERS OF INFLUENCE

GAPAs and SAPAs operate within an integrated network where like-minded professionals, movers and shakers in business and philanthropy, congregate through mutual friendships to share ideas with each other.

This is a tightly knit group where network members grow toward their highest potential, and are quite deliberate in these growth initiatives. They schedule meetings with colleagues to push them civically and professionally. No quid pro quo arrangement exists in this world of sacrificial betterment. Personal agendas, especially if they concern money, are distasteful and can lead to expulsion from the group because etiquette is breached or informal rules of conduct are not followed.

Generationally wealthy adults don't attend our workshops, but their kids enroll in our financial life skills summer camps. We have had situationally wealthy adult participants take part in our workshops. They have advisers, but wanted to improve their knowledge of comprehensive life and financial planning topics.

GAPA children embrace the wealth-creating process, even if their parents take great measures to avoid discussing it. Wealthy children, unless guilt has crept in, don't view their life of privilege from an adversarial perspective. Investment options with a higher risk-and-return profile, such as hedge funds, private equity, and other accredited offerings, aren't seen as deceptive trap magnets.

In the chapter "Primary Sensory-Learning Drivers," I discussed faith and touch as the two primary components to make a financial connection with GAPAs. Faith is an intangible attribute that affirms what they already know: Wealth principles work through patient endurance. GAPA children see them in action every day; they are an integral part of their world.

Through sensory and interactive experiences in our camps, affluent children easily grasp higher-level financial terms that align with their sense of purpose and legacy responsibilities. They have just as much fun as poor and middle-class kids have playing our financial wellness apps, but their focus is different. They see economic empowerment from a macro or big-picture lens. Their poor or the middle-class peers often view the lessons from a micro or short-sighted perspective.

It's time we get serious about our nation's wealth gap and stop trying to score political points. Republicans are quick to talk about the good ole days under former president Ronald Reagan. Democrats yearn for an economic renaissance akin to the Bill Clinton era, when middle-class wages and their resulting financial harmony were more in sync.

I'm sorry to bust your political bubble, assuming you have one, but the days of these two storied presidencies are long gone. We now live in an interconnected environment. What happens in China, Japan, Europe, or the Middle East affects the United States, and vice versa.

Americans need a new playbook to deal with twenty-first century demands. The Internet and e-commerce. Economic shocks. Unexpected job layoffs. Manipulation of the money supply by central banks. Political divisions. Homegrown and international terrorism. Natural disasters. Are you prepared to financially handle surprises the future is sure to bring? The informed wealthy and their offspring are, and we'll need the GAPA or SAPA playbook to navigate an economic terrain that is likely to change. The financial experts and wealth advisors I interviewed in the "Investment Planning" section provide a pretty good template.

20

RETURN ON INVESTMENT

*The outcome that an individual expects or accepts
from a financial outlay in percentage or monetary
terms, or as part of a broader legacy narrative*

"What Do I Have to Lose?"

The word choice, "What do I have to lose?" speaks volumes about GEDAs' mindset when assessing their return on investment (ROI) for a financial come-up. This attitude has a dual nature. On one hand, it's fatalistic. On the other hand, it's impetuous.

The poor think of investment losses in relation to outsized investment gains, which might explain how they justify playing the lottery, gambling, or thinking of the next hustle. The financial outlay or energy expended pales in comparison with the anticipated payout. In effect, the poor minimize their real losses and maximize their expected profits.

This is the culture of poverty. Any ray of hope to escape economic distress can't be incremental in substance. No way. It must be grand and full of excitement, and of course, fraught with many perils, which seemingly go unnoticed by GEDAs. Those dopamine triggers to win big have such a euphoric stranglehold on their mind and body that a loss isn't factored into the investment analysis equation.

Wealth attainment is conceptual to the poor, because they have tremendous difficulty grasping the process of transgenerational asset accumulation. First, they see it as too much work and something that takes too long to achieve. But it is doable. Second, the poor lack wealth accumulation role models to show them legitimate escape routes, so they stick to what they know. Third, many GEDAs are mired in economic hardship, mental anguish, senseless violence, and personal brokeness that constantly canvasses their landscape, guarding against them leaving their environment. Loyalty to the cause of suffering is a real phenomenon that many poor people won't readily admit.

LaMont Hardiman says a mentality that embraces a quick hustle or relies on lucky breaks is used by the poor to bounce out of a financial pit. But, in reality, these measures often set GEDAs back instead of propelling them forward. Self-set traps that even Houdini could never escape from are par for the course to those living in poverty.

This mentality also shows up when GEDA parents push their children to focus on career paths in sports or entertainment as the ultimate financial come-up. They believe losses are minuscule in relation to the monetary benefits. Of course, the odds of success are rarely considered. Successful sports figures like Lonzo Ball, Kevin Durant, Neymar da Silva Santos Junior, Michelle Wie, and Conner McDavid are called sports prodigies for a reason. They were born with a special talent and developed a unique skill-set to earn millions in their respective sports.

Opportunity cost and risk assessment are punishing forces in poverty. Money, time, and energy are often squandered by GEDAs chasing a financial windfall, repeating behavioral norms and accepted practices passed down generationally.

Let's take a close look at the anatomy of economic dysfunction. You do have a job, though it doesn't pay well. You get caught up in the vicious cycle of taking your paycheck to a pawn shop or check-cashing place to pay back a loan or catch up on utility bills. Investing never enters your mind. Economic distress compounds as you bind yourself even tighter to an anticipated jackpot. You play the lottery or slot machines every day. You are guided by the gut in your stomach instead of the brain in your head.

Losses are viewed in the dark, and GEDAs don't realize how much they spend gambling. This is immaterial, they think, because the forthcoming jackpot will cover the losses. I'm reminded of Oscar, played by Will Smith in the animated movie *Shark Tale*, who amasses a huge debt before his date with destiny arrives. Instead of paying the loan back, he wagers on a seahorse named Lucky Day, who comes up inches short from winning a race. Oscar's big payday ends in disappointment. His money problems and appetite for relevancy compound the problem. Down on his luck, he looks for another financial hustle and miraculously finds it as the Sharkslayer. Oscar finds fame and riches, but they always come with a hefty price tag and character test. He wasn't ready for either of them.

Outsized gains lure the poor in, offering an enticement for players to bounce out of financial hardship while unfortunately keeping them stuck in it. They remain trapped in a vortex that sends them farther down the economic abyss. Time for an updated frame of reference to break the cycle.

> "Poverty is hard to wash off because of the ingrained, multigenerational mindsets that are inherited by children and grandchildren."
>
> **–LaMont Hardiman**
> Financial Advisor

In critiquing the poverty mentality, it is easier for the poor, in some respects, to achieve financial freedom once they've been exposed to the right information and a scaffolding mindset than it is for the middle class.

You can't go any lower than poverty. That's the ground floor. With the right game plan, focus, and mental endurance, you're likely to escape. Granted, the desire to leave must be more intense than the comfort of staying.

"What Do I Have to Risk?"

Generational income-stability Americans tend to think of investment risks in relation to anticipated losses. Their internal dialogue expresses all the reasons why they shouldn't invest in the stock market, from losing money, which they are sure will happen, to having little control over a process that could affect their lifestyle when their investments decline in value. They're confident that they will figure something out in retirement. Time, GISAs presume, is on their side.

That thought process should take place now while they adequately prepare for an economic future sure to punish the ill-prepared retiree. By all accounts, it'll be more challenging if the Social Security and Medicare entitlement programs run into major solvency problems within the next two decades as many prognosticate.

The entrenched middle class places an inordinate amount of trust, as noted throughout the book, in the bank or credit union holding their money. They put faith in liquid assets but fear marketable securities without guaranteed protection of principal. They should be asking, "How much of our standard of living are we willing to give up today to live a secure life in the future?" They must step back from their emotions to see the future clearer, and if they do, investment decisions should be easier to make.

Most people define risk as the loss of principal. They don't factor in purchasing power risk, which potentially is a more debilitating risk because of inflationary pressures in our economy. GEDAs' and GISAs' time horizon is short-term, while the informed wealthy have a long-term focus and plan for an environment where goods and services will cost more tomorrow. They take measures to hedge against inflation, which takes a bite out of purchasing power, and intuitively understand that $1 today will more than likely be worth far less in the future.

SOCIOPSYCHONOMIC FILTER
A fiduciary is the highest form of stewardship. Sometimes that may mean an advisor or planner tells clients the hard truth about their financial condition, even if it's difficult to digest.

Another risk that catches the middle class off guard is reinvestment rate risk that arises when a bond or certificate of deposit matures and the capital must be deployed elsewhere.

One of Beth Spark's clients was so adamant about protecting his principal that he couldn't foresee reinvestment rate risk, but she did. The risk: Interest paid, and thus income, in the future could be significantly less than in the past as the bond or certificate of deposit (CD) matures.

Beth's client parked the money in a 10-year CD, with an interest rate paid of almost 10 percent. She says, "When the CD matured, he had to reinvest the $100,000 at 5 percent. He invested himself into the lower or struggling middle class because of reinvestment rate risk, which is a measure of interest rates, and thus, how our economy is performing and how investors are rewarded. I recommended that he split it 50-50, half the money in a CD and the other half in equities. Or he could have invested 75 percent in a CD and 25 percent in equities. Obviously, there's no guarantee. But had he taken my advice, he would have been in a better financial situation."

Understanding that equities (stocks and mutual funds) are a hedge against inflation is one of the most glaring differences among social classes. Wealthy investors fully comprehend hedges against risk that exist in our economic marketplace. GEDAs and GISAs often concern themselves only with dollars at their disposal, which are impacted by various economic forces.

Why does the middle class assess investment opportunities from the lens of risk-loss realities instead of risk-gain possibilities? Before I attempt to answer this question, perhaps the disconnect has something to do with their lack of appreciation for the Rule of 72. Beth explains, "The compounding effects of this rule are undeniable. In the beginning interest grows slowly, but as time moves along, especially over many decades, it is a beautiful thing to behold. There's no guarantee of course, but a portfolio can double or triple or quadruple in value several times over two or more decades."

> GEDAs are punished by compound interest on cash advances, while GAPAs use it to their investment advantage.

GEDAs are punished by compound interest, paying exorbitant fees on cash advances. GISAs who abuse credit cards feel the impact of compound interest, too. An interest rate of 18 percent will double the debt amount, assuming no reduction in principal is made, every four years using the Rule of 72. This is good for lenders, but bad for borrowers. (Seventy-two divided by the interest rate tells you how long, in approximate terms, it'll take for money or an asset to double in value.)

This is the fundamental difference between GISAs, GEDAs, and GAPAs when ROI is the backdrop. The informed wealthy take advantage of compound interest, and it usually works for them. The traditional middle class doesn't like taking chances with their money unless a guarantee is promised or assumed, which is rare. Income-oriented stocks aren't risk-free but they do offer investors a dividend, lucrative in some cases. Dividend-paying stocks also offer upside potential.

Buying a stock without an income stream is a hard sell to GISAs. But if a dividend or tangible benefit is attached to it, the purchase makes more sense because this added component speaks their language and calms their fears. Income stability provides financial harmony to GISAs. Inconsistent or unknown income stimulates financial disharmony. GISAs guard against this, which may explain their reluctance to invest in risky offerings without a cash reward. Or, just as likely, the advisor did a poor job with messaging.

"Clients need to hear how this vehicle will maintain or enhance their lifestyle, or better yet, their overall financial wellness," Beth says. "Speak more about the income possibilities and less about the underlying asset."

The middle class finds comfort in setting and achieving attainable goals, such as getting out of debt or saving more money. However, reaching for bodacious financial goals that stretch us past our comfort zone are frightening to tightrope walkers conditioned to taking baby steps with their money. These types of goals require a certain amount of risk-taking.

GISAs are too quick to shortchange themselves on what's possible financially. My wife, with her blue-collar roots and concerns, offers a plausible explanation for their fears of investing in the stock market.

"Growing up in the middle class, you often feel this way of life is as good as it gets for your financial situation," she says. "Besides, contentment of needs should be enough, right? One of the reasons we feel this way is that we may not measure up to the class above us. Wearing the middle-class label is where we stay, afraid to take chances with our money. We set low expectations on what's financially possible outside of a paycheck. We deprive ourselves of the amenities and luxuries that can result from wealth creation. But I think another reason, though few of us will admit it, is we fear losing our middle-class associations if we become wealthy or adopt an affluent mindset. It took me a long time to realize that I didn't have to abandon my core, middle-class values, but I did have to upgrade my mindset."

PROS VS. JOES

Managing an investment account yourself is possible, if you have the time and diligence to construct, monitor, and rebalance the portfolio when necessary.

Online brokerage houses have made it easier for retail investors desiring to take investment matters into their own hands, offering low fees on trades and general advice on the world of investing.

The reality show *Pros vs. Joes* captivated viewers as former star professional athletes, many well over the age of 50, competed against weekend warriors. It was comical because, in most instances, the Joes were so overmatched that you couldn't help but laugh. Here's what is not funny. I remember watching an episode featuring former NBA enforcer and jump-hook extraordinare Kevin Willis, who knocked the wind out of me during my rookie year with a blow to my midsection with his forearm, which I returned in like form but just a tad harder on the very next play down the court. During the episode, Kevin pulverized the Joes as if he were still in the league, and was so physical that it looked like he was throwing them around like rag dolls.

It's one thing for Joes to dominate other Joes. But testing your bravado, even against over-the-hill pros, is a lesson in futility. The pros are called pros because they know what they're doing and have the experience to prove it. So, yes, retail investors can manage their investment portfolios, but do they have enough game in them to do it well?

Beth says retail investors average roughly a 4 percent annual return on their investments. Not bad for the do-it-yourselfer. Now, let's compare this to the pros. Institutional investors, which include endowments or professionally managed retirement accounts, average annual returns of about 9 percent. What explains the difference? Beth says the professional investors have a disciplined approach that prevents emotions from manipulating their actions. The average investor, on the other hand, lets emotions guide his or her actions.

> "It's not that people have a comprehension deficit. Most financial planners and investment advisors have an explanation deficit."
>
> **–Beth Sparks**
> Financial Expert and Wealth Advisor

Average investment Joes with a do-it-yourself attitude can improve in specific financial areas, but they will still likely need assistance from the experts. As my wife often tells me when I train young athletes, "It's easy for you to demonstrate a difficult move or technique, but not for them. It comes naturally to you, because you were a pro. These kids need step-by-step guidance until it becomes second nature. This takes a great deal of practice, which you already know."

The disconnection GISAs have with the benefits of stock investing and financial wellness may very well be a communication gap. "The financial planning industry was birthed in the 1970s. Since that time, the industry overall has done a decent job educating the middle class on the benefits of what we offer. Most people know what a stock broker does. However, they do not understand the amount of value that a comprehensive, certified financial planner can provide," Beth says.

Cash flow management and emotional IQ are foundational pillars in the wealth creation playbook. Without allocating your extra funds, investment opportunities remain stuck on the shelf and are viewed from a distance. They can, at times, however, come with an expiration date to capitalize on what is likened to as the eighth wonder of the world—compound interest.

Managing cash flow, the difference between money coming in and going out, is a prerequisite for getting out of a financial rut and onto the path of economic freedom. Without cash flow, the investment game plan doesn't work. That's why unnecessary spending is identified and plugged so clients can manage their wealth, says Tyler Cook. "To become wealthy, you must first save it. The hardest dynamic is to train people's brain to save or invest increases—pay raises, bonuses, and lucrative commissions—from their employment income," he adds.

> "Cash flow management is the biggest problem we have with clients."
>
> **–Tyler Cook**
> Certified Financial Planner

Instability affects performance, which is why pro athletes spend off seasons building and strengthening their core and skills. It's no coincidence that the amazing things they do on the court or field result, in large part, from a rock-solid core—strong abdominal and lower back muscles. The same is true in the world of investing.

Market turbulence tests your core and your emotional IQ that must be strong to prevent irrational decision making. So, financial planners must model a strong core to clients, whose support is needed most during periods of intense turmoil. "Whether it's a stock market downturn or job layoff or death in the family, we have to be disciplined and even-keeled ourselves," Tyler advises.

COLLEGE DEBT AT A CROSSROADS

Middle-class parents usually wait too late to plan for their children's college costs. Maybe mom and dad were hoping the investment in tutoring and private sports training would pay off with a full academic or athletic scholarship for their child to attend a Division I university. The likelihood of this happening is low. GISA and GEDA families ought to be proactive in devising a realistic game plan for their children's higher education plans. We're not talking about tuition costs only, but for their kids to graduate from college with a beneficial degree and a manageable debt load.

There are four ways a student can graduate without any college debt: she's super smart (academic scholarship), super talented (athletic scholarship), super poor (need-based grants), or super wealthy (family assistance or estate trust proceeds).

Very few incoming college students are talented or smart enough to leave the college scene without any debt. Besides, there are only so many scholarships available to hand out each year.

I believe children should shoulder a fair share of their college debt even if parents or grandparents are wealthy and can afford to cover the full tuition. Being a perpetual bailout machine stunts a child's growth and sense of personal responsibility. Don't do it.

GISA parents also may irreparably harm their looming retirement as they make incredible financial sacrifices so their kids can attend college. Middle-income children have time to pay back student debt, but their parents' retirement countdown begins the moment they turn 50, just as their investment prodigies typically enter or leave college.

What about GAPAs and GEDAs? The wealthy prepare years ahead on where their children or grandchildren might attend college and estimate how much it will cost for post-secondary educational expenses. For the poor, LaMont Hardiman says there is no college planning and academic scholarships are rarely pursued. Most of the attention, he says, is paid to athletic scholarships. "Nowadays, you must be more than a good athlete; you need smarts, too."

Paying for college entails many options. A popular choice is 529 savings plans, where the earnings in these accounts grow tax deferred, with qualified distributions for higher education expenses that are exempt from taxes. There are drawbacks to 529s, and one of the most glaring is the effect they can have on other forms of monetary support.

"People don't realize that the money in 529 savings plans counts against their child's or grandchild's financial aid eligibility at a university. This reduces the amount of merit- or need-based tuition assistance students could potentially receive from that school," LaMont says. He adds that millions of dollars are not rewarded to eligible students because they failed to complete the Free Application for Federal Student Aid, or FAFSA, correctly. (In the sequel to this book, strategies and tools will be highlighted to help readers create a college tuition game plan for their children or grandchildren.)

> ## DID YOU KNOW?
> Merit-based scholarships are extremely hard to secure. Not only does a child have to be really smart with an ACT score north of 30, but other factors such as extracurricular activities, communication skills, and even race can impact a school's scholarship decisions.

Hands-on training and apprenticeship programs at area businesses are great tools to help children identify potential career fields early, Tyler says. This eliminates young people from wasting time trying to find themselves in college, unsure what degree they'll pursue. Unfortunately, far too many students graduate with a boatload of debt and meaningless degrees piled on top of it. Pre-emptive planning for college saves money and offers families peace of mind.

Banks are culpable as well in the college-debt game, providing loans with high default rates to students and co-signing parents. In an exasperated tone, Tyler says, "College debt has surpassed credit card debt as the second largest type of personal debt. Something's got to give because college will be, if it's not already, too expensive for the struggling middle class."

One of the side benefits of our financial summer camps is exposing middle and high school students to a broad range of career paths in graphic design, culinary arts and food services, philanthropy, financial planning, corporate sales, marketing, law, accounting, engineering, real estate, office and home design, and many other fields. Several students have even landed internships in the process.

"What Do I Have to Gain?"

When investing for personal, financial, or business reasons, the mega affluent think of gains in relation to commensurate risks. They don't look at investing as a losing proposition. Of course, GAPAs and SAPAs are keenly aware that some of their investments will sizzle while others fizzle. This is the nature of the wealth game.

The über wealthy play the weighing game, a filtering process in which activities and opportunities are judged based on their value-added benefits and return on time invested. Here's what I mean.

Money is not the overriding issue in evaluating the merits of an investment, donation request from a worthwhile charity, tutoring service, or athletic development opportunity for children or grandchildren. It always comes back to the GAPA playbook: Does the opportunity fit into their legacy game plan? After a thorough deliberation, the generationally wealthy make room for opportunities that save time, add peace of mind, and protect their brand from scarring. GAPAs are fanatical about every aspect of their heritage.

They avoid peddlers promoting riskier investment products under the guise of risk-free options. That word—guarantee—is not in their lexicon as they move up the risk-reward continuum: stocks, real estate, commodities, precious metals, master limited partnerships, private equity, and hedge funds. In private equity or high-structured finance arrangements, it's common that three to four deals out of 10 will prove lucrative, but they will more than make up for the six or seven that turn out to be duds. Even when there are no strings attached, the generationally affluent expect a return. They are incredibly deliberate about their time, money, energy, and effort.

HOW WEALTHY ARE YOU?

When you ask a person how wealthy he is, the question elicits reactions that range from braggadocio to surprise to outright offended. That's because most people associate this question with their financial health. Some see it as an indictment, others as a ploy to compare their score with someone in a better situation economically. GAPAs, and those with an affluent, holistic mindset, don't view wealth entirely from a financial perspective.

The generationally affluent don't look at wealth per se in terms of a number. Yes, we, outsiders, tend to describe them from income statement or balance sheet vantage points, knowing they are way up there while we struggle to make ends meet down here. This is offensive to GAPAs, and rightly so, because wealth is multifaceted in their world. It covers the gamut.

Wealth is a state of being for GAPAs, inside and out. Their financial condition reflects their philosophical beliefs about what constitutes true wealth. There's personal wealth. Spiritual wealth. Emotional wealth. Psychological wealth. Social wealth. Professional wealth. Relational wealth and several more I'm sure I am forgetting.

"Everybody defines wealth differently. If you ask so-called rich people if they're wealthy, I bet they would say no. If your perception changes based on your environment or who you're around, then your definition of wealth changes, too. It all comes back to the core, as you aptly state," Tyler says. "Our tagline at John Sestina and Co. is 'Managing to be Wealthy.' As our founder, an avid Harley-Davidson fan, likes to say, 'It's not the destination; it's the ride.'"

> Financial wealth is a microcosm of GAPAs' values, beliefs, and mindsets.

True wealth in life should be such an exhilarating ride that it takes our breath away, arriving at a destination where we look back and can honestly admit, "I fulfilled my potential in every area of life." How's your journey coming along? Are you producing a verifiable return on the investment on this cherished possession we call life?

THE ROI BRAIN

The return on investment (or ROI) brain that characterizes each social class follows, with notable differences in how GEDAs, GISAs, and GAPAs respond to and handle opportunities to accumulate wealth.

The Explosion Factor

The ROI brain of GEDAs gravitates toward dramatic escape routes. An outsized gain on a small wager is the ultimate financial come-up. That's why casinos, the lottery, and other forms of gambling are popular money-making (or investing) options for the poor. While they are the social class that can least afford to lose money, it doesn't stop them from fantasizing about a rags-to-riches, fairytale ending that a big payout might bring. This keeps them coming back to slot machines and racetracks, despite the insurmountable odds gaming venues offer.

Poverty's topography teems with self-laid traps, navigational roadblocks, and never-ending construction zones. That's why trampoline measures are pursued by GEDAs seeking to bypass the harsh terrain of perpetual lack. However, rarely do such propulsion methods provide economic relief for those most in need.

The Equilibrium Factor

The ROI brain of GISAs seeks shelter in stability measures that are predictable—reliable job, dependable cash flow, and an anchored lifestyle. Obviously, this cautious approach can become disrupted when economic vertigo appears, which unsettles the traditional middle class.

A horizontal framework relies upon financial harmony, a symbiotic bond shared between GISAs' money and their standard of living. Safety in their number—what's required annually to fund a level of material and social comforts—is paramount.

When this number is compressed or threatened, their monetary vestibular system is placed on high alert. This may explain GISAs' aversion to the stock market because so many of them literally are one missed paycheck away from financial ruin. Foul odors and loud noises—gyrating equity markets and troubling economic forecasts that wreak havoc on their olfactory and auditory mental senses—are avoided by tightrope walkers. They must focus their energies on the next immediate step in front of them, or paying their monthly bills.

> The tightrope approach is used by GISAs to keep monthly inflows in perfect harmony with their standard of living.

The Endowment Factor

The ROI brain of GAPAs is influenced by the endowment factor. Endowment is commonly used in philanthropic circles, but conveys a broader meaning beyond a charitable bequest or monetary donation. Synonyms include legacy, inheritance, aptitude, capability, competency, genius, qualification, and virtue.

The generationally wealthy have an uncanny ability to pass down attributes, financial resources, and lucrative opportunities to key stakeholders within their tightly regulated inner circle—family, professional, and social relationships.

The endowment or legacy filter rules the GAPA mindset. It takes vision and meticulous planning to generate an investment return with a financial perpetuity focus.

HOW DO SOCIAL CLASSES DEAL WITH FINANCIAL ADVICE?

With an optimistic outlook, GAPAs always envision things going well. They see and take every step on the staircase, without any reservations, to reach a successful goal. They deal with problems quickly and learn from their investment mistakes.

The informed wealthy need neither convincing that asset acquisition is a good investment tool nor financial advice wrapped in persuasive speech; they get it. Investment recommendations that align with GAPAs' asset allocation and diversification playbook are implemented. Period.

The generationally affluent always believe there is something to gain even when they lose; life lessons and growth markers are often uncovered under the rubble of financial setbacks.

The middle class and poor seek reasons to avoid investing. They may interpret investment overtures as scams, setups, or desperation tactics to extract money from them. In some cases, their concerns are legitimate. It's better to pass on a money-making opportunity that isn't explained in a language they fully comprehend, and as a result, can't verify or trust.

Contemplating financial information or investment advice overwhelms GISAs, because they realize it's necessary to reach their goals but convince themselves the timing is just not right. Economic vertigo has crept in and keeps them from moving forward, so they pass up potentially life-changing opportunities to achieve financial freedom.

Outright rejection or hostility is how the poor respond to financial advice because they feel there's little point to it and surmise they will always be broke. The GEDA environment convinces them to give up.

A monumental mistake is made by gatekeepers who serve the poor. They depend too heavily on incentives to generate participation in anti-poverty programs versus the takeaway lessons and tools learned to break free from the shackles of economic despair.

In a memorable phone conversation several years ago with the CEO of a nonprofit organization with a national footprint, the two of us discussed a financial empowerment program for her constituency here in Central Ohio, most of whom were single-parent mothers and teenagers living in abject poverty. Part of our dialogue went like this:

> **Me:** We have a financial life skills program that can assist your organization. It covers the basics of life planning and financial management. It also provides participants with a working knowledge on building wealth as well as ... (She stops me in mid-sentence.)
>
> **CEO:** Okay, I get what you're saying, but let me play devil's advocate. A single-parent mom may say, "I can barely feed my kids. What good is this information going to do for me right now?"
>
> **Me:** The single-parent mom in poverty needs a game plan to get off the crisis carousel. Dysfunction won't go away on its own. We both know that in many cases, it's generational.
>
> **CEO:** We do have a budget for your program. What do you think if we also provide a hook or cash stipend to each person who participates?

I was disappointed by her co-signing request, that she would want me to sign off on a cash enticement as the driving participation benefit, not the development of financial life skills. Instead, I suggested establishing deferred savings accounts for the participants. Why? Because immediate financial hooks tend to perpetuate the poverty mindset, not change it. Personal improvement is the real reward, not a few bucks that will get spent as soon as they leave the workshop.

As the CEO of a nonprofit, I also understand the numbers game. Donors and grant providers want to know how many people are served by their financial support. However, this is problematic as goodies—and not life-transforming information—become the sole basis for attracting constituents.

Let's pause and clarify a theme in *Sociopsychonomics* that hopefully dispels an unfounded myth: All rich people are the same. The generationally affluent are a distinct subset in the so-called rich category, and in many respects, stand above the fray. They don't fawn over their wealth as some believe. Does extreme wealth give them a certain amount of cache and power? Indeed. But these shouldn't be misinterpreted as signs that they are emotionally tied to money. Most of the time, GAPAs distance themselves from it, not as an appeasement to outsiders, but as an enduring rule and personal conviction to remain true to the intangible nature of generational affluence. True wealth isn't ostentatious; it needs no introduction.

However, it's a different scenario for those with little to modest amounts of money. In those instances, emotional attachments are clearly visible. Fearing the loss of their money exacerbates the financial decisions GISAs make, or paralyzes them from taking calculated investment risks. Less of something, money in this case, can cloud our judgment in making more informed decisions with better long-term outcomes.

> ## SOCIOPSYCHONOMIC FILTER
> The poor often don't see the value in financial knowledge unless an immediate, monetary incentive is attached as a participatory requirement.

A DEFICIT WORTH FIXING

The poor often have fundamental deficits that must be addressed before they can even consider scaffolding options to wealth creation. These deficits include writing, reading, communicating, calculating, and networking. The steepness of their deficit slope indicates the pain threshold they're willing to tolerate to improve baseline skills. If GEDAs get tripped up at the baseline, frustration inevitably sets in and the opportunity to create a positive experience is lost. Here's what I mean.

Monya and I envisioned a dual purpose when creating our financial life skills curriculum, a decade ago. We wanted to educate underserved communities about economic empowerment, and to help children and adults build their math skills.

Their deficits in math, or analytical processing skills, were so pronounced that we had to redesign our apps. Our high school participants displayed great difficulty in rounding numbers. We had to show them how to do it so they could calculate the hypothetical shares of stock they could purchase using make-believe money. Rounding numbers should have been learned in third or fourth grade.

Visibly frustrated, many participants checked out and didn't want to go on with the investment lesson, no matter how hard I tried to sell the most exciting part of the game—the chance to watch their portfolios significantly go up in value.

Persuasion didn't work as participants struggled in front of their peers with simple rounding calculations. It was heartbreaking to watch them save face in front of classmates, or lay their head on the desk as if to say, "We give up!" Opportunity lost to change lives and legacies possibly forever.

I am not keen on handicapping poor kids. But in this instance, programming an app to do automatic calculations saves time. It's also advisable on several fronts. First, this was the first introduction for many of these kids to the stock market and portfolio income. A bad experience could negatively affect their possibility filter and cast a dark shadow over their financial potential. Memories retrieved later might have negative associations, triggering GEDAs' penchant to avoid wealth-building opportunities that they assume involve too much work. Second, they were so embarrassed by their math deficit that it caused participatory paralysis. When you get in a room with like-minded individuals, behavior mimicking is contagious. Third, we realized that you can be right and still be wrong. Our goal to improve their math skills was laudable, but a 90-minute presentation isn't going to solve a math deficit that has been accruing for many years.

We've since tempered our enthusiasm to transform baseline deficits when time to do so isn't on our side. However, we remain effective showing participants from economically distressed communities that their unfortunate predicament can have a happy ending.

Poverty needn't be a permanent and debilitating economic condition. The poor can get out, but the room for error is very small. The return on investment for those who do escape will produce untold dividends for them and their offspring, hopefully decades into the future.

Their escape from the poverty plantation benefits our nation in profound ways. Fewer people incarcerated. More taxpaying Americans. A greater sense of personal well-being for those once written off. Each day, I thank the Good Lord for helping me to get out.

INSURANCE PLANNING

21

INSURANCE STRATEGY

*The methodology employed by a social class
to deal with insurance risks*

Risk Retention

Just as they do with other facets of financial matters, the underclass takes incredible risks with their insurance strategy. The poor often employ a gambler's mentality and roll the dice, believing they can beat the odds of being underinsured or uninsured on the premise it's unaffordable and unnecessary. Their lack of money, as a result of limited job opportunities, is symptomatic of a much larger and incredibly dangerous narrative that I refer to as the indoctrination of fatalism.

This mentality holds that preventative measures do little good to counteract fate, a pervasive belief among the poor. They accept the notion that unfavorable outcomes are part of their composition. Life is inherently unfair, and so are the financial systems in which they must pay to play. The law says merely possessing a car doesn't validate one's ability to operate a motor vehicle; a valid driver's license and proof of financial responsibility do.

That's nice to say, but for the poor it's backward thinking. For them, a car is secured first, a driver's license second, and auto insurance last. Thinking through the outcomes of driving without insurance is just an abstract concept and rarely factored into a GEDA's decision-making filter. Remember, feelings, perceptions, superstitions, and instincts dictate the outcome. Thus, low-probability events that might result in loss don't conjure up the same fears high-probability events do, say like failing to pay the rent in the middle of winter. That, my friends, is a tangible reality for the entrenched poor and something they have witnessed many times.

> "In disadvantaged neighborhoods, eviction is to women what incarceration is to men: Incarceration locks men up, while eviction locks women out."
>
> **–Matthew Desmond**
> MacArthur Foundation

I remember several evictions in the housing project of my youth where a family's belongings, furniture, and other household items got kicked to the curb as onlookers gasped in disbelief. The embarrassment and shame on their faces were palpable. I felt so bad for them. If these families didn't secure their belongings by sunrise, some of their more valuable items—bicycles, televisions, and clothing—would be snatched up by pillagers in search of free goodies. Armed with fresh fodder, gossip peddlers quickly spread the news throughout the neighborhood. Humiliation and trepidation followed the evictees, but in the broader context, the evictions created a frame of reference for other residents that made paying the rent their top (and most expensive) priority in lieu of competing alternatives, such as buying groceries, dining out, clothing, grooming expenditures, and of course, liability insurance. For the poor, liability insurance protection above the state minimum isn't a big deal since a car accident seems far-fetched and won't happen anytime soon.

What the poor don't see is that they absorb a huge risk when choosing a higher insurance deductible. Cost is typically the presumptive reasoning behind the decision. That sounds strange, but in the insurance world premiums and deductibles are inversely correlated. Higher deductibles result in lower premium payments (and lower payout risk to insurers), and vice versa. GEDAs often select the higher deductible to reduce how much they pay for the premium.

Liability, collision, and comprehensive are the three types of automobile insurance coverage. Every state sets a minimum threshold for liability coverage. In Ohio, it is 25/50/25, which refers to the maximum dollars the policy will pay on a claim. If one person is injured in an auto accident, the liability limit is $25,000; if more than one person is injured, the limit is capped at $50,000; and for property damages, the ceiling is $25,000. Minimum coverage can result in maximum financial pain.

The market for minimum auto coverage has expanded in recent years, and it's easy to understand why poor people take advantage of it. So what's the problem? The poor are likely to have assets and a net worth (negative in many instances) far less than these limits. If they hurt someone in an accident and got sued and lost, their assets and wages could be garnished to cover damages, medical costs, and legal fees. However, this setback might be the furthest thing from a GEDA's mind since job prospects often lead to minimum-wage paychecks. Without sufficient assets, the plaintiff's collection efforts would likely be futile.

The poor typically only have liability coverage without collision or comprehensive protection, according to Donna Harlan, a property and casualty specialist with the Dan Coonfare Agency, a Nationwide Insurance affiliate. However, she says there is a bigger issue.

With thousands of customers, Donna writes policies for every socio-economic class and says many lower-income individuals let their insurance policies lapse. "Unfortunately, they are then placed in a non-standard pool of high-risk drivers and pay more for coverage because they can't get into a standard market. Maybe they couldn't afford their premium payments for two months to deal with a more pressing financial matter," she adds.

Poverty often leaves its victims immobilized in the web of chaotic life events—the law of unintended consequences—where they turn the corner and another unexpected problem appears more daunting than the last one.

Risk Transfer

When it comes to insurance, GISAs prefer a cruise-control approach once the risk to insure an asset—or income stream—has been transferred from them to an insurance company.

Dee Miller, a standout football player at Ohio State who had over 2,000 receiving yards as a two-year starter in the 1990s, operates the Dee Miller State Farm Insurance Agency in Hilliard, Ohio. He provides insurance advice to more than 3,000 customers and agrees the middle class fears change.

"I asked a client, 'You've been with State Farm for 25 years with very few claims. Why do you have such a low deductible?' This client could have saved thousands of dollars in premium payments through the years by raising his deductible just a few hundred bucks, which would most likely not have affected his financial situation one bit," he says. In-motion habits are hard to change.

A man whom I've grown to love—Chris Fairrow—is the proverbial middle-class retiree. You may recall his story in Chapter 4, "Your Fascinating Brain." I have never met a more dedicated, loyal, and time-compliant person as Chris. Seventy-one years old, his work ethic defies conventional logic. My father-in-law likes what he likes and is resistant to change. His motto, consistent with GISA ideology, maintains that "if it ain't broke, don't try to fix it."

At times, I've taken the reins from him to navigate his financial and nutritional ship in the right direction before they veered off course indefinitely. I assisted him several years ago with a life and financial plan. Analyzing his insurance needs showed he was underinsured given his asset base and liability coverage exposures. He was retired but working part-time and renting an apartment back then. In the world of insurance, "If it ain't broke" invites intense scrutiny because life's events bring change. A first, second, or third marriage, the birth of a child, buying a new home, or early retirement should trigger GISAs to review their coverages with their insurance representatives.

DID YOU KNOW?

Standard auto liability coverage in most states is 100/300/100, which could still pose tremendous risks to policyholders if they are found at fault in an auto accident.

In Chris's case, his auto liability coverages were 50/100/50, above the legal limit but below the industry standard. His risk profile is an insurer's dream. He hadn't filed an insurance claim for 10 or more years and paid his premium like clockwork. However, life offers no guarantees that circumstances won't change. I advised Chris to increase the liability coverages on his auto and renter's policies as well as secure an umbrella policy for additional protection. He called his insurance representative two days later. The cost differential for the bundling of his auto and renter's policies was well short of $100 for the year. And gaps in coverage were eliminated, while liability protection increased dramatically.

Insurers profit through the law of large numbers where the probability of outcomes is reasonably predicted based on the results of a very large sample size with similar characteristics. Human beings have free will, but we behave in predictable patterns. Insurers know this, factoring in social class dynamics, locale (suburban, rural, or inner city), age, occupation, gender, life status (single, married, widow or widower, retired, etc.), weather patterns, and previous claims to assess the likelihood of future payouts. Obviously, they are pretty darn good at this.

Risk transfer protects a policyholder up to the insured amount. The insurance company assumes the coverage risk and in return, policyholders agree to pay a fee for the coverage. The traditional middle class is a huge proponent of risk transfer. They have embedded fears of being on the wrong side of any transactional relationship—work, homeownership, and retirement. They hedge their bet based on the financial resources available to them. Unfortunately, they often leave themselves exposed to unnecessary risks while trying to save a few dollars. Insurance is a quid pro quo, interdependent transaction, built on cooperative fairness where each side agrees to keep their end of the deal. It provides security and peace of mind to GISAs, which they count on to ensure that their cherished savings and assets remain protected.

Risk Mitigation

The Merriam-Webster dictionary defines mitigation as "to make less severe or painful." GAPAs take pain's consequences quite seriously, especially when legacy assets and the family's brand are on the line.

The informed wealthy mitigate risk because they have a comprehensive plan where latitude is given to absorb or transfer an insurable risk. They are quick to intervene when a problem first appears and won't wait around to see if something bad materializes. Intuitively, they think, "What are my liability exposures? How can I mitigate them?"

They see the good in others from afar, but are quite cautious in their business and personal relationships. Character flaws are red flags to them because of the inherent risks. Better to be safe than sorry, as the saying goes.

Background checks on potential business (or even life) partners, domestic workers and hired help, and even guests attending exclusive events on their stately premises are standard protocol. I've attended several private get-togethers over the years that were hosted by GAPAs on their home turf. Nothing escaped my observant eye. As an outsider, the experience was memorable. The well-manicured lawns, check-in guards, and security cameras and undercover security personnel in dark glasses with ear buds immediately caught my attention.

SOCIOPSYCHONOMIC FILTER

GAPAs take proactive steps to mitigate high- and low-probability threats to legacy assets and their carefully crafted brand.

A normal way of life for the generationally wealthy, but to step inside a mansion with over 30,000 square feet of living space, opulent furnishings and expensive decorations, multimillion-dollar artwork throughout, and dozens of wait staff who have very little interactions with family members and guests beyond work-related duties quickly let me know that I was in another world. It's reminiscent of my first encounter on the NBA hardwood playing against Michael Jordan. It didn't seem real, as if the game was being played in slow motion. Truth be told, I even got a bit light-headed and star-struck by MJ when standing next to him my rookie year. He had that "air" about him that was mesmerizing.

For the generationally wealthy, risk mitigation is not just about insuring an asset or income stream; it encompasses a whole lot more. Children and grandchildren are obvious ransom targets, so even their daily activities and friendships and interactions outside the home must be closely monitored.

The elimination or minimization of liability exposures is an elaborate strategy with moving parts that need constant attention. GAPAs are conditioned to deal with life from an offensive and defensive strategy. The security clearances. The ongoing monitoring of potential threats. The insulated and tightly controlled network. The impressive balance sheet or net worth statement. Advisors at their beck and call to keep everything running smoothly.

Great financial blessings come with a huge price tag, which GAPAs willingly pay for their life of grandeur and stewardship. It's a world that I admire, but only from a distance.

22

RELATIONSHIP WITH INSURANCE PROFESSIONAL (SPORTS ANALOGY)

The manner in which social classes view their association with an insurance representative from a sport's perspective

Opponent

"Why are you taking more money out of my pocket for coverages I don't need or want?"

I played against some of the greatest NBA basketball players of all time, including Michael Jordan, Shaquille O'Neal, Patrick Ewing, Hakeem Olajuwon, Karl Malone, Tim Duncan, Charles Barkley, David Robinson, John Stockton, and Kobe Bryant. Opponents also surface off the court.

The generationally impoverished often have an adversarial relationship with authority figures and business professionals based on misplaced trust. Remember, in poverty, betrayed trust can create irreparable damage because, the poor assume, people will always let them down or take advantage of them. Their cynicism toward outsiders is a real hurdle to leap when working with GEDAs, who are conditioned to doubt the intentions of people who haven't earned their trust or can't be trusted. It can be challenging to convince the underclass, as well as the middle class, to plug insurance gaps. Plus, the poor are trying to stretch every dollar. "Son, you can't get blood out of a turnip," as my mother would often say when our monthly welfare check was dwindling down.

DID YOU KNOW?

A crucial component in an insurance premium is a policyholder's zip code. Higher crime areas, educational standing of residents, and income level contribute directly or indirectly in an insurer's risk assessment of likely claim payouts.

The primary (and largest) asset the poor typically insure is an automobile with minimum liability coverage. This is a start, but more protection is needed for their prized possession and future livelihood.

As a child, I distinctly remember auto insurance being an optional coverage. Proof of insurance back then wasn't a requirement by the Ohio Bureau of Motor Vehicles to operate a "moving vehicle." Most of the people in our neighborhood who owned a car didn't have insurance, and if they did, they probably let it lapse to cover their rent payment or buy groceries or purchase statement assets, clothes and shoes primarily. Today, it is mandatory, although the minimum limits of coverage are woefully inadequate.

Insurance isn't on a GEDA's radar screen generally even when the upside is clear. My friend Dee Miller put it this way:

> "They may consider bundling auto and renter's together if it makes sense. I'll provide an auto quote for $100 per month. They balk, so I ask if they have an apartment and would consider renter's insurance. They'll respond, 'No, I only have a certain amount to spend on auto insurance.' I provide a renter's insurance quote and then give them a multi-line discount for the auto. Now the monthly expense is $99, or $1 cheaper than what I originally quoted them. Some people will still only want the auto insurance instead of bundling it. I don't get it, but then again, maybe I'm not explaining this correctly because it defies common sense."

Referee

"Can you provide clarity and objectivity to help me with this insurance situation?"

For the middle class, they seek clarity, objectivity, and impartiality when their economic foundation is cracking. GISAs expect someone like a union representative, political candidate, service provider, or business professional to intervene on their behalf when it appears a situation is unfair.

A basketball referee is an arbiter who ensures game rules are followed on the court. A good one avoids favoritism and ignores pressures from outside influence—whether they are the coaches, players, or fans. He is praised when the right call is made and vilified when a call changes the momentum of a game. I've played in dozens of basketball games through the years and can distinctly remember calls made by a referee that contributed indirectly to a loss. For the most part, he did his job correctly, but our team blamed him, not our sloppy play, for the loss.

> "Some clients look at me like I'm responsible for premium increases. I don't have anything to do with corporate decisions."
>
> **–Dee Miller**
> Insurance Representative

Dee says insurance professionals sometimes bear the weight of consumers' angst over premium increases. "They see me as either an opponent or the referee who has influence to intervene on a matter related to a premium increase or an unsatisfactory claim payout."

Bad things can happen in the blink of an eye, and accidents happen to even the most cautious drivers. Tragically, the emotional and financial scars left often are exacerbated without sufficient insurance protection. The insurance professional, or referee, offers an intervening voice of reason to prevent a disastrous outcome. I don't know how many times a referee, without calling an offensive foul, warned me about something wrong I was doing. "Funderburke, be careful using your right arm to push away the defender's hand when you're driving to the basket," he might say, and I heeded his advice every time. He corrected the bad behavior and let me stay in the game. Consider your approach toward insurance protection the same way.

An insurance representative told me a story that illustrates the importance of excess coverage beyond standard or typical liability limits.

Mary (not her real name) had moderate 100/300/100 auto liability and property damage coverage. This protects an at-fault driver up to $100,000 if she injures one person, $300,000 for two or more people, and $100,000 for property damage. The legal coverage for many states is only 25/50/25.

She never envisioned the day when her auto liability coverage would be needed, but then the unthinkable happened, and Mary killed someone in an auto accident. She received a letter from the insurance company stating that all her liability limits had been exhausted. Frantic, Mary called her insurance representative and inquired about the letter.

Because one person was killed in the accident, Mary's policy allowed for $100,000 to be paid out in an accident where she was at fault and there was one injury. The problem, the insurance representative said, is that she could be responsible personally if the victim's relatives decide to sue for more than the $100,000 payout.

"Oh, I understand now," was her response.

Mary now sees the importance of higher liability limits as well as an umbrella insurance policy, which would have provided additional protection once the auto liability limits were exhausted. Ironically, one month before the accident Mary's insurance representative had called her for a third and final time about adding higher liability coverage. She never returned this last call.

Teammate

"How can I/we protect ourselves from insurance risks?"

The mega wealthy don't treat insurance professionals as an opponent because protecting their income statements and balance sheets and family legacy come with a cost.

John Sestina, a personal mentor and legend in the world of fee-only financial planning, candidly says, "I ask clients if they have the cash or marketable assets to make themselves whole again after a large-scale loss for which they were not insured against. If they say no, then they need liability protection and shouldn't mind making premium payments that in the aggregate, may exceed tens—if not hundreds—of thousands of dollars. This conversation usually justifies the need for insurance coverages, even if a claim hasn't been made or paid out for years."

The generationally wealthy take a holistic approach to insurance. This includes auto, homeowner's, health, disability, long-term care, umbrella, professional (or errors and omissions), and officers and directors protection. The super wealthy also buy liability coverage for their fine art and antiques. Additional protection will be needed for chauffeurs, nannies, groundskeepers, and anyone else who works for them on a day-to-day basis at a personal level.

Teammates inspire, encourage, assist, motivate, and protect each others' blind side. From little league sports through the pros, I was fortunate to play with teammates who fit the description. You trust a teammate's insights and know he has your best interest at heart. Sometimes, however, his advice appears counterintuitive. Taking a page out of the GAPA and SAPA playbook, I followed the suggestion of a trusted teammate, an insurance professional, to go with my head instead of my heart.

Some time ago, a representative from a local nonprofit contacted me about joining its board of directors. Like LFYO, this service provider has a passion for empowering inner-city youth. I asked her if the organization's insurance covered its board of directors and if so, what was the coverage limit. She says the group did not have such coverage; I declined to join for this reason alone. The risks were simply too great and outweighed the benefits. Suppose an employee was arrested on child molestation charges or accounting irregularities were exposed. Each could tarnish the board members, and if a lawsuit were filed, the plaintiffs might go after anyone with deep pockets and connected to the nonprofit. Insurance provides just-in-case protection. She thought my concern should have been overlooked in lieu of the organization's greater good and empowerment endeavors. Indeed, their goals to assist disadvantaged youth aligned with ours. I reiterated the rationale and urged her organization to look into insurance coverage for the board members.

Multiply my liability exposure by several dozen and you get an idea why GAPAs must go to great lengths to protect their assets, legacy, and family brand. My concern may seem farcical on the surface, but some risks, however absurd, are no laughing matter. They aren't worth taking.

23

INSURANCE SYNONYMS

*How a social class sees, believes, or perceives
the role insurance plays in their lives*

Trap

Insurance is seen as another trick in a long line of deceptive practices that rich companies and dishonest salespeople employ to keep the poor, well, poor. Buying something with no instant benefit is difficult for the poor to grasp. What they can't physically touch, taste, or experience right away doesn't make practical or financial sense. Insurance, where one waits for something bad to happen before collecting, seems downright unfair to GEDAs. Perception matters more in poverty than reality.

By now you know that feelings dominate the landscape of economic distress for the poor. It's true that impoverished areas experience a higher incidence of crime than do wealthier sections of a city. On a percentage basis, more cars and homes are burglarized in inner-city communities, and more murders and senseless acts of violence committed. Hopelessness and despair that tomorrow won't be any better are entrenched mindsets. This was my world for 18 years, which couldn't pass by fast enough. I couldn't wait to get out.

Growing up in poverty, you are conditioned not to trust outsiders. Your world of lack—money, jobs, role models, structure, peace of mind, and nutritious foods—prevents you from seeing the benefit of insurance coverage beyond a trial period. The poor are punished once again by the law of unintended consequences.

Here's a sampling of questions and comments GEDAs make about insurance in general, or when filing a claim: "My possessions aren't worth insuring." "Just send me my check for the damage done to my car—don't you believe me?" "Why does a claims adjuster need to come out and investigate?" "What good is insurance if you can't use it right away?" "I don't want nobody getting rich off my death. You're crazy if you think I'm gonna let you be the beneficiary of an insurance policy on my life."

> "Poverty is bleak and cuts off your long-term brain."
>
> **–Linda Tirado**
> Author, *Hand to Mouth*

For the poor, insurance is an abstract concept where deferral of benefits is synonymous with denial of benefits, which all translates into a big waste of time. They pay cash to bind coverage on an asset that may take months or years to reap the benefits. In their mind, they are being played by the system.

Gary Trent, a friend and former NBA player, who also grew up in abject poverty as a child, provided this quote in my first book, *Hook Me Up, Playa!* He says, "Insurance is the biggest game in town, until you need it." Gary has some of the most memorable one-liners that I've ever heard, but this one summarizes how many people living in poverty truly feel about insurance.

Donna Harlan has witnessed GEDAs' reservations firsthand. "Skepticism and confusion of what we offer as property and casualty representatives may be tied to their level of education, which speaks to the understanding of the importance of insurance," she says.

Tradeoff

The middle class faces an ongoing economic dilemma each month that forces them to weigh what financial obligations to meet against the backdrop of cash shortfalls. Paying a premium for additional coverage is bypassed to pay for the mortgage, credit card balances, groceries, utilities, gas, and childcare. Here's the problem: Most GISAs depend primarily on a single income stream from their employer to pay monthly bills. Instead, they should create at least three supplemental income streams and ensure no coverage gaps exist that could upset their financial equilibrium. Tradeoffs often lead to insurance blind spots; you never see them until it's too late.

If you've ever played football and had your bell rung, you can relate to this. Football was my first love as a kid. I remember in eighth grade getting leveled by a blocker I didn't see while focused on tackling his teammate who was headed for the end zone. That runner had my undivided attention and I was gaining ground fast when I got crushed. I was airborne for a few seconds before landing flat on my back. The blocker was my blind spot on that field.

Dee Miller equates helping customers with their insurance blind spots to doctors preaching the value of a preventative health regimen.

SOCIOPSYCHONOMIC FILTER

Insurance blind spots can derail the most cautious financial strategy. Unfortunately, the middle class often fails to see just how problematic their play-it-safe approach really is.

"It's tough sometimes convincing the middle class or underclass to incorporate a more holistic approach to their insurance needs," Dee says. "I often use the analogy that a doctor will recommend lifestyle changes to combat a chronic health condition. She may tell a patient to eliminate harmful foods from his diet or start exercising more. Some patients acknowledge the doctor's opinion after leaving the office, but don't take any of the suggestions to heart.

"I point out the gaps in coverage and provide suggestions on how best to fill them. Period. Before our meeting ends, I tell them, I am their partner and not the enemy and want to protect them from a large-scale loss that would be financially detrimental to the family and way of life. All the while, my eyes focus on the wife, who will usually outlive her husband by several years and might be more emotionally receptive to my advice. It's just so sad, and shocking really, that people have these glaring insurance blind spots."

Let's revisit a familiar theme that may bring GISAs' blind spots into clearer focus: analysis paralysis.

The middle class will rationalize why they don't need the extra expense for excess coverage right now. They convince themselves that a potential loss is unlikely to happen anytime soon. It's not that they believe in bending the odds of loss avoidance in their favor as the poor mistakenly attempt to do; GISAs simply don't believe that the benefits will ever justify the means.

Dee says he keeps the lines of communication wide open with his customers so they never feel left in the dark, especially when he's talking with them about additional coverage. In those instances when a client stalls or overanalyzes an insurance decision, Dee documents the correspondence and the coverage he's suggesting for the client. "It's absolutely imperative that I protect myself and the company," he notes.

Dee had a married couple with a business who wanted to convert a whole life policy with a small death benefit to a term policy with a much larger death benefit, which he thought would better protect their assets.

"I met with them on several occasions—keep in mind, they called me about upgrading their life insurance coverage—and they didn't want to continue, telling me they felt as though I was trying to get more money out of them. Even the middle class can look at me as an opponent who is taking money out of their pocket, although they know in the back of their minds that more coverage is needed," he says.

SOCIOPSYCHONOMIC FILTER

Large-scale loss protection comes with a cost, although GEDAs are quick to discount low-probability outcomes while GISAs tend to waver between the expense and justifiable benefits.

Life insurance isn't a retirement plan in the traditional sense, but it can provide financial security and peace of mind after the death of a spouse or family member when these attributes are most needed.

Donna of Coonfare Insurance says, "The middle class may struggle financially but they will find a way to pay their bills. Unfortunately, they may not have riders, or additional coverage, for items like jewelry or other expensive valuables if they are damaged or stolen."

That does not apply to all GISAs, of course.

The law of diminishing returns forces GISAs to make insurance tradeoffs with potentially devastating consequences. Dee says a small subset of his middle-class clients with an affluent mindset see the value of excess coverage, particularly if they have a teenage driver in the home. They're not taking any chances with their financial livelihood.

Tradition

For the generationally wealthy, insurance is synonymous with tradition, a tool they use to protect assets, preserve their heritage, and safeguard loved ones from danger. Along with tax and estate planning strategies, insurance also has a multifaceted function. It is used to mitigate liability exposures, pay exorbitant death taxes, fund philanthropic causes, and operate in a marketplace with far-reaching tentacles that can cover several continents. For those reasons alone, business, investing, and travel considerations need a comprehensive game plan to tackle a wide array of circumstances.

An important component in their life and financial planning toolkit, specialty coverages are likely to include excess liability insurance, cyber insurance, kidnap and ransom insurance, travel insurance, trade credit insurance, key employee insurance, and concierge health insurance, among many others.

A brief description of these coverages follows:

- **Excess Liability Insurance:** Also known as umbrella or add-on insurance, it provides coverage beyond specified limits of an underlying policy, which must be exhausted first. It can shield wealthy and middle-income families from liability claims or frivolous lawsuits.

- **Cyber Insurance:** The generationally affluent and the companies they own are supersensitive about losing data and getting hacked. We've seen data breaches where customer information is stolen and ends up costing a company millions. Both the tangible—items that can be felt or touched—and intellectual property of digital information need vigorous protection.

- **Ransom Insurance:** That's hard to believe, right? But if it weren't a concern, then no insurance market for it would exist. Sadly, Americans traveling outside the country are kidnapped and held for ransom. It doesn't happen often, but GAPAs must take precautionary steps that protect their legacy tradition and fulfill the mandate set long ago by their patriarchal or matriarchal family member.

- **Travel Insurance:** Canceling a vacation, getting sick outside America, or losing your luggage are some of the reasons travel insurance offers peace of mind on international trips. GAPAs don't participate in the game of negligible chance outcome avoidance. Premium payments for off-the-beaten-path insurance are a hedging strategy.

- **Trade Credit Insurance:** This coverage relates to American companies engaged in commercial transactions with foreign suppliers and manufacturers. It is an extension of trade credit or a deferral payment arrangement that offers customers temporary reprieve from immediately paying cash for a good or service. There are several reasons for its employment, but two of the more common ones include the varied accounting practices and standards in foreign jurisdictions, plus political unrest and how it affects their financial markets, which oftentimes fluctuate more wildly than what we see in the U.S.

- **Key Employee Insurance:** The disability or death of a senior executive or CEO can devastate a multibillion-dollar company. He can't be replaced, but at least the projected value of his impact on overall profitability going forward can be recouped by the payout benefit.

INSURANCE TOOLS KEEP A LEGACY IN PLAY

You may not be all that familiar with this type of insurance, but it's been around for nearly two decades. Also known as pay-as-you-go or white-glove healthcare, it lets patients pay a monthly or annual retainer fee and the cost for each visit to the doctor of their choice where they receive one-on-one care. It's available to anyone who can pay for the service, which isn't as expensive as one might think. Sounds great and it fits GAPAs well because they are willing and able to pay for exclusive service and care. But as more physicians adopt the model, this will invariably lead to a doctors' shortage, and it's the poor who overcrowd emergency rooms for non-threatening sicknesses that will suffer.

The financial success of SAPAs and GAPAs, as well as the protective measures they must implement to preserve wealth, are quite evident in professional sports. In spite of guaranteed television contracts and licensing deals in the billions of dollars, they don't play games when it comes to their most prized assets: the athletes. I can only imagine what Jerry Reinsdorf, owner of the Chicago White Sox and Chicago Bulls, paid to insure the contracts of Michael Jordan, Scottie Pippen, and coach Phil Jackson. It was estimated

Michael's economic impact on Chicago from his rookie year in 1984 until his first retirement in 1993, a 10-year window, topped $1 billion. Like fairy dust, his golden touch landed on hotels, restaurants, department stores, and just about every downtown establishment and let them get rich off of his basketball prowess. Today's stars—Kevin Durant, Stephen Curry, Aaron Rodgers, Matt Ryan, Bryce Harper, and Clayton Kershaw—command huge contracts and endorsement deals that are insured against an injury, illness, or death since profitability forecasts are made in advance by the team as they capitalize on their athletic talent and drawing power.

Insurance blind spots are unlikely with GAPAs, but are noticeable when someone moves from a poor or middle-class upbringing into situational affluence. With the euphoric jump, they often forget to insure liability risks that could devastate their newfound wealth. The lapse is a self-inflicted wound, or at worse, an obvious disregard to use insurance to guard against potentially damaging economic repercussions. GAPAs don't typically make this mistake and employ safeguards against every conceivable exposure that might appear and threaten the family legacy.

24

INSURANCE MISCONCEPTIONS

*The erroneous assumptions that are characteristic of
a traditional social class in regard to the protection of
an asset, income stream, or legacy attribute*

"It's An Unneccessary Expense"

Why do some people, the poor in particular, treat insurance as an unnecessary expense? Perhaps the intangible nature of insurance, so different from anything they are accustomed to buying, tops the list.

"With insurance you are buying a piece of paper with ink on it," says Dan Coonfare, owner of the insurance agency that bears his name.

It's harder for many poor people to grasp the importance of insurance since the benefits are usually delayed until a loss occurs. The poor should justify buying insurance to protect their loved ones and personal assets, but they don't. In fact, the decision is already made before alternatives—like purchasing food and other tangible items they can touch or feel immediately— are ever considered. Their decision-making filter doesn't necessarily contrast short-term options alongside long-term consequences.

The key to helping economically distressed Americans is weighing the value of consequences and benefits in proper context. Persuading them must be initiated in their language of emotion (fear primarily), although logic is critical to buy-in and longevity.

Short-term distractions often appear in their world and at the most inopportune time to short-circuit the process of sustained success (paying premiums or investing in personal development practices), just when a GEDA incorporates a ray of hope for a brighter tomorrow. For example, a single-parent mom making ends meet on a minimum-wage income wants to increase liability coverage on her automobile, that is, until a close family member asks to borrow $200 to stave off an eviction threat from an apartment. Like her, this family member is taking care of three kids without any assistance from the children's biological fathers.

> ## SOCIOPSYCHONOMIC FILTER
> Insurance is most needed in an environment of perpetual stress and higher-than-average probabilities for human error: impoverished communities.

Dee, the Hilliard-based insurance representative, says the most glaring misconception to him is the number of people who believe they must have a lot of money or assets before buying or adding insurance coverage. "People have more than what they think they have. People are worth more than they think they're worth. And if you never correct this misconception, then you are creating a pattern that your children and grandchildren will emulate years into the future; this is a learned behavior with devastating consequences."

The law of unintended consequences disproportionately punishes the poor more than any other social class. Insurance and estate planning are not huge concerns for them. They may look at renter's insurance as an unnecessary expense that can be bypassed to pay a cable bill. The immediacy of needs clouds their judgment in analyzing the merits of protecting personal property if a large-scale loss occurs, which baffles Dan Coonfare.

"If they can't afford $150 for an annual tenant's or renter's policy, then how will they come up with the money to recoup $5,000 of possessions lost in a fire?" he asks. "Every winter our local news stations report on fires at apartment complexes, one after the other. The buildings likely are insured, but the tenants' contents are probably not. They are responsible for everything inside their apartment."

The risks are too high when the behaviors of others, neighbors in this instance, can't be controlled or regulated.

There are social class dynamics at play on why some people aren't adequately protected through insurance. However, cultural implications can also play a part.

In the African-American community, most of us don't have sufficient insurance protection. We don't consider the importance of insurance products until we need them, and when we die many leave behind a trail of debts that with proper insurance planning could have been minimized or avoided.

"People will die without any life insurance and some family member must come up with $8,000 to $10,000 for the burial expenses," Dee says. "This would not happen with sound planning. I'm not against Starbucks, but I see people spend $5, three to four times each week for a Frappuccino without ever thinking twice about protecting themselves or their family from a large-scale loss. A church offering plate or GoFundMe account shouldn't be the default financial arrangement to bury someone."

"It Can Wait"

The middle class waits for a triggering event to buy life insurance or to increase their liability coverage. "A lot of times people think a low-probability disaster will never happen to them; it's always the other guy or family who will be on the short end of the large-scale loss stick," Dan says.

Consider a couple of stories that illustrate the necessity of plugging those insurance gaps.

An insurance representative shared with me, who wished to remain anonymous, a story about a client who had a garage sale one sunny afternoon at her East Coast suburban home. She was well off but wouldn't be classified as generationally or even situationally wealthy. During the garage sale, a customer filed a lawsuit after breaking an ankle on her property by stepping in a crevice on the brick-paved driveway. The plaintiff was awarded a seven-figure payout in punitive damages beyond the hospitalization and medical costs to repair the broken ankle. Fortunately, the homeowner had sufficient insurance protection to avoid a potentially devastating financial loss.

Dee Miller had a new client who wanted to increase his umbrella insurance policy from $1 million to $4 million. The cost differential for the year wasn't significant relative to the upgrade in protection, and it was commensurate with his net worth. Conducting an *insurance needs analysis*, which identifies potential liability exposures and areas of deficiency, Dee noticed the client's auto policy lacked medical payments coverage. That means the client would be on the hook for hospitalization expenses occurring from an auto accident in which people are injured and he's found at fault. The umbrella policy would not cover the client, thus a gap in coverage existed and would need to be filled immediately.

The client went ahead and added medical payments to his umbrella policy, but a more skeptical client with a cost-first-and-risk-mitigation-second approach would vacillate between the need for additional coverage and the expense. Still, clients rationalize away the need as unnecessary, telling themselves that what happened to Dee's client wouldn't happen to them. Insurance professionals and financial planners can't use guilt or compulsion to persuade someone to act. However, they can paint a picture that explains human error and unnecessary financial suffering in a logical fashion that makes theoretical sense based on the law of averages.

Buying life insurance is a deeply emotional decision, and most people prefer not to go there. Even financial planners struggle with it. It's a delicate topic, but the alternative of scrambling to replace a decedent's income can be a nerve-wrecking ordeal for a family. It also may very well be the overriding factor an advisor or representative highlights as a conversation starter to broach the subject.

Thinking about what isn't going to happen instead of what possibly could happen is a big problem for GEDAs and GISAs. The number of adults in America without adequate life insurance is alarming: "More than 4 out of every 10 people do not own a life insurance policy of any amount," according to bestliferates.org. And a large percentage of these life insurance policies are secured at work or through a group membership plan. "Not right now" or "I have it at work" are common phrases to deflect attention from life insurance blind spots.

Dee says most workers aren't quite sure what type of insurance they have at work: life insurance or accidental death insurance. These are two policies with completely different death benefit triggers. He adds, "Most of the time an insurance policy offered by an employer is 1.5 times annual salary, thus an employee earning $100,000 in a given year would have only $150,000 in life insurance. This person may have a home with a mortgage that is significantly more than the life insurance policy offered by her company. If she were to die, the beneficiary would inherit the house as well as the associated debts."

So, what's the purpose of life insurance and how much is typically needed? As Dan and Dee both point out, life insurance is based on a person's or couple's economic standing in life—their current and future ability to earn an income stream. If the primary or even secondary breadwinner dies, how will those left behind survive financially? Whatever the financial plan (or lack thereof) the decedent leaves behind, a family must live with the benefits or repercussions.

> ### Did You Know?
> A rule-of-thumb average for life insurance is 10 times an individual's or couple's gross annual income.

Fast forward to the future. What does your financial picture look like? Have you taken adequate measures to provide for the lifestyle needs of loved ones in the event of your death? If what you envision looks good, then you probably did fine. If it isn't, then you probably need to sit down with a qualified insurance representative to come up with a game plan to protect loved ones who depend on your income stream. Financial planners recommend that people buy life insurance coverage 7 to 10 times their gross annual income. That's a rule-of-thumb average and recognizes that every situation is altogether unique.

I updated a life insurance policy several years ago. A nurse came to our home to administer a series of tests to determine the state of my health, an underwriting requirement. No coverage will be granted until this occurs and the results are processed.

Obviously, I won't benefit from distributions of an insurance policy on my life. As the expression goes, "No one ever saw a Brink's truck following a funeral procession." Unless you are generationally wealthy and can afford to self-insure, life insurance makes sense for the vast majority of Americans, but it amazes me how many families don't have the financial resources to bury a loved one. This topic, including the methods some families use to pay for a funeral, will be revisited in greater detail in the "Estate Planning" section. Death, like life, is also very expensive.

A legacy is far more than what someone leaves behind for others to inherit. Financial burdens add salt to emotional wounds that may never heal.

"Every Conceivable Insurable Risk Has Been Accounted For"

Can the wealthy miss the mark on comprehensive insurance planning? Well, it depends which subset one is addressing. The generationally wealthy are unlikely to have coverage gaps or insurable risks that need plugged. It's very probable that situationally affluent- and functionally affluent-positioned Americans have some gaps in coverage. Unlike GAPAs, they weren't reared in an environment where risk prevention is the norm. The generationally affluent have teams of professionals to mitigate or eliminate known exposures and risks that arise through unlikely circumstances. Maximum insurance coverages are implemented to protect individual family members and other assets: automobiles, homes, antiques, and businesses. Lawsuits, as you can imagine, are always a concern.

By now, you know that income and wealth are not synonymous terms. It's easy to generalize and place high-income earners and asset generators in the same group. Six- and seven-figure wage earners with gaps in insurance coverage can't be generationally wealthy. GAPAs don't gamble with their legacy assets or family brand; too much is at stake—it must be carefully protected. However, the situationally and functionally affluent can have insurance gaps as they move up the socioeconomic ladder. Significant wealth and better risk mitigation strategies are positively correlated. This doesn't mean that a less robust or negative net worth and less stringent protective measures are likewise positively correlated. In fact, insurance can protect future income streams and the resulting higher net worth from asset gains as time goes by.

Now, GAPAs' legacy continuity is an asset for them that insurance can't protect. An insurance policy can't insulate a legacy from the individual and free will choices the next generation makes. Estate planning trusts with spend-thrift provisions can limit family members' access to legacy assets, but the generationally affluent can't predict with absolutely certainty who their children and grandchildren will become.

TAX PLANNING

Author's Note

President Trump has vowed to make good on an election pledge to overhaul the Tax Code. At the time of this book's publication, tax law changes are being vigorously debated in Congress. If enacted, some of the points of emphasis highlighted in the "Tax Planning" section will be amended or rendered obsolete.

25

TAX DOCUMENTATION HABITS

The degree to which a representative social class keeps track of important documents and related materials for tax-filing purposes

Disorganized

Poverty is a chaotic environment and one I lived for nearly 20 years. To insiders, it's a normal routine full of head-scratching inconsistencies. Outside of work and school, time is flexible and impulsive; you fill it as you see fit. Structure is rigid, a straightjacket that holds its prisoners hostage. This may explain why mealtime and bedtime are moving targets. Dinner could be served as late as midnight and dependent on what's available to eat. Imagine eating a high-caloric meal with little nutritional benefits—every night before bedtime—that ultimately disrupts the body's circadian rhythm or sleep-cycle equilibrium. Of course, it's hard to function without adequate nutrition and rest.

So it might not be a surprise that the poor are typically disorganized when it comes to compiling needed tax documents. You don't know where things are because no system exists to track them. They could be anywhere and you find yourself scrambling to retrieve them when tax time approaches, especially when you're expecting a refund. Sometimes they can't be located. Fortunately, an IRS audit is unlikely for most low-income earners with few (if any) itemized deductions and struggling to make ends meet each week.

SOCIOPSYCHONOMIC FILTER

One of the biggest challenges facing impoverished communities come tax time is information overload, the difficulty or inability to manage multiple aspects of this stressful process simultaneously, which of course is so foreign to their language filter and way of thinking.

Betty Collins, a certified public accountant (CPA) with Brady Ware & Co., works with hundreds of clients across the socioeconomic spectrum. She's supportive of organizations that empower single mothers and women who have escaped abusive relationships. Some clients, Betty says, get flummoxed filling out their taxes.

"I have a client who makes $22,000 a year, and while Columbus isn't an expensive place to live, her income doesn't go very far here. Her biggest problem is that she can't comprehend what is required to complete her tax return; the process of filing taxes overwhelms my client. She doesn't want to go to H & R Block or use a family member to file a return. Instead, she wants a professional who will make sure she is compliant," Betty notes.

Distrust and skepticism are common in generational poverty. They may share too much information with those on the inside—family members, friends, and neighbors—but are quite hesitant to divulge important information to a tax representative. Betty understands this well. "I have some clients classified as the working poor who question me about the significance of a document and whether it's needed. I have no idea what drives the disorganization and distrust, but they are definitely present," she says.

What's fascinating about our Sociopsychonomic filter is that it demonstrates how we are entrenched in a certain social class based on our annual income or net worth and yet display the mindsets and behaviors of a different class. Is that frame of reference consistent with our upbringing or one we hope it will replace? Tax documentation habits, being organized or disorganized, is a perfect example.

So you made it out of poverty but can't overcome perpetual disorganization. Or you earn a middle income but aspire to take control of your own economic destiny by investing in the stock market or starting a business. Affluent people tied emotionally to their middle-class upbringing fret over nickel-and-dime expenses that seem trivial given their wealth profile. They got catapulted to affluence but weren't reared in it. They haven't quite learned how to compartmentalize their middle-class ways and habits into their appropriate categories. The transition is still a work in progress.

Organized

I need look no further than my wife Monya to see the impressive organizational skills of the middle class on display. In our household, she pays the bills and keeps the records. At tax time, Monya organizes each document in its appropriate category—personal, business, charity, or investment—that our accountant needs to complete our personal and nonprofit tax returns or file an extension. Her process saves time, money, and peace of mind. It is also a welcomed relief in the Funderburke household as April 15 draws near. In fact, Monya will often send requested information and documents to our CPA several months before tax day. Accountants charge by the hour, which means more time spent compiling a tax return equates to a bigger tax preparation bill. As a self-proclaimed cheapskate, I am delighted by every dollar we can save as a family.

Let's explore the rationale behind GISAs tax documentation habits and compliant nature to avoid IRS scrutiny. The traditional middle class follows instructions well and does what they're told in a timely fashion. I've incorporated this attribute into my personal and professional activities because of the diligent efforts of my soulmate. As a teenager, though, I had the reputation of doing my own thing and was labeled a nonconformist

> IRS compliance and their much-needed tax refund are the two driving forces for GISAs as Tax Day—April 15—approaches.

by my high school and college coaches—Scott Weakley, Chuck Kemper, Bobby Knight, and Randy Ayers. I had a selectively compliant obedient filter, which is common among the poor and based largely on superficial feelings. In my case, I often interpreted their commands as threats that were intrinsically unfair or devoid of substance.

GISAs, by nature, play it safe even knowing that retirement and potential Social Security shortfalls will likely cause them to outlive their money. They still cling to the safe choices of savings accounts, certificates of deposit, and federal bonds as their primary income streams. Starting a business is a terrifying predicament since most start-ups fail within their first three years. Likewise, compliance guides their tax documentation habits, a predictable pattern foundational to their economic DNA.

Betty says the acquiescent nature of the middle class ensures they follow the rules and file their taxes in a timely manner. "The middle class, those earning between $75,000 and $175,000, are very organized when it comes to tax information," she says. "They want the process of filing taxes to be over with; they don't want it to drag on any longer than is necessary. They come prepared, fully aware of the laws, which they obey. The vast majority of them do not want to file an extension beyond April 15 and anticipate a tax refund, which is their ultimate prize."

The poor and middle class respond to fear, but for different reasons. You may recall that fear is one of the six primary emotions. Located in the temporal lobe of the left and right hemispheres, the amygdalae control the emotional response of fear. It's part of the limbic system, where emotional reactions trigger physiological changes as the body prepares for an aggressive or passive response.

The temporal lobe is the auditory and internal dialogue processing center. This area of the brain can be GISAs worst enemy when they are overcome by analysis paralysis and outcome loss. Our sense of balance resides in the ears. Threatening words—incoming or outgoing—that could potentially disrupt their financial equilibrium are paralyzing to GISAs, for example, an IRS inquiry or self-inflicted disaster scenario. This singular issue may garner their undivided attention until it is resolved and economic balance restored. Anything related to the ears—listening, memorizing, recalling, internal chattering, or balancing—is a function of the temporal lobe.

I met Gerald while doing a presentation on money and emotions for his social organization, which hosted a free workshop to low-income residents who live near the King Arts Complex near downtown Columbus. After the event, Gerald casually mentioned that he was an IRS agent, which caught people off-guard. He says keeping receipts and other tax documents can validate a paper trail to show the IRS, should it have questions about your return. What you hear largely determines how you move.

An IRS inquiry isn't necessarily going to alarm GEDAs, but for GISAs, it's another story because the middle class fears unexpected punishment. A fine, penalty, or audit would disrupt their allocation of resources that they must carefully protect. GISAs don't want any problems with the IRS, which may explain why they're so organized come tax time, thanks in large part to their fear-based internal dialogue center.

Compartmentalized

For the generationally wealthy, everything is compartmentalized or arranged based on the income type and how the IRS Tax Code will affect the following income categories: ordinary (income from a job or business), portfolio (income from investments), and passive (income from rental or commercial real estate, royalties, patents, and other intellectual property). They have a system in place that keeps track of their tax liability throughout the year. It is usually flawless.

"The super wealthy look at it in terms of compartmentalizing. What are they going to spend year-end based on what they've already paid in taxes during those first nine months of the year," Betty says. "Or they will hold onto cash and pay the outstanding tax liability on April 15. The affluent are intentional with everything."

> ### SOCIOPSYCHONOMIC FILTER
> Compartmentalization is the process of aggregating, and then separating, documents in an orderly and systematic manner, which pays huge dividends for GAPAs and SAPAs come tax time.

GAPAs and SAPAs track tax legislation so that they can plan ahead to deal with it. The informed wealthy, she says, expect their CPAs and family offices to keep them abreast of proposed changes in legislation. "This is what we as CPAs are paid to do. Obviously, this brings a great deal of risk for my profession since we must always be on top of our game. No wealthy individual, family, or corporation enjoys being audited by the IRS. It's a grueling ordeal."

A wealthy individual or family has a much higher chance of being audited by the IRS than the poor or middle class do. With more wealth comes greater scrutiny to report all forms of income (and losses), regardless of the source.

In terms of financial planning areas outlined in this book, intentionality and deliberateness of action are what separate the three social classes. The poor believe life is random, where winners and losers are determined by luck. Outcomes are final as superstitions and feelings dominate their beliefs, attitudes, and behaviors. The traditional middle class operates their lives according to chance, which is predicated on what they can and cannot control. They depend on the collective efforts of interdependence to maintain a status quo existence occupationally and financially.

The mega wealthy believe destiny is on their side, where actions and activities lead to favorable circumstances that result from due diligence. Destiny and risk are positively and conditionally correlated. They are prudent in their risk taking and calculated efforts. GAPAs place absolute trust in the professionals around them to do a good job in managing their affairs while providing objective advice at the same time.

26

TAX CODE STRATEGIES

*The tools social classes are likely to employ to maximize
their tax refund or net income throughout the year, or
minimize a tax liability when completing a federal tax return*

Personal Exemptions, Standard
Deductions, and Credits

Providing people with a real-world experience to supplement or supplant their current economic frame of reference is the goal of our Mr. Fundy's Financial Life Skills™ curriculum. We believe this may be the best opportunity to overturn the fatalistic mentality embedded in generational poverty; GEDAs assume wealth accumulation is beyond their reach. Money, even in a hypothetical setting, can kick-start their financial dreams.

In the game Taxes Owed or Refund Due? each participant calculates their tax liability or refund based on the choices selected in the Reality Days game, where participants deduct taxes from their gross monthly income. The remaining cash flow is used to select a housing option, transportation, and contend with other expenses from childcare to insurance to groceries, for instance.

> **SOCIOPSYCHONOMIC FILTER**
>
> Earning a higher monthly income that results in paying more income taxes is a liberating feeling for the poor, even in a hypothetical game setting.

We've made several observations of those taking part in the Taxes Owed or Refund Due? game. Our findings follow:

- Computing a tax liability or refund was initially daunting for participants because the concepts were foreign to them, but their anxiety level subsided and confidence grew as we moved through the calculation.

- Children from wealthier backgrounds were more empathetic to the plight of the poor when they, too, had to make economic decisions on a very limited income.

- Participants who received an Earned Income Tax Credit were ecstatic by this bounce of good fortune, while those who did not receive the credit felt shortchanged.

- Participants from impoverished backgrounds with high-paying jobs in Reality Days could better visualize how they want their lives to unfold and the associated obligations required of taxpaying Americans.

- Children and young adults were very interested in learning more about how taxes are collected and used by government authorities.

- Participants from middle-class backgrounds were more apt to shore up savings, take a vacation, or spend the tax refund on their children.

- Overall, participants looked at their tax refund as a bonus to save more money, contribute to a retirement or investment or college savings account, live in a better neighborhood, or purchase depreciating assets like a car or flat-screen television. (Depreciating assets go down in value shortly after they're bought.)

Above-the-Line Deductions, Itemized Deductions or Standard Deductions, and Child and Dependent Care Credits

People can take advantage of a variety of deductions and credits that may reduce how much they pay each year to the federal government: standard deductions, itemized deductions (state and local taxes, mortgage interest, charitable donations, and property taxes to name a few), child and dependent care credits, the Earned Income Tax Credit (or EITC) that helps low- to moderate-income households with children. Above-the-line deductions that reduce annual gross income include alimony; student loan interest; IRA contributions; books and supplies teachers buy for their classrooms; contributions to self-employed retirement plans; and Health Savings Accounts (HSA) contributions, among others.

For illustrative purposes, let's examine a hypothetical middle-class family to see how these moving parts fit together to complete a modified 1040 tax return. First, take a deep breath. You'll need it.

John and Mary have been married a little over one year. He went through a bitter divorce with his ex-wife two years ago and has full custody of their six-year-old son, Micah. John pays $1,500 in alimony each month to Elaine, his former wife.

In 2016, John, a project manager, and Mary, a grocery store clerk, had a combined annual income of $130,000. Now they must figure out whether they'll have a tax liability or get a refund from the federal government. The first step they'll take is calculating their adjusted gross income (AGI), which is the last line on the front page of a 1040 or 1040 EZ tax form.

Above-the-line deductions of $25,500 for John's alimony payments, interest on student loans, and IRA contributions for 2016 reduce the couple's AGI to $104,500 ($130,000 − $25,500). To figure their taxable income, Mary and John must decide next whether they'll take the standard deduction for a married filing jointly couple of $12,600, or if higher, itemize their deductions. The Tax Code allows taxpayers to deduct whichever is greater, the standard deduction or itemized deductions. They can also deduct another $12,150 for three personal exemptions.

Now if the couple chooses to itemize all their deductions, $28,160, and claim the $12,150 in personal exemptions, they will see their taxable income dip further to $64,190, a much better situation for John and Mary. Taxes due from the couple on $64,190 are $8,701, according to the IRS. The pair had $22,445 in federal taxes withheld during 2016 and is eligible for $4,000 in dependent care and child tax credits. In the end, the family is going to receive a tax refund of $17,744 ($8,701 − $22,445 − $4,000). Not too bad. However, with better tax planning throughout the year, John and Mary could have enjoyed more cash to meet lifestyle obligations instead of providing the IRS with an interest-free loan, which in theory equates to a tax refund. In other words, a tax refund is simply an overpayment of taxes.

Capital Gains, Deferral of Income, and Loss Carry-Forwards

The wealthy can't permanently avoid paying taxes—and those who do defraud the government face stiff consequences—but they can shift or reinvest income that has already been taxed at the federal level. Paying a lower tax rate on capital gains and deferring income is perfectly legal and delays the immediate payment of associated taxes. The poor and traditional middle class will likely lack the financial resources or appetite for risk to pursue these options. That's too bad, because an enticement for them is that the tax rate they would pay on qualified dividends would be either zero percent or 15 percent, depending on their adjusted gross income. Sounds like a good deal to me if they have the money and stomach to take on risk in the stock market.

GAPAs and SAPAs go to great lengths to minimize their tax liability. They look for opportunities to step down—but not step over their obligation to pay taxes—from their current marginal tax rate of nearly 40 percent to the lowest rate possible on long-term investment gains or qualified dividends for taxpayers in their income bracket, which currently is 23.8 percent. (This 23.8 percent tax on long-term capital gains is broken down into two parts, the first consisting of a 20 percent tax on qualified dividends. High-income earners must also pay a surtax of 3.8 percent on investment income, a mandate instituted in the Affordable Care Act to help fund this law.)

The working poor and middle class typically earn all of their income from a job. Employment earnings are taxed at the federal and state levels. For different types of investments, including the length of time an investor holds them, they can be taxed at a much lower rate than employment income. The qualified dividends that a wealthy investor receives from a stock or mutual fund are currently taxed at a maximum rate of 23.8 percent.

Investing involves risk, including the loss of principal, but this does not deter SAPAs and GAPAs. They understand the tradeoff between risk and reward, which they manage quite well in conjunction with their tax minimization strategies. For business or investment purposes, the wealthy employ a property schedule, as stipulated by the Tax Code, as another strategy to reduce net income and delay payment of a potentially huge tax bill well into the future. Depreciation on an investment in land or a building reduces net income since it is treated as an expense. However, an asset's accumulated depreciation must be recaptured if sold at a profit. Stay with me now.

The amount of depreciation taken against the asset—which must go down in value over time and be used for business or investment purposes—will be recovered if the property is sold at a gain. Again, the Tax Code is not set up to allow the wealthy to walk away permanently from their obligation to pay taxes on an investment gain. However, affluent investors can defer payment of tax on the proceeds from a sale until the doctrine of constructive receipt comes into the picture.

Backlash directed at the wealthy stems from, or so it is assumed, their ability to defer tax on income that they immediately control. Income maneuverability should not be confused with income accessibility. In the 'hood, a popular saying is "Don't hate the player, hate the game." Deferred income, whether from selling an asset, an employment bonus, qualified retirement account, or stock option, must get taxed at some future point when access to the income is realized. Until then, the IRS will always keep a close eye on the trail of deferred income, even years or perhaps decades after the wealth initiator's death. Uncle Sam has a long memory when it comes to taxes that haven't been collected yet. Trust me, he will eventually get paid.

The doctrine of constructive receipt sounds more complicated than it really is. When an individual has access to earned income, or money inherited from a trust for example, then a tax becomes due. Income that has been credited to an individual's account is the same thing as constructively receiving it. Access is the key word. In this realm, it's the immediate ability to spend, save, protect, invest, or donate the money as one pleases. As long as the action is legal, the IRS couldn't care less what is done with the money; they just want to collect the tax as soon as access is granted to enjoy or delay the income's benefit. Once shielded income steps outside the shade of tax protection, it is fair game.

SOCIOPSYCHONOMIC FILTER

Access to income is the litmus test for the doctrine of constructive receipt, an often misunderstood issue in the income-inequality debate.

The informed wealthy are hyper-vigilant about reducing their tax liability for any of the three income buckets: ordinary income, investment income, and passive income. A capital loss is when an investment sells for less than what the owner paid for it. Individuals can carry capital losses forward indefinitely but net capital losses are limited in the offsetting of taxable income. Affluent investors, with the guidance of their CPAs and financial representatives, can discuss how best to offset capital gains with capital losses.

Offsetting is perfectly legal and it's available to any taxpayer who can use it. Of course, capital at risk can be a frightening proposition for the traditional middle class, regardless of the offsetting benefits. Take another breath—this will make more sense with the following example.

John, a very wealthy investor, purchases stock in Pear Inc. He's owned the stock for a little more than a year and now wants to sell some of his shares. The price John paid for each share of Pear stock on Dec. 15, 2015, was $50 and totaled $50,000 (1,000 shares x $50). He sold the stock on Dec. 20, 2016, at $75 a share. In aggregate, the value of his Pear shares rose to $75,000 (1,000 shares x $75). His profit after selling the shares was $25,000 ($75,000 − $50,000). Not bad.

Let's shift our attention to the long-term loss incurred when he sold his Equip Source stock.

The per-share price he paid for the Equip Source stock on Dec. 14, 2015, was $120, which totaled $60,000 (500 shares x $120). He sold the stock on Dec. 21, 2016, and incurred a long-term loss in the process. Each share was sold at $90 a share, $30 less than what he initially paid for the stock. The value of his Equip Source position was now $45,000 (500 shares x $90), and his loss totaled $15,000 ($45,000 − $60,000).

John's net long-term gain on the two stocks he sold in 2016 was $10,000 ($25,000 − $15,000), consisting of a gain on the sell of Pear stock and a loss on the Equip Source stock. For this particular transaction, the long-term gain tax that he paid was $2,380, or a 23.8 percent tax rate ($10,000 x .238). Had he held onto the stocks for less than a year, John's gain would have been taxed as a short-term gain at a marginal tax rate of 39.6 ($10,000 x .396 = $3,960). Pay careful attention to the huge difference between long-term capital gains and marginal tax rates above certain income thresholds. The generationally and situationally affluent do.

Many affluent individuals and families didn't become wealthy overnight. Theirs is a long-term wealth journey, and they are very good at playing money ball in incremental steps.

CHAPTER

27

TAX WITHHOLDING COMFORT LEVEL

The comfort level that a representative social class employs to achieve one of three outcomes: mitigate the effects of a tax liability, maximize the amount of a tax refund, or manage cash flow while enjoying the benefits of a refundable credit

Too Little

I grew up in a home with no male influence, though my mother did the best she could to care for my three older sisters and me. I empathize with single-parent mothers facing stress-induced financial challenges amid households where fathers are no-shows. It's even more difficult—a near impossible task—to do this earning a minimum wage or insufficient income.

I have great admiration for the working poor. They take great pride in earning a paycheck instead of depending on a welfare check. As a former welfare recipient myself, I'll never oppose it, but welfare should offer only temporary financial support to a family until reliable employment and some semblance of a stable living situation are secured. As taxpayers who understand and abide by the dictates of compassion, our government is obligated to help the poor. However, this should never disempower them. Welfare in America is not a generational birthright of perpetual dependency.

The working poor typically withhold too little in federal taxes from their paychecks because they need the extra cash for monthly bills and groceries. Fortunately, they rarely will have a tax liability because they earn too little, but likely will receive a tax refund each year, thanks in large part to the Earned Income Tax Credit (EITC). The EITC is a refundable credit beneficiaries receive even though they haven't paid any taxes at the federal level outside of Social Security and Medicare.

Tax refunds are overpayments of the taxes employers withhold from a wage earner's paycheck based on two factors: yearly compensation and the information or allowances provided on an Employee's Withholding Allowance Certificate, or W-4 form.

The W-4 can be updated throughout the year; it's a responsibility that rests solely on the shoulders of employees, not the employer or HR department. The W-4 may need tweaked depending on how much more or less cash an employee wants withheld to meet her needs, which oftentimes is shaped by a change in her life status because of a divorce, hours worked, or a new baby, for example.

Too Much

According to a 2015 *CNN Money* report, "84 percent of those [who made] less than $50,000 [for the year] received a refund in 2012."[22] While the poor withhold too little from their paychecks, the middle class typically withholds too much, which diverts cash away from managing their monthly financial obligations throughout the year. They are likely to receive a tax refund each year, as do the poor. IRS compliance, fear, and a forced-savings mentality highlight the middle class's default tax withholding strategy.

I often ask middle-class adults who participate in our financial wellness workshops if they receive a tax refund. Most nod their head in the affirmative and enthusiastically share the amount of the refund with me when no one else is listening. As a general observation, I've found that the refund amounts to roughly 8 percent to 12 percent of a couple's annual income.

Accountants hold two schools of thought on the subject of tax withholdings. One side believes giving the government an interest-free loan makes no sense. Why pay more in taxes to have your money returned to you at a later date without an economic benefit? They advocate employees have withheld as little as possible. CPAs who work with more wealthy clients tend to side with this view.

"If you do proper planning, you shouldn't get a tax refund. But if you do, then it should be minimal relative to your overall annual income," Betty Collins says. Sound advice, to be sure.

Accountants in the other school of thought believe forced savings are a good thing. They understand the traditional middle class's logic in securing a tax refund; the accomplishment of a goal matters more than the methods used to reach it. The CPAs feel it's unnecessary to berate a taxpayer who withheld more in taxes from each paycheck if this was her intended purpose with or without a change in life circumstances. These CPAs appear to be in the minority.

> An interest-free loan to Uncle Sam is how many accountants view a sizable tax refund.

Chris, my father-in-law, shared his tax withholding's comfort level. "I had extra taxes taken out of each paycheck for decades so that I would get something back. I looked forward to the refund check every year. That money went for three things: a summer vacation or trip to an amusement park with our four kids, back-to-school clothes, and a boost to strengthen savings."

Now, let's highlight a few tactical maneuvers the middle class can deploy with the extra tax savings they'd have throughout the year, thanks in part to an updated withholding strategy:

- They could contribute more to their defined contribution plans, such as an employer-sponsored 401(k) or 403(b) plan. It's possible that an individual retirement account (IRA) could be established alongside their 401(k) or 403(b).

- Cash flow forecasting, or aligning monetary inflows with outflows, could help in paying off debt and related interest charges sooner rather than later.

- Extra tax savings could fund the start of a side business that doesn't interfere with GISAs' primary work responsibilities.

- More money in GISAs' pocket each month could lessen the financial burden and reduce stress levels.

Too Exact

SAPAs and GAPAs want to know their tax liability ahead of time and pay it monthly, quarterly, or on April 15, the traditional tax liability due date. The wealthy always have their economic and political pulse on matters that affect their tax bill. They compare last year's taxes while simultaneously meeting with their wealth-protection team to discuss the tax liability game plan.

"Their withholdings and estimates will be 100 percent of the federal taxes paid last year or 110 percent of the previous year's taxes if income has risen," Betty says. "Affluent business owners will do year-end planning in the fourth quarter, or the last three months of the year, to reduce their tax liability by spending money on repairs and needed expenditures. The tax burden is really huge right now on the affluent."

Betty talks about a client once classified as a middle-income earner. This client's wages increased significantly, but she never asked Betty how much to withhold until her quarterly federal tax estimates rose dramatically. Significant income gains translate into higher taxes and greater due diligence to report accurate information on a tax return with a kosher paper trail. Like it or not, it's the way our progressive tax system works in a capitalistic environment.

THE JOCK TAX

I paid a lot of taxes as a former NBA player blessed to have earned a seven-figure income for several years. Roughly half my income went to Uncle Sam. Half of a lot was still a lot, but this didn't mean I had to keep my mouth shut in regard to the taxes—federal, state, local, Medicare, and Social Security—that were deducted from those paychecks every two weeks.

I played my first seven years for the Sacramento Kings in California, which has very high tax rates on income above a certain threshold. What most people don't know is that professional athletes, entertainers, and other high-income earners are subject to the jock or entertainment tax. This isn't a separate tax outside of what high earners already pay, but refers to the process authorities use to tax their income, which is quite interesting, to say the least.

Officials know when pro teams are coming to their state or city, how long they'll be there, and when they are coming back. In today's social media world, athletes can't escape their whereabouts and can be tracked by the hour or minute. Some jurisdictions tax athletes on the number of days they are physically in the area.

For example, a sports team may arrive two days before the game is played. It's possible an athlete's income will get taxed for the three days he is present in that city, not just the day of the game, which would appear to make more logical sense. Players have no say deciding when to enter or leave a city leading up to or after a game. Adding to the insanity, pro athletes are even required to file a tax return for almost every locale where they play. I remember the agony quite well, and the thousands paid to my accountants to keep every tax return straight.

28

TAX PREPARER

The nonprofit organization, company, or person a taxpayer uses to prepare a 1040 tax return, either pro bono or as a fee-for-service contractual engagement

Uncompensated Preparer

The working poor may use an uncompensated friend, family member, or free service offered by a nonprofit organization to complete their tax return. They also will use enrolled agents for the mass-market tax preparation providers. In some cases, the fees charged will be significant, on a percentage basis, relative to the amount of the refund. I will revisit this again in the next section on enrolled agents.

If there are no itemized deductions, the working poor's tax return should be fairly straightforward to complete as long as it contains the standard deduction elected for her filing status, personal exemptions taken, federal and payroll taxes paid for the year, and available credits secured. There is even free file software available through the IRS website, irs.gov/freefile, for those wanting to complete their own tax return.

Uncompensated tax preparers are likely to have a basic knowledge of tax matters, and some may have received a cursory introduction to the Tax Code. To truly empower the poor, however, free tax preparation offerings by nonprofit organizations should be combined with a game plan to build wealth-appreciating assets instead of wealth-depleting assets that perpetuate generational poverty. These feel-good assets—cars, electronics, and clothes—decrease in value once bought. After bills or debts are paid, the poor often turn their attention to these assets to boost their spirits.

Enrolled Agent

Mass-market tax preparation services are the domain of enrolled agents. An enrolled agent is a tax advisor who is authorized by the U.S. Department of Treasury to assist taxpayers with their 1040 tax returns. Along with CPAs and attorneys, enrolled agents can also represent their clients before the IRS in the event of an audit or dispute. There's a place for enrolled agents, the H & R Blocks and Jackson Hewitts of the world, which offer differing levels of expertise when handling your tax return. In general, a CPA will have more in-depth knowledge than an enrolled agent about tax and financial matters.

Some mass-market tax preparation services charge clients, predominately low- and middle-income families, a higher than average fee for uncomplicated tax advice, though the expense isn't always commensurate with the level of assistance provided. To be fair, sometimes it is. There are many mass-market locations strategically placed in geographic and socioeconomic settings that speak the language of their demographic. These quick-service providers satisfy a need in the marketplace when a tax refund is sought without delay. However, most people don't exactly know what they're getting. Preparing a basic, rudimentary tax return shouldn't cost more than a few hundred dollars, even for middle-market taxpayers in cities where the cost of living is higher than the national average.

"With mass-market tax preparation companies, their biggest selling feature is the same-day tax refund that day, but the fee can be as high as 30 percent," Betty Collins says. "If someone goes to one of these places and takes advantage of the Earned Income Tax Credit and gets a $3,000 tax refund,

$1,000 of it may go directly to the tax preparation company. Our firm ran the numbers on what it would cost to do a basic tax return, for example, itemizing mortgage interest, charitable deductions, and the like. It would be $75 for some items, Schedule A related items would be $25, e-filing would be this, and so on. The total fee out the door at our Columbus firm would be about $450 or $500, but the person or couple filing jointly might have to wait several weeks for the tax refund. People pay a steep price when they are in a hurry, which some tax preparers capitalize on to satisfy the huge demand."

> Tradeoffs exist when a same-day tax refund is the ultimate prize. Immediate cash in hand comes with an added cost.

The average employee with just a few itemized deductions might be well served in completing their own 1040 return using Turbo Tax or similar software by an IRS-approved vendor. For a nominal fee, these do-it-yourself offerings provide step-by-step instructions for those with very little income outside of a W-2 or employment income.

Millennials don't want to do anything by hand; they prefer to complete a tax return online—their world—as opposed to the mundane process of filling out and then mailing in printed forms. Betty taught her own kids how to complete their returns using Turbo Tax, where the IRS finds errors quickly. Given the trepidation many poor and middle class people have come tax time, they are unlikely to complete a return without the handholding guidance of a face-to-face tax advisor, regardless of costs.

Certified Public Accountant (or CPA)

Income streams, lavish estates, and business dealings around the world require a high level of sophistication and attention to detail to prepare a complicated tax return for a SAPA or GAPA. My experience filling out tax returns in each city I played pales in comparison to what the super wealthy face. They need experts to comply with tax matters at the federal, state, local, and international level.

The mega affluent need advisors, particularly CPAs, tax attorneys, and family office professionals, to handle various aspects of their highly complex, financial situations. Some would argue that IRS scrutiny is more pronounced with the wealthy than either the poor or middle class. More income and assets call for a more thorough understanding and interpretation of the Tax Code, which currently entails more than 75,000 pages. SAPAs and GAPAs realize the value a CPA provides them. Time is perhaps the most valuable asset the wealthy don't have in abundance, so they rely heavily on tax professionals to complete nearly every task of a tax return for them.

CPAs are a different breed. They are microscopic in their analysis of numbers, aimed at staving off an IRS inquiry. Their expertise includes financial auditing and planning, corporate finance and governance, estate planning, and forensic accounting, among many other areas that are boringly interesting to number geeks, which includes me. They are the kind of teammates you want as the tax return shot clock winds down and possession of the money ball is critical, a continuous moment for SAPAs and GAPAs, who always are cognizant of tax time even if April 15 is many months away. To them, tax planning is ongoing. They retain CPAs indefinitely to help them stay out of the tax return rat race. Unfortunately, the poor and middle class get stuck in it every year.

CHAPTER

29

INCOME RECOGNITION, TAX FORMS, AND SCHEDULES

The tax documents that must be filled out or filed by taxpayers to complete a 1040 individual return

A brief discussion of many of the key features of the 1040 income tax return will be discussed next, followed by a chart summarizing and comparing each social class's propensity to receive or complete various tax forms.

A W-2 shows the amount of taxes withheld by an employer from an employee's paycheck for the year. Withholdings—weekly, monthly, or quarterly—should be made throughout the year to prevent underpaying taxes to the federal government. However, the working poor may have very little if any federal taxes deducted from their paychecks because of favorable exemptions, the applicable standard deduction, and available credits.

Form 1099 speaks primarily to independent contractors and the income they receive working on behalf of a company or organization. The contractors are responsible for paying the taxes due. Other 1099 income sources include interest and dividends from savings accounts, stocks, or mutual funds. Withdrawals from retirement accounts, which the wealthy are likely to have, and state income tax refunds and unemployment compensation that primarily benefit the working poor and traditional middle class are additional 1099 income sources.

Schedules, also known as attachments, will depend on the taxpayer's necessity to file them. Outside of the Schedule EITC, which identifies whether a taxpayer is eligible to receive the Earned Income Tax Credit, the working poor are unlikely to complete any of the other tax form schedules. SAPAs and GAPAs will likely file attachments along with their 1040 return that run the gamut, from itemized deductions to capital gains and losses on investments to taxes owed for the employment of domestic workers—nannies, security personnel, chefs, etc.

The following chart provides a summary of the glaring differences representative social classes display in regard to income recognition, tax forms, and schedules as April 15 draws near each year:

Categories	The Working Poor	The Traditional Middle Class	The Situationally and Generationally Wealthy
W-2 Taxes Withheld by Employer	Maybe (but could be zero)	Yes	Yes
1099 Independent Contractor for Work Performed	Possibly	Possibly	Possibly
1099-INT Interest Paid	Very Unlikely	Possibly (but likely very small)	Yes
1099-DIV Dividends Paid	No	Maybe	Yes
1099-R Retirement Withdrawals	No	Possibly	Yes
1099-G State Refund & Unemployment Compensation	Possibly	Possibly	Unlikely

Categories	The Working Poor	The Traditional Middle Class	The Situationally and Generationally Wealthy
Schedule A Itemized Deductions	No	Likely	Yes (but adjusted gross income exceeds benefit threshold)
Schedule B Interest & Dividend Income	No	Maybe (but probably would be insignificant)	Yes
Schedule C Profits & Losses for Sole Proprietorship and Single-Member LLC	Maybe	Maybe	Maybe (but unlikely to operate a sole proprietorship because of risks)
Schedule D Capital Gains & Losses on Investments	No	Maybe (but probably would be insignificant)	Yes
Schedule E Income from Rental Real Estate & Royalties	No	Maybe	Yes
Schedule F Profits & Losses from Farming	No	Maybe (but likelihood is very low)	Maybe
K-1 Income & Losses from Pass-Through Entities	No	Maybe (but likelihood is very low)	Yes

Categories	The Working Poor	The Traditional Middle Class	The Situationally and Generationally Wealthy
Schedule EIC Eligibility for Earned Income Credit	Yes	Maybe (but probably would be insignificant)	No
Schedule H Taxes Owed for Employment of Domestic Workers	No	No	Yes

Most of the middle class, who comprise a solid majority of the population, don't believe they can climb any farther up the economic ladder. They are content, unable, unwilling, or lack the confidence to travel beyond this financial point and reach their economic potential. "This is their comfort level. I was that way a long time in my life before I found my purpose and passion in life, and I've never looked back," says Betty Collins.

She alludes to GISAs' ingrained and self-defeating feelings that drown them in the quagmire of life's circumstances, while GEDAs believe they are trapped by them. A tax return, although not based on empirical evidence, often tells the story on how committed we are to reaching our financial potential based on the schedules or attachments used to complete it.

30

TAX CODE MISCONCEPTIONS

*The erroneous assumptions that are
characteristic of a traditional social class in
regard to the Tax Code*

"I Should Have Received a Larger Tax Refund"

By now, you should be familiar with the Earned Income Tax Credit (EITC), a refundable tax credit many low-income Americans qualify for with or without dependents. The Additional Child Tax Credit is another refundable credit for those with children whose incomes are near or below the poverty threshold. For a family of four in 2016, the federal poverty guideline was $24,300 and $11,880 for singles.[23] Obviously, it is incredibly difficult to survive on these thresholds in lieu of housing, food, and other living obligations. Tax credits provide incentives for the poor and struggling middle class to work instead of collect welfare benefits.

The EITC is also a dignity play. To generate a paycheck through legitimate work and receive a tax refund is liberating to the human soul, especially in an environment where unemployment runs rampant. As a kid living in a housing project, I can't recall any person who got up in the morning and went to work, though I'm sure there were a few. Drive down the street of any impoverished neighborhood today and you'll still see a high number of adults traversing the landscape, seemingly aimless, without a job or the inclination to find one.

> ## SOCIOPSYCHONOMIC FILTER
> Earning a paycheck instead of receiving a welfare check is a critical step in breaking the cycle of generational poverty.

Inner-city communities comprised largely of blacks, Hispanics, and Appalachian whites, need our help. The challenge for nonprofit and profit-driven organizations is to help the residents increase their employable skill-sets and economic frame of reference so they can earn and maintain a dignified wage. The next step is showing them how to create a sustainable wealth path and contribute more tax revenues to the government, which requires a mindset shift. In my sequel to this book, I will offer practical tips and solutions to help them achieve this goal.

The working poor and low-skilled employees may not fully understand why they don't receive a larger tax refund. Betty Collins had a conversation with her pastor son, Andrew, on this subject. He is more focused, and rightly so, on saving souls rather than making a lot of money. Betty says, "He earns a very modest income and shared his concerns with me one day on why he doesn't receive a larger refund from the IRS. I told him, 'You don't pay federal taxes because your income falls below a certain threshold; you are just filling out forms because you have to.'"

Tough love from a woman who is a fine mother, avid philanthropist, and very good CPA to boot.

A federal income tax is levied on employment earnings above a certain threshold. People with lower incomes often pay little or no federal tax when deductions, personal exemptions, and credits are considered. The refund that low-income workers receive is capped because they typically withhold minimal federal taxes throughout the year. Without the earned income and dependent care credits at their disposal, the working poor would have an even bigger economic hole from which to climb out. They certainly could use a bigger tax refund even though they're not entitled to one.

"The Tax Code Is Only for the Rich and Well-Connected"

Many poor and middle-class Americans, and the politicians who cater to these two voting blocks, embrace the misconception the IRS turns a blind eye on the misdeeds of the mega wealthy that fail to pay their fare share of federal income taxes. The top 20 percent of income earners pay over 80 percent of federal taxes.[24] As noted, beyond a certain income, no tax breaks exist on ordinary income for the super wealthy.

GAPAs and SAPAs are adept at shifting income and their residency in some cases, a tax mobility play to friendlier jurisdictions. They aren't afraid to relocate to a state (or country) that welcomes disgruntled taxpayers. Texas and Florida, two states without a personal income tax, have seen an influx of new residents over the last few years compared with those Texans and Floridians who left the states.

Mindy, a middle-income earner for years, worked for a company head-quartered outside the U.S. that went bankrupt. She asked her former employer if she could continue the relationship with customers since the company wouldn't be servicing them anymore. The company agreed, and over the next two years Mindy grew the business and was paying taxes on earned income equal to the salary she previously received from her former employer. This catapulted Mindy into the rarified world of high-income, six-digit earners. She asked her accountant how to minimize her tax liability. The response: "Not a whole lot."

Mindy realizes that her significant income increase leaves very few alternatives for minimizing taxes when an individual or couple earn a sizable salary. She and her husband, Dave, could take advantage of one option by setting up a pension that would let them defer income for their retirement because a 401(k) alone may not be enough for their golden years. A few other options exist to defer income, and thus, taxes. Also, Mindy's boost in earnings means deductions and credits available to the poor and middle class may not be available to employees in her income stratosphere. She is learning that her acrobatic jump in income isn't as advantageous from a tax minimization perspective as she once thought.

Public outcry is growing louder by the day that the super rich, who earn more than $100 million a year, are to blame for the wealth gap in America. Critics lament that this group makes insane amounts of money but doesn't actually create wealth for the average person who builds, makes, or designs tangible things our economy uses and needs. Besides, the super wealthy can afford to pay more in taxes, the argument goes. This is why we have such a divisive political climate, driven largely by rhetoric and well-packaged sound bites that create an environment of back-and-forth finger pointing, while nothing gets done and the wealth gap widens.

For anyone not well-connected, envy can creep in and cloud their economic opportunity filter. It's human nature and GISAs may feel disconnected from opportunities that are afforded to the mega wealthy. They sacrifice just as much as their affluent peers in terms of work ethic and family obligations, but the financial payoff or benefits don't always measure up. The middle class has a right to feel shortchanged, especially when lifestyle expenditures exceed their monetization efforts by a wide margin.

> ## SOCIOPSYCHONOMIC FILTER
> For anyone not well-connected, envy can creep in and cloud their economic opportunity filter.

Betty Collins's daughter Erica is a schoolteacher, one of the hardest professions around. Although not much is left from each paycheck, Erica does save 10 percent of her income consistently. Betty didn't shy away from helping her daughter understand a profound truth about supply and demand.

"You've chosen to be a teacher. You don't save everything today for tomorrow. This is accomplished over a lifetime," Betty says. "I married your stepfather, a post office worker who will retire early in a few years, because he saved diligently for two decades, although my mother initially wanted me to marry a businessman until she learned that her future son-in-law had more money in the bank than his soon-to-be CPA wife did. Your stepfather did what he needed to do over time, and is reaping the benefits today. He chose to become a post office employee and to use what he has and make it work financially. You assume the life-changing benefits and financial drawbacks associated with your occupation."

Income is a supply and demand issue. Lower supply of highly skilled workers with technical expertise and greater demand equate to high-income professions, while an abundant supply with moderate demand lead to low- or middle-income occupations.

Since retiring from the NBA, I've worked as an educator and now as a business owner. Each has been more gratifying than my time on the basketball court despite the precipitous drop in income. Compensation is based on what an employer is willing to pay you, not necessarily what you're worth. Hard work and equitable pay are not synonymous terms.

No person in his right mind can argue against the fact that a committed schoolteacher in an inner-city community is more valuable to our society in comparison with the exploits of a pro athlete making ridiculous amounts of money playing a kid's game. Our system isn't perfect, but it's the best we've got among available alternatives.

"GET IT OFF THE GLASS!"

As role players in the context of sports analogies, the middle class needs to be more vigilant and resolute in how they view and pursue wealth accumulation without selling their souls in the process. They are key players in helping their companies amass huge fortunes, particularly those with mandates to increase shareholder value, but must become their own wealth-building advocates despite promises made by elected officials to help Main Street America. Who's really looking out for these folks? It needs to be the person standing in front of the mirror, squinting at her own reflection.

I can relate to middle-class angst as a role player during my time in the NBA. Yes, I had my moments of glory, but they were few and far between. When they did come, I had to be ready. Known as Mr. Instant Offense when I came off the bench my rookie year, I had to defer to Mitch Richmond if we were on the court together, our team's best player that season. An on-court exchange we had during a game against the Minnesota Timberwolves follows:

> **Me:** Mitch, didn't you see me running the court hard? I was open. Why didn't you pass me the ball?
>
> **Mitch:** Fundy, my bad—I didn't see you.
>
> **Me:** (I'm open a second time under the basket.) Mitch, you missed me again on the mismatch. I had a mouse in the house. ("Mouse in the house" refers to a taller player being guarded by a shorter opponent.)

Mitch: Again, my bad.

Me: (I'm really upset as Mitch takes a jump shot immediately after our eyes meet. Had he passed me the basketball, I could have scored very easily.) Bro, I can't believe you didn't pass me the ball—you looked right at me.

Mitch: Fundy, listen. You have to get it off the glass, my man. ("Get it off the glass" was a kind way of saying that I had to rebound his missed shot attempts.)

I shook my head in disbelief at his candor, but he was right. If I wanted to impact the game, it was up to me to capitalize on the opportunities. No set plays were called for me, so I had no choice but to hustle and carve out my own niche. My time on the court was limited, and I had to maximize it. Although a role player, I worked just as hard as Mitch during practice, but he was the superstar. His shot attempts each game were decided in advance; mine were not. He was the face of the franchise, while I played a supporting role. He was the highest paid player, while I was not. He took the heat for the team's lackluster play, and I had the luxury of walking quietly by reporters who pressed Mitch for post-game comments.

It's flawed, but it's the way our system works in sports, business, and life. Fairness is not built into the capitalistic model because economic success isn't a zero-sum game. In other words, financial opportunities are not limited to the so-called privileged few. You don't have to be born into wealth to become a wealthier you. The moral of the basketball story is this: The poor and middle class should pursue the money ball, comprised of ordinary income from a job; portfolio income from stocks, bonds, or mutual funds; and passive activities such as rental real estate and intellectual property. Building significant wealth may take a while, but it's doable, and I know dozens of people who've achieved this goal on modest incomes. They profited from compound interest, instead of being a slave to it. Money ball shot attempts from a person's rebounding efforts are positively correlated. Cheering wildly in the stands, Uncle Sam will always be high-income taxpayers' biggest fan. You'll see why at the end of the next section.

> Income mobility isn't guaranteed in America, but the opportunity is. Don't let anyone convince you otherwise.

"The Working Poor and Lower Middle Class Pay Hardly Any Taxes"

Former presidential candidate Mitt Romney alleged during the 2012 campaign that 47 percent of Americans don't pay federal income taxes. What he failed to articulate was those people did pay FICA (or payroll) taxes, better known as Social Security and Medicare.

The poor are disproportionately hurt more by lifestyle taxes then either the traditional middle class or affluent. Gas and sales taxes, also known as regressive taxes, pinch resources the poor desperately need to get by. They also endure what I call the *punishment tax.*

A stressful living environment, lack of education and financial acumen, low-paying jobs, high incarceration rates, children born out of wedlock, too few positive role models, frequent trips to purchase high-margin items at nearby convenient stores, declining mental and physical health, and a vision that doesn't stretch beyond a week are brutally taxing to those enduring poverty's plight. Those earning a seven-figure income live outside of

> The *punishment tax* is a brutal condition the poor must endure to cope with life's unfortunate and, at times, unfair predicaments.

poverty's walls and have little clue what it is like to survive in the land of economic misery. The question to ask the super wealthy is if they would like to trade places with someone in a lower tax bracket.

The mega wealthy shouldn't feel guilty about their fortunes in contrast to the misfortune of the poor. Most SAPAs and GAPAs have worked hard and played by the rules. They have every right to voice their concern about the burgeoning tax gap. Budget shortfalls at the state and federal level make the wealthy easy targets to generate more tax dollars for government coffers. However, the very fact of being in the top echelon of earners is a cherished (and sometimes enviable) place in American society.

"I tell clients, 'Look, you are paying 50 cents on the dollar on total taxes. At least you still have 50 cents in which to spend or invest.' High-income earners and the super wealthy have advantages that they don't clearly see at times," Betty notes.

Before I close out this chapter, an important point needs to be made about tax misconceptions, which are symptomatic of a deeper problem most people are unaware of, or frankly, could care less about. In my conversations with people across the socioeconomic spectrum, all of them, to some degree, feel their payment of taxes is inherently unfair. The working poor and struggling middle class can barely keep their head above water in a sea of rising financial responsibilities. Many of them believe the wealthy should be taxed into oblivion since they were direct beneficiaries of tax cuts under former President George W. Bush (and to a certain extent, even President Ronald Reagan). Critics argue tax cuts and the war on terror have contributed to a record national debt. The wealthiest wage earners in America point out that their share of the federal income tax burden is onerous. As noted, the top 20 percent of wage earners pay the bulk of all federal income taxes. What about the bottom 20 percent of wage earners? Well, they typically receive a tax refund from Uncle Sam. This, too, many SAPAs and GAPAs fume, is unfair.

David Stockman, who served as the director of the Office of Management and Budget under President Reagan from 1981 to 1985, is not well liked today by Democrats or Republicans. He resigned from his post over 30 years ago because he couldn't convince fiscal hawks masquerading as big-government spenders in his party to pull back the purse strings. His pleas fell on deaf ears. David has since been sounding the clarion call for decades. Still, today he doesn't believe lower taxes for the wealthy or even middle class can ever work given our annual federal deficits and skyrocketing national debt. This annoys Republican leaders and right-leaning commentators greatly. David urges spending cuts across the board, even entitlements, to save our federal government a few needed bucks, infuriating those on the political left, too. One thing is certain: We're in big trouble folks.

ESTATE PLANNING

CHAPTER

31

BIGGEST ESTATE CONCERN

The overriding challenge or concern that a
socioeconomic group has when a loved one dies

Funeral Expenses

The biggest estate concern among the poor upon the death of a loved one is paying for the funeral. A full-court press is employed to find enough money for a respectable home-going for the decedent. Family members and friends are called, while GoFundMe accounts are established to generate empathy and cash. Businesses and nonprofit organizations are tapped to help pay for the funeral, which on average will cost between $8,000 to $10,000—an unexpected (or perhaps anticipated) expense the poor just can't meet.

One such incident I vividly recall occurred on a Sunday in late winter of 2016 as I was leaving my former church, The Wave Ministries, which was located in Whitehall and co-pastored by former NBA star and Olympic gold medalist Michael Redd and his best friend, Daniel Ortiz.

Whitehall is an economically challenged suburb on the east side of Columbus that has undergone a major transformation over the last two decades as inner-city residents have been pushed outward from the capital city to make room for revitalization efforts in and around downtown. In many respects, this suburb has some of the same challenges as inner-city communities shackled by generational poverty: low-income residents on government assistance, expanding hopelessness, rising fatherlessness, an overburdened school district, and senseless acts of violence that defy human logic. The suburbanization of poverty in America is a phenomenon that has been occurring for the past twenty-five years.

I was speaking with Jason Tyree, whom you read about in the section on functionally affluent-positioned Americans (FAPAs), near the front door next to the church parking lot. Two visibly distraught white young adults in their early 20s, a man and woman, entered the building and approached us. The man asked if he could speak with someone at the church. As filters, we asked if there was anything Jason and I could do to help. He told us a family member was recently

> "How someone dies is a key distinction between the social classes."
>
> **–Eric Seabrook**
> Life Coach and Attorney

killed by a madman with a machete, caught in the middle of a dispute between a female acquaintance and her boyfriend. The family didn't have any money to provide their loved one with a decent burial; the body had been in the county morgue for days. We were stunned by his frankness, recalling in graphic detail how this young person was brutally murdered.

Benny White, a funeral home owner and director with nearly 40 years of experience, is well-versed in estate matters, especially of low-income to middle-class families. He offers a socioeconomic perspective about the state of affairs for the typical impoverished family.

"A lot of times in poverty, the families don't have full-time jobs with benefits, life insurance for example, and they can't pay for the funeral," he says. "Their primary focus is making ends meet, providing a roof over their head and food in their bellies. Paying for the final expenses of a loved one is the farthest thing from their minds.

"They never think or plan ahead; it's about living life for today. They're reactive instead proactive, and their kids and grandkids grow up and follow in their footsteps because they don't know anything different," Benny says.

Some people consider financial solicitations through social media platforms, such as GoFundMe, to be embarrassing and distasteful. Critics assert it's inappropriate to ask people with no ties to the decedent to help pay for the funeral. During my NBA days, I received more than a dozen calls asking me to help someone with funeral expenses of an extended family member or acquaintance that I either had never met or seen in decades. I was never upset with the request but bristled at the underlining guilt that shrouded it. Was I obligated to intervene given the good fortune I enjoyed as a professional athlete, years removed from the debilitating clutches of poverty in the Sullivant Gardens housing projects? Sometimes I helped; at other times I did not.

A key reason a dignified funeral is so important to the poor is because they don't feel their lives are valued to the same degree as the middle class and wealthy. When the poor die, some leave behind a trail of heartache and misery that family members and friends can hardly bear. But how many of us in the middle and upper class really care?

As highlighted throughout the book, feelings or perceptions matter more to the poor than do the realities of empirical evidence. The poor do have a legitimate reason to feel their lives are without purpose, especially when the microscope zooms in on the lack of meaningful job opportunities, decent housing, safe neighborhoods, and low expectations set for them by those with little knowledge about the trauma associated with economic despair and perpetual stress. That's why I refuse to let participants from impoverished backgrounds who attend our self-empowerment programs trip over the bar of low expectations. Not under my watch!

Burial Arrangements

Too many people overlook this three-part plan when death enters the picture: How will our family pay for the funeral? Where will the deceased family member be buried? Which family member will serve as a point of contact and oversee burial arrangements?

The cost of saying goodbye isn't inexpensive. Pre-paid funerals and cremations are a growing market segment of the funeral home industry. Including end-of-life planning into your long-term financial strategy might alleviate potential monetary burdens children and family members are likely to absorb.

The middle class will usually have the resources to pay for a funeral. They have decent jobs that provide modest incomes and benefits. If their employer offers group life insurance, the employee and his spouse as well as children might be covered. They are more insulated or protected economically than the family in poverty. The bigger issues for them include the executor of the will (if one exists), overseer of the decedent's financial assets, and coordinator of the funeral and burial arrangements. Each can cause GISAs more angst than you might think.

Nobody wants family members bickering among themselves at the funeral of a loved one, but it happens. Common causes include sibling infighting, severing relationships with those who have alternate viewpoints, and threats about taking a family member to court. I have witnessed more than a dozen middle-class funerals that fit this description. The backlash reverberates long after the funeral has ended.

Estate Settlement

The generationally wealthy, or charities mentioned in the decedent's elaborate estate plan, will inherit significant assets, including cash, common stock, bonds, personal property, and life insurance proceeds, among many lucrative benefits.

Arguably, GAPAs' overriding concern when a key family member dies is whether the estate settlement matches the spirit and specifications of the will and trust documents. This arrangement is done in an orderly and efficient manner that, to an outside observer not acquainted with the ways of legacy wealth, can be misconstrued as callousness or insensitivity because it appears that the grieving process was bypassed or short-circuited to follow the minutest details per estate distribution or liquidation stipulations that were predetermined years, if not decades, in advance.

The generationally affluent are able to compartmentalize their despair so that feelings don't get in the way of structure and legacy continuity. I've attended numerous funerals of the poor and insanely wealthy. The intensity of wailing and sobbing that takes place is much more pronounced in poverty than affluence. Emotions may boil over during funeral proceedings for GEDAs, while GAPAs tend to keep a tight lid on supercharged feelings to avoid even the slightest attention-generating faux pas. Etiquette and decorum are always on display with GAPAs, regardless of the occasion. Death is final, yet funeral manners live on and must be followed with religious zeal. They, too, are learned through protocol and can't be compromised, no matter the circumstance.

32

ESTATE PLANNING TEAM

The key member(s) responsible for settling or overseeing the decedent's estate

MTP

The estate planning team for GEDAs usually consists of the MTP, or Most Trusted Person. This responsibility falls onto the shoulders of a parent, domestic partner, relative, or close friend. The higher up the socioeconomic ladder one goes, the more likely the team includes plenty of players with professional designations.

Decedents on the poor side of town likely will die without a will, which is known as dying intestate. In these cases, a probate court judge appoints someone to oversee the estate, which is inventoried and valued, and includes background information on heirs and communication with creditors. Excluded from the court's accounting are jointly held property with survivorship rights and payable upon death accounts. Life insurance policies and retirement accounts, whose assets are disbursed to named beneficiaries, bypass probate as well.

Clearing an estate through probate is an arduous process that can take months, if not years, to complete. This task is not for the faint at heart.

Overseeing administrator duties for someone in poverty may be an emotionally draining and time-consuming responsibility, even if the estate has but a few assets. The administrator must be organized, patient, emotionally stable, committed to filing paperwork promptly, and perhaps most important, able to follow concrete instructions.

MRC, MAC, AND STS

The traditional middle class designates an MRC, MAC, or STS to handle an estate's end-of-life affairs. The MRC (Most Responsible Child) typically oversees the care needs of an aging parent and settles the estate. Factors that help determine the MRC's worthiness include career path, personal discipline, organizational skills, emotional profile, and financial stability. The aforementioned factors might be bypassed for the selection of an MAC (Most Available Child), an important consideration if siblings live out of state. The STS (Spouse that Survives), whether ready or not, will manage all aspects of the estate when children aren't available, can't be trusted, or the cost of professional assistance is prohibitive.

You'd like to think that settling an estate would be a smooth process, and that is the case most of the time. However, it also can change on a dime when family caregivers feel entitled to certain assets that the decedent hasn't promised, or some of the children feel shortchanged and blocked out of the will. That is why contested wills, where one sibling believes another sibling unduly influenced an aging parent, are more prevalent today. Families may contest a will or trust document where the language is ambiguous and open to interpretation. If it ends up in court, family members might fight over the remains of the estate. It's something with which attorney Eric Seabrook has witnessed on numerous occasions.

"This speaks to what should be in a will," says Eric, who has nearly two decades of past experience handling estate matters. "A contest forfeiture clause might be instituted that says if a person contests the will, he forfeits his interest. This creates an incentive to accept your inheritance, even if you feel you deserve more."

Settling an estate is never an issue in generational affluence, but it can be quite problematic for the poor and middle class. Eric's clients have included hundreds of low- and middle-income individuals, and he says settling an estate can be an issue with GEDAs and GISAs. "You would be amazed how often an estate never gets settled. Someone will be driving the car of the decedent for months before the state notifies him to change the name on the registration and do a clean title," he says.

Eric estimates that about half the middle class dies without a will, which is surprising considering their educational and professional standing, and no-tably, conservative nature. They know it's important but delay getting it done.

For those who do set up a will, a short list of standard items is usually highlighted: a car, house, home equity, personal property, a modest savings or checking account, and a retirement account with a relatively small value.

"The real x-factor," Eric says, "do they have a life insurance policy? If it is through their job, it might be one-and-a-half times income or between $50,000 to $75,000. If there is a life insurance policy outside a job, it might not cover the funeral." One last point. Some families are barely able to cover the funeral costs. However, they'll spare no expense to look good at the home-going ceremony—a new wardrobe, an updated hair weave, and colorful fingernails that sparkle in the light.

CFP, FOP, CPA, WMA, CLU, JD, and PTB

The generationally wealthy have complicated estates with millions or billions of dollars in assets that must be preserved and protected by their team of experts. Key players of a GAPA's estate team include a CFP (Certified Financial Planner), FOP (Family Office Professional), CPA (Certified Public Accountant), WMA (Wealth Management Advisor), CLU (Chartered License Underwriter), JD (Juris Doctor/lawyer), and PTB (Personal Trusted Banker). A CFP or FOP manages the team. The CPA handles tax matters relating to the decedent's estate. The WMA distributes income-generating assets to vested beneficiaries, including the surviving spouse, children, and charities. The CLU discusses the particulars surrounding insurance proceeds. The JD is the lawyer who oversees legal matters. The PTB makes sure surviving family members have access to cash or assets in the trust.

I was meeting with a Planned Giving Representative (PGR) two years ago who expressed an interest in learning more about our nonprofit organization. A PGR helps the mega affluent donate money to charities aligned with their core values, while also offering insight on favorable tax considerations for philanthropic-minded GAPA and SAPA individuals and families. Part of our conversation follows:

> **Representative:** I have a client who sold a business for more than $100 million. But this opportunity didn't create the happiness he thought it would and said the accumulation of his newfound wealth was a hassle.
>
> **Me:** What do you mean?
>
> **Representative:** My client said most of his time is spent protecting the wealth instead of enjoying it. Meetings with accountants, lawyers, and financial advisors are a headache.
>
> **Me:** Interesting headache to have. (We laughed in agreement.)

This particular client is situationally wealthy. He amassed his fortune after selling a lucrative business, I presume, that catapulted him from the middle class to affluence. Obviously, SAPAs and FAPAs are entirely different from GAPAs, although most people see the three subsets from the same financial lens. However, key distinctions exist when estate planning enters the picture.

Civic duty and legacy continuity are not drudgery to GAPAs. Wealth is altruistic, an opportunity not to show off affluence as a fragrant offering of arrogance, but to emit an aroma of genuine compassion that is pleasing to the human soul. As noted, many GAPAs are giving the majority of their estate away by pledging it years before they die. To relinquish a sizable amount of their wealth by giving it to charitable entities speaks more to GAPAs' insistence to stay clear of handicapping their descendants with the trappings of inherited affluence than anything else. The situationally and functionally affluent, meanwhile, rarely move up to generational affluence because wealth is squandered by descendants who were never groomed for the task of legacy continuity.

33

LEGACY PROJECTION

The image and identifying traits that best describe how the decedent or loved one will be commemorated by family members, friends, colleagues, and community stakeholders

"Personality Lives On"

When someone dies in a poor community, his or her outward features are celebrated at the funeral and long after the death occurred.

Commemorative qualities might include the person's sense of humor, athletic talents, culinary skills, charisma, street cred, and even procreative abilities. Pictures of the former athlete are displayed next to the casket. Family members, friends, and homies share stories and eyewitness accounts regarding the decedent's wit, charm, and penchant for having a good time.

What's so interesting about this form of self-expression is the manner in which these traits and habits are employed during life to divert attention from the person's depressing economic predicament while standing out or standing up to their peers, which is something I know very well. Shifting attention from the pain or internal turmoil of fatherlessness and financial misery and lack of opportunity is an acceptable and natural reaction in poverty.

An individual's memory is kept alive through graffiti murals, community demonstrations, tattoos, and T-shirts. Eric Seabrook shares, "I have a friend who owns a screen-printing business. We had a discussion one day about this phenomenon you identify in *Socio-psychonomics*. One of the things the poor do, particularly in the black community, is that we'll create a rest-in-peace T-shirt to celebrate

> A life sets a legacy in motion, while death continues it.

the death of a person. A T-shirt is significant for a very brief moment because it'll fade when it's washed, gets lost, or eventually, is thrown away. It is a physical item that represents the transition from life to death."

As the T-shirt fades, so do the memories of the loved one who died because his legacy footprint—a bankable commodity in which others can (and should) draw from—was never firmly established during life. A life sets a legacy in motion, while death continues it.

"Character Lives On"

At a middle-class funeral, mourners reflect on the inward qualities of the decedent who embodied the spirit of sacrifice. They pay their respects with praise, describing the decedent with what my wife calls middle class buzz words—loyal, responsible, faithful, reliable, dependable, trustworthy, and hard worker. These types of qualities forever endear me, a poor kid from the ghetto, to the middle class.

Two men, John "Fatman" Hardiman and Phil Henry, former little league coaches of mine on opposite sides of the racial spectrum, profoundly helped shape my blue-collar work ethic and commitment to others. Their funerals were attended by hundreds of people, each reflecting on their life of service. John, an African-American, was a father to three children and a surrogate dad to several hundred white and black children living in the "Bottoms," a poverty-stricken community in West Columbus near downtown. He was a tireless social servant who worked extended hours at Gladden Community Center and other social service agencies for decades, but without the commensurate overtime pay. Didn't matter. John cared only about saving the lives of children that society wrote off as hopeless misfits, destined for a life of teen pregnancies, crime, and revolving incarceration. Sitting in the back of the church at his home-going, I wept as his eulogy was read. He was the catalyst behind our nonprofit entity, the Lawrence Funderburke Youth Organization (www.LFYO.org). He helped us secure our tax-exempt status in 1998, and we are still changing legacies, not just lives. I am still very close with Peggy, John's widow, who was married to him for 34 years. Rest in peace with the Lord, Fatman. Job well done.

Phil was a white Columbus Police Department officer for several decades. Although he and his family lived in the prestigious Upper Arlington suburb, Phil was a native of the Bottoms, a blend of inner-city blacks and Appalachian whites who shared one thing: economic distress. It was a place where the welfare recipients and underpaid workers struggled to make ends meet each day. For the kids, participating in sports at the Westside Boys and Girls Club was a racial unifier back in the early 1980s, just a little more than a decade removed from the Civil Rights Movement. Other than skin color, there weren't many differences between poor blacks and poor whites. Poverty's residual effects then and now don't discriminate on the basis of race, gender, or religion.

Phil embraced us as our Little League football coach, just as he did his four children. For a white guy and a police officer, he had a peculiar air about him, though it wasn't pretentious. He tilted his police cap to the side like a "brother." His measured walk displayed confidence as well as give-and-take respect. We only saw him in a police uniform at practices, which he attended after work. For the black players, Coach Phil was the only white police officer that we knew and trusted personally. In the 'hood, cops were viewed as troublemakers, but he certainly changed our perspective.

Coach Phil did a lot to keep us poor kids out of trouble. He even allowed the entire team to spend the night at his home, which incidentally, was my first trip to an affluent suburb. His funeral was an honor to attend, complete with heartwarming tributes from colleagues and dignitaries befitting a man of valor.

"Heritage Lives On"

Whereas poverty is outwardly focused on personal qualities, the legacy of affluence projects forward. GAPAs take measures to ensure the family's brand, heritage, and goodwill continue unabated from one generation to the next. This systematic approach to legacy continuity moves children and grandchildren to fulfill their potential—personally, educationally, financially, and philanthropically. GAPAs embody the spirit of former Ohio State football coaching legend, Woody Hayes's pay-it-forward doctrine. This duty isn't optional for GAPAs but obligatory, a rite of passage required by each family member regardless of gender.

Commemorative traits of GAPAs include philanthropist, investor, visionary, legacy progenitor, trendsetter and change agent, proactive, and altruistic. Accolades are highlighted in the funeral program without pretense. Family members, friends, and colleagues praise the decedent for a life well lived, free of the trappings of material wealth but full of personal enrichment in helping others achieve success. Attendees measure the weight of the decedent's balance sheet by his compassion for humanity and the charitable causes his wealth will support well into the future.

While laughter is perfectly appropriate at a home-going for a GEDA, it may be quite distasteful at a GAPA's funeral ceremony, where the atmosphere is somber and serious. The tone, tenor, and temperament of a clergy member presiding over a funeral proceeding for a GEDA of African-American descent will resemble an emotionally charged Sunday sermon with references for attendees to accept the Lord Jesus and turn away from their misdeeds since no one knows the day or the hour of death. I've attended a few GAPA funerals and must admit that an emotional plea isn't the preferred method to change someone's heart. In fact, introspection and self-reflection, in their way of thinking, are individually inspired. Sustained transformation is rational and happens organically. The legacy progenitor and change agent in the customized casket wouldn't have it any other way.

CHAPTER

34

INHERITORS' INHERITANCE

The dreams, debts, and duties beneficiaries receive or are required to fulfill after a family member passes

Dreams

The death of a child, regardless of the age, leaves behind unfulfilled promises, unrealized potential, or tragic outcomes, which then are usually inherited by a parent, grandmother, or trustworthy relative.

The child may have been seen as the proverbial meal ticket or financial savior born to take care of the family. The pressure a child born into poverty feels to be the family provider when a special talent or gift of his has been identified is challenging but surprisingly manageable. I speak from experience.

In my case, being the family meal ticket was something I embraced. I never felt pressured or forced to accept this responsibility. In fact, it was an honor to fulfill a promise I made to my mother as a little boy, that I would buy her a home one day if the opportunity presented itself; she'd never have to live in the projects again. I never regretted the economic support that I provided Ma Dukes and my sisters as a professional athlete. As the "man of the household," it was my duty, though I had no idea what the responsibility entailed. Like most other aspects of authentic manhood, this, too, was a trial-and-error experience.

I know of 10 people I grew up with who were murdered or died before they reached 25. One of my neighborhood peers, "MeeMee," who lived just a few apartment buildings over from our unit, was one of them. MeeMee was smart, beautiful, and possessed an angelic smile that lit up a room. She was the dream girl of every boy in Sullivant Gardens without a doubt, and an incredibly talented singer with a promising music career. Her life was cut short by an enraged boyfriend, jealous of the attention she was receiving on the national and international level. She was ready to sever the relationship, but not before he took her life.

SOCIOPSYCHONOMIC FILTER

Roughly 70 percent of inner-city children in the African-American community are born out of wedlock. Fatherlessness is an epidemic of jaw-dropping proportions, scarring the male and female children born to absent fathers for the rest of their lives.

As a child, I attended the funeral of my neighbor and friend, Shawn Farmer. He died before the age of 12, and I'm still not sure about the cause of death, although I believe it was accidental. Shawn was smart and had a magnetic personality that deterred neighborhood enemies. He had a knack for making friends with jocks and troublemakers alike. He could dance, which attracted attention from the young ladies in our housing project.

His death had a profound impact on my life because it seemed so unfair to see someone my age lying in a casket. Also, as I was riding in the car to the funeral home with several of Shawn's family members, I'll never forget the sickening perfume of a woman sitting next to me. Literally, it almost made me gag. She must have sprayed the entire bottle on her blouse, a putrid rose-scented fragrance. I had to plug my nose until we arrived at the funeral home. In a weird way, I equated Shawn's untimely death with her odorous perfume. Both smelled really bad and will always be entrenched in my memory bank.

I could describe countless examples of other young people from impov-erished communities—inner city and Appalachian—who died too soon and left behind their unfulfilled dreams. What is so sad is that the vast majority of them didn't even make it to 40. Drug overdoses, suicides, drive-by shootings, savage beatings, and being caught at the wrong place at the wrong time snuffed out a life of promise and unlimited potential.

I visited the London Correctional Prison 10 years ago to direct a documentary. My life went one way and a high school teammate of mine, Lonnie Jones, took a completely different path. An outstanding basketball player in his own right, Lonnie got caught up in the drug game, the fast life of easy money, and the trappings that come with each. He spent near-

> The phrase "gone too soon" is an unfortunate and often unavoidable predicament of the landscape of generational poverty.

ly a decade in prison but has since turned his life around and accompanied me on several speaking engagements to enlighten inner-city youth on the perils of the thug life. He now holds a steady job and keeps himself away from trouble that could send him back to prison. Lonnie says, "I wasted nearly a decade of my life behind bars." Prison or a juvenile facility, not just a graveyard, is another place where a young person's potential gets buried.

Ben Wilson was a basketball phenom from Chicago in the mid-1980s, a can't-miss recruit who had every Division I powerhouse pursuing him. One of my teammates with the Sacramento Kings, Nick Anderson, himself a top-five prep star, played on the same team with Ben at Simeon High. I'll never forget the conversation Nick and I had about Ben during a flight to play an out-of-town game.

Ben was a silky smooth player whose potential had no bounds. He was shot November 21, 1984, outside a convenience store in Chicago and died the next day from complications. I asked Nick about the shooting.

"You know how it is in the 'hood," Nick said. "He got shot for no good reason. Man, he would have been a huge NBA star if he were still alive. No question about it."

Today, senseless violence in the inner city and rising drug overdoses in rural communities are derailing the goals and dreams of impoverished children who carry them until their untimely demise. What a tragedy it is for our country to witness tens of thousands of our young people never making it to their Second Quarter of Life.

"From 2011 to 2016, we've presided over 50 funerals for people younger than 25 years old," says Benny White. "Now multiply this times the number of other inner-city funeral homes scattered across the country and you'll get tens of thousands of funeral proceedings. We are in the business of burying the dead, but we wish this weren't the case for these young men who, quite often, lived a very short and confusing life.

"You would think that a young person who sees one of his peers laying in a casket in a permanent state of sleep would want to change his life. No, he cries at the funeral and then goes right back out to the street seeking revenge and never learns the lesson that death is final—game over. Life is not valued, theirs or anyone else's. These young people are looking for an identity, something or someone to relate to while they attempt to fill the void or pain in their own lives," Benny says.

Debts

Death brings challenges to the middle class, and those who inherit the decedent's assets and debts are left pondering a slew of questions. Will mom be able to stay in the house? What financial resources are available to help mom through this transition in her life? Who will take the lead in dealing with mom's elder care and financial needs? When mom dies, will someone be emotionally attached to the home? These types of questions may have been asked before a loved one's death, but without exploring a clearly defined strategy to deal with them.

Even without a legal or an enforceable document in place, GISAs will still honor the intangible and tangible debts of the decedent. Typically, intangible debts are connected to a personal or relational asset—a physically challenged surviving spouse unable to care for herself or a beloved pet. Tangible debts are attached to a physical or material asset, such as a house or automobile. A mortgage, auto loan payment, or another maintenance expense would be paid by the debt-holder to carry on the decedent's legacy. This financial and emotional burden can create enormous friction and infighting between vested beneficiaries if the responsibility falls to the family member with the "deepest pockets" or most accommodative schedule. Invariably, he or she or they will feel that the weight of this responsibility isn't fairly distributed.

Randy Brooks, the prototypical GISA, grew up in a tight-knit, blue-collar neighborhood in Central Florida. He is a close friend and a stand-in big brother to me. Randy handles the estate of his deceased mother, Lauretta

O'Brien, who went home to be with the Lord on October 17, 2014. She was one of the funniest and kindest people I've ever met and will always hold a special place in my heart.

Before she died, Lauretta left Randy and his sister, Kim, with clear-cut directives, although no estate plan existed before her death. Before she passed, Lauretta gave them specific instructions to keep the house for emergency purposes in case one of her children falls on hard times, gets sick, or needs a place to stay. The brother and sister feel obligated to honor the intangible and tangible debts associated with their mother's wishes. However, Randy thinks the responsibility should be more evenly spread among all the siblings. He says, "Kim and I pay the property taxes and maintenance bills. But there are three other children in the picture who could potentially benefit if misfortune comes their way and they need temporary lodging. We need a solution to this situation because what exists presently isn't working financially."

> An inheritance of debts encompasses more than just financial obligations; sometimes they include emotional and sacrificial responsibilities as well.

Fortunately, the house does not have a mortgage attached to it and Randy holds the title. He might be the exception rather than rule because for many middle-class families, an active mortgage exists after the death of a beloved family member. They may have equity in the home, but who can pay off the house or maintain the property? This could prove more challenging when children live in different cities or states. Will a home be sold or signed over to a nursing home to pay for the care of an aging parent?

Duties

We know the generationally wealthy have a duty to carry their legacies forward, so when a patriarch or matriarch dies, their wishes are reflected in trust documents that spell out the civic, cultural, and career duties survivors must fulfill.

These traditions are based on GAPAs' values, and are carefully constructed with the utmost care. They do fret about their children catching affluenza, a psychological condition that recognizes the feelings of social isolation, guilt, and lack of motivation some wealthy people might experience. However, a more pressing, deep-seated worry for the generationally wealthy is passing the legacy baton: Will the transition be seamless or fumbled?

Sports fanatics stand in amazement as they watch their favorite athletes electrify the crowd with game-winning goals in a championship game. The civic duty in which GAPAs carry out their legacy is nothing short of astonishing as well. The commitment to improve the lives of others through philanthropic efforts isn't done for media exposure, fanfare, or recognition. No, the generationally wealthy often support charitable causes, donating billions of dollars to worthwhile causes, in the spirit of anonymity. Cultural duties encompass the ethnic struggles and triumphs that have shaped each GAPA's philanthropic identity, while no journey is taken without the compass of faith and fortitude. These qualities belie a confident assurance in a GAPA's ability to succeed in every endeavor of life and are carved from career duties that include continuous learning and fulfilling one's economic potential. GAPAs gravitate to professions without an income ceiling—business, law, finance, and medicine—while expecting family members to follow.

SOCIOPSYCHONOMIC FILTER
Duty, not drudgery, is an embedded component in fulfilling a GAPA decedent's wishes to the minutest of details.

GAPAs apply the same diligence and detail to the spirit of civic pride as they do in the creation of new or continuing wealth. What will remain into perpetuity is a family's brand and legacy, which are distinctions that separate GAPAs from every other socioeconomic class subset. They work together in a synergistic fashion, binding together unique values, traits, and beliefs that form GAPAs' philanthropic DNA. Legacy fulfillment and continuity are the inheritors' responsibilities to further the family brand.

Although he wasn't born into generational affluence, Les Wexner is the first person in Columbus, Ohio, that comes to mind when this classification is mentioned and perhaps that's because he is the CEO of L Brands, a Fortune 500 company. Or maybe it's because he turned a $5,000 loan from his aunt in 1963 into a multibillion-dollar empire in less than 40 years while increasing shareholder value exponentially. Or perhaps as one friend who works for the company put it, "Les isn't afraid to shake things up. Initially, his suggestions may defy common sense, but the outcomes are usually quite beneficial."

Attorney Eric Seabrook asks, "What will Columbus look like after Les Wexner dies?" In the world of philanthropy, his fingerprints touch every corner of our state's capital.

"It's going to be interesting to see who acts as the surrogate or replacement for his charitable footprint, which should, in all likelihood, continue its present course," Eric notes. "Perhaps the overseer will be his wife Abigail or one of his children. Whoever it is, he or she or they will stay on message. The script will be followed to the exact detail."

Indeed, Les Wexner has had such a profound influence on Central Ohio in so many ways, including at our alma mater, The Ohio State University, in New Albany, voted the best suburb to live in America, and countless nonprofit organizations. Eric's rhetorical question is a movie reel getting repeated by GAPAs across the country, whose charitable footprint will continue long after their passing.

CHAPTER

35

BUSINESS CONTINUITY

The plan (or lack thereof) for a successor to operate or grow a business in the event of an owner's incapacity, illness, or death

Stop

A misconception exists that every one who is poor receives some type of government assistance or taxpayer-funded support. In fact, some GEDAs are business owners. The working poor operate small businesses all across this landscape we call America, and they struggle daily to generate enough cash to keep the doors open. They often don't generate enough revenues to pay themselves a living wage. In essence, they are wage poor. They work hard, but are held captive to the whims of recessions, consumer spending levels, deeper-pocketed competitors, neighborhood blight, criminal mischief, and a predominately low-income customer base.

A business closing in my neighborhood always piqued my interest as a child. One day it was there; the next day, it was gone. I never knew the reason. Was the catalyst an unforeseen misfortune, or as many people in economic misery would call it, bad luck? As I got older, I gained further insight on the perplexing nature of poverty. Life, health, food, appearance, relationships, skills, opportunities, jobs, and money seem to last only for a time when you're poor. Enjoy or hold on for dear life to the moment while it lasts, because it does come with an unknown expiration date that eventually will break your heart. Why would running a business be any different?

Poverty is suffocating and overly cynical. Yes, it's possible to develop a middle-class or affluent mindset; the choice is always available but not easy to make. This is why *Sociopsychonomics* was written. However, the fear of poverty never leaves even when you escape its surroundings. A new frame of reference must supplant the old way of thinking. As one pastor shared during a Sunday morning sermon, "Something familiar doesn't automatically have to be fatal."

Success doesn't have to come with an expiration date and can extend from one generation into perpetuity if deliberately planned. However, it won't happen by accident or a series of fortuitous events.

Businesses fail for a variety of reasons. Look at Silicon Valley where failure is celebrated. Why? Lessons are learned by entrepreneurs, and an updated frame of reference can be used to navigate around or avoid future problems. Of course, some actions should never be repeated while inactions to do the right thing at the right moment are contributing success killers, too. It's certainly easy to pursue a business dream when you have an MBA from an elite university and the financial backing and mentoring support from venture capitalists as a backstop. But the poor don't have access to these amenities, which are glaringly obvious regarding business continuity. They often run their operations through a hit-and-miss strategy, where an orderly system of checks and balances is rarely considered. Oftentimes, the owner is the business. No wall of separation exists between the two, and when he or she dies, so does the venture.

From the standpoint of poverty, the following factors explain why business ends at death or when the owner is incapacitated or ill for any length of time:

- The business was built on the name recognition of the owner.

- Succession planning is never (or rarely) considered.

- Expertise is not shared with employees or family members, especially the ingredients and formulas that make the business successful. Betrayed trust is a huge problem in poverty to overcome.

- Financing options are unavailable to keep the business going when cash flow dries up.

- Guidance from mentors to operate, maintain, and grow a successful business were never offered to or accepted by the owner.

Pause

It's a little different for businesses guided by owners with a middle-class mindset. If he or she should die, the business may go through a transitional period until another leader emerges to run it. The collective skill-sets by committee, an employee group, or family members keep operations going in the interim. Customers still get serviced and payroll is met. Like their GEDA brethren, GISA business owners might think about

> This shouldn't be the case, but succession planning is a back-burner issue for the typical middle-class business owner.

a succession plan while they're alive, but they fail to incorporate it before they die. It's very hard for them to relinquish control of the business to someone, even a blood relative, who hasn't put in the same level of financial resources and sweat equity.

Succession planning recruits and grooms employees to move into positions of leadership pending the departure of an owner or other key employees. They are chosen in advance, and by the time their predecessor leaves, they know what to do, how to do it, and when to do it, making sure the company doesn't skip a beat. Succession planning is a vital tool for small and large businesses.

Provisions may have been made to transfer legal ownership of the business to heirs, but the blueprint to maintain and grow the business was never discussed. Or, the next generation may have operational control but lack the skills and expertise to keep the business going. If it's a family business, is it a self-sustaining entity or does it require active involvement by family members who inherit a portion of the entire operation? In this type of business, it is only as strong as the surviving family members holding operational control.

"There's a family-owned business here in my hometown of Augusta that is run by several brothers," Eric Seabrook says. "The father who founded the company died several decades ago, and the business has never had consistent growth. It provides a living for the brothers and their extended families, but they have to work the business. In effect, they are employees and not business owners. There is no such thing as being a silent partner or sideline equity owner with their business arrangement."

Our new economy requires a certain level of sophistication in a highly competitive marketplace where customer loyalty isn't a sure bet as in the past. New-school inheritors—their children and grandchildren—may be short on skills but tall on vision, a stark contrast to their parents and grandparents. Children are more apt to outsource to a manufacturer the family's secret recipe that has been built or protected in-house for decades. The parents are old school and prefer a hands-on approach to every aspect of the business, though times are changing as profit margins get squeezed further. The two sides stand generations apart on a business succession plan that should merge operational values of the past with modern touches of the present. It will take patience and trust for this to happen, but it needs to occur before it's too late.

Play

Business succession planning in poverty for mom-and-pop operations is a non-thought; it's not considered. For the middle class, it is an afterthought, not on the radar screen until a triggering event occurs. For the informed wealthy, it is forethought because they leave nothing to chance.

Dave Thomas, the face of Wendy's right up until his death, appeared in hundreds of commercials for the company that helped boost its market share. He was a guest speaker in my business marketing class at Ohio State and discussed his company's values and provided us with several keys to personal and professional success. He ran Wendy's by middle-class attributes and the motto his grandmother instilled in him as a child that said, "Don't cut corners."

The passing of Dave Thomas may have had a negative impact on short-term sales and the company's stock price over this same period, but his death didn't permanently cripple the company. Pre-emptive measures taken by legacy-minded board members were implemented to account for Dave Thomas's declining health. According to a *CNN Money* article written by Lenora Chu, "Wendy's board had in years prior [to his death] already moved [him] out of the operational leadership role and named a longtime veteran to the company's chairmanship."[25]

Some businesses never recover when a company founder dies, especially if he or she were featured in memorable commercials pitching products
and services to captivated customers. Companies without a finely tuned succession plan will have a tough time surviving in our current marketplace.
The perfectly timed moment is unlikely to appear for an in-depth discussion
of this sensitive subject. However, somebody has to come forward and run
the risk of stepping on someone's toes, even those of a revered founder or
company executive.

Death is inevitable. The generationally wealthy start with the end in mind.
A succession plan marks the end of the oxygen journey, but the lifeblood of
a business founded by a GAPA never dies. In fact, the brand's way of doing
business—it's operational DNA—is self-perpetuating. Once policies and procedures for business excellence are set in motion, success continues its course
as if the GAPA-decedent were still alive, according to the blueprint of the
wealth progenitor.

Remember, the situationally and generationally affluent see time as a
continuous loop, a nonrenewable resource that cannot be replenished. That's
why they'll pay whatever amount to compress the effect time has on their
tight-knit schedules by purchasing a fractional interest or outright ownership
in a private jet, planning their calendar one year in advance, or hiring a family
office to manage their financial affairs. Time is worth far more to them than
money. On the whole, the poor are ambivalent to time; they see it as static
and elastic. The middle class maintains a stop-start perspective on time. How
people see time typically is representative of the social class in which they were
reared as a child, which often spills over to every aspect of their adult life,
including the world of business.

Business continuity for the generationally wealthy is a seamless transition.
Like their legacy, it is transgenerational. A business doesn't stop or pause upon
the death of family members, regardless of their positional authority within a
company or social circle. Included in succession planning is how the business
ownership will get transferred or sold at death. A cautionary approach by the
mega wealthy always considers the well-being of others first. They ensure
surviving spouses, family members, shareholders, and carefully crafted legacies
are protected in a business transaction.

Business attorney Michael Anthony has been a close friend since high
school. His family welcomed me into their home in the suburbs to see another
world that was far different from mine. He says what should go into a succession

and ownership transfer plan for solely owned or partnership agreements rests upon the business's size, scope, and value. Forward thinking owners, not just the super wealthy, would be well-advised to consider either a buy-sell agreement or cross-purchase plan. A buy-sell agreement arranges for a third party, key employee, or partner to purchase a partial or complete interest in a business. Cross-purchase plans typically use life insurance proceeds to buy out the decedent partner's interest or proportionate share.

Mike says legal disputes can become really terse between the surviving family and the business's other partners, especially if a competent business attorney is not employed.

"It can get real nasty if documents aren't in place to protect both sides when a business owner or partner dies," he says. "A spouse or family member may want to wrestle control away or exert undue influence on a business she may know nothing about." The generationally wealthy have likely instituted a business continuation or transfer plan that would prevent such a headache from ever happening. They are always thinking about the pros and cons of their many business dealings that transcend both the life and death of any single family member.

CHAPTER
36

PHILANTHROPY

The process by which an individual, family, or organization administers, receives, or initiates a charitable offering

Receiver

Growing up in abject poverty, our family had to rely on benevolent offerings to supplement our welfare check. We would not have been able to survive without charitable assistance. In economic distress with no relief in sight, you're always thinking about being on the receiving end of charity and philanthropy, never initiating them. For the generationally poor, the necessities of life are so great that the focus is more inward rather than outward. This is not the case with the situationally or functionally poor who refuse to be seen as charity cases. Pride prevents them from accepting any semblance of a handout, even when they need or are entitled to it.

The entrenched poor know how to navigate the benevolence landscape to fulfill their needs. Government assistance programs and charitable organizations that provide food, clothing, and housing are sought out. Eric Seabrook notes, "They know the sources to go to, so they learn how to operate in their sphere of sustenance, but they never move past immediacy of needs or the basics of life. And to a large extent, this also applies to the middle class with their over-reliance on education and a secure job with guaranteed benefits. How do you get people to move toward self-sufficiency financially?"

There's always a small contingency of the poor who escape the clutches of economic distress. The key is to enlarge these numbers so that the vicious cycle is broken forever.

> "Charity is impulse-driven giving; philanthropy, on the other hand, is intent-driven giving with a strategic purpose."
>
> **–Steve Moore**
> Director for Donor Services and Development
> The Columbus Foundation

"BEAM ME UP, MR. FUNDY"

How do you help the poor develop a legacy mindset of self-sufficiency while moving beyond immediacy of needs? The solution isn't as daunting as one might assume. Enlarge their frame of reference, change their Sociopsychonomic filter in how they handle financial opportunities and setbacks, and reprogram their financial GPS to escape the land of lack but go back to pull others out. The atmosphere of wealth creation must be non-threatening and full of merit-based encouragement. False praise handicaps the poor even more.

Abstract or theoretical concepts work well in affluence but usually have difficulty gaining traction with the poor when first introduced. To appreciate the language of wealth, the poor must understand and retain it through a salient experience that is easily recalled from their hippocampus, where long-term memories are stored. These memories are often triggered by the emotionally charged amygdala and olfactory bulb, where the sense of smell resides. Both are housed in the temporal lobe. The poor must be transported from their landscape of perpetual need—literally, figuratively, and emotionally—and shown what economic success looks like from an aerial vantage point with clearly defined boundaries, roadblocks, and destination markers. Of course, they also need people strategically placed along the journey to cheer them on when their emotions scream, "Give up now! You'll never make it!"

Facilitator

Most government and nonprofit employees typically come from middle-class backgrounds, but never see themselves on the same plane as the wealthy, regardless of their annual income and interaction with them. GISAs assume that to do so would rub against their blue-collar nature and positional standing on the socioeconomic ladder. They avoid financial extremes, preferring the safety and security middle income provides, which is comfortably above the poverty threshold but well below a life of abundance.

As noted throughout the book, the fragility of their financial world hinges on a stable job with benefits, adequate savings to support lifestyle demands, and homeownership that they think will supplement retirement shortfalls. Most middle-class Americans also are woefully behind in funding their children's college expenditures and wait until college is upon a child before considering a tuition payment plan. A similar track is taken with estate planning that many of them ignore until a triggering event like a death occurs.

I am equally comfortable being around GEDAs, GISAs, and GAPAs. A person's socioeconomic status does not affect my level of comfort in their presence; it's how I've interacted with each since I was a teenager. Although her circle of connections is extensive, my wife is most at ease with those who, like her, grew up in the traditional middle class. It is a safe space for her. Being around extreme poverty or in the presence of mega wealth can be discomforting to Monya.

SOCIOPSYCHONOMIC FILTER

The mega wealthy may set up a fund at a charitable entity, but will in all likelihood not work there.

Although a segment of middle-class facilitators believe they have a peer-to-peer relationship with SAPAs and GAPAs, many GISAs who administer benevolent offerings on behalf of the wealthy display a mindset of deference, particularly if they have a longstanding connection to the world of affluence without growing up in it.

They may have attended elite private schools together and played on the same sports teams with affluent children, but the subliminal message reverberating within the ears of the typical, servant-oriented GISA is this: "I am content being the facilitator of charitable donations made by affluent philanthropists to disenfranchised communities. I am too proud to be on the receiving end of benevolent support, but too scared of the responsibility that über wealth brings in providing financial assistance to organizations that serve the poor. I'm in a stable place right now."

Donor

The generationally wealthy do care about the poor, but don't fully understand the challenges GEDAs face due to their insulated lives. I'm reminded of a cartoon I saw as a kid where a king and queen lived in a castle with a moat around it. Entrance to or from the castle was over a drawbridge using a lever inside the castle. GAPAs may assume—wrongly, I might add—that the complexities of affluence are too daunting for the average person to grasp. Thus, wealth-empowerment programs for the poor aren't necessarily high on their charitable radar screen. Why not?

A 2013 article in *The Atlantic* magazine said "not one of the top 50 individual charitable gifts [in 2012] went to a social service organization or to a charity that principally serves the poor and the dispossessed."[26] GAPAs, like the poor and middle class who give to religious or social service organizations, donate money to causes within their sphere of influence. Affinity giving—not the intentional neglect of the poor—is usually the underlying theme of the planned giving habits of the mega wealthy. Charitable support and bequests are given in concert with their philosophical and intellectual footprint, which is a world away from the plight of poverty. However, the irony here is that organizations GAPAs support are often located within a few miles of poorer communities, especially in or near the heart of their respective cities.

The wealthy attend philanthropy celebrations and cocktail receptions in honor of their generosity while taking the safest route possible to reach their intended destination. They may drive by the face of poverty, which doesn't register with GAPAs' logical way of thinking. Explain poverty to the wealthy in their language without emotional guilt, however, and see what happens.

Their charitable frame of reference will be enlarged to support causes that assist and empower the poor. Exposure to empowerment programs that enable the poor to build personal and financial assets is the key, which GAPAs have in abundance and GEDAs desperately need to escape poverty's clutches.

The following characteristics and attributes, each starting with the letter "h," are common among generationally wealthy donors:

- **Harmony:** charitable giving is always aligned with family values, traditions, and strategic initiatives.

- **Humility:** often prefer public anonymity when making charitable donations.

- **Homework:** due diligence is required before considering a donation to a nonprofit organization.

- **Honesty:** recipients of charitable dollars must be good stewards of the financial support and provide an extensive accounting of the money's use.

- **Hands-On:** entire family, across multiple generations, is involved in the charitable-giving process.

- **Hierarchy:** consultants and planned giving representatives (PGR) follow a chain of command in the administration and execution of the charitable-giving process.

- **Habitual:** logic, not emotion-based giving, is the filter used in the charitable-giving process.

- **Heritage**: legacy continuation is a critical and enduring component of the charitable-giving process.

CHAPTER

37

ESTATE PLANNING MISCONCEPTIONS

The erroneous assumptions that are characteristic of a representative social class in regard to incapacity, end-of-life, and charitable donations

"I Don't Have Anything; Only Rich People Need Estate Planning"

The poor make the mistake of thinking they don't need estate planning. They do. Unfortunately, they typically don't have the financial resources to pay a lawyer to create a will, advance directives, and designate healthcare and financial power of attorney documents. A basic estate plan can cost between $500 and $2,000—depending on the depth of expertise sought. Fees associated with incapacity and end-of-life plans vary by region.

Jim Feibel is an estate attorney and personal friend with nearly 60 years of experience helping clients across the socioeconomic spectrum. His typical client has a net worth between $1 million and $5 million, but recently Jim assisted a poor family in a probate court proceeding that took several months to resolve. He offered the services pro bono and encourages more attorneys to do the same for impoverished communities given their lack of knowledge in estate matters, though an ominous or early death (with plenty of warning signals) is a regular occurence in the land of economic heartache.

"The state initiates a will for the poor or anyone who dies without creating a valid will," he says. "Even at the most basic level, the poor should have a will drawn up because the one that the state oversees may not be suitable for their situation."

Jim says the estate value of the family he helped was less than $50,000, but sibling dynamics complicated things. The parents passed and left their five adult children with a home that was worth only $36,000. One of the five children was nearly beaten to death over a drug deal gone bad and had to spend a considerable amount of time recovering in the hospital. For much of his life, Jim points out, he's been involved in illegal activities.

"If the parents had thought about it, they probably wouldn't have left anything to this child. Let's assume he had significant debts and a creditor placed a lien on the house; then the other four kids are put in jeopardy for their portion of the home. This particular scenario happens more often than you think," Jim says.

Guardianship of children or dependents is another area of estate planning that few low- and middle-income families address. Very few parents want to go there. A dependent includes a child younger than 18 or an adult family member who cannot care for himself. A legal guardian would be responsible in caring for the needs of a dependent.

SOCIOPSYCHONOMIC FILTER

If you have a body with oxygen in it and just even a few prized possessions, then you, too, still need an estate plan.

Selecting guardians for our children in case something fatal happens to both of us was one of the hardest decisions my wife and I have made. Shared values, the guardians' age, residency, and competency were important considerations we used in the decision-making process. Fortunately, we have family and friends willing to hold this power of appointment. We trust the representatives selected would be good stewards in the development and surrogate parenting of our children.

Finding suitable guardians to care for a decedent's child(ren) is a limited option for the poor. If a child has a special need, who will take care of her? Who will make healthcare decisions on behalf of a parent when he is unable? The poor are trying to stay afloat in turbulent financial waters, and estate planning is the farthest thing from their minds. "It's the iceberg that most of them never see coming; it's headed straight for their small boat," says Benny White, owner and director of White's Funeral & Cremation Services here in Columbus.

"We'll Eventually Get to Estate Planning"

An early (and tragic) death is more common in poverty than the middle class. GEDAs accept death as inevitable, while GISAs prefer to not think about dying until a triggering event forces them to deal with it. They don't consider estate planning a pressing consideration since their date of death isn't something they can predict, but eventually plan for it to occur sometime in the Fourth Quarter of Life. They'll calculate how much life they have left to live when the horn sounds for the end of the Third Quarter of Life, somewhere between the age of 60 to 65. The funeral home has been contacted to estimate the cost. Burial plots are prepaid as the lens of dying clears. They assume death will result from cancer, heart disease, diabetes, or mental illness. They're sure of it because genetics has prophesied their likely cause of death. (As highlighted in the wellness chapter, I am a huge fan of epigenetics. Evidence suggests genetic markers for various diseases and illnesses can be short-circuited through a healthy lifestyle that includes nutrition, exercise, and an optimistic attitude.)

> ### SOCIOPSYCHONOMIC FILTER
> The assumption is that the middle class will eventually get to estate planning. Unfortunately, it usually gets to them first.

Benny White says GISAs take a second-half approach to end-of-life planning. "Unfortunately, the middle class has a 40-year estate planning window, age 25 to 65. A family is usually started and a decent job secured around the age of 25, which is when estate matters should initially be planned," he advises. "However, they drag their feet, waiting until retirement or age 65 before they do anything about it."

Attorney Eric Seabrook talks about a friend in his early 60s, an executive with a major healthcare company, who is facing changes he never expected at this point in his life, which also illustrates the vagaries of living despite planning for them.

"Money is not an issue for him," Eric notes. "He had a child late in his mid-50s. He is facing some different kind of challenges. He is in his third marriage and never planned for growth pains to occur in the Fourth Quarter of Life. He assumed all of his growth issues would be resolved once he reached this milestone in life. Having a child near retirement presented a unique set of obstacles that he didn't envision dealing with. Estate planning notwithstanding, assumptions can be very difficult, costly, and dangerous for the middle class to overcome."

SOCIOPSYCHONOMIC FILTER
Growth challenges later in life are unexpected obstacles that can be disruptive forces to GISAs' monetary vestibular system.

GISAs claim to be risk averse but take huge risks when they neglect basic estate planning matters. The warning signs are always present, but they refuse to see them. These warning signs are hidden from the poor, but faintly visible to the middle class. When an aging parent can't take care of herself or she dies, GISAs ask themselves, "Why didn't I intervene sooner?"

Monya epitomizes the typical middle-class upbringing and comments, "They don't understand the critical nature of goal insulation. Unforeseen problems can obliterate their savings and retirement comfort. Their I'll-deal-with-it-eventually mentality is largely to blame for their feet dragging."

Eric shares a farcical (yet serious) story about a middle-class couple and their analysis paralysis.

"I met with them five times to discuss several estate documents and it was frustrating. At the conclusion of our fifth meeting, I said, 'There is nothing else I can say or do to help you two make a decision. Do you want to continue?' Again, they left my office without making a critically important decision that could cause enormous emotional and financial pain. To make matters worse, they even called into question my motives to make money from the estate plan. Unfortunately, this couple's actions mirror many of their peers in the middle class."

"Charitable Giving Makes a Lasting Difference"

Wealthy donors with the means to assist worthwhile nonprofits have tremendous disdain for those who take advantage of their generosity. Their affluence, in the majority of cases, wasn't amassed because of an inheritance charity case or birthright bonanza. It's precisely why they incorporate policy statements and return on donation measures into their charitable giving playbook. Not surprisingly, this keeps emotionalism and organizational ineptitude at bay.

Community foundations are another buffer that follow the letter of the law set forth in each wealthy donor's Declaration of Charitable Giving. The foundations are not impressed by feel-good stories that fall short in producing positive outcome measures. Their litmus test: What verifiable methods are used by nonprofits in need of financial support that prove their assistance is, in fact, changing GEDAs' lives? Employment and family stability measures— observable benefits of an upgraded mindset—are used to determine if an organization's methods line up with its mission. A disconnect between the two is a red flag and cause for alarm, regardless of a nonprofit's best intentions to help impoverished constituencies.

GAPAs distribute their charitable resources in methodical, strategic, and time neutral ways. Their world is not predicated on feelings or impulsivity, and needy charities must first submit to a rigorous screening process before seeing a dime. If a nonprofit doesn't like that, it can look elsewhere. That sounds harsh, but it's how a GAPA mind works. Compassion is a measured reaction, not a flood of emotions. Strategic giving is not necessitated by merit but based on preselected boundaries that prevent impulse-driven giving. To deviate off course would violate the spirit that binds together a wealthy individual's or family's legacy values and commitment to goodwill.

The Columbus Foundation oversees $2 billion of charitable and philanthropic dollars, making it the seventh largest community foundation in the nation. The irony of its proximity, within walking distance of some of the city's most dangerous streets, never escapes me.

Over a decade ago, Monya and I established two donor-advised funds through the foundation to empower disadvantaged communities. As donors and empowerment facilitators, we often are invited to various events to mingle with other aspiring change agents and learn how we can make a bigger difference in the community while leveraging the power of the foundation's influential brand.

Monya and I attended a Columbus Foundation luncheon one afternoon to hear Robert Lupton speak, a Caucasian pastor and community-empowerment specialist in Atlanta, who heard a calling decades ago to embolden the poor and impoverished families, empowering them to take hold of the dignity each human being deserves. Leaving behind the comforts of suburban America, he and his wife went into Atlanta's inner core, a land of chaos, dysfunction, and unrelenting despair. The predominately African-American residents resisted and were quite skeptical of Robert's efforts, but eventually embraced his two-way giving entreaty with open arms: Beneficiaries of empowerment support are obligated to help themselves and others break free from the shackles of economic misery.

> "Giving to those in need what they could be gaining from their own initiative may well be the kindest way to destroy people."
>
> **–Robert Lupton**
> Community-Empowerment Specialist

Robert shared with the audience several heartwarming and thought-provoking excerpts from his book, *Toxic Charity: How Churches and Charities Hurt Those They Help (And How to Reverse It)*. He then opened it up for questions and comments. Although a near-impossible task, I waited patiently until he acknowledged me. I stood up, introduced myself, and gave a brief overview of my life story—eerily similar to Atlanta residents bound by the spirit of poverty—to the room full of middle-class and affluent donors. The escape route Robert eloquently shared to audience members, seemingly glued to his impassioned words, is the same path I took to get out, though obvious scars still remain. By now, you know what some of them are.

Can charity be toxic to the human spirit of personal responsibility and self-sufficiency? Like Robert implies, I believe it can. Dependency is a result when nonprofit entities and social service agencies, financed by federal tax dollars and wealthy (and middle-class) donors, do for the poor what they have the power to do for themselves. I witnessed it growing up in an impoverished environment for nearly two decades where the compassion road, paved with good intentions, may have unintentionally tripped up or disempowered the very people they graciously served.

These organizations help the people they serve but they don't always empower them, and that is a real distinction between the two. Charity can certainly be toxic if it creates a perpetual state of dependency.

Compassion should be extended to those in need, but how do we move the poor toward self-sufficiency and away from self-pity once they are on their feet? It's a delicate process that my wife and I have carefully administered over two decades while empowering the poor and middle class to accumulate legacy assets that build personal and financial wealth instead of squandering them.

Our charitable dollars are being used to finance the God-directed mission we were placed on this earth to accomplish. Donors must do more than change lives; they must change legacies, too!

POST GAME

ACKNOWLEDGMENTS

A big man I am, but a special shout out goes to The Big Man Upstairs. Thank You for showing me each social class mindset in the biblical account of the Israelites' transition from Egyptian bondage (poverty), through their Wilderness experience (middle class), and for some of them, to the Promised Land (affluence). All praise and credit belong to You—God the Father and Your Son, my Lord and Savior, Jesus Christ—for being there for me when my biological father was not. I exist to give glory and honor to You.

To my soulmate and better half, my wife Monya, your love and devotion mean the world to me. I would not have been able to complete this project without your genius. I'm so fortunate and grateful to have you in my life.

To my two children, Nyah and Eli, thank you for your patience as I toiled for over two years to complete *Sociopsychonomics*. So much work is still left to be done to help people live a life of purpose. Of course, the two of you inevitably come first.

To my loving mother, Laura, aka "Ma Dukes," thank you for believing in me. Your timely words of wisdom were instrumental in shaping my personal and spiritual development. To my sisters—Adele, Gina, and Tamara—thank you for your support through the years.

To my editors, Ingrid Case and Craig Lovelace, I appreciate your tireless efforts with the manuscript and diligence in helping me become a more polished writer.

A special thanks to those of you who contributed directly or indirectly to this book: Michael Sr. and Fran Anthony, John Sestina, Chris Fairrow, Starr Powell, Sue Kaufman, Robert Sr. and Missy Weiler, Tony Payne, Ric Dillon, Jason Tyree, Kioshi Smith, Dr. Ian Krajbich, Dr. LaMont Clay, Dr. Augustus Parker, Dr. Linda Reese, Peggy Hardiman, Lonnie Jones, Nate Mitchell, Jeff Blackwell, Gary Lewis, Chef Jim Warner, Danny Levitt, Fred Fairrow,

Eric Seabrook, Dan Schilling, Jeff Talbert, Cecil Gouke, Mike Uckele, Katie Morton, Leah Wilcox, Kevin Kroos, "Maria," Roger Blackwell, Thad Matta, Toshia Safford, Jerry Saunders, Beth Sparks, Dave Houze, Tyler Cook, Stephen Lukan, Chris Boyd, Kenny Crump, Ron Stokes, Derek Sharp, LaMont Hardiman, "Bennett," Michelle Moore, Dee Miller, Dan Coonfare, Donna Harlan, Reggie Thomas, Betty Collins, Benny White, Randy Brooks, Michael Anthony Jr., Drew Stevens, Jim Feibel, and Steve Moore. I can't thank you enough for sharing your insights to paint a clearer picture of social class dynamics in America.

Finally, I am grateful for the life lessons poverty taught me. Had I not been reared in economic distress, I would not be who I am today. Nor could I empathize with those who are trapped in it.

NOTES

1. U.S. Census Bureau. 2016. "Poverty Thresholds by Size of Family and Number of Children."

2. Lam, Bourree. "How Much Wealth and Income Does America's 1 Percent Really Have?" *The Atlantic.* 12 March 2016. Web. 24 May 2017.

3. U.S. Census Bureau. 2016. "Poverty Thresholds by Size of Family and Number of Children."

4. Luhby, Tami. "Republicans want the poor to work for their government benefits." *CNN Money.* 30 May 2017. Web. 15 June 2017.

5. Elkins, Kathleen. "Here's how much the average American has saved for retirement." CNBC. 12 September 2016. Web. 14 April 2017.

6. Retrieved on 8/25/16 from http://www.city-data.com/neighborhood/Milo-Grogan-Columbus-OH.html.

7. Retrieved on 8/25/16 from http://www.city-data.com/neighborhood/Milo-Grogan-Columbus-OH.html.

8. Walter, Mikel. "A Charmed Life." *The Jeffersons.* Online video clip. YouTube. 28 November 2016. Web. 10 February 2017.

9. *The Wizard of Oz.* Dir. Victor Fleming, George Cukor, Mervyn LeRoy, Norman Taurog, and King Vidor. Perf. Judy Garland, Frank Morgan, Ray Bolger, Bert Lahr, and Jack Haley. Metro-Goldwyn-Mayer, 1939. DVD.

10. Geto Boys. "Mind Playing Tricks on Me." *We Can't Be Stopped.* Rap-A-Lot Records, 1991. CD.

11. Hornsby, Bruce. "The Way It Is." *The Way It Is.* RCA Records, 1986. LP.

12. Cooley, Aaron. "War on Poverty." *Encyclopedia Britannica.* Web. 11 August 2017.

13. Kirkpatrick, Curry. "Funderburke vs. Knight." *Sports Illustrated.* 22 January 1990. Web. 14 June 2016.

14. Turner, Cory. "Teachers Are Stressed, And That Should Stress Us All." *NPR*. 30 December 2016. Web. 24 February 2017.

15. "Rise Up: A SportsCenter Special." *ESPN*. Bristol. 14 February 2016.

16. Khazan, Olga. "The Luxury of Waiting for Marriage to Have Kids." *The Atlantic*. 17 June 2014. Web. 19 October 2016.

17. Kincaid, Ellie. "Why having kids later is a really big deal." *Business Insider*. 30 June 2015. Web. 19 October 2016.

18. Mann, Leslie. "Study finds nearly half of Americans not drinking enough water." *Chicago Tribune*. 5 June 2013. Web. 25 May 2017.

19. "Vestibulocochlear nerve." *Healthline*. 9 March 2015. Web. 15 June 2017.

20. Vasel, Kathryn. "6 in 10 Americans don't have $500 to cover savings." *CNN Money*. 12 January 2017. Web. 15 May 2017.

21. "The Financial Status and Decision-Making of the American Middle Class." *Consumer Federation of America*. 17 September 2012. Web. 18 June 2017.

22. Sahadi, Jeanne. "Nearly 8 out of 10 U.S. taxpayers get refunds." *CNN Money*. 14 January 2015. Web. 8 November 2017.

23. U.S. Department of Health and Human Services. 2016. "Poverty Guidelines."

24. Saunders, Laura. "Top 20% of Earners Pay 84% of Income Tax." *The Wall Street Journal*. 10 April 2015. Web. 10 August 2017.

25. Chu, Lenora. "Newman's Own: Preparing for life after Paul." *CNN Money*. 22 July 2008. Web. 26 April 2017.

26. Stern, Ken. "Why the Rich Don't Give to Charity." *The Atlantic*. April 2013. Web. 22 March 2017.

CONTACT

Visit MrFundy.com for more information on Lawrence's outreach efforts, speaking opportunities, personal and corporate wellness programs, and book orders.